For-Profit Philanthropy

For-Profit Philanthropy

Elite Power and the Threat of Limited Liability Companies, Donor-Advised Funds, and Strategic Corporate Giving

DANA BRAKMAN REISER AND STEVEN A. DEAN

OXFORD
UNIVERSITY PRESS

OXFORD
UNIVERSITY PRESS

Oxford University Press is a department of the University of Oxford. It furthers the University's objective of excellence in research, scholarship, and education by publishing worldwide. Oxford is a registered trade mark of Oxford University Press in the UK and certain other countries.

Published in the United States of America by Oxford University Press
198 Madison Avenue, New York, NY 10016, United States of America.

Library of Congress Control Number: 2022919941

ISBN 978-0-19-007450-0

DOI: 10.1093/oso/9780190074500.001.0001

Printed by Sheridan Books, Inc., United States of America

We dedicate this book to our friends, family, and colleagues and to all those fighting for a brighter future.

Contents

Acknowledgments

Every book is a product of far more people than those whose names appear on the cover. Researching and writing largely during these often-isolating pandemic times made us even more grateful for the time and energy our colleagues and interlocutors devoted to help us make it better. We could not possibly thank all of them here, but we particularly acknowledge the assistance, comments, and insights of Brad Borden, Evelyn Brody, Julie Battilana, Tricia Bromley, Heidi Brown, Roger Colinvaux, Kathleen Darvil, Jean Davis, Brian Galle, Jill Grennan, Debbie Grossman, Phil Hackney, Daniel Hemel, Garry Jenkins, Claire Kelly, Brian Lee, Ben Leff, Sharon Lincoln, Ray Madoff, Ruth Madrigal, Johanna Mair, Roberta Mann, Jill Manny, Lloyd Mayer, Kim Meredith, Ariel Meyerstein, Ingrid Mittermaier, Lara Patil, David Reiss, Charles Sellen, Mark Sidel, Norm Silber, and those who organized and participated in the dozens of conference panels and workshops at which we received valuable feedback on portions of this book. The thoughtful editors and staff at Oxford University Press, Newgen Knowledge Works, and Arc Indexing made the book markedly better. Our research assistants, Bianca D'Agostaro, Josh Hamlet, Yifan Lin, Heather Lanter, Christie McGuinness, Gita Miller, Melissa Sheridan, and Yin Yu have our appreciation as well. In addition to those individual contributions, we especially want to thank Brooklyn Law School for the unstinting support that made this book possible.

We each feel so very fortunate that we have built a scholarly partnership together. As coauthors, we have been able to do what neither of us could have accomplished alone. Of course, thanks are also due to our friends and family—Jeff, Charlotte, John, and Jen in particular—who indulged our fascination with a corner of the law not often explored, sometimes at the expense of time together. Their patience and good humor were indispensable. Finally, we thank our readers in advance for engaging with our ideas and continuing the conversation.

ACKNOWLEDGMENTS

Introduction

> This is the way the world ends
> Not with a bang but a whimper.
>
> —*The Hollow Men* by T.S. Eliot

The size of the US philanthropic sector hints at the pivotal role it has long played in American society. Americans gave almost $485 billion to charities in 2021 alone, a record-breaking outpouring of generosity sparked by the global pandemic but not out of step with typical annual totals.[1] The nonprofit sector employs well over 10 percent of US private workers,[2] and grantmaking foundations hold more than $1 trillion in assets,[3] with billions more held by operating charities.

Disasters like the COVID-19 pandemic bring the contributions of this sector—to research, public health, job training, and community support—into sharp relief. Philanthropic institutions have the power to change lives and shape policy, fueled by a combination of private funding, government subsidies, and public goodwill. It has been a hallmark of American society since Alexis de Tocqueville identified it as unique in the 1830s.[4] Yet, for all its power, a crisis now looms over the future of the philanthropic sector itself.

Practices, players, and norms native to the business sector are migrating into philanthropy, muddying the distinction between commerce and charity and eliding the regulatory framework designed to keep them separate. Philanthropies organized as limited liability companies (LLCs) like the Chan Zuckerberg Initiative (CZI), donor-advised funds sponsored by investment company giants like the nearly $50 billion Fidelity Charitable,[5] and strategic corporate philanthropy programs that align charitable giving by multinationals as diverse as Citigroup, Google, and General Motors to their business objectives reveal a transformation of this cornerstone of American society. Their for-profit philanthropy shatters the long-standing divide regulation has maintained between business and charitable activities.

For-profit philanthropy represents a threat the scale of which has, until now, gone unrecognized. Experts have unearthed compelling evidence of its broad impact but have failed to appreciate that they have described one conflagration rather than many. Accordingly, they have tailored solutions to what they see as discrete regulatory failures, not realizing that each merely represents an isolated

For-Profit Philanthropy. Dana Brakman Reiser and Steven A. Dean, Oxford University Press. © Oxford University Press 2023. DOI: 10.1093/oso/9780190074500.003.0001

front in a broader struggle. All the while, the unraveling of a pact between elites and the public that fueled half a century of philanthropic achievement has accelerated unnoticed.

That crisis threatens the trust that has always been central to charity law, allowing donors to give without hesitation even when they know little about a charitable organization or its leaders. Charity law's "nondistribution constraint," for example, ensures that those leaders may not enrich themselves at their charity's expense. With that particular worry set aside, would-be givers can donate to a public charity with the same ease that they might purchase shares in a public company, confident that whatever may happen, their donation (or investment) will remain dedicated to a cause (or to generating profit).

In recent years, charities have been forced to grapple with a rising tide of "slacktivism." In the summer of 2020, Blackout Tuesday filled social media streams with black squares. To some, those squares represented a powerful statement in support of Black Lives Matter. Others dismissed them as cheap theater—virtue signaling—displacing giving and other concrete steps to support racial equity.

For-profit philanthropy can be "a willingness to perform a relatively costless, token display of support for a social cause, with an accompanying lack of willingness to devote significant effort to enact meaningful change,"[6] and has seduced many of the country's wealthiest individuals and largest corporations, undermining trust not in the charities receiving philanthropic capital but in the elites supplying it. The erosion of that trust can be seen in the rising political fortunes of taxes targeted at the richest Americans, ranging from Senator Warren's wealth tax to the billionaires income tax proposed by Senator Wyden. For the last half-century, Americans have been content to let elites put their wealth into private foundations to benefit the public. Today, they seem increasingly open to the possibility of deciding for themselves where that wealth goes rather than leaving the choice up to General Motors or Bill Gates.

For-profit philanthropy explains what has made the public more inclined to dismiss elite philanthropy as so much virtue signaling, hollow measures to burnish reputations rather than sincerely charitable acts. Simply put, elites have brought this on themselves by setting aside philanthropy law's equivalent of the nondistribution constraint—the private foundation—created by the 1969 Tax Reform Act. This legislation should be understood as a Grand Bargain that enabled elite philanthropy to reassure the public that their purported altruism would indeed benefit ordinary Americans. When for-profit philanthropists spurn this Grand Bargain, they do not merely opt out of a burdensome tax regime. They threaten the future of what has been one of the cornerstones of American society for hundreds of years.

Key to the Grand Bargain's success was constructing the regulated—albeit lightly—private foundation form in which to conduct of elite philanthropy.

Opting into foundation law's strictures on targeting, timing, and transparency allows philanthropists to credibly commit to using a share of their vast resources to serve public ends rather than private ones.

- Targeting requirements limit the purposes to which purportedly philanthropic funds may be directed. Although the bounds of foundations' permissible charitable activities are quite capacious, both dealings with founders' related businesses and political contributions are placed clearly beyond their limits.
- Timing requirements impose a schedule for putting philanthropic assets to active use. They do not demand quick and wholesale distribution of a philanthropic endowment, but they do preclude foundations from merely hoarding wealth to magnify the power and influence of their donors.
- Transparency requirements force elite philanthropy into the sunlight, where the media and the public can test its claims of public benefit.

Accepting the Grand Bargain's conditions also granted elite philanthropists tax advantages, reputational protection, and a shot at immortality. And it empowered no less an authority than the federal government to punish those who deviated from the terms of the deal.

But where for decades elite philanthropy was the province of private foundations, today it is as likely to be practiced within philanthropy LLCs, commercially affiliated donor-advised funds, and strategic corporate giving programs. Each operates outside the foundation model, unwedded to the Grand Bargain's terms. No longer walled off from the influence of American capitalism by philanthropy law, for-profit philanthropy deploys the arsenal of business in service of charitable goals.

For-profit philanthropy's rebuff of the Grand Bargain presents a combination of enormous potential and grave risk. Freed from the regulatory requirements imposed on traditional philanthropic foundations, for-profit philanthropy can unlock innovation and attract capital that donors might otherwise keep in their pockets or pass on for future private use. Yet eliminating philanthropy law's bright line between the private—and public—regarding activities of affluent families and influential firms makes accountability elusive. Philanthropy has accomplished much for many, and for-profit philanthropy could mark its end.

Improbably, federal tax laws constraining the targeting, timing, and transparency of philanthropy have preserved the public's trust in wealthy donors for more than fifty years. Increasingly, for-profit philanthropy allows individual and corporate donors to sidestep such requirements when it suits them. Undermining this regime risks a catastrophic loss of public trust in the value of private philanthropic endeavors. For-profit philanthropy threatens the very idea of philanthropy as a public good distinct from private gain.

This book highlights three noteworthy for-profit philanthropic developments, identifies the strains they place on the federal scheme—the Grand Bargain—which has regulated traditional philanthropy since it was brokered in 1969, and proposes pathways for regulators and philanthropists themselves to respond.

Business Practices, Players, and Norms Migrate into Philanthropy

The impact of business practices, players, and norms on modern philanthropic activity cannot be overstated. Philanthropists, either themselves or through their lineage, all trace their wealth to some venture's financial success. These triumphs understandably lead them to view the tools of business favorably.[7] Those individuals and entities still in the throes of managing successful businesses see every day that financial returns can be combined with other worthy objectives—creating jobs, building new markets, and enhancing capacity and communication. That they would aspire to employ business strategies to fulfill the philanthropic sector's promise of immense and enduring impact seems almost inevitable.

When Mark Zuckerberg and Priscilla Chan pledged their vast wealth to the public interest, they declined to follow in the footsteps of generations of tycoons before them. Upending the conventional wisdom of pursuing philanthropy through a nonprofit, tax-exempt foundation bound by the Grand Bargain's terms, they formed the Chan Zuckerberg Initiative as a for-profit limited liability company (LLC).[8] Not only can this philanthropy LLC make traditional charitable grants, but it can also make impact investments and political contributions to "help solve some of society's toughest challenges—from eradicating disease and improving education, to addressing the needs of our local communities."[9]

The Chan Zuckerberg Initiative can hold unlimited quantities of Facebook stock and create synergies with Facebook and other related properties. And it need only reveal to the public those activities and successes its founders seek to tout. Traditional foundations, by contrast, must navigate a complex web of restrictions and regulations the Grand Bargain imposes on their investment, spending, and management practices and must make public detailed accounts of both these activities and the foundation's supporters.[10]

Many of the same forces that make an LLC appealing to ultra-high-net-worth individuals have attracted billions in contributions from somewhat less well-heeled donors to commercially affiliated philanthropic vehicles like Fidelity Charitable.[11] These commercial sponsors accept funds and appreciated assets from donors and hold them in "donor-advised funds" earmarked for future distribution to charity.[12] Donors receive an immediate tax deduction on terms closer to those applied to operating charities running soup kitchens and conservation programs than those that apply to elite private foundations under the Grand Bargain. Donors also retain the right to advise the sponsor who holds the funds on who should ultimately receive the donated assets and how they should be invested in the meantime.

Fidelity Charitable and other charitable sponsors act as custodians, faithfully following the advice they receive. At the same time, their affiliated investment companies provide investment and administrative services for a fee. Donors enjoy the best of both worlds—the foundation-like benefits of controlling an endowment for grantmaking but on decidedly more flexible terms and with more generous tax advantages than those the Grand Bargain brokered. Donor-advised funds face no requirement to pay out a percentage of their assets annually, as do private foundations.[13] Although a private foundation's grants and donors are matter of public record,[14] disclosures regarding donor-advised funds are far less transparent. Fidelity Charitable dutifully files reports of the grants it issues with federal regulators, but its aggregated data obscure the identities of specific donors and their individual grantmaking decisions.

The pull of flexibility came together with the external push of the corporate social responsibility (CSR) movement to drive corporations to align their philanthropic efforts to their business models. Although corporate philanthropy has long been a staple of business practice, large and multinational firms have transformed their giving into strategic corporate giving programs that marry business objectives with charitable ones. No longer simply the province of altruism or even public relations, the full range of corporate departments now routinely use corporate giving for purposes as diverse as attracting and retaining talent, developing new products and markets, and smoothing supply chains.

In another era corporate giants might have highlighted donations to a museum but today firms strategically fold their philanthropy into increasingly robust CSR departments designed to showcase the firm's responsiveness to stakeholders of all kinds. Recapping its 2020 efforts in a Global ESG Report, Citigroup explained: "We're more committed than ever to using our corporate voice and our core business capabilities—and strategic philanthropy—to address societal challenges head-on, with bolder actions and positions than we have taken before."[15]

A combination of corporate foundation grants and direct corporate giving can be carefully calibrated to align with the firm's business needs and goals. Direct corporate giving is eligible for tax deductions as if it were conducted in a tax-exempt entity, but subject to none of the Grand Bargain's timing, transparency, and targeting limitations applicable to foundations. A corporate foundation, like any other, must make mandatory annual payouts, endure prohibitions on self-dealing, and provide transparency around grants and donors. Direct corporate giving can be enmeshed with profit-making on any timeline a firm prefers, and only selectively disclosed.

Corporations can choose for-profit philanthropy one grant at a time, sacrificing nothing while gaining unparalleled freedom. But a few have gone all-in for the brand of flexible, unregulated philanthropy direct giving offers. Google announced it would shift its corporate philanthropy away from its corporate foundation in 2008,[16] eventually shuttering it ten years later.[17] Pearson closed its foundation in 2014 and General Motors did the same in 2017.[18]

Philanthropy LLCs, commercially affiliated donor-advised funds, and strategic corporate philanthropy illustrate the broad appeal of for-profit philanthropy. Collectively, they reveal tremendous creative energy and resources deployed toward prosocial goals, presenting opportunities for massive investments directed toward charitable ends. Unfortunately, they also demonstrate how for-profit philanthropic innovations allow individual and corporate donors to avoid regulatory structures designed to constrain the power philanthropy grants to elites. Without the accountability long supplied by the Grand Bargain, even the most venerable philanthropic institutions become vulnerable.

Philanthropy's Grand Bargain

The antidemocratic nature of philanthropy has long been a source of concern. The concept at its core relies upon high-net-worth individuals, affluent families, and prosperous firms to identify and combat social problems. These same individuals, families, and firms do so with the spoils of their economic victories or those of their predecessors—plunder unshared with workers and consumers who could as easily vilify their greed as laud their generosity.

The last transformative innovation of American philanthropy produced the general-purpose foundation at the turn of the twentieth century. Its pioneers included the Rockefellers and Carnegies—individuals, families, and firm founders whose economic power was much maligned by the public. On the national stage, these efforts reached their apex when John D. Rockefeller failed to convince Congress to grant his foundation a federal charter.[19]

On the eve of World War I, Congress feared that Rockefeller's philanthropic foundation would betray the public trust just as T. S. Eliot's *Hollow Men* soon would. In his devastating poem, Eliot skewered cataclysmic failures of leadership that led the world to war. Congress worried that Rockefeller would prove to be just such a Hollow Man. Today's for-profit philanthropists, trading foundations for slacktivism, could finally realize that long-ago Congress's fears.

A century ago, state legislatures proved more open to Rockefeller's notion (displaying the same eagerness they would later show to serve as midwives at the birth of benefit corporations, low-profit limited liability companies, and other hybrid social enterprise vehicles as detailed in chapter 5). Eager for the influx of giving to provide social supports in their communities, they acceded to this innovation. Newly minted millionaires saw vindication in philanthropy and, over time, state-chartered general-purpose foundations became elites' philanthropic vehicle of choice.

The embrace of foundations by state legislatures did little to ease fears that philanthropists would betray the public trust. Rising along with the antielite tide of the Red Scare and racist responses to critical foundation support for the civil rights movement, eventually demanded a federal response. By the late 1960s, Congress was poised to act. The Grand Bargain embodied in the sweeping 1969 tax reform legislation responded to blistering criticism of the philanthropic sector.[20] Although Congress clearly valued the resources foundations invested in relieving society's ills, legislators perceived their freedom from public control and entanglement with business as grave threats.

Congress preserved a robust philanthropic sector by dividing charitable activity into two distinct statutory categories. Distinguished by a broad base of donors or substantial revenue earned from conducting charitable operations, "public charities" retained something closer to pre-1969 tax treatment.[21] More solipsistic "private foundations"—supported by a small number of donors, substantial investment income, or both and pursuing charitable purposes though grantmaking rather than direct operations—found tax benefits more vigorously curtailed and regulatory oversight heightened.[22]

Distinguishing between public charities and private foundations allowed Congress to impose timing, targeting, and transparency requirements on the latter to deliver public accountability even when the public did not hold a charity's purse strings. These accountability measures bolstered public trust in foundation efforts and activities. They did so in large part by imposing sharp demarcations between donors' philanthropy and their private lives and businesses, facilitating the scrutiny needed to distinguish altruism from indulgence.

Under the federal tax regime the Grand Bargain brought to life, private foundations operate in perpetuity, but not as storehouses for wealth their founders can exploit personally or commercially. Spending rules demanded a percentage of assets be expended yearly in service of the foundation's declared charitable mission.[23] The grants that most easily satisfy this timing requirement flow to the public charities the 1969 Grand Bargain deemed trustworthy by virtue of their broad public support.

The foundation rules ushered in by the 1969 Act also address how foundations' largesse should be targeted. Spending that raises the specter of foundations serving their donors' and managers' interests rather than those of the broader public—like grants to individuals, lobbying, or campaign expenditures—trigger stiff penalties. Investment rules limiting the stakes foundations may hold in businesses[24] and regulating their investment activities[25] likewise ensure that foundations avoid entanglements with markets. And management rules prohibiting even arm's-length transactions as inappropriate self-dealing constrain donors' and leaders' capacity to use their foundations for personal enrichment.

Walled off from donors' business and private lives, foundations also find themselves subject to the unforgiving glare of expansive transparency requirements. Ironically, private foundations must file the most comprehensive annual informational tax returns with the IRS of all tax-exempt entities and make all of their content available to everyone. These requirements allow authorities, the public and—critically—the media to verify foundations' claims they act in the public interest. The GuideStar website further enhances accessibility, with foundation disclosures now available to anyone with just a few clicks.

Any successful bargain requires concessions by both sides. The 1969 Act's private foundation rules offered the public accountability thanks to a clear divide between elites' public philanthropy and their personal fortunes and a legal regime to test elite philanthropy's bona fides. In return for complying with those regulatory burdens, donors secured protection from a threat of taxes—just emerging in Rockefeller's day—that had risen to levels unimaginable by today's standards, as high as 77 percent on individual income.[26] Philanthropists also beat back pressure to limit foundations' lifetimes, safeguarding the privilege of perpetuity for donors keen to use philanthropy to achieve immortality.[27] Despite the timing, targeting, and transparency requirements the Grand Bargain imposed, elite donors retained substantial philanthropic autonomy and a powerful tool to bolster their reputations. .

A half-century of philanthropic achievements can be traced to this legislative compromise. Its vision of accountable philanthropy fostered confidence that allowing the wealthy to place big bets—like the Gates Foundation's on vaccine development,[28] malaria eradication,[29] and HIV treatments[30]—could yield prizes far richer than those that could be produced if the private sector and the government were to act on their own. Striking such a balance between liberty and equality allows donors an extraordinary degree of freedom to gamble with resources that might just as easily—and more democratically—be deployed in and by the public sector.[31]

Collecting taxes at steeply progressive rates could alternatively have dramatically shrunk the Gates Foundation's more than $55 billion stockpile.[32] The result would put some—perhaps most—of that capital under direct public control, leaving the government to pursue the public good with its increased share while Bill and Melinda French Gates and Warren Buffet (who contributed $32.7 billion to the foundation over fifteen years)[33] do the same with what remains in their hands.

The Grand Bargain instead offered elite philanthropists the autonomy to pursue ambitious social goals largely of their own design, as long as they targeted their efforts within a publicly acceptable range of charitable goals, conducted their activities on a publicly acceptable timeline, and provided the public with transparency around their actions. Doing so has yielded prizes that neither private enterprise nor the public sector would have produced on their own. Our 911 emergency response system offers a striking example of the rich rewards the public has enjoyed thanks to the bold efforts of philanthropists.[34] Without the accountability long preserved by the Grand Bargain, future social innovations could be lost as the public and private sectors part ways to make smaller wagers on their own.

In 1969, with both the ambition of the US income tax and discontent over philanthropy's influence at their zenith, the private foundation preserved the public's trust in elite philanthropy. Simply put, lawmakers exercised restraint so the wealthy could continue not to. The Grand Bargain assured the public that elites would prove to be more than Hollow Men and that they would pursue ambitious public ends rather than narrow private ones. Just as important, the Grand Bargain gave ordinary Americans the power to tell the difference.

Opting Out of the Bargain

Increasingly, though, donors have rejected the Grand Bargain's austere diet in pursuit of new philanthropic flavors. A century after Rockefeller failed to secure a federal charter for a general-purpose philanthropic foundation, at the stroke of a pen wealthy elites can order up a philanthropy LLC free from both tax and regulatory oversight. Although it has chosen to make billions in charitable grants since its inception in 2015 and detail them on its public website at least since 2018,[35] the Chan Zuckerberg Initiative need never pay out any assets to charity or disclose any of its philanthropic assets or activities to anyone. It can use those assets for investments (the terms of which it does not detail publicly), engage in political activity, and utilize its close relationships with Facebook in the process. Chan and Zuckerberg could even—one day—draw their contributions back out. Unthinkable, perhaps, but not impossible.

Unlike the donors to philanthropy LLCs, donor-advisors cannot reclaim the assets they assign to a donor-advised fund or deploy them for their own benefit or to fund political activity. But Fidelity Charitable, a donor-advised fund sponsor operating in affiliation with Fidelity Investments, can continue providing investment services to these funds indefinitely. It can leave the questions of when and whether to deploy even one penny of the vast and growing assets under its control to serve the public interest entirely in the hands of its "donor" customers.

These customers qualify for tax deductions at the moment they deposit their funds with Fidelity, but their activities—and indeed existence—remain obscure. Under current law, any individual donor-advisor's identity and the causes and programs they support will be impossible to determine, unless they choose to publicize them.

When corporate philanthropy flows through its core corporate bureaucracy, we have only the firm's word that its giving represents altruism rather than marketing, employee benefits, or product or business development. Unmoored from the foundation payout requirement's demands to favor public charities and foundation restrictions on self-dealing, programs and expenditures touted as corporate philanthropy can just as easily be win–win CSR that enhances brand value, retains employees, and maintains a firm's social license to operate. In extreme cases like GM, Pearson, and Google, which dismantled their corporate foundations entirely, the Grand Bargain's targeting, timing, and transparency obligations disappear completely. The public interest can be fully subsumed into firm interest, yet a tax deduction comes along with either funding approach.

Shouldering the Grand Bargain's restrictions imposed on foundations to gain access to tax advantages has become far less attractive after decades of steadily decreasing tax rates. Even the steeply progressive reforms championed by the Biden Administration and some in Congress do not contemplate marginal rates taxing well over half of each dollar earned. Just as importantly, it would take an overhaul of the tax code far more comprehensive and an injection of funds for enforcement far more massive than those President Biden has sought to give teeth to any higher rates Congress imposes.

The mid-1990s saw nearly every enterprise—business and philanthropic ventures alike—gain the freedom to choose for itself whether or not to pay the corporate tax. This levy became essentially optional, easily avoided by structuring an endeavor as an LLC and checking the proper box on a tax form. That marked a dramatic departure from a 1980 proposal that would have imposed what was then a 46 percent corporate tax on LLCs such as the Chan Zuckerberg Initiative.[36] This advantageous treatment has by now become so firmly entrenched that more LLCs are formed in the United States than any other type of business entity.[37] Fifty years after the Grand Bargain, the rise of the LLC's "tax nothing" and the fall of tax rates on individuals and corporations to 37 percent and 21 percent, respectively, make the relative rewards of the Grand Bargain look like a bad deal for elites.

Embracing for-profit philanthropy's new legal technologies over those of the 1969 Grand Bargain has—for the moment—granted philanthropists such as Chan and Zuckerberg, donor-advised fund sponsors like Fidelity Charitable, and corporations embracing strategic giving approaches from Citigroup to Google new freedom to place the bets they choose. But they cannot do so on their own. If the public loses faith in philanthropy, they may yet decide to withdraw the financial support implicit in the Grand Bargain.

Trust

Today's receding regulatory tide makes the short-term costs philanthropists must bear to skirt the Grand Bargain's requirements quite modest. Taking the public's trust as a given suggests the long-term costs will be too. But confidence that the fear of Hollow Men that doomed Rockefeller's federal foundation and ultimately brought the Grand Bargain to life will never return may be misplaced.

The risks posed by for-profit philanthropy for the public—typically dashed expectations—tend to be easy for ordinary Americans to understand. Today's wealthy donors, by contrast, would be hard-pressed to picture themselves in a world once inhabited by titans like Rockefeller: a world where trust has been lost and the entire project of private philanthropy has become suspect. For-profit philanthropy collapses boundaries—philanthropic counterparts to the depression-era Glass-Steagall barriers that, until a decade before the 2008 financial crisis, separated consumer and investment banking—carefully constructed by the Grand Bargain. When corporations conduct philanthropy through each of their business divisions, when investment companies offer charitable giving accounts to their mutual fund customers, when donors opt for an LLC as the hub of their philanthropic operations, the lines between charity and business become murky.

Cavalierly discarding the private foundation as the entity of choice for insular donors strips away the regulatory oversight and public scrutiny they once attracted. Accountability measures that once bolstered trust seem to have been dismissed as irrelevant. Without the assurance these guardrails provide that donors' philanthropic lives will remain subject to public scrutiny and distinct from their business empires and personal fortunes, the public's trust in elite visions of the good becomes vulnerable. If lost, the public may demand that it control distribution of a greater share of elite wealth, endangering the project of philanthropy writ large. Such a shift would not only undercut for-profit philanthropy's compelling new paradigm but could take much of traditional philanthropy—and its redemptive power—along with it.

In the absence of an architecture of trust, the public may lose faith that elites who once grew wealthy at their expense will act in a meaningfully different way when they engage in philanthropy. And trust matters. Consider similarly innovative efforts to blend profit and purpose in the social enterprise space that unintentionally highlight the limits of good intentions.

Over the past decade, most states have created one or more hybrid organizational forms to house ventures committed to pursuing more than one bottom line.[38] These legal technologies promised to provide mission-driven entrepreneurs with the ability to tap into vast US capital markets by building trust with investors. Yet, each form allows either investors or entrepreneurs to unilaterally defect from the blended value vision and pursue profit alone.

Predictably given the resulting absence of trust, none of those dozens of hybrid forms has been embraced as a vehicle for lasting collaboration between social enterprise founders and investors. Unable to broadcast a reliable signal of key parties' commitments to blend profit with purpose, hybrid entities—even Delaware's much-anticipated version, dubbed the public benefit corporation[39]—have failed to deliver the accountability the Grand Bargain once did. Ever more widely available, fewer than 10,000 ventures nationwide have actually used them.[40] Entrepreneurs continue to form mission-driven businesses that require capital to grow and scale. Both these entrepreneurs and their potential investors need to trust in each other's commitments to blending profit and purpose, but the new forms offer little reassurance and remain little used.

For-profit philanthropy's trust problem will be no easier to untangle. Venturing beyond the safe confines of the Grand Bargain into today's relatively gentle regulatory wilderness by employing philanthropy LLCs, commercially affiliated donor-advised funds, and strategic corporate philanthropy courts a public skepticism philanthropists may only recognize too late. Trust represents an immediate problem for social enterprises as entrepreneurs must raise capital upfront from skeptical markets. Over time, for-profit philanthropy may trigger a different reckoning.

By jeopardizing the Grand Bargain's delicate balance, and the trust it forged between philanthropists and the public, the rise of for-profit philanthropy threatens a grim future. Imagining its Hollow Men pleading with the public in "dried voices . . . quiet and meaningless as wind in dry grass"[41] to be believed may seem far-fetched. But Rockefeller's experience shows it is not.

And it would be the public that would suffer. Without that trust, the benefits of philanthropy's experimentation could be lost as well. The autonomy philanthropy enjoys to transform private resources into public benefits in unconventional ways—acting as countless laboratories of social good—relies on trust. For-profit philanthropy allows influential actors to circumvent the Grand Bargain's minimum accountability standards, endangering that trust. Without it, it would be all too easy for the pendulum to swing from today's permissive approach to tomorrow's burdensome regulation.

Of course, not all efforts to combine profit and purpose falter. Collapsing once distinct categories might actually succeed too well, a lesson the ESG investing boom can teach us. The past five years have witnessed exponential growth in investment products promising to marry financial return and concern for environmental, social, and governance (ESG) factors.[42] This growth has not been driven by promising concessionary returns—lower financial gains traded for environmental stewardship or power-sharing with marginalized communities. Rather, the promise is "doing well by doing good" with ESG delivering rather than substituting for financial returns. ESG, such funds insist, aligns with financial return, serving as a proxy for long-term profitability and astute management of risks and opportunities.[43] In essence, they claim that policing the line between profit and social good has become irrelevant as the categories have collapsed.

Not all investments that promise financial gain and environmental, social, or governance benefits will require a trade-off. Investors assured that some offerings will do just that might not be blamed for flocking to them. But if investors demand market rate financial returns from ESG investments, fund managers will cultivate those ESG traits compatible with market rate financial gains. Reducing a company's dependence on traditional fuels or diversifying boards might fit that bill, but other environmental, social, and governance efforts will not.

There exists, of course, a risk of crowding out. Win–win ESG investments could displace investments that would secure greater social good by sacrificing private gains. If confused for philanthropy, they could even crowd out charitable contributions. As long as ESG investing brings new assets into the prosocial arena, that such investments will pursue only the thin slice of the ESG pie that aligns with financial return raises few concerns. But for-profit philanthropy presents the same risk of monoculture, with more troubling consequences.

If the business and charity categories collapse, the focus of philanthropy might similarly contract. Philanthropic dollars may flow only toward charitable projects that map well to the private and corporate interests of donors, requiring neither trade-offs nor leaps of faith. Educational technology projects can enhance learning in poor communities and open new markets of consumers for tech companies. Marketing donor-advised fund accounts can attract new assets for management and (eventually) new charitable spending.

But it is hard to make money feeding the hungry. And business metrics will inevitably do a poor job capturing the benefits of combatting structural racism. Even if the public can be convinced that the border between philanthropy and private profit need no longer be militarized, the shape of the philanthropic sector that such a remade landscape might nurture would look quite different from our own.

Worse, for-profit philanthropy's math might dictate choices at odds with the public's vision of charity. Should Mark Zuckerberg and Priscilla Chan decide the surest way to achieve their laudable aims would be for one of their children to run for higher office, CZI, a philanthropy LLC rather than a foundation, could devote all of its resources to fund that campaign. Without doubt, the public would view that as a betrayal.

Over time, more subtle breaches of the Grand Bargain may persuade voters to assert control over philanthropic resources. Higher taxes and more burdensome regulation would translate into a reliable—if unspectacular—flow of public benefits. Philanthropists will likewise continue to promote their values with their curtailed freedom and smaller bank accounts. But the big bets the Grand Bargain once made possible will be lost.

The Paths Forward

The myriad risks posed by the disruption of for-profit philanthropy invite just as wide a range of responses. Government actors could reform philanthropy regulation to enhance oversight and accountability when players, practices, and norms native to the for-profit sector migrate into philanthropy. High-net-worth individuals, affluent families, and major corporations engaged in these practices can use private ordering to draw their own boundaries for the targeting, timing, and transparency of their giving. Even in the current low-tax and low-tax-enforcement era, a new bargain remains within reach because a loss of trust would benefit neither elites nor everyone else.

Rather than endless attempts to plug holes in a Grand Bargain suited to the needs of yesteryear, policymakers could use their regulatory authority to enhance trust by alternate means. Commercially affiliated donor-advised funds, strategic corporate philanthropy, and philanthropy LLCs may have already grown too big to dismantle, yet their growth makes them a tempting target and an opportunity for regulatory innovation. And that regulation need not follow the Grand Bargain's playbook.

Timing-focused legislation designed to nudge assets in donor-advised funds out the door to operating charities and the funds themselves back toward the Grand Bargain's vision could just as easily target distribution of dormant funds to Black-led charities or underserved communities. The Grand Bargain, of course, never attempted to challenge racial inequality in that way. Even more modest changes such as applying donor-advised fund disclosure rules fund by fund would increase transparency, perhaps publicizing worthy but underfunded charitable recipients. In the near term, pinpoint efforts like these may be sufficient to preserve trust and stave off more profound change. But such timid responses to for-profit philanthropy will not tame the grave risk it poses to the Grand Bargain.

Whether as a complement to or a substitute for such focused regulatory efforts, a range of privately developed solutions could also deliver some portion of the trust the Grand Bargain provided for half a century. Philanthropy LLC founders and corporate donors can empower independent boards to police the targeting of their largesse. Commercially affiliated donor-advised fund sponsors can require donors to designate default charities to whom their unspent contributions will be distributed after some reasonable time has elapsed—even without a government mandate to do so. For-profit philanthropists of all stripes can undertake transparency commitments, enlisting third-party information providers like GuideStar to assist.

If such efforts take root, timing, transparency, and targeting constraints once imposed by statute might simply be embraced as best practices. Third-party certifiers could emerge to measure compliance. Of course, the success of such efforts will necessarily vary. Without the benefit of potent public interventions like the nondistribution constraint or the Grand Bargain, it may be too much to hope regulatory nudges and private pledges can subdue the threat posed by for-profit philanthropy.

If targeted regulation and private ordering prove insufficient, more systemic solutions may be necessary. Whether or not recent interest in a wealth tax can be linked to the rise of for-profit philanthropy, such a tax could provide the foundation for a reinvigorated Grand Bargain or an entirely new one. In his 1889 essay, *The Gospel of Wealth*, Andrew Carnegie famously made a similar prediction about the power of the estate tax.[44] His hope, of course, was that the tax would generate philanthropy rather than revenue. Today's wealth tax—or some other steeply progressive tax—could do the same by applying the lessons of the Grand Bargain to for-profit philanthropy. Commensurate with the scale of the threat posed by for-profit philanthropy—and our society's massive inequality—systemic reforms might also reach beyond the tax code to check the power of wealthy elites directly. Reforming election law or campaign spending rules to diminish elite power could deliver a More Perfect Bargain for philanthropy in the process.

For-profit philanthropy's new hybrid philanthrocapitalism represents a bold gamble on philanthropy's future. Casting aside the traditional tools of philanthropy as Mark Zuckerberg and Priscilla Chan did to the private foundation when they launched their philanthropy LLC in 2015 could, as they hope, end disease as we know it.[45] As we will show, the failure of the Chan Zuckerberg Initiative could also mean the end of philanthropy as we know it. Gambling with $45 billion—free even of the minimum standards on timing, transparency, and targeting imposed by the 1969 Grand Bargain—could shatter the truce brokered between philanthropists and the public half a century ago.

A Roadmap

The remainder of this book proceeds in three parts. Part I (chapters 1, 2, and 3) traces three case studies: making the abstract notion of for-profit philanthropy concrete with real-world people and projects. These chapters reveal the extent to which for-profit philanthropy's growth has undermined the Grand Bargain.

The Chan Zuckerberg Initiative and the other philanthropy LLCs detailed in chapter 1 enjoy favorable tax treatment not so different from a private foundation while sidestepping its moderate demands with respect to targeting, timing, and transparency. Fidelity Charitable and other commercially affiliated sponsors of donor-advised funds—an innovation poised to do for donating what the credit card once did for spending—take the stage in chapter 2. These vehicles allow donors to manipulate the timing of charitable giving while retaining, and sometimes improving upon, its tax advantages and privacy. Finally, chapter 3 recounts the rise of strategic corporate philanthropy generally, and the decline the corporate foundation specifically. These developments highlight the freedom corporate donors enjoy to judge for themselves what passes for philanthropy and the discretion they maintain to selectively disclose their activities.

Part II (chapters 4 and 5) shows first what for-profit philanthropy jeopardizes, then how. Chapter 4 details how the Grand Bargain's minimum standards of transparency, timing, and targeting came to nurture trust in philanthropy for half a century. Probing deeply into the caverns and recesses of the 1969 Tax Reform Act, it reveals both the clarity of its categories and the power of its regulatory controls.

Chapter 5 reveals the risks of the Grand Bargain's collapse. It first identifies the value secured by the private foundation's commitment device: trust. Foundation law's tripartite accountability regime reassured policymakers and the public that elites could be trusted to pursue public good with their fortunes, rehabilitating elite philanthropists' reputations from bullying to benign. It then offers two quite different visions of a philanthropic sector without trust. A loss of trust might foretell either the either philanthropy's demise or its troubling rebirth.

Part III (chapters 6, 7, and 8) turns toward the future. Given the challenges outlined in Parts I and II, the way forward will not be an easy one. Even modest disruptions could upend a long-standing balance—both between liberty and equality and between innovation and regulation—that lends philanthropy its potency. Fortunately, there are many paths forward, and regulators and philanthropists can traverse them simultaneously. Chapter 6 explores how targeted regulatory solutions could take on those risks surgically, finding new ways to bring targeting, timing, and transparency to for-profit philanthropy. In the process, it highlights opportunities to deliver regulatory innovations responsive to modern concerns.

Recognizing that the mere threat of enhanced regulation may spur for-profit philanthropists to preempt it, chapter 7 offers ways to enhance public trust through private ordering. Although private ordering solutions tend to be nonstarters in the realm of public goods, if sufficiently motivated, elite philanthropists have the ample resources needed to take on such an expensive project. The biggest risk—not only to them but to all of us—if neither approach curbs the excesses of for-profit philanthropy lies in a loss of confidence that philanthropy serves public interests rather than private aims. Chapter 8 explores the systemic reforms a catastrophic loss of trust in philanthropy might usher in, including tax hikes and more direct efforts to curb elite power.

Without a way to ensure that philanthropy remains focused on solving public problems, on a public timeline, with opportunities for public oversight, philanthropy could appear—if not become—no more than a series of vanity projects more worthy of skepticism than acclaim. If virtue signaling supplants virtue, the Grand Bargain that secures public trust in elite philanthropy seems destined to collapse with the proverbial whimper.

Without efforts by regulators, philanthropists, or both to reassure the public, for-profit philanthropy could jeopardize the whole project of philanthropy, leaving tomorrow's elites Hollow Men as impotent as Rockefeller found himself a century ago. Through a comprehensive overview of this important but overlooked legal phenomenon, this book offers the historical and theoretical context necessary to understand the profound threat for-profit philanthropy poses and a roadmap for how the law can address it.

PART I
ELITE PHILANTHROPY IN THE TWENTY-FIRST CENTURY

1
The Philanthropy LLC

Like the famed philanthropist John D. Rockefeller, the limited liability company (LLC) now trending in elite philanthropy circles began its rise in the oil industry.[1] Modeled after legal forms pairing flexible governance and liability protection for owners overseas, state legislatures began offering the new form to entrepreneurs in the late 1970s. Today, more new businesses start as LLCs than in any other legal form.[2]

The LLC cemented its dominance among business firms after the Clinton Administration determined that the entity could be ignored for tax purposes, with profits taxed only in the hands of its owners. Chapter 5 explains how this radical notion, which came to be known as a "tax nothing,"[3] helped inspire generations of avant-garde legal forms. This chapter shows why for those with everything, nothing has proven to have a potent appeal.

The Chan Zuckerberg Initiative (CZI) can lay claim to being both the best and least known philanthropy LLC. News outlets buzzed with questions about the until-then little heard of use of LLCs for philanthropy when it was first established in December 2015.[4] But most casual observers took no note of the philanthropy's unusual form.

The outcry among those that did, questioning its founder's motives, inspired Mark Zuckerberg to offer his own explanation in a Facebook post. "By using an LLC instead of a traditional foundation, we receive no tax benefit from transferring our shares to the Chan Zuckerberg Initiative, but we gain flexibility to execute our mission more effectively."[5] That mission straddles initiatives in three areas—education, justice and opportunity, and science—which CZI pursues through grantmaking, impact investments, advocacy work, and engineering.

For ultra-rich donors like Chan and Zuckerberg, the LLC improves on conventional philanthropic platforms. A generation before, creating a philanthropic vehicle without securing a tax exemption for it might easily have been legal malpractice; tax-exempt foundations represented the obvious choice. By the time of the Chan Zuckerberg Initiative's founding, the philanthropy LLC had become a proven alternative. Chan and Zuckerberg, trumpeting their adoption of the form across their social media empire, left no doubt that the age of the philanthropy LLC had arrived, presenting great value to founders and grave risks for the public.

For-Profit Philanthropy. Dana Brakman Reiser and Steven A. Dean, Oxford University Press. © Oxford University Press 2023. DOI: 10.1093/oso/9780190074500.003.0002

LLC adopters tout its operational versatility as the key to its appeal. And employing a philanthropy LLC undoubtedly eliminates countless burdens the traditional foundation format imposes. Since 1969, a series of excise taxes have served as lighthouses marking hidden shoals—entanglement with business or politics—perceived as existential threats to philanthropy.[6] Philanthropy LLCs blithely ignore those risks and the safeguards built to guard against them. Their funders accept a moderately higher tax burden in exchange for freedom to pursue their vision of the good unfettered by foundation law's limitations.

The power an LLC form preserves for its founders figures prominently in its allure. An LLC can be formed by a single person, a couple, or a group. Its founder or founders may manage it directly. No pesky board of directors need get in the way of their vision, and any fiduciary obligations an LLC's managers owe will be to the founders themselves. It can spend its assets down at breakneck speed, seeking to exhaust its resources during the founders' lifetimes. Or it can take the long view, engineering a big payout in the distant future.

LLC founders also retain the ultimate power: exit. For all the claims by philanthropy LLC founders that assigning their funds or shares to their LLCs are donations, assets so transferred can be as easily returned to founders' accounts. An LLC can be terminated, with any assets remaining after clearing its debts returned to its member or members.

Such a transaction has no tax consequences, and it need not be reported to anyone. Legally, it represents nothing more than moving your wallet from one pocket to the other. For ultra-wealthy celebrity philanthropists like Chan and Zuckerberg, the public relations challenge of such a move could be significant. But of course, we only know what they choose to tell us.

A philanthropy LLC bestows on founders the power to tell their own stories. An LLC founder faces no legal obligation to inform anyone of its formation, other than the secretary of state in which the entity will be formed, who must receive its bare-bones articles of organization.[7] The actions—and indeed existence—of the philanthropy LLCs explored below emerge only from the disclosures they and their founders choose to make and the efforts of journalists.

In sharp contrast, federal law requires foundations to make annual reports on their assets, activities, personnel, and donors.[8] More telling, these disclosures become public documents, reviewable by anyone with a little time and internet access through the GuideStar website.[9] Every good businessperson understands the value of controlling the narrative; it is certainly not lost on the ultra-high-net-worth individuals opting for philanthropy LLCs.

For philanthropists seeking to flexibly deploy their stratospheric wealth in pursuit of their idiosyncratic visions of the good, the benefits of using an LLC inevitably offset its tax disadvantages. Revelations about the irrelevance of the tax laws to the wealthiest Americans[10] underscore why a philanthropy LLC's benefits will outweigh the notional tax costs of foregoing the conventional alternative: a tax-exempt private foundation. Tax nothing treatment means assets donated to a philanthropy LLC continue to be treated as those of the donors, attracting no notice from the tax laws.

Any net income the LLC earns will be taxed to its owners. By the same token, an LLC's donors may avail themselves of a charitable contribution deduction when and to the extent their LLC actually makes a charitable grant. They do need to wait to enjoy this benefit until such time as the LLC actually makes a donation—in contrast, funding a foundation entitles a philanthropist to an immediate deduction—but when the wealthiest Americans pay no income tax at all, that hardly matters.

Estate taxes might capture assets held by an individual controlling a philanthropy LLC at its owner's death. If the owner has not made provision in their estate plan to donate these assets to charity or undertaken estate tax-minimizing strategies, the estate tax stands ready to seize control of a meaningful portion of their fortune. Currently, estates worth up to $12.06 million for individuals and $24.12 for married couples pay no tax at all.[11] Although shockingly high amounts, Chan, Zuckerberg, and the other philanthropy LLC adopters described here will easily surpass them. If those individuals fail to plan ahead to minimize estate tax on the LLCs' assets at death, they will have only themselves or their lawyers to blame for their tax bill.

Well-heeled and well-counseled philanthropists can minimize the tax costs of opting for an LLC. What costs remain will often be far outweighed by the operational versatility, control, and privacy the LLC option provides. The option value of the LLC—to do what you want, to change your mind, to tell your own story—may or may not persuade billionaire philanthropists to give away more of their wealth than they otherwise would. Choosing that option inarguably reduces the public's ability to target their largesse, mandate its timing, and impose transparency obligations necessary to verify their actions.

The Philanthropy LLC's Provenance

Given Zuckerberg's household name status as founder and CEO of the world's largest social media platform, CZI's renown is unsurprising. But its notoriety should not be mistaken for novelty. Philanthropy LLCs had already quietly been deployed for other Silicon Valley fortunes—two of them for more than a decade.

Offering perhaps the greatest contrast in PR style to CZI is the Emerson Collective, a philanthropy LLC formed by Laurene Powell Jobs in 2004. With assets largely traceable to her marriage to the late Apple founder and CEO Steve Jobs, Emerson "deploys a wide range of tools—from impact investing to philanthropy to advocacy—in pursuit of a more equal and just America."[12] It utilizes these tools across a diverse philanthropic agenda: education, immigration, climate change, and cancer research. According to its famously private founder,[13] each of these are "[c]omplex systemic failures" that "require flexible approaches, new models, and improved public policy."[14]

Also in 2004, Pam and Pierre Omidyar used their eBay wealth to embrace the opportunities presented by the philanthropy LLC. The couple combined their preexisting private foundation with a new LLC into a hybrid they christened The Omidyar Network. It too emphasizes the LLC structure's value in enhancing the range of tools it provides "to build more inclusive and equitable societies—for the benefit of the many, not just the few—across the globe."[15] The foundation continues to make grants to public charities, while the LLC engages in impact investing and advocacy work. The decision to layer an LLC alongside the existing private foundation was driven by a desire "to support early-stage organizations that catalyzed economic and social change, and the autonomy to work flexibly across the returns continuum" with "an 'impact first, tool second' approach, centering systems and impact, and deploying relevant tools as needed."[16]

Other tech billionaires quietly followed their examples. Facebook cofounder Dustin Moskovitz created Good Ventures LLC as a vehicle for impact investing after leaving the company in 2012, together with his partner (now wife) Cari Tuna. Along the lines of the Omidyar Network, Good Ventures is linked with a charitable foundation engaged in grantmaking.[17] Through this combination, they seek to "give and invest for maximum impact,"[18] guided by counsel from philanthropy advisors Open Philanthropy and GiveWell.

Together with his wife Connie, Microsoft cofounder Steve Ballmer founded the Ballmer Group in 2014 with a focus on education. They, too, opted to organize as an LLC. The group combines charitable grantmaking with impact investing and policy work "to improv[e] economic mobility for children and families in the United States."[19]

The LLC trend continued after CZI's splashy entrance. John and Laura Arnold announced plans to bring their foundation under a larger LLC umbrella in 2019. The couple, whose fortune is drawn principally from the profits of the hedge fund John Arnold led, have broad philanthropic interests tied to increasing opportunity and reducing injustice. They "focus on correcting systemic failures through evidence-based solutions,"[20] with the LLC coordinating the grantmaking efforts of their preexisting foundation, as well as a donor-advised fund and an advocacy group.

When the ravages of the COVID-19 pandemic spurred billionaire and then-Twitter and Square CEO Jack Dorsey to jumpstart his philanthropy, the LLC was again the vehicle of choice. Dorsey's explanation rings familiar, citing the form's "flexibility" to make disbursements either from an affiliated "Start

Small Foundation or the LLC directly based on the beneficiary org."[21] Dubbed #startsmall (he is a former Twitter CEO after all), Dorsey's announcement also committed to a radical do-it-yourself kind of transparency that would track his contributions and their purposes publicly and in real time.

Even two of the philanthropists most highly identified with the foundation form have embraced the advantages of the philanthropy LLC. The announcement of Bill and Melinda French Gates's divorce in 2021 provoked greater interest in the LLC vehicles each had founded individually: Breakthrough Energy and Pivotal Ventures.[22] Although they will continue to be involved in the massive Gates Foundation, the two LLCs align with each of their personal passions—Bill's for clean energy and Melinda's for women's empowerment. The entities' LLC structures allow their founders to nimbly combine philanthropic and investment approaches and, until recently, keep them under the radar.[23]

With much of her net worth deriving from Amazon shares, MacKenzie Scott's fortune is growing at a rate difficult for her giving to match—though she is making a valiant effort.[24] Several waves of contributions disclosed between July 2020 and March 2022 through posts on Medium describe direct gifts of over $12 billion to more than 1200 charitable organizations across a wide range of areas.[25] Scott has thus far publicized only donations to charities, so it is uncertain whether these constitute all or only a part of her efforts to complete her 2019 giving pledge to "keep at it until the safe is empty."[26] Some of her giving has been channeled through her donor-advised fund, the subject of chapter 2, and Scott has not revealed whether she employs an LLC. Either way, her efforts to enhance her flexibility and control over her giving have much in common with the public LLC adopters described already. By likewise eschewing a traditional foundation, she equally disregards its capacity to generate accountability and maintain public trust in philanthropy.

The concerns raised by the LLCs profiled in this chapter apply equally to elite philanthropy conducted without the benefit of any organizational structure, though it is unlikely many elite donors will elect to proceed in this manner. Small, direct charitable contributions from individuals are a cornerstone of the nonprofit sector. For those making million-—or billion-—dollar contributions, however, the benefits of a legal structure and the liability shield that comes along with it are a powerful draw to formal organization.

The LLC's particular appeal to wealthy donors connected to Silicon Valley and the technology sector can be explained—at least in part—by its iconoclasm. Those earning great wealth in technology have long seen themselves as disruptors, toppling the conventional wisdom to make way for radical new visions. The mere fact that the LLC allows a philanthropist to reject fusty traditional approaches in favor of the unexpected strikes the same nerve as Facebook's aggressive "move fast and break things" and Apple's more contemplative "think different." Private foundations have changed little in the new millennium, indeed since 1969. For today's tycoons, that might be reason enough to reject them; but LLCs' far greater operational versatility, control, and privacy deliver a host of more tangible benefits.

Operational Versatility

Alongside theoretically significant tax benefits, the obligations imposed on tax-exempt organizations—and private foundations in particular—can be daunting. A sprawling regulatory framework conceived more than fifty years ago obligates foundations to keep their distance from business, stay out of politics, make consistent payouts to charities, and disclose much of their conduct to the public. For billionaires operating at the level of those described here, the costs of lawyers and accountants needed to comply with these regulations should hardly register. The forgone opportunities foundation law's confines impose matter much more.

That can be seen in the choices these philanthropists make. Unconstrained by limits on the nature of their business relationships and political activities, for-profit philanthropists using LLCs behave differently. Even when their current actions look like their peers using conventional foundations, an LLC form preserves for founders the valuable option to venture into unchartered philanthropic territory in the future.

Investing at Scale

Philanthropy LLCs offer their founders the flexibility to wield whatever tool best serves their lofty objectives. For many, investments in for-profit firms have proven attractive.

Together with traditional philanthropy like contributions to a range of education initiatives, the Emerson Collective has made some bold and surprising business deals. Emerson's investment in online municipal bond broker Neighborly and its acquisition of a majority stake in *The Atlantic* both made quite a splash.[27] Flourish, "a venture firm investing in entrepreneurs whose innovations help people achieve financial health and prosperity," advances the Omidyar Network's philanthropic vision.[28] Spun off in 2019 to form an independent firm with funding from the Omidyar Network, Flourish invests in for-profit ventures that focus on everything from insurance to digital currency.[29]

Connie and Steve Ballmer took to the pages of the *Chronicle of Philanthropy* to trumpet the Ballmer Group's investment in Social Solutions, an Austin software company that works with nonprofits and governments. They explained:

> Our support will allow Social Solutions to accelerate development of Apricot, an off-the-shelf software package, and allow it to better integrate with data from other sources to provide a 360-degree view of a family's challenges. Because our financial stake will help ensure the product is sold in high volume, we can be sure it will stay up-to-date and affordable.[30]

The $59 million investment was to be split between operational support to develop products and hire staff and a pool of funds for matching grants to enhance nonprofits' access to the software developed.[31]

LLCs' capacity for investing at scale cannot be matched by private foundations. Tax law's awkwardly named "excess business holdings" regime ensures that tax-exempt foundations can own no more than 20 percent of any business—even less if their leaders or substantial owners also own shares.[32] By design, the consequences of violating these rules can be devastating, but not quite in the manner one might expect.

Exceeding the excess business holdings threshold does not necessarily endanger the tax-exempt status of a foundation. Breach instead triggers a special tax on the value of the excess holdings. Initially, a tax of 10 percent is imposed on any excess business interests. If the foundation continues to hold more than these rules permit, the penalty rises to a breathtaking 200 percent. At this point, of course, although nominally a tax, the excess business holdings rules become a cudgel, making the intentions of Congress to steer foundations away from deep entanglements with businesses unmistakable. Another two-tiered tax penalizes both foundations and their managers for imprudent investments that "jeopardize the carrying out of any of its exempt purposes" by imperiling its financial position.[33]

Perhaps no entity has struggled more mightily with the excess business holdings rules' limitations than Newman's Own Foundation. When Newman's Own launched its highly successful brand in Paul Newman's barn, with the actor mixing a vat of salad dressing with a canoe paddle to give away as Christmas presents, it set itself on a difficult path.[34] Since then, the business has generated and given away hundreds of millions of dollars. But the structure it embraced, funding philanthropy out of the profits of a for-profit venture the foundation owned, clashed with onerous excess business holdings restrictions.

After Newman's death, the Newman's Own Foundation took direct and complete control of the for-profit company. This obviously posed a problem. Owning 100 percent of a for-profit company's stock represented a clear violation of the excess business holdings rule setting a 20 percent ceiling. The foundation faced compelled divestiture.

An eleventh-hour legislative solution saved the day when finally, in 2018, Congress created what many justifiably now refer to as the Newman's Own exception. It gave foundations permission to hold 100 percent of for-profit companies, provided their stakes are acquired by gift and the companies remain independently operated. This tailor-made exception fits Newman's Own like a glove but otherwise leaves the excess business holdings rule—and its daunting consequences—intact.[35]

LLCs, in contrast, face no limitations on the investments they may hold—whether to capitalize enterprises pursuing donors' desired social impacts or to fund the LLC's operations. This smooth path, however, does not mean LLC investments will always succeed. Impact investments can prove prescient and return both financial and social value, but they can also disappoint on either or both fronts. In the years after Emerson's investment, Neighborly pivoted away from its initial focus on municipal bonds to blockchain technology and then to telecom infrastructure and eventually ran out of money.[36] Ballmer's Social Solutions investment may revolutionize social services and return a profit; it may do only one; it may do neither.

The Chan Zuckerberg Initiative's inaugural impact investment has since demonstrated the challenges in marrying mission and profit. Andela was founded with a "strategy . . . to identify high-potential talent on the African continent, train them in software development (with a heavy emphasis on remote work and soft skills) and then place them as full-time distributed engineers"[37] and CZI invested in several rounds of Andela funding. The firm remains afloat, but just five years after its creation and three years after it was CZI's first investment, Andela made "an extremely difficult decision as it relates to a number of talented junior engineers," closing training programs in three African countries and eliminating 250 employees as part of "a strategic shift in how we think about talent."

The LLC offers philanthropists an option unhindered by private foundation law's regulatory framework. It empowers for-profit philanthropists to bet big—on both impact investments and their own investment philosophies. Like all high stakes wagers, some will fail spectacularly but others will pay off. The freedom to take on risk in the name of seeking vast societal rewards defines this way of doing the business of philanthropy.

Keeping the Corner Office

The excess business holdings rules cause an additional headache for moguls intent on helming both major firms and philanthropies. Take Zuckerberg, who remains CEO of Facebook (though now rebranded as Meta) and has indicated no intention to cede control over his creation.[38] An LLC structure allows Zuckerberg to make the headline-grabbing donation to CZI while retaining his majority voting position at the firm.

Had he contributed his $45 billion in Facebook stock to a private foundation instead, those shares and their votes would have fallen under the control of the foundation's board of directors. These fiduciaries would owe their prudence and loyalty to the foundation's charitable mission. That might or might not align with the interests and preferences of Zuckerberg or any other CEO.

Perhaps even more painful for Zuckerberg, tax law's excess business holdings regime would force a foundation recipient of his shares to divest its stake in Facebook to the extent it exceeded 20 percent of the company. This ceiling on the stake a foundation may own falls further to account for amounts owned by substantial contributors, managers, and their relatives (read: Mark Zuckerberg and Priscilla Chan) control. Once excess business holdings exist, the clock begins to run on the brief period during which the foundation must sell off shares until its stake falls below the acceptable limit.

The affront this forced divestiture regime would represent to Zuckerberg can be read in the fact that he at first declined to transfer his voting control over Facebook even to the LLC he formed with Chan. Rather, he initially persuaded the Facebook board to reorganize the company's capital structure to add a new class of shares that would be economically valuable when contributed to CZI but would not dent Zuckerberg's control over the company.[39] Shareholders sued in protest and the plan was eventually abandoned. Still, the lengths to which at least one highly successful entrepreneur went in order to retain tight control over the leadership of his firm powerfully illustrates the value an LLC's flexibility delivers. Dorsey's initial announcement that he created #startsmall with a contribution of Square shares and that he would "need to pace the sales over some time" suggests a similar desire to conduct divestiture on his own schedule.[40]

LLCs preserve for founders the freedom both to pursue their philanthropy and to fund it through controlling stakes in for-profit ventures. Unmoored from tax law's restraints on this tool, LLCs can leverage the extraordinary power of capital markets to fuel a philanthropic mission, though not without risk. The lack of diversification of CZI's assets may not always be a winning investment strategy, for example, if antitrust efforts to break up tech giants prove fruitful.

Leveraging Business Assets and Acumen

The highly successful founders of philanthropy LLCs can offer more than dollars to the causes they support. Especially younger donors still leading the business empires that made their fortunes also see the value their firms' products and know-how can contribute. Again, CZI's experience shows how.

CZI has been a major supporter of Summit Schools, a charter school operator in California and Washington State,[41] granting it and its related entities tens of millions of dollars to date.[42] Summit began developing an online personalized learning platform for its own use. When Mark Zuckerberg became aware of the organization's needs, he offered Facebook's engineering prowess to assist.

Facebook's engineers helped Summit Public Schools launch what became the Summit Learning Program for its own network and for licensing by other schools. In 2017, CZI transitioned to a direct role as Summit's "long-term technology partner."[43] Teams of engineers, product managers, designers, and data scientists with links to Facebook's vast talent stores and technology tools took part. The philanthropy LLC, as Summit's evolving partnership with CZI demonstrates, can provide a depth of in-kind support and technical assistance a foundation's strict limits on transactions with donors and managers were designed to prevent.

Philanthropy LLCs undertaking large-scale investments in for-profit firms, engaging in co-creation by partnering with grantees, and brokering relationships with founders' firms on their behalf, comes with the potential for reputational damage, self-dealing, or both. Expansion of Summit's learning platform in schools beyond its network has generated some disapproval. Contractual requirements that partner schools share deidentified student data with Summit and its partners—including CZI—proved particularly problematic. That harvesting of student data raised troubling questions that the information—potentially reidentified—might be used in future ventures.[44] Such concerns about the CZI–Summit relationship have caused friction for CZI with grantees and employees.[45] So has the overlap between CZI and Facebook.

With an entity as large as CZI and a founder as influential as Mark Zuckerberg, criticism comes as no surprise. Pointing out that its interactions with Summit have raised eyebrows does not suggest that CZI has done anything untoward. Similar questions could be raised about the unconventional investments Emerson, Omidyar, and Ballmer have made in The Atlantic, Flourish, and Social Solutions.

Transactions between each pair could easily be designed to help for-profit businesses thrive in service of the philanthropy LLC's social goals. CZI might provide low-cost intellectual property licenses courtesy of Meta while the Emerson Collective could provide office space on favorable terms. An LLC is purpose-built to enable such mutually beneficial arrangements.

Had these founders employed a conventional foundation structure, such transactions could easily violate strict tax rules limiting transactions with related parties. Careful vetting would be essential. For example, foundations that purchase or lease property from for-profit businesses connected to their donors or managers—described by tax law as "self-dealing" whether or not the insider receives a benefit—will trigger hefty penalties.[46] The initially modest 10 percent (5 percent on managers) tax on the transaction ratchets up to 200 percent

(50 percent for managers) if not corrected. Should the transaction even demonstrably benefit a philanthropy and its aims, the penalties stand. Intentionally overbroad and punitive, the self-dealing rules offer assurance that private foundations will steer clear not only of conflicts of interest but of even the potential for them.

Obviously, it would be regrettable if student data CZI harvested from Summit enriched Zuckerberg and Chan (or worse yet, Meta). But the self-dealing rules also prohibit entirely benign transactions clearly advantageous to foundations and their charitable goals. Bright-line rules designed to make an emphatic statement about the poorly drawn boundary between philanthropy and commerce, these restrictions err on the side of caution.

A noble purpose will not transform excess business holdings into permitted investments. The same holds true here. Clear evidence that a low-cost license of valuable intellectual property favors a foundation will not shield a transaction from tax penalties targeted at self-dealing. These rules decisively separate profit-seeking from philanthropy, standing in sharp contrast to the LLC's embrace of for-profit philanthropists' symbiotic visions.

CZI, or its portfolio companies, might benefit by capitalizing on Facebook's technology at favorable rates. The same goes for real estate and all the other resources ambitious ventures need to succeed. Even if CZI decides not to engage in such transactions, choosing for-profit philanthropy ensures that it could. By using an LLC rather than a private foundation, its founders retain the freedom to envision the optimal degree of integration between their business and philanthropic pursuits.

Unleashing Advocacy

Breaking another traditional taboo in the sector, philanthropy LLCs engage in direct political advocacy and even campaigns.[47] That involvement reflects a conviction that philanthropists, as The Omidyar Network puts it, "have to do everything we can to support those on the frontlines of change."[48] The versatile LLC vehicle places every possible route toward societal improvement at philanthropists' disposal.

When the Emerson Collective chooses to embrace political advocacy, it faces no more regulatory obstacles to doing so than any individual might. It can lobby for or against specific pieces of legislation, latitude it has embraced to advocate forcefully on immigration issues. The Collective pushed hard to support the passage of the DREAM Act in Congress.[49] Powell Jobs spoke out on her own and also took action through the Collective that "commissioned polling, lobbied Congress, urged President Barack Obama to take action and funded a documentary about undocumented youth."[50]

Like the individual behind it, Emerson can also support or oppose candidates. Federal election law treats contributions by tax nothings as though made by their owners.[51] The Center for Responsive Politics indicates that the Emerson Collective contributed nearly a quarter of a million dollars to national Democratic Party organizations and more than $30,000 more to Joe Biden.[52]

Information about the Collective's political activities remains incomplete. Its political contributions must be disclosed under election law, but unearthing lobbying information is more difficult and the Emerson Collective does not publish detailed information about its lobbying activities. Given its focus on immigration and its more general statements, though, it would be reasonable to assume that some significant part goes toward advancing congressional efforts on immigration reform. No matter whether Emerson's political activities represent something to be praised or feared, both campaign contributions and substantial advocacy programs remain out of reach even for mega foundations like Gates and Ford.

John and Laura Arnold highlighted the importance of combining advocacy with grantmaking when reorganizing their philanthropic efforts under the Arnold Ventures LLC umbrella.[53] The press release announcing the change described an evolving philanthropic strategy. "[W]e realized that in order to create change that lasts, we would need to remove barriers between data and decisive action, working swiftly across the policy-change spectrum."[54] Arnold Ventures' communications describe their work as limited to advocacy—not political campaign contributions—addressing a wide range of issues. Its criminal justice reform efforts contributed to passage of the federal FIRST STEP Act, and its advocacy work both in Washington and in state capitals across the country concerns topics as diverse as gun violence and prescription drug pricing.[55]

As their LLC ramped up its advocacy, the Omidyars chose to make more details of this activity freely available. In October 2020, the LLC published a list of thirteen entities to which it provided funding for lobbying and other advocacy efforts in 2019. The purely voluntary disclosure included the names of the organizations and briefly described the types of projects funded through each, though it did not include the amounts contributed. In its own words:

> Policy, politics, and direct advocacy are critical ways for [Omidyar Network] to leverage our resources to support the change we want to see in the world. . . . Because our investments in organizations such as 501(c)(4)s come from a private, for-profit company, we are not required to disclose them in the same way we disclose the grants given from our private foundation. But that goes against our commitment to transparency and true democracy, so we are voluntarily disclosing them here.[56]

The Omidyars, who report their last contribution to an individual candidate or party was in 2011, also disclosed their own personal contributions to advocacy groups in 2020.[57] Both the donors and their LLC have committed to continue to operate transparently in this space.

The advocacy efforts of other LLCs are more difficult to pin down. The Arnold Ventures website stresses the importance of "relationships with key policy-making officials at all levels of government" and "providing support for ongoing advocacy or defending against efforts to repeal or legal challenges to the policy changes [Arnold Ventures advocates] through strategic litigation."[58] Readers can learn more about this work, however, only through highlighted stories about the LLC's advocacy leadership.

The Ballmer Group's site describes its work as "employ[ing] levers of change that hold promise for long-term system improvements" including advocacy but only individually discloses charitable grants, though details of some of its other activities can be found in occasional features and blog posts.[59] When asked in connection with a 2019 feature, "[o]fficials from the Ballmer Group [] told Education Week they would not commit to publicly disclose all the organization's grants, investments, lobbying work, or support for elected officials and campaigns."[60]

Policy reform and political change are powerful levers to advance visions of the good. Using an LLC allows philanthropists the choice of whether to reach for them. This degree of freedom contrasts starkly with the punishing limits enforced against private foundation advocacy and campaigning.

The treacherous rocks Congress marked in 1969 included investments and business transactions made by private foundations. Congress also seemed to find political spending particularly threatening. Support for civil rights by prominent foundations in the preceding years drew attention to the influence wielded by philanthropic organizations. And as with the regulation of foundations' business relationships described above, the prohibitions imposed on their political expenditures take a sweeping approach.

A tripartite prohibition on spending private foundation resources on politics makes no attempt at subtlety. If a substantial part of any tax-exempt charity's activities consists of influencing legislation, it will not qualify for tax-exempt status. Together with a prohibition against supporting candidates for public office, also known as the Johnson Amendment, this statutory barrier starkly limits the freedom of all charities to engage in political activity.[61]

But for private foundations, Congress has gone even further. An escalating excise tax mirroring that imposed on excess business holdings, jeopardizing investments, and self-dealing transactions targets amounts spent by private foundations to influence legislation and political campaigns. Tiered to first offer a warning to the foundation then to brutally punish recalcitrance—the second-tier tax rises to 100 percent—this excise tax sends an unambiguous message that no amount of political activity by private foundations will be tolerated.[62] As with jeopardizing investments and self-dealing, the political expenditure rules target not only the foundation but also individual managers involved in suspect transactions. Burdening managers with a tax as high as 50 percent on the organization's political spending underscores the ferocity of tax law's insistence that foundations avoid entanglements with politics.

Despite long-standing prohibitions and harsh penalties designed to prevent it, philanthropists remain intent on influencing policy. Foundations find ways to advocate for policies that align with the particular visions of their funders. Although doing so requires navigating an unforgiving array of potentially existential threats and much lies out of bounds, private foundations retain access to a variety of political weapons and have amply demonstrated their ability to wield them.

The rise of the Common Core educational standards highlights the influential policymaking role private foundation spending can play regardless of tax law's attempts to limit it. In 2008, Bill Gates met with reform advocates who persuaded him that "academic standards varied so wildly between states that high school diplomas had lost all meaning" and offered a solution.[63] The results of that meeting were astonishing: "one of the swiftest and most remarkable shifts in education policy in U.S. history."[64] A number of factors figured in the success of the push to encourage states to adopt the Common Core. Support from President Obama and Education Secretary Arne Duncan played a role.[65] The $200 million devoted by the Gates Foundation to the effort helped dissolve long-standing resistance from teachers' unions and conservatives alike.

In just a few years, the Common Core standards had been adopted in all but a handful of states. Despite constraints designed to ensure otherwise, the Gates Foundation evidently enjoyed great freedom to influence policy decisions. Although it may have violated the spirit of rules designed to prevent political advocacy, the Gates Foundation's effort did not trigger any sanctions. The explanation may simply be that "because of the way education policy is generally decided, the Common Core was instituted in many states without a single vote taken by an elected lawmaker."[66] Advocating for the Common Core simply did not implicate rules prohibiting a private foundation from spending money to promote either legislation or legislators.

The Gates Foundation's involvement in the adoption of the Common Core education standards shows that fearsome limits on political activity can be conquered with guile—at least under certain circumstances. The protections that prevent political activity by private foundations remain imperfect. But a philanthropy LLC eliminates them altogether.

The LLC transforms a fraught strategy suited only to a small subset of policy issues into a simple matter of writing checks. When this ability to unleash advocacy combines with the other freedoms a philanthropy LLC grants to its founders, its allure becomes obvious. Not only can elite philanthropists who opt for an LLC invest for social good at scale, retain leadership of their firms, and leverage the business assets and acumen of those firms, they can pursue their policy agendas directly through lobbying and campaign contributions. Unbelievably, the advantages do not end there.

Preserving Control

A philanthropy LLC grants its founder or founders unparalleled control over the implementation of their charitable visions. As the LLC's owners, they can design the entity's governance, dominating it should they wish to do so. This authority controls not only to whom and for what purposes the LLC's funds will flow but also the timeline for their distribution. It also grants them the power to exit. LLC members may dissolve the entity and reclaim its assets for themselves at any time.

Controlling Governance

An LLC observes the rules laid out in its operating agreement—which its founding member or members may design in any way they desire.[67] Founders can choose to empower a board or another group to supervise the LLC. Or they may choose to manage the organization entirely on their own. The operating agreement can establish any objectives its founders choose. It can also raise, lower, or even largely eliminate fiduciary obligations on the part of those managing the entity.

This operating agreement need never become a public document. As a result, precious little information can be divined about the governance arrangements of the philanthropy LLCs described here. Founders must file their articles of organization with the state in which they form their entities, and these documents do become publicly available. But they provide only the most basic information, confirming the existence of the entity and an agent to receive legal communications but little more.[68] Although a philanthropy LLC's founder can share control over their creation with outsiders, enhance fiduciary obligations, or impose other accountability features, the voluntary disclosures of those discussed here provide no hint that they do.

Controlling When Funds Flow

Philanthropy LLCs also provide their founders unfettered discretion over the speed at which they spend their money—a freedom that runs in both directions. The specter of the estate tax all but ensures that they will set their own lifetimes as the maximum duration for their LLCs. Whether they will reach that endpoint quickly or slowly, smoothly or in fits and starts, is up to them.

For some adopters, this flexibility dovetails with a desire to distribute assets quickly. John and Laura Arnold have made accelerating their philanthropy a key goal. They speak publicly about the importance of having "today's philanthropists help solve today's problems today," noting that "[w]e think people should give more money. There are many future billionaires and wealthy people who will help solve tomorrow's problems tomorrow."[69]

The Arnolds became the first to join a global campaign called "Give While You Live," orchestrated by Global Citizen in 2021. The effort urged major donors to commit to giving 5 percent of their total wealth to charity each year.[70] The Arnolds would almost certainly have exceeded that modest threshold without that public commitment, but they made the pledge anyway.

They have a proven track record for spending down their wealth. Forbes found John Arnold had given more than 20 percent of his wealth to charity, one of only ten philanthropists reaching this highest level of giving.[71] As discussed in more detail in chapter 2, the couple has also been involved in advocacy efforts imploring Congress to incentivize others to do the same.

Although we do not know the particulars of the philanthropic vehicles MacKenzie Scott employs, she too has been both an advocate and a practitioner of giving fast. When reflecting upon her Giving Pledge commitment, she highlighted not only its scope but its speed. "Last year I pledged to give the majority of my wealth back to the society that helped generate it, to do it thoughtfully, to get started soon, and to keep at it until the safe is empty."[72]

The magnitude of the need generated and revealed through the COVID-19 pandemic and the movement for Black lives intensified her desire to act immediately. It also informed a determination to empower the recipients of her donations. She made six-figure gifts to hundreds of organizations in just a single year's span and included no restrictions at all on their use.

Many traditional foundations likewise freed grantees from contractual restrictions to enable them to nimbly respond to the unprecedented demands of 2020, but a shift to frontloading giving contrasts sharply with the mainstream foundation culture, where perpetuity is deeply ingrained. Indeed, the quiet acceptance of foundations' perpetual life is perhaps the most important compromise Congress struck in its watershed 1969 foundation legislation. Rather than explicitly imposing a limited lifespan on private foundations or openly endorsing their perpetual existence, it imposed a requirement that a foundation's adjusted net income or at least 6 percent of the value of its assets be spent in each year.[73] The required spending—intended to capture actual or imputed returns on a foundation's investments and designed to vary with market yields—was soon fixed at the current rate of 5 percent of a foundation's endowment.[74]

Without such rules, philanthropy risks mutating from altruism into a perverse form of privilege. Wealthy patrons could forever dangle the promise of charity with no obligation to provide it. Critics of university spending policies highlight that risk.

Elite institutions like Harvard and Yale have been derided as little more than hedge funds with universities attached,[75] prompting Congress to impose a 1.4 percent tax on the income of the largest university endowments in 2017.[76] Private foundations pay a nearly identical tax on their investment incomes,[77] yet unlike Harvard or Yale, they must also spend—or simply forfeit—a minimum amount of their endowments each year.

That 5 percent spending requirement still allows prosperous foundations to achieve—or at least aim for—immortality. And many do. The Ford Foundation, for example, routinely earns more than 5 percent on its investments.[78] Spending 5 percent of the value of its assets each year limits its growth, rather than its lifespan. Founded explicitly to endure in perpetuity, Ford will continue its charitable mission ostensibly forever.[79] When a foundation's initial donor inscribes perpetuity into its formative documents, trust or corporate law will also demand that its managers not distribute too much at any one time.[80]

There are, of course, foundations that aim to make themselves irrelevant. Some are established with a goal of spending down their assets; others have shifted away from a perpetual vision over time. The brief, four-year lifespan of the Rockefeller Sanitary Commission for the Eradication of Hookworm Disease offers an early template. Its creators effectively declared victory and closed up shop having, as its name boldly predicted, all but eradicated the disease.[81] Some foundations in our own times—even highly influential ones—have adopted plans to aggressively spend down. The John M. Olin Foundation seeded a new conservative intellectual movement and made a lasting impact all while committed to close the foundation within twenty-five years of its founder's death.[82] Bill and Melinda French Gates once committed the Gates Foundation to spend the resources they provide to it within twenty years of their deaths.[83] Whereas the couple's divorce appears poised to impact their future giving to the foundation they created together, their commitment to spending down remains: in early 2022, the foundation announced plans to maintain its grantmaking at the elevated level adopted in response to the COVID-19 pandemic or higher.[84]

These efforts illustrate that a commitment to distribute philanthropic assets speedily is certainly possible within a foundation structure. But the pull of perpetuity is strong. Consider the actions of five other leading foundations—the Ford Foundation, the John D. and Catherine T. MacArthur Foundation; the W.K. Kellogg Foundation; the Andrew W. Mellon Foundation; and the Doris Duke Charitable Foundation—in the face of the COVID-19 pandemic's global disruption. Unlike many, these foundations not only wanted to help but had the resources to make an enormous difference. They sat atop billions, and in some cases tens of billions, of dollars earmarked for the arts, education, and public health at a time of urgent need.

These prominent philanthropic organizations very publicly pledged to increase their giving significantly. But with the bulk of their endowments invested for the long term, the stock market downturn that marked the early days of the pandemic gave them pause. They proved reluctant to liquidate investments with markets at a low ebb. Instead, given that interest rates had fallen along with equity markets, the group of five chose to borrow to finance their increased giving.[85] Issuing long-term debt to finance today's crisis illustrates that even when foundations recognize the urgency of current problems, they continue to envision remaining a viable force in the philanthropic world for the long haul.[86]

Although some philanthropy LLC founders rely on the form to give fast, it also empowers philanthropists to give leisurely. The value of the philanthropy LLC option emerges vividly when juxtaposing the Ford Foundation and Dorsey's #startsmall LLC. Dorsey created #startsmall during the pandemic and in response to the urgent needs it created. And like the Ford Foundation, it deployed roughly 10 percent of its endowment in response.[87] But eventually, pandemics recede. The Ford Foundation will shift from a wartime to a peacetime footing. Presumably, the same will be true for #startsmall. But how should the LLC behave in relatively lush times to prepare for lean years certain to come?

The Ford Foundation, like all private foundations, enjoys some flexibility to credit amounts beyond the minimum required spending in one year against the demands of future years. But tax law's payout rule will require at the very least that the foundation consistently distribute a portion of its endowment.[88]

#startsmall could vary the rate of its giving far more. Dorsey might decide that, in a world filled with risk, the wisest course in more prosperous times would be for #startsmall to build its stores. Doing so would ensure that in future crises, it would be armed with the resources needed to combat disease or famine or flood. An LLC structure leaves this decision entirely to him.

The Chan Zuckerberg Initiative provides another real-life example. It reports making $2.9 billion worth of grants in just its first six years of existence,[89] and $2.9 billion represents a colossal sum. But had Chan and Zuckerberg given their Facebook stock or its cash equivalent to a private foundation, that hypothetical philanthropy would have had to contribute much more to charities. Five percent of the $45 billion Chan and Zuckerberg estimated their contribution to be worth in 2015[90] would be $2.25 billion *per year*. Moreover, between 2015 and 2020, the price of Facebook's shares more than doubled. We can assume that a foundation recipient of their donation would have begun divesting its Facebook shares into a more diversified portfolio of holdings immediately. Still, the foundation payout rule would have required that private foundation that never was to have given away more in a year or two than CZI has in its entire existence.

If the value of Meta shares continues to grow, CZI will grow along with it. Unless Zuckerberg and Chan make ever bigger distributions and find other ways to significantly accelerate their giving, they will have a hard time keeping up. Perhaps a philanthropic balloon payment will come due. CZI may find a charitable cause worth spending a huge portion of its funds to pursue. But if current trends continue, CZI would exist until, presumably, its assets are poured into estate tax deductible vehicles at the latter of Chan and Zuckerberg to die.

Controlling Exit

This, of course, assumes Silicon Valley's most famous couple stays together. As the Gates divorce jarringly reminded the charitable community, not all philanthropic partnerships are "til death do us part." When the couple announced their split, they assured the foundation and the public that they would continue to work together amicably on the Foundation's behalf.[91] It remains to be seen whether this will be possible. Predictions vary from expectations of limited impact to concerns one or both Gates will transfer their attention and energy to other projects, including those of their philanthropy LLCs. So much so that the couple announced a contingency plan: Melinda will receive assets from Bill to pursue her philanthropy on her own and step down from the foundation if they cannot continue working together after two years.[92]

However disruptive the Gates divorce turns out to be for the Gates Foundation's day-to-day operations or the strategic vision of its founding couple, the assets they have already contributed to their philanthropic entity will remain locked in. Contributions made to a foundation (like donations to any other charitable nonprofit) simply cannot be clawed back for private use. This ensures any Buffet shares already donated to the foundation will likewise survive his resignation from its board and any further fallout that may ensue.[93]

Should conflicts one day separate the interests of the co-founders of CZI or the Ballmer Group, they will possess a far greater degree of freedom. Assets given to a philanthropy LLC would be just as easy to retrieve as they were to give. To the extent an LLC owner comes to prefer an alternative use for its assets, they can simply remove them. Or they could check a box on a tax form to have the LLC treated like a corporation for tax purposes and deploy its assets like those of any other corporation.

Exit becomes relevant not only in the context of a troubled marriage or other partnership. It also gives philanthropy LLC founders the ultimate luxury—to simply change their minds. Single-member LLC owners can take back their assets and members in multiple-member LLCs can take back their share of the assets, subject only to any limitations on exit provided in the operating agreement.[94] That agreement can be amended should it foreclose opportunities the LLC's member or members desire at a later time.

Perhaps one day Laurene Powell Jobs will decide her assets would be better used to form a media company of her own, to buy a baseball team outright, or simply to pass on to her loved ones for their own private use. If so, no more than paperwork will stand in her way. She remains free to pull her assets from the Emerson Collective and deploy them elsewhere.

It must be said, again, that the words and actions of the LLC founders described here in no way suggest plans to reclaim the assets they have transferred to their philanthropic ventures. Quite the opposite. Especially those who have made public announcements of their gifts have done so in terms reflecting strong resolve. The reputational cost of walking back those promises would be significant, possibly devastating. But the future remains uncertain, and no legal barrier stands in the way.

The LLC offers donors extraordinary freedom to control their own destinies. That makes them irresistible to the elite philanthropists chronicled here. The better question might be why more wealthy donors do not use one. But then again, maybe they do.

Telling Your Story

Should anyone be inclined to know, they would have no way to determine the number of philanthropy LLCs that have been formed or that currently operate across the United States. As noted earlier, an LLC's formative documents must be filed with the secretary of state in the jurisdiction in which it is established. But these filings need not hint at philanthropic intentions or disclose the names of founders. Hundreds of thousands of LLCs spring into existence each year,[95] filed with secretaries of state scattered across fifty-plus jurisdictions. The choice to broadcast the creation or existence of a philanthropy LLC lies entirely with its founders.

MacKenzie Scott exemplifies this phenomenon. She may use an LLC, but unless she decides the public should know, it will not. She may or may not be among the rarefied circle of philanthropy LLC founders.

Thus far, her philanthropy has been both transparent and opaque. Scott describes her giving as assisted by a team of nonprofit advisors, and news stories identify some of her giving as occurring through a donor-advised fund.[96] Her Medium posts list the organizations she supports and amounts given to them (in more granular fashion in some posts than others). But even grant recipients report receiving calls from an advisor out of the blue and receiving an unexpected—and often huge—windfall of unrestricted funds.

Scott's efforts deserve the effusive praise directed her way. She gives big, gives in ways that empower charitable recipients close to the ground, gives fast, and reports gifts publicly. Yet by forgoing the conventional philanthropic form, she has displayed a troubling commitment to secrecy. The public knows only what she chooses to share about her giving, when she chooses to share it.

That secrecy has proved a great temptation to scam artists. Taking advantage of the excitement Scott has generated by surprising recipients with large unsolicited gifts, they have targeted vulnerable individuals falsely claiming a fortune in donations awaits them if they deposit money in a fake bank.[97] Of course, the scammers take the deposit and leave the would-be recipient in the lurch.

Whether or not Scott chooses to use an LLC or simply acts as a private individual, there are certainly philanthropy LLC founders who share far less information. The LLC form caters to guarded philanthropists who give quietly from within its cloak of privacy. The Emerson Collective came close to this description for a long time.

The Collective's investments described earlier have made headlines and its website has long highlighted stories of its projects in a variety of mission. But it has still earned a reputation as highly secretive.[98] Powell Jobs's passion on immigration issues appears to have convinced her to take on a more public role of late, though Emerson still does not provide comprehensive disclosures of its activities.

Even when they make no effort to keep their philanthropy secret, choosing an LLC means donors can present information about their activities on their own terms. These selective disclosures vary widely according to the tastes of individual philanthropists for the spotlight, by type of project or issue, or even over the passage of time. Steve Ballmer's reported rejection of a call for full transparency has not stopped the Ballmer Group from selecting highlights from its work for presentation on its public website. Nor its founders from speaking and writing frequently about its mission and projects in the press.

Other LLCs have taken on transparency as part of their brands. The Omidyar Network offers the strongest example. In its view, the organization's core principles demand a considerable level of openness.[99] Highlighting transparency as a key part of its approach, it explains this practice "enable[s] those who work with us—and those who might disagree with us—to have clarity on what we are trying to achieve." The LLC's voluntary disclosure effort extends beyond its advocacy work. The Network's website provides a list detailing charitable grants, advocacy grants, and investments by area of focus, all sortable by recipient name, geographic focus, year, and amount contributed.[100]

Good Ventures insists that "philanthropy could have a greater impact by becoming more transparent."[101] Its site includes a downloadable database of details on the foundation's grants as well as a more general listing of the LLC's investments. In both cases, links to the Open Philanthropy website provide additional information.

CZI too has come to embrace greater transparency. It now publishes information on the recipients, amounts, and general purposes of its charitable and advocacy grants.[102] It continues to hold the details of its investment portfolio more closely, only listing the names of its investments in for-profit entities.[103] Although less fulsome, this list tells us a great deal about CZI—the recipients overwhelmingly operate in the education technology space.[104]

The variability of LLC disclosure also allows for innovation. When Jack Dorsey created his #startsmall philanthropy LLC in 2020, he simultaneously launched an online spreadsheet to detail precisely which causes received contributions, when they received them, and why.[105] In a Twitter post, he explained the evolution of his views on transparency in giving. "It's important to show my work so I and others can learn. I've discovered and funded ($40mm) many orgs with proven impact and efficiency in the past, mostly anonymously. Going forward, all grants will be public. Suggestions welcome."[106] By the end of 2020, Dorsey had made more than one hundred contributions and by the end of 2021 had added well over one hundred more, representing more than $400 million in donations tracked in a public Google sheet.

Had any of these donors instead used a private foundation exclusively for their giving, disclosure would be formal, mandatory, and consistent. Tax-exempt status does not free an organization from what many consider the most burdensome feature of US tax law—filing a tax return. Whereas churches enjoy the benefits of tax exemption without a filing requirement[107] and small charities can use a short and straightforward reporting document,[108] the disclosure obligations for private foundations are real and substantial. Their Form 990-PF returns demand—and ultimately reveal—details of a foundation's investments, its grants, its donors, and its interactions with those in control.[109] These disclosures document foundations' compliance with the prescriptions and proscriptions detailed above and provide a consistent reporting structure allowing for comparisons across the sector.

For those giving away billions, the out-of-pocket costs of bearing this bureaucratic burden would mean little. Unlike the excise taxes and penalties applicable to foundations, the compliance costs of disclosure would be no more than a rounding error to many elite philanthropists. The true burden imposed by foundations' transparency mandate lies in the fact of disclosure itself.

The significance of the required disclosures transcends the financial details it implicates. Tax-exempt foundations must not only file returns with tax authorities, they must also make those returns available to the public. Forms 990 frequently serve as a critical source of information about the finances of charities. The Internal Revenue Service itself warns that "[h]ow the public perceives an organization . . . may be determined by the information presented on its return."[110]

Moreover, for a private foundation, those disclosures also become a reflection of its funders. Unlike all other tax-exempt entities, the schedule listing foundations' donors is a public document. Although the Supreme Court struck down a California requirement that charities disclose donors to state regulators on First Amendment grounds in 2021, it did not disturb IRS disclosure requirements, including those for foundations. The majority indicated the possibility of a very different outcome should the federal tax regime be challenged, as "revenue collection efforts and conferral of tax-exempt status may raise issues not presented by California's disclosure requirement."[111] For now, foundation donors must continue to sacrifice some of their ability to mold perceptions of their philanthropy in exchange for tax-exempt status for their philanthropic vehicles. Notwithstanding the uncertain outcome of future challenges to federal disclosure requirements, the transparency they currently demand is surely a more meaningful burden to a billionaire than even the most exorbitant accountant's fees.

Control over the narrative has value even for those elite philanthropists who pride themselves on transparency. The #startsmall tracker provides as much or more information about the amount and timing of each transaction than a private foundation. #startsmall also made those disclosures far sooner than the law would have demanded. Still, the public Google sheet does not tell us much of what a private foundation would be required to disclose. As a result, Dorsey enjoys considerable freedom to shape perceptions of his philanthropy. The Omidyar Network and CZI likewise control the information they provide and can use their stances on transparency to differentiate their philanthropic brands.

The power to control the narrative also makes it less daunting for Dorsey's #startsmall and the others—if their founders chose—to do precisely what the foundation rules prohibit. Unlike a private foundation, a tax nothing could, for instance, license proprietary technology on favorable terms without triggering excise taxes and with no obligation to report. To be clear, yet again, nothing about #startsmall or the other contributions reported here suggest a disregard for these strictures. But the spreadsheet that serves as the virtual home of #startsmall lacks the granular detail on relationships between funders and ventures that a private foundation must make available to the public.

Mandatory reporting requirements can help to ensure consistency even when they do not increase the overall degree of transparency. Even if a philanthropy

LLC were to provide the same level of transparency as a private foundation, it would enjoy the freedom to present that information in whatever format it wishes. Without the ability to compare apples to apples across philanthropic ventures, disclosures may prove less helpful even if they do provide an unvarnished view of a philanthropy LLC's activities.

Voluntary transparency can be comprehensive or superficial or anywhere in between. It can highlight areas of founders' greatest satisfaction or the public's greatest concern. It can aid comparisons or frustrate them. It bears repeating, though, that the voluntary disclosure pursued by a philanthropy LLC remains just that: voluntary. The option it provides donors to use disclosure strategically and to thereby shape their own story is one of the greatest assets of the LLC form.

The Price of Freedom

Like any other option, wealthy donors pay a price for the many freedoms a philanthropy LLC provides. These costs come—perhaps predictably—in forgone tax benefits. The extent of these missed opportunities, though, may not be nearly as large as might be expected. For billionaires especially, the value of the LLC option has proven well worth the expense.

Income Taxation

Income tax benefits for philanthropists choosing private foundations come in two distinct types. First, private foundations enjoy almost complete exemption from taxation on the income they earn. Private foundations manage endowments in the millions or even billions of dollars, throwing off massive amounts of dividends, interest, and capital gains. Yet, they pay only a nominal tax on all the income their portfolios generate. Currently, the rate is 1.39 percent.[112]

In addition to the entity-level tax benefit of exemption, contributions generate deductions for a foundation's donors.[113] When an individual contributes to a private foundation, they can deduct the value of their donation from their income in determining their tax liability. Moreover, the benefit of this incentive for charitable giving skews toward the wealthy. Its structure as a deduction means its impact will be greater the higher the marginal tax rate of the taxpayer claiming it.[114]

From 1990 until 2020, the charitable contribution deduction was available exclusively to those (predominantly affluent) taxpayers who itemized their deductions. Itemization requires a taxpayer to identify each of his deductible expenses one by one. This additional layer of complexity in preparing one's taxes is only worthwhile for those who would deduct expenses of more than the standard deduction all filers can claim as a matter of right. This group of taxpayers who can take advantage of the charitable contribution at all was further reduced when the standard deduction was more than doubled as part of the 2017 Tax Cuts and Jobs Act.[115] The CARES Act legislation adopted in the throes of the COVID-19 pandemic modestly improved this situation. It provided nonitemizing taxpayers access to the charitable contribution deduction in 2020 and was extended to 2021 as well, but the deduction was capped at just $300 and has since expired.[116]

Opting for a philanthropy LLC appears at first to give up these valuable tax benefits: an LLC neither enjoys an exemption from tax on its income nor boasts charitable status providing its donors deductions for contributions. But it is a tax nothing. Either disregarded entirely (if the LLC has a single member) or eligible for pass-through tax treatment like a partnership (if it has more),[117] the tax consequences of an LLC's actions attract little or no tax. This allows philanthropy LLCs and their founders to retain much of the tax benefit of a private foundation while enjoying the freedom and flexibility of an LLC.

It is true that income earned on donated assets held by a philanthropy LLC will be taxable and the LLC's owners will be the ones with the tax bill. But philanthropy LLCs may not generate significant taxable income from their investments. A portfolio of risky impact investments may well post net losses. Still, if The Ballmer Group sees financial returns from its Social Solutions investment, the Ballmers will have to include them in their income tax calculations. Any gains from Emerson Collective's investment in The Atlantic or CZI's in Andela will be taxable to their owners as well.

Likewise, if #startsmall should sell shares of Square, Dorsey could have quite a large tax bill to pay—even larger if proposals like those President Biden put forward in 2021 eventually succeed in increasing capital gains taxes for those at the highest levels of income and wealth.[118] The tax nothing status of the LLC would attribute and tax the shares' increase in value while held by the LLC to Dorsey himself. This situation compares terribly with the consequences of private foundations selling appreciated shares contributed by their donors.

The gift of an appreciated asset to any tax-exempt charitable entity allows donors to avoid recognizing and paying income tax on the asset's growth in value while in the donor's hands. Selling the asset would trigger taxation, but donating it to a qualifying charity does not.[119] The charitable recipient can then sell the appreciated asset, enjoy its increased value, and pay little or no tax. The associated capital gains thus escape taxation permanently: a feature of the tax treatment of charities that has been loudly condemned by critics but is understandably prized by donors.[120]

Donating to a philanthropy LLC also will not generate an immediate deduction as a donation to a private foundation would do. Indeed, contributing assets to a single-member LLC owned by the donor would—for tax purposes—be a nonevent. Again, the tax benefits available for private foundation donors appear vastly superior. A taxpayer who contributes appreciated assets—stock in a valuable tech company, for example—to a private foundation can deduct their contribution against their income when calculating the income tax they owe, up to a certain percentage of their income per year.[121]

The value of deductions based on noncash charitable contributions varies by the type of asset contributed and, most important here, the charitable entity receiving the donations.[122] For gifts to public charities, donors may often deduct the fair market value of the donated asset. For gifts to private foundations, though, full market value deductions are available only for gifts of appreciated stock in public companies. Deductions for other noncash donations to private foundations are limited to the donor's cost of acquisition or "basis."

This initial consideration suggests the philanthropy LLC option will cost founders dearly. #startsmall's sale of appreciated Square shares donated by Dorsey would seem to deprive him of tremendous tax benefits. But it need never do any such thing.

Dorsey and other philanthropy LLC founders need only be patient to recapture much of the benefit of the charitable contribution deduction. His donations of Square shares to #startsmall will not create an immediate income tax deduction, but when and to the extent #startsmall makes a grant to a tax-exempt charity, the benefit resurfaces. The LLC pays no taxes, so it can claim no deductions. Contributions by #startsmall will instead flow through to Dorsey. He can set those deductions off against his other income up to the relevant percentage limit the tax code applies. Staging contributions to the LLC using an as-needed approach timed to coincide with distributions to charities can bring the moment of contribution and the moment of deduction ever closer together.

A strategy directing #startsmall to make its charitable contributions in the form of the donated Square shares themselves can even secure for Dorsey the benefit of avoiding capital gains. Assume—we have no idea—the LLC sold some number of the Square shares Dorsey contributed at their $250,000 market value to obtain the funds it used for its donation to Aim High, an organization that runs a summer enrichment program for low-income students in the Bay Area.[123] If Dorsey's cost of acquisition was zero, the $250,000 capital gain from the sale would be taxable to him, but he would also be entitled to a $250,000 charitable deduction once the grant was issued. If #startsmall instead transferred the Square shares directly to Aim High, Dorsey would recognize no income yet still be entitled to the $250,000 deduction. In fact, because the percentage limits on charitable deductions are lower for donations to private foundations than for donations to public charities like Aim High,[124] using an LLC in this way might even provide donors with greater benefits than would a private foundation.

How valuable such a strategy will be will depend on the specifics of individual transactions and the cost to donors of waiting for future deductions versus securing them straightaway.

Of course, all this assumes elite philanthropists are concerned about income taxes at all. With their vast fortunes, one might imagine even the payments top marginal tax rates demand would be of little moment to those at the highest levels of wealth. But ProPublica's investigation into billionaires' tax returns suggests quite the opposite. Demonstrating both a considerable appetite and capacity for managing their taxes, many of the richest Americans report strikingly little income.[125] The tax avoidance the ProPublica investigation unearthed relied on perfectly legal maneuvers, including but not limited to charitable deductions. Operating through an LLC may close off some of these tax-minimizing strategies, but many avenues remain to fold this flexible vehicle into a broader income tax minimization plan.

Transfer Taxation

Income taxes are not the only taxes out there, of course. We also levy taxes on transfers of wealth through lifetime gifts and death-time bequests.[126] Rates for the unified federal gift and estate tax currently top out at 40 percent, though reformers on both sides of the aisle would like to shift them in one direction or the other. As noted above, these taxes will never affect most taxpayers, as a unified lifetime credit shields transfers of up to $11.7 million for individuals and $23.4 million for married couples. To ultra-high-net-worth philanthropists described here, however, transfer taxes certainly matter.

Charitable contributions, including those from estates, qualify for an unlimited deduction from these transfer taxes.[127] No matter how many billions of dollars one leaves at death, those devised to tax-exempt charities (along with those gifted during life) will avoid taxation entirely. But philanthropy LLCs are not tax-exempt, and they are not charities, so they do not qualify for the deduction. Gifts to an LLC fall within the gift tax and the assets of an LLC "tax nothing" are includable in its owner's estate.

Again, a deeper understanding of the law involved and the tax planning opportunities available to philanthropy LLC founders will blunt these concerns. Assets exchanged for an LLC membership need not be treated as a gift at all. Considering the valuable control rights received in return, these are not gifts but purchases for value fully outside the purview of the gift tax. For donors at this level, one can also expect a careful estate plan. A simple provision in one's will or other documents donating the LLC's assets to a charitable recipient on the owner's death will allow those assets to qualify for the deduction—neatly escaping the estate tax too.[128]

This does set death as the practical endpoint for philanthropy LLCs, however. Married LLC owners can extend the time somewhat, as the unlimited marital deduction will avoid application of the estate tax to the assets of the first spouse to die.[129] At the death of the last surviving spouse co-owning a philanthropy LLC, however, its assets must either be transferred to a tax-exempt entity or be subject to the estate tax. Unlike a private foundation, so commonly and easily deployed in perpetuity, a philanthropy LLC must end with its members. For donors like the Arnolds, who have committed to "give while they live," a lifetime limit on the (tax-free) accumulation of assets for philanthropy will only increase its attraction. For founders seeking a substitute for a private foundation's reach and longevity, this cost of the LLC option is worth underscoring.

Conclusion

For-profit philanthropy, and the philanthropy LLC in particular, represents a new chapter in a long and complex story. The Gates Foundation, created just a year before the US Treasury announced the radical changes that would bring the LLC into the mainstream, bookends an era that began in Rockefeller's time. The strengths and the weaknesses of the federal regulatory framework Rockefeller never lived to see—the Grand Bargain—are illustrated by the fact both that the Gates Foundation exists and that it may be the last of its kind.

The freedom delivered by the LLC appears to make the choice faced by today's wealthy philanthropists an easy one. Where the foundation mandates accountability, the philanthropy LLC delivers autonomy. A foundation faces prohibitions and sanctions, while an LLC provides founders an extraordinary degree of discretion, including the ability to reclaim their assets down the line. An LLC can exercise its many freedoms from behind a protective veil of privacy, while a foundation's compliance is made subject to public scrutiny. A tax-exempt entity does enjoy some benefits unavailable to a tax nothing, but both receive favorable tax treatment.

These differences can be thought of as an option. Whether the freedom to change one's mind or to engage in political activity or to gamble on a potentially lucrative investment draws any given philanthropist to choose an LLC over a foundation, the options for-profit philanthropy provides have value. Robert Merton and Myron Scholes shared a Nobel Prize for offering a formula to determine the value of a much simpler option,[130] and doing so here would be infinitely harder.

Fortunately, for-profit philanthropy's precise option value does not matter. It is clear that the emergence of the LLC has sharply reduced the price. Unsurprisingly, the most sophisticated philanthropists are increasingly choosing to pay that lower price by forgoing tax-exempt status in favor of the operational versatility, control, and privacy a philanthropy LLC promises.

CZI, Good Ventures, #startsmall and the rest highlight not only the disjunctures involved in a shift away from the private foundation but also some continuities. Resourceful philanthropists operating within foundations have found ways to advocate for policy reform, own for-profit ventures, and ensure the long-term expansion of their endowments despite rules designed to prevent exactly that. But the philanthropy LLC brings the potential for much more dramatic shifts, allowing philanthropists not just to push boundaries but to completely erase them.

The rise of this tax nothing also highlights broad changes in tax law that tend to make for-profit philanthropy a less costly proposition than it would have been a half century ago. Income and estate tax rates, of course, have fallen across the board. The ability of elites to transmute highly and currently taxed salaries into lightly and later taxed capital gains reached new heights in the age of Facebook and Twitter. Together, those changes have dramatically eased the cost of the option for-profit philanthropy represents, forever changing the face of elite giving in the United States.

The remainder of Part I (chapters 2 and 3) explores two distinct additional examples of for-profit philanthropy. Commercially affiliated donor-advised funds and strategic corporate philanthropy have much in common with the philanthropy LLC. In each instance, players, practices, and norms native to the business sector are deployed in philanthropic spaces to enhance donor flexibility, control, and privacy.

2
Commercially Affiliated Donor-Advised Fund Sponsors

New technologies are disruptive. That is no less true when the technology in question is legal. The limited liability company (LLC) illustrates the breadth of the impact a change in law can produce. Once unleashed by state legislators, the LLC transformed the business landscape. As chapter 1 shows, it now appears poised to do the same for philanthropy. This chapter turns its focus to another innovation that threatens to upend the established order of charitable giving.

The donor-advised fund (DAF) works like a credit card—or perhaps a debit card—for charitable spending. Donors transfer assets to a sponsor entity, which holds the assets in an account until the donor advises the sponsor to contribute them to a charity. In the meantime, the sponsor invests the assets subject to the donor's instructions. Sponsors were originally community foundations providing guidance to donors on needs and organizations in their local regions. Today, the field is dominated by sponsors affiliated with commercial investment firms.

Before credit and debit cards existed, we dined out, bought airline tickets, and fueled our cars. Now, we would be hard-pressed to manage those simple tasks without the help of corporate behemoths like Visa or MasterCard. Recent years have seen what may be the beginning of a similar transformation. By 2017, DAF sponsors affiliated with commercial entities had come to account for four of the ten largest recipients of charitable funds in the United States: Fidelity Charitable, Goldman Sachs Philanthropy Fund, Schwab Charitable Fund, and the Vanguard Charitable Endowment Program.[1]

One can easily imagine a world in which donating money without Fidelity comes to be just as unthinkable as spending it without Visa. This chapter takes a careful look at the role this new breed of intermediary already plays in charitable giving, explaining both the forces that gave rise to the DAF and the likely impact of its commercially affiliated variant in years to come. Situating these funds in the broader context of for-profit philanthropy shows the challenge they pose to the Grand Bargain and helps paint a picture of the future of charitable giving.

For-profit philanthropy—here in the form of the commercially affiliated DAF—challenges our understanding of what is and is not charitable. The origins of DAFs highlight both the importance and the limitations of the Grand Bargain.

For-Profit Philanthropy. Dana Brakman Reiser and Steven A. Dean, Oxford University Press. © Oxford University Press 2023. DOI: 10.1093/oso/9780190074500.003.0003

The philanthropy LLC rejects its rigid framework and the tax benefits the law offers in exchange. In a sense, the DAF does the opposite, seizing the tax benefits available to charitable entities without fitting neatly into any of the law's categories. The commercially affiliated DAF has made that appealing combination widely available.

As this chapter shows, decades of conflict over the nature of these funds has yet to provide satisfying answers to even basic questions of when and who. The philanthropy LLC threatens to upset the Grand Bargain from the top down. With its mass-market appeal, the rise of the commercially affiliated DAF stands poised to do the same from the ground up.

Uncharitable Charities

Commercially affiliated sponsors of DAFs like the Vanguard Charitable Endowment Program qualify as public charities under federal tax law but do no charitable work. Instead—like a through-the-looking-glass credit card provider—they hold donated assets awaiting future distribution to operating charities. In the meantime, they invest those assets in return for fees. They are independent from their affiliated for-profit companies but share their names, customers, and platforms and contract with them to provide investment and administrative services for the funds they hold. Commercially affiliated DAF sponsors have experienced massive growth over the last two decades, and at the end of 2020 held more than $100 billion in assets.[2]

These entities present merely affluent donors with all the benefits that attract ultra-high-net-worth individuals to the philanthropy LLC: greater flexibility, control, and privacy. Unlike the LLC vehicles discussed in the last chapter, here those gains can be achieved with no increased tax burden. Indeed, DAFs offer a tax advantage over their closest alternatives.

Of equal, if not greater, interest in this story is the allure of DAFs for their affiliated investment funds. The traditionally philanthropic area of grantmaking has proven such a fertile ground for profit that it has attracted Fidelity, Vanguard, Schwab, Goldman Sachs, and virtually every other player in the investment industry. The fortunes of this industry, and those who lead it, depend on the value of the assets under their management. As contributions to DAFs keep growing,[3] posting increases every year for more than a decade, creating affiliated DAF sponsors has proven a wise extension of investment companies' businesses. Mistakenly leaked information from Goldman Sachs Philanthropy Fund confirms these entities are even attracting billion-dollar donations.[4] And the demand for these funds has surely not yet been exhausted.[5]

When for-profit players see money to be made in the traditionally philanthropic sphere, they will predictably rush to corner the market. Their efforts may bring new and greater assets into the charitable sector. But replacing mission-oriented stewards of philanthropic funds with profit-focused counterparts can also have a powerful, perhaps even transformational, impact on the charitable sector.

The Community Foundation

Donor-advised funds sound like a product dreamed up by today's high-octane investment industry—and to be sure, commercially affiliated DAFs are exactly that—but the origins of these vehicles can actually be traced to a very different time and place. A century ago in Cleveland, Ohio the community foundation was born. Frederick Goff, who had been an attorney for John D. Rockefeller and Standard Oil and a leading trust banker and president of the Cleveland Trust Company, established the Cleveland Foundation in 1914.[6]

Goff's community foundation tweaked the general-purpose foundations being pioneered by the great industrialists of the time, including his former employers the Rockefellers. This first community foundation was organized as a group of charitable trusts, managed collectively by a community board of trustees that represented the public and used a single bank to manage the foundation's assets. It solicited and accepted contributions from local donors of far more modest means than the Rockefellers, aggregated and invested the donated assets for growth, and made grants of the income to local charitable organizations to improve the Cleveland community in which it operated.

Goff evangelized his Cleveland experiment widely, and it was quickly replicated in cities and regions nationwide. Just six years after the Cleveland Foundation's founding, nineteen of the twenty-one largest US cities boasted community foundations of their own.[7] Over time, other legal models garnered adherents; today, community foundations are also organized as single trusts or nonprofit corporations rather than multiple trusts, and many utilize the investment services of multiple banks rather than a single one.[8] Still, the philanthropic concept pioneered in Cleveland remains the pattern for community foundations around the country today, and the model has proliferated.[9]

Although community foundations share a name with philanthropies endowed by the largesse of a single individual or family to pursue its view of the good in perpetuity, they have always been designed for quite different purposes. Community foundations draw donations from a wide network of contributors and—true to their name—pursue communal visions. The very local focus of community foundations allows them to become expert on the charitable needs and resources of their home city, region, or state. They not only aggregate donors' assets but advise on their best deployment and innovate to solve local problems.

At their core, community foundations are asset aggregators, investors, and distributors that act as intermediaries for civic-minded individuals without the means to establish philanthropies. These features made them a natural place for the development of DAFs.[10] The New York Community Trust claims to have created the first DAF in 1931,[11] an assertion the philanthropic community seems to have universally accepted.[12] Although the "donor-advised fund" term did not become his widely used until much later, the idea of allowing donors to make gifts to a community foundation and recommend the grants that should be made out of these donated assets dates back nine decades.

Neither Public nor Private

The major reforms enacted in the 1969 Grand Bargain sent shockwaves through the philanthropic sector, and community foundations lay above a key fault line. Chapter 4 will provide a comprehensive discussion of the many elements of this reform, but the key one here is the identification of two flavors of tax-exempt charitable entities: public charities and private foundations.[13] Unless an entity falls into one category or the other, it is not a tax-exempt charity. Community foundations, as decades of disputes have demonstrated, fit neatly within neither.

Public charities enjoy clear—and very intentional—advantages over private foundations. They and their donors receive the most favored tax treatment and lightest regulatory touch. Private foundations and their donors—viewed with skepticism because of concern that the capital they wield might serve the interests of those donors rather than benefiting the public—are given pared-down tax breaks and are subject to greater regulation and harsh penalties.

Private foundations must pay out at least 5 percent of their assets annually and a host of rules limit their investment activity and expenditures. This new second-class status even stripped them of their right to full tax exemption; ever since, private foundations have had to pay a small tax on their investment income. Their donors also lose out. They are eligible for smaller deductions than donors to public charities and their access to some of the richest charitable tax benefits, such as those available for contributing appreciated assets to public charities, is limited.

The decidedly less favorable private foundation designation applies as a default to every organization exempt under Internal Revenue Code § 501(c)(3). To escape it, an exempt organization must meet one of various tests for public charity status. Again, chapter 4 provides more details on the operations and consequences of these tests. Suffice it to say here that meeting them requires an exempt organization to prove, in one of a number of highly technical ways, that it derives considerable support from—and in theory is therefore accountable to—the public, as opposed to answering only to a small number of generous donors. Their sources of funding would prevent most of the organizations that call themselves foundations or that would be described as foundations in nontechnical discussions from passing any of the public charity tests. Community foundations, however, managed to escape the gravitational pull of private foundation classification.

Their liminal status arguably should have resulted in private foundation treatment for community foundations, but a little luck and a lot of advocacy prevented that. Another Clevelander played a pivotal role in this development.[14] Norman Sugarman was born in Cleveland in 1917 and became a lawyer for prominent donors there after serving the predecessor to the Internal Revenue Service. When the 1969 tax reforms passed, Sugarman began advising community foundations to confirm their public charity status, and a number did so through the agency's private letter ruling procedure.[15] This process allows individual taxpayers to submit a set of facts to the IRS and receive the Service's interpretation of how tax law would apply to them.

Over time, regulations yielded two ways that a community foundation could qualify for the more desirable public charity status. It could demonstrate that a third of its support came from small donors and public sources. Or it could demonstrate that its lower level of public support (as low as 10 percent) was buttressed by facts and circumstances demonstrating it was "organized and operated so as to attract new and additional public or governmental support on a continuous basis."[16] A community foundation could meet this requirement by seeking contributions from a wide spectrum of donors in its area, including through intermediaries.

But community foundations could clear these hurdles only if their many separate funds were treated as a single entity. If each fund were required to meet the public charity test individually, many if not most would fail. Treasury regulations went on to identify a series of requirements necessary to obtain single entity treatment.[17] To qualify, a community foundation must operate and receive funds under a common name conveying the community foundation idea. In addition, all component funds must be subject to a common governing instrument and governing body, which holds what is known as the "variance power."[18] This is the power to

> modify any restriction or condition on the distribution of funds for any specified charitable purposes or to specified organizations if in the sole judgment of the governing body . . . such restriction or condition becomes, in effect, unnecessary, incapable of fulfillment, or inconsistent with the charitable needs of the community or area served.[19]

Finally, component trusts or funds must be created by gift to the community foundation, with no material restrictions or conditions on their use.

Who

The intent of these requirements could not be any clearer. They aimed to provide an answer to an elemental question posed by the DAF: whether a DAF sponsor should be acknowledged separately or disregarded as a mere agent of its donors. To obtain public charity status, a community foundation could not be a mere custodian of funds continuing to be controlled by its putative donors.

In other words, the community foundation must be more than a conduit. It must be treated as an independent actor capable of engaging in charitable acts, and it must be the ultimate owner of funds donated to it, with the power to direct their use and distribution. Even among community foundations organized as a single nonprofit corporation, it is not uncommon to find bylaws demanding an independent community board, control over donated funds, and the availability of the variance power.[20] Indeed, these have come to define the concept of the community foundation and are among the accepted best practices within the industry.[21]

The significant donor power found in DAFs is clearly in tension with the idea of control over donated assets by a community foundation and its board. But Sugarman's ultimate goal required governmental assurances that offering such funds would not threaten a community foundation's ability to secure public charity status. He saw the 1969 classification regime as an opportunity for community foundations. Persuading existing foundations and future donors not keen on complying with the new private foundation rules to transfer their contributions to community foundations could open a huge supply of assets for communities. These donors would certainly like to benefit from the more generous public charity treatment of community foundations, but many would balk at turning over direction of their charitable funds to entities with whom they had little prior relationship and over whom they had no ongoing control.

Devising a neat compromise, Sugarman obtained the IRS's blessing of a type of DAF in a private letter ruling secured for the Cleveland Jewish Federation. In it, the Service opined that a donor could contribute assets to create a fund within a community foundation but retain the power to recommend distributions from the fund over time, without scuttling the community foundation's tax-favored public charity treatment. The IRS was clear that "[s]uch recommendations shall be solely advisory, and [the Cleveland Jewish Federation] may accept or reject them, applying reasonable standards and guidelines,"[22] but the door was opened.

Donor-Advised Funds' Tax Benefits

Once community foundations were free to operate DAFs while maintaining their status as public charities, their value for donors only increased. The most obvious benefit of utilizing a DAF to make charitable contributions is tax deductibility. A $100 (or $1,000 or $100,000) donation to a DAF is treated exactly the same—for tax purposes—as if it were made to the American Heart Association, a local homeless shelter, or the Catholic Church. The contributed amount can be deducted from a taxpayer's adjusted gross income on their itemized tax return, yielding a benefit proportionate to their marginal tax rate.

Percentage limitations cap the tax value of DAF contributions, as they do for gifts made to other charitable entities, to only a portion of a taxpayer's income. But because DAF sponsors qualify as public charities, more generous percentage limitations apply. Cash gifts to DAFs are subject to a 60 percent limit, versus a 30 percent limit for cash donations to private foundations. Gifts of appreciated property to DAFs face a 30 percent limit, but the same gifts to a private foundation are capped at 20 percent.

As chapter 1 discussed, donations of appreciated property to public charities give rise to two different types of tax benefits. First, the amount of the tax deduction available to donors of appreciated property varies depending on whether the recipient organization is a public charity or a private foundation. Other than for gifts of publicly traded securities, a private foundation donor's deduction is limited to their basis (usually the property's cost of acquisition). But public charity donors—including contributors to DAFs—can deduct both publicly traded securities and other kinds of donated appreciated property at fair market value. No matter what the taxpayer expended to acquire the property or how difficult it will be for the charitable recipient to liquidate, their deduction will be the property's full current valuation. Second, all donors of appreciated property avoid taxation on the value of the property's appreciation. If a donor sells their appreciated property and donates the proceeds, they will have to pay tax on the gains in its value over their basis in the property sold. Donating the property instead allows them to escape taxation on any increase in its value.[23]

Despite the obvious appeal of the double benefit attendant to charitable gifts of appreciated property, taking advantage of it can be challenging. Gifts of appreciated property valued at over $5,000 require a qualified appraisal, which not every donor knows how to obtain.[24] More important, imagine the strain on a local soup kitchen of managing the gift of shares in a privately held business, a work of art, or real estate in a distant jurisdiction. Many charitable recipients simply will not accept gifts of appreciated property—particularly appreciated property other than publicly traded securities—as the costs of liquidating these assets can be substantial.

Donor-advised funds are a particularly attractive vehicle for securing the especially generous tax treatment charitable gifts appreciated assets receive. Unlike operating charities, DAF sponsors are often well situated to receive gifts of appreciated property and to assist donors in taking advantage of the double benefit they carry. Commercially affiliated sponsors are singularly qualified to take in such contributions. They are already experts in the investment space and operating at an immense scale, unlikely to be daunted by the tasks of securing appraisals and liquidating assets. Unsurprisingly, these sponsors are actively courting this part of the DAF market[25] and succeeding. Fidelity boasted in its 2021 Giving Report that "more than $1.6 billion in contributions were non-publicly traded assets, such as private stock, limited partnership interest or cryptocurrency," 11 percent of overall contributions received.[26]

As noted in the last chapter, other than the $300 above-the-line deduction instituted for 2020 and 2021 in response to COVID-19, none of these tax benefits are available to taxpayers who do not itemize their deductions. Taxpayers filing individual or joint returns have the choice whether to tote up their deductible expenditures, like charitable contributions or state and local tax payments, and be prepared to justify them with documentation. Alternatively, they may claim a standard deduction in amount set by law and available to all with no questions asked. Donors who make contributions which, when combined with their other deductible expenses, do not rise beyond the level of the standard deduction, will gain no tax benefit by itemizing.

While no self-respecting billionaire would fail to itemize, the increase in the standard deduction in the 2017 Tax Cut and Jobs Act by a factor of two (to $12,000 for individuals and $24,000 for couples) made forgoing itemization a real possibility for many affluent taxpayers. When it took effect, 29.5 million fewer households claimed itemized deductions than had the year before.[27] Charities and their leaders expressed concern that this change, although not directly revising the charitable contribution deduction at all, would depress charitable giving as the real tax benefit of charitable contributions disappears for the ranks of new standard deduction takers.[28]

When

Closely linked with the question of who is the question of when. And that is important because when a donation is made matters. The changes made to the tax laws in 2017 underscore why timing is important. Donor-advised funds offer individuals a mechanism for altering the timing of a charitable gift in order to alter its tax consequences. Treated as more than a mere conduit for donations, DAFs allow donors to achieve tax results they otherwise could not.

The simplest illustration of why timing matters is the technique referred to as "bunching." A couple that plans to donate $10,000 per year may not have sufficient deductible expenses to justify itemizing under the new $25,000+ standard deduction regime. If they fail to itemize, however, they will lose access to the charitable deduction. By planning ahead and bunching donations into a DAF, they can use the charitable deduction and the higher standard deduction strategically. For example, in Year 1, they can donate double or triple their annual charitable contribution budget to a DAF and avail themselves of the charitable deduction by itemizing in that year. In Year 2 (and perhaps Year 3), they need not make any contributions and can rely on the standard deduction. They can still, however, direct the DAF sponsor to spend down their fund in Year 2 (and perhaps Year 3), making the planned $10,000 donations to the charities of their choice at those later times. A number of advisors suggested the bunching strategy in the press in the short period between enactment of the Tax Cut and Jobs Act and the close of 2017.[29] A spike in contributions to DAFs suggests many donors heeded their counsel.

This bunching strategy is a new spin on the long-standing practice of using DAFs to smooth giving over time. For those with sufficient disposable assets, a DAF can operate not only like a credit or debit card, but like an endowment. Invested prudently, the funds' assets can grow sufficiently to allow for a relatively even flow of contributions to charities, despite the ups and downs of market cycles. Advising powers may also be transferred at death by the donor. A DAF whose advisor can pass on their power to recommend distributions to their heirs at death is an extremely durable giving device.

Timing, of course, is not only important to donors, but to the vital work of charitable recipients. While a DAF donor will receive a tax deduction immediately upon contribution of assets to a sponsoring organization, when those funds will become available to fund the work of actual operating charities is anyone's guess. A donor-advisor may prize immediacy and issue advice to pay out a grant from her DAF directly after contributing the necessary assets, or those assets may languish forgotten and unused but growing.

This timing issue has existed since the establishment of the very first DAFs nearly a century ago. And not all experts agree that a potential delay in DAF distributions is cause for concern. Delayed expenditures can give donors time to make more considered grants or to design them to pursue needs expected to arise in the future. They might enhance donors' ability to inculcate a legacy of giving in their descendants. But even those offering qualified support to current DAF regulation accept that "DAF funds unspent as a matter of inertia, through procrastination or forgetfulness" are troubling unless the value of spending those funds later exceeds that of spending them today.[30]

A 2021 study by Professors James Andreoni and Ray Madoff argued that the exponential rise of DAFs with commercially affiliated sponsors has exacerbated it considerably. Using data from Giving USA, the National Philanthropic Trust, and federal tax filings, they found that had operating charities "received donations at . . . the average rate that they received in the 5-year period before commercial DAFs[], they would have received an additional $300 billion" between 2014 and 2018.[31]

Donor-Advised Funds as For-Profit Philanthropy

Like philanthropy LLCs, DAFs offer their creators an appealing mix of flexibility, privacy, and control when compared to private foundation alternatives. They neatly avoid regulation intended to ensure philanthropic outlays will be timed to ensure societal benefit commensurate with its tax advantages. They preserve for donors nearly all the tax advantages that apply to contributions to public charities operating actual charitable programs. Until 2006, DAFs actually did avoid all of the private foundation rules' restrictions on investment and spending. After legislative changes at that time (and which will be discussed in Congressional Action) DAFs still remained free of most of them—including the payout requirement.

They are also more private.[32] Although the public charity of which a DAF is a part remains within federal and state regulators' purview, individual DAFs are subject to no direct oversight. Tax disclosures are made at the sponsor level, not fund by fund. The transparency this aggregate disclosure requirement provides is, thus, frustratingly partial. Individual donors cannot be tied to specific contributions as would be the case if donors instead established a private foundation.

Despite the fact that a DAF does not allow a donor to create their own institution, staff it, and set its priorities, the control they exercise remains considerable. Technically, donors must relinquish control over DAF assets and have no legal power over the sponsor organization that holds them, but in practice donor advice tends to be powerful and rarely ignored. As such, a DAF can be seen as a kind of a "mini" private foundation[33] or perhaps a (not very) poor man's private foundation—with superior tax advantages.[34]

A Win-Win for Donors

Predictably, the win-win DAFs offer to donors has continued to attract attention. Donors are flocking to the form, wooed by commercially affiliated sponsors poised to ensure their new customers can extract every possible advantage from the system. Defying the rigid Grand Bargain framework that preserves philanthropy law's targeting, timing, and transparency, commercially affiliated DAFs have drawn skepticism from regulators, legislators, and the public—right up through today.

Testing the Limits

After the initial post-1969 rulings and regulations, the IRS's skepticism over who and when in the DAF context fueled a series of exemption battles. The seminal victory for DAFs came in the 1987 case of *National Foundation, Inc.* (NFI) *v. United States.*[35] NFI was designed to extend the DAF model beyond the community foundation context. It received funds from donors (often existing private foundations or would-be foundation founders) and used them to initiate "projects," typically for charitable purposes recommended by donors. In the year it applied for tax-exemption, over half of the funds that NFI distributed went to operating these projects.

The NFI board had to approve any donor-initiated project and would evaluate proposals based on qualification for exemption under § 501(c)(3), serving public rather than private purposes, adequacy of documentation and scope, and the ability of NFI to administer it. Donors were required to make an initial $500 contribution, which was held in escrow during the review process, and pay a nonrefundable $100 fee. If a project proposal was rejected, the donor could roll their contribution over into a new proposed project, or have the funds returned.[36] When a project was approved, the contribution would become subject to the control of NFI. Contributed funds could be used for other charitable purposes at NFI's discretion, but donor recommendations would "ordinarily be honored."[37]

Donors were advised that only funds turned over to NFI's complete control could qualify for the charitable tax deduction, and NFI sought an IRS ruling of exemption. It did not need to qualify under the community foundation regulations for treatment as a single entity, as the project funds it operated were separate for accounting purposes only. NFI operated as a single nonprofit entity under state law. Still, the IRS notified NFI that it planned to reject its application for exemption, and the two parties went back and forth over the question. Before they could reach a final resolution, NFI went to court seeking a declaratory judgment confirming its entitlement to tax-exempt status.

The IRS protested but the court sided with NFI. To qualify as exempt from taxation under § 501(c)(3), an entity must be both organized and operated for an exempt purpose under the Code, including "religious, charitable, scientific, testing for public safety, literary, or educational purposes, or to foster national or international amateur sports competition . . ., or for the prevention of cruelty to children or animals."[38] The entity also must eschew inurement of its net earnings to private individuals or entities, substantial lobbying, and any political campaign activity.[39] The NFI articles of incorporation repeated these requirements as its own, meeting the organizational test, so the question of its operations controlled. The IRS argued that NFI should not be understood to operate for charitable purposes itself but rather to serve as an agent providing a service to wealthy clients.[40] NFI's services allowed donors to undertake the activities of a private foundation while avoiding regulation as such. The court vehemently disagreed, finding NFI's distribution of funds not dissimilar to the activities of long-exempt organizations like the United Way.

Perceiving not one potentially charitable actor but many, the Service also balked at the multiplicity of exempt purposes asserted by NFI in its operations. Unwilling to allow the NFI board to take its place deciding whether project proposals would qualify for exemption, the IRS argued that each project should separately apply for tax-exempt status. It feared that an umbrella exemption would risk mistaken characterizations allowing nonexempt activity to go on within NFI on a tax-favored basis. The court blithely rejected these claims, noting that NFI's innovative form should not preclude exempt status. In fact, it opined that "NFI truly functions in the 'spirit of charity.' "[41]

Central to the IRS's claim was the issue that Sugarman finessed decades earlier: donor control. The IRS argued that NFI's clients did not give up control of the funds transferred to it and thus their transfers did not qualify as completed gifts eligible for the charitable deduction. In its view, NFI served instead only as a "conduit" for their donations, "circumventing the authority and responsibility of the Commissioner of Internal Revenue" and not deserving exemption as a charitable entity.[42] The court saw things quite differently, finding the record amply supported NFI's position that donors relinquished to it all control over donated assets at the time of their donation. The court also had no problem with NFI's practice of deferring to donor advice on distributions, especially considering the organization's requirement that each project comply with its own Board's criteria for initiation.

The holdings in *NFI* set the stage for the widespread adoption of the DAF model outside traditional community foundations, and innovations continued. Two of these innovators pushed the limits enough to also end up in court. *The Fund for Anonymous Gifts* (The Fund) v. *IRS* involved an entity formed to allow donors to make anonymous gifts to tax-exempt public charities. In contrast to NFI, however, The Fund's donors were permitted to place conditions on their grants, which could grant donors ongoing control over the distribution and investment of donated funds and were binding on the sponsor. The IRS objected to this, as well as other elements of the Fund, and initially won its case on grounds that these binding conditions precluded it from being operated exclusively for charitable purposes.[43] Donations with binding conditions were not gifts at all.

The Fund appealed, however, and during oral argument offered to change its governing documents to remove donors' ability to insert such conditions.[44] The Fund followed through on this offer and spent over a year in unsuccessful settlement negotiations with the IRS. The appellate court eventually vacated the original decision and ordered the trial court to enter summary judgment in favor of The Fund's exemption. The appellate court had harsh words for the government and served the IRS with what appeared like a humiliating defeat.[45] Yet, the case did draw a bright line that DAF sponsors cannot cross—formal, legal control in the hands of donors will scuttle exemption.

A few years later, it was the fund sponsor's turn to feel the sting. Among other things, California DAF sponsor New Dynamics Foundation was designed to obtain contributions to DAFs when it sought charitable tax exemption in 1996.[46] It was finally denied three years later on grounds of donor control, akin to that found in *The Fund*, but also because it was found to serve private rather than purely public interests. New Dynamics' promotional materials, and particularly statements and literature by its founder Robert Henkell, suggested to donors that assets contributed to these funds could be used to personally benefit them or their family members.

New Dynamics sought relief in court, and this time the government prevailed. Taking into account the practices of New Dynamics under Henkell and later management at the helm at the time of the case, the court found it was not entitled to tax exemption.

> [T]he donors in question did not truly relinquish ownership and control over the donated funds or property. Rather, they were allowed to treat NDF as a conduit for accomplishing the twin tax avoidance goals of building up their assets tax-free and then siphoning off the accumulated wealth to pay for personal expenditures.[47]

Donor advice is consistent with tax exemption and charitable deductions, but private goodies for donors are decidedly not.

New Sponsors Jump In

Long before Visa and MasterCard, legend has it that Frank McNamara found himself at dinner with clients but without his wallet and the experience inspired him to create the Diners Club Card, "the first multi-purpose charge card."[48] The rise of the commercially affiliated DAF from its humble Cleveland origins invites the comparison. With the legal groundwork laid, the arrival of commercial intermediaries may have been inevitable.

Skirmishes like *The Fund* and *New Dynamics* reinforced the prohibitions on private inurement and formal donor control, but the war had effectively been won in 1987. Once NFI obtained public charity status as a national entity coordinating large numbers of accounts funded by individual donors with significant practical (but not legal) control, so could any number of sponsors. The race had begun.

First off the starting blocks was Fidelity. The Fidelity Charitable Gift Fund (now operating as "Fidelity Charitable") incorporated the lessons of *NFI* and anticipated the lines drawn in *The Fund* and *New Dynamics*. Its broad mission to support charitable activities in virtually every possible area echoes NFI's multiplicity of purposes. Fidelity Charitable, in its own words, operates

> to facilitate, support and increase charitable activities in the following areas; health and human services, children, youth and families; social welfare; education; scientific research; culture, arts, and humanities; religion; civic and community affairs; environment; wildlife and animals; testing for public safety and consumer affairs and *other charities that support causes that represent the philanthropic wishes and geographic regions of [its] donors.*[49]

Like NFI (and the revised operations of The Fund), Fidelity Charitable holds all of its assets for charitable use and requires donors to relinquish legal control over any assets donated to it. The donors do retain the power as advisors to recommend charitable recipients as well as investments for their DAFs, which advice is usually followed. Private benefits like those that were the ultimate downfall of New Dynamics, however, are prohibited. Other commercially affiliated sponsors followed suit: the Vanguard Charitable Endowment was established in 1997; Schwab Charitable in 1999; the Goldman Sachs Philanthropy Fund in 2001; and many more.

As these funds came before the IRS seeking exemption, the familiar issues of donor control and potential noncharitable or donor-benefiting uses of donated funds were easily resolved. Existing case law made clear that all sponsors must hold the ultimate power over donated funds and needed to take steps to ensure their proper distribution. These applications, though, brought up new issues unique to commercially affiliated sponsors, for which community foundation sponsors provided no ready analogue.

Could a commercial sponsor's relationship with its affiliated investment company undermine its charitable purpose? Might it generate substantial private benefits to the affiliated for-profit that would preclude its exemption under § 501(c)(3)? On what terms could an investment company provide services to its affiliated DAF sponsor? Still no case has come to court raising these interpretative questions, but the dialogue between the IRS and commercially affiliated sponsors seeking exemption demonstrates their salience to regulators.

The story of the Vanguard Charitable Endowment (the Endowment) application provides the most public example. It received an advance ruling of exemption and public charity status after months of back and forth with the IRS, much of which was ultimately published.[50] A considerable amount of the correspondence between the Service and the Endowment focuses on the latter's relationship with The Vanguard Group, Inc. (Vanguard).

At the time, Vanguard provided investment services to a family of more than thirty funds and had more than $300 billion in total assets, and it was heavily involved in the creation of the Endowment. It contributed startup assistance, including an interest-free loan of $750,000. The Endowment additionally benefited from free use of Vanguard office space and staff time and a royalty-free license to use the Vanguard name. Vanguard also sent a promotional mailing about the Endowment to select clients. The relationship between the two reached the apex of each entity; John J. Brennan, CEO of the Vanguard Group, was one of the three Endowment trustees.

The Endowment and Vanguard planned to continue their relationship past the start-up phase primarily through a service agreement. Under it, Vanguard would provide investment management and administrative services to the Endowment. The investment management services were to be provided at cost, using the same approach Vanguard did for funds in its mutual fund family.[51] Administrative services rendered by Vanguard, namely, daily pricing and recordkeeping services, were to be provided for modest fees.[52]

The IRS inquired about all facets of the connection between Vanguard and the Endowment. It demanded the details of the service agreement between the two entities, asking about the rationale for awarding the service agreement to Vanguard as well as specifics on fee structures and other benefits the investment company would receive from the deal. The Endowment reassured the Service that the fees for Vanguard's services—although not secured through any kind of competitive bidding process—were a bargain that would redound to the benefit of the donors and charities it served. Although not all costs could be estimated at the time, it repeatedly characterized the services as being provided at-cost and offered a variety of metrics demonstrating they were below market.

The IRS also inquired about more indirect benefits of the relationship, asking questions about the Endowment's plans to solicit Vanguard's mutual fund clients as donors and the likelihood of overlap between the two groups. The Endowment described its plans for seeking out donors from among Vanguard's clients as limited to the promotional letter mentioned above and the posting of information about the Endowment on Vanguard's website. The Endowment maintained that it was committed to maintaining a separate existence that would not be seeking to cross-appeal to Vanguard mutual fund clients.

These responses sufficiently reassured the IRS in the Vanguard matter, and their fellow commercial sponsors successfully navigated these issues as well. Obtaining exemption as a commercially affiliated sponsor has become routine. Some isolated litigation involving commercial sponsors have arisen lately, but customers rather than the government originated it. These cases challenged asset management practices at commercially affiliated sponsors but were ultimately unsuccessful.[53]

Growth

Today the DAF field is dominated by sponsors created by mutual funds or other financial firms, each of which conveniently provides the investment and administrative services required of its own affiliated sponsor.[54] The National Philanthropic Trust runs an annual survey of DAFs, and breaks sponsors into three categories: national charities, community foundations, and single-issue charities. The national charity category, which is primarily made up of commercially affiliated sponsors, predominates. In the words of the 2020 Report, "the number of DAF accounts at National Charities is five times the number in the other two types of charitable sponsors combined. National Charities distribute more grant dollars and have higher aggregate charitable asset values."[55]

The growth of assets held by DAFs has been striking across all types of sponsors in recent years, reaching a total asset size just shy of $160 billion in 2020. The number of funds has been growing steadily for the past decade, along with contributions by donors and grants to charitable organizations. Donor-advised funds paid out more than $34 billion in grants in 2020 and received more than $47 billion in contributions—both all-time highs. Donor-advised funds had "outpace[d] the field in giving"[56] as early as 2017, "receiv[ing] about 8 percent of all dollars donated by Americans."[57] As individual charitable giving has remained relatively constant, dollars that once would have gone directly to charities are instead being channeled through DAFs and other intermediaries.

The rise of commercial sponsors has been downright stunning. In 2016 and 2017, the *Chronicle of Philanthropy*'s Philanthropy 400 list crowned Fidelity Charitable as the top recipient of charitable funds in the United States.[58] Each year's list reported the charities that raised the most money during the prior year. During Fidelity's reign, it bested household names like United Way, the Salvation Army, Harvard University, and St. Jude children's hospitals. And it was not alone. Of the top ten recipients of charitable funds on the 2017 list, four were commercial sponsors of DAFs. Fidelity has also become an enormous force in grantmaking; by 2017 it paid out more in grants than any other US grantmaker save the Bill & Melinda Gates Foundation.[59]

After two years of Fidelity taking the top spot, the *Chronicle* changed its methodology. Redubbed a ranking of "America's Favorite Charities," gifts to DAFs were explicitly excluded.[60] United Way regained the top spot and household name charities like Catholic Charities, the Mayo Clinic, and Stanford University filled out the top ten. There is little doubt that without this methodological change, DAF sponsors would have continued to take over the top echelon of the *Chronicle*'s leaderboard.

Charitable giving generally and giving to DAFs in particular boomed in 2017, due to a combination of stock market performance and the anticipation of new tax rules under the Tax Cuts and Jobs Act. Fidelity Charitable cited an 83 percent year-over-year increase in donors that year, powering its receipt of a record $8.5 billion in contributions.[61] Its DAFs' charitable grants also rose sharply, by 27 percent to $4.5 billion. Other commercial sponsors saw similar increases. Although these record increases may have been outliers driven by an unusual confluence of events, the expansion of DAFs has continued.

Controversy

The legislative attention to DAFs struggled to map them onto the charitable terrain. Donor-advised fund sponsors are not technically private foundations, but they are also a very unusual type of public charity. Congress has been made keenly aware of the charitable timing problem DAFs pose and the potential they raise for other kinds of abuse.

Congressional Action

This classification problem came to the fore in in the very first federal legislation to address DAFs explicitly. In order to incentivize giving after the devastating Gulf hurricane, The Katrina Emergency Tax Relief Act temporarily waived the percentage limitations on deductions for charitable contributions to public charities.[62] Donations to DAFs, however, were specifically excluded.[63] Although DAFs were public charities, they "were not the right sort of charity" which would "spend the money quickly and not accumulate the funds."[64]

The issue arose again in response to the COVID-19 pandemic. The deduction for charitable contributions for all taxpayers regardless of itemization as part of the 2020 CARES Act legislation likewise excluded DAF contributions.[65] The capped $300 deduction ($600 for married couples) was small and short-lived. Yet the law carefully disqualified contributions to DAFs from its benefit. The simultaneous increase of the percentage cap on deductions of cash gifts to public charities likewise did not apply to contributions to DAFs.

Despite this snub, COVID-19 prompted a flood of giving from DAFs. One study of community foundations and national sponsors found that in the first half of 2020, DAF distributions increased 29.8 percent over the same period the prior year, to $8.32 billion, "nearly doubl[ing]" the already impressive 16.7 percent year-over-year growth from 2018 to 2019.[66] The National Philanthropic Trust breathlessly reported that in 2020, "Grants Pass $30B for the First Time."

Some community foundation and commercial sponsors also urged their donor-advisors to activate giving in response to extraordinary needs.[67] Philanthropists Jennifer and David Risher put their own money on the line, pledging to disburse matching grants to charities supported by donors who contributed 50 percent or more of their DAF balances in 2020. Other philanthropists joined the matching pledge and #HalfMyDAF reported grants of "$8.6 million from DAFs [went] to nonprofits in five short months, helped by $1.4 million in matching funds" and promised even greater success in the future.[68]

By 2020, Congress had already enacted legislation targeting DAFs twice. In addition to the post-Katrina legislation, the 2006 Pension Protection Act (PPA or the Act) provided a formal definition, turning on three essential attributes that remain unchanged today.[69] Under it, a DAF is owned by a sponsoring organization, a term the statute also defines,[70] which legally controls the assets it contains. Each DAF the sponsor holds is "separately identified by reference to the contributions of a donor or donors," and the fund's donor or the donor's designee has the power to advise the sponsor on the fund's distributions and investments.[71]

With the target of its regulation thus established, the PPA's provisions then lasered in on addressing perceived abuses. It prohibited distributions to individuals and limited permissible recipients of grants from DAFs to tax-exempt public charities or government entities, unless the sponsoring organization engages in "expenditure responsibility."[72] Expenditure responsibility is a concept drawn from private foundation law and entails substantial due diligence prior to and after the distribution of funds to ensure they are used for charitable purposes.[73] Grants to international charities likewise require additional vetting. Some sponsoring organizations are willing to engage in expenditure responsibility to accommodate the giving preferences of donors to their DAFs, generally for an additional fee.[74] The extra time and costs required for such diligence led many to take the administratively easier route and permit distributions from DAFs they hold only to US public charities.[75]

The 2006 legislation also took aim at abuses whereby donors benefited from their own funds. It imposed penalty taxes on donors, donor-advisers, and related persons or entities if they received more than an incidental benefit from a DAF. Recipients of such improper benefits are subject to a 125 percent penalty tax on it, and fund managers who agree "to the making of a distribution, knowing that such distribution would confer a benefit" are subject to a 10 percent tax as well.[76] Taking a belt-and-suspenders approach, the legislation applied a preexisting regime penalizing public charity self-dealing to DAFs as well.[77]

The PPA also applied the excess business holdings rules discussed in the last chapter to DAFs. As explained there, these rules limit a foundation's total holdings of any single business to a maximum of 20 percent. The legislation extended this regime to DAFs on a fund-by-fund basis.[78] As for private foundations, the 20 percent ceiling is reduced by holdings of related parties and increased if control of the entity lies in unrelated hands.

The final thread of the legislation's DAF provisions looked toward the future. At the time, little information was available about the size and scope of DAFs and their sponsors, and Congress was left with many unanswered questions. The Act mandated sponsoring organizations to begin reporting annually aggregate figures on the number and value of the assets they held in DAFs, contributions received, and grants made, on the publicly available Form 990.[79] New applicants for public charity status were also required to disclose whether they would sponsor DAFs.[80]

This information made it possible to track DAFs much more closely, a job Treasury was specifically assigned. The statute commanded that Treasury study and report on the appropriateness of the deduction for donations to DAFs, including whether donors' advisory rights were consistent with a proper deduction, and on the advisability of adopting an annual payout requirement.[81] Although Congress instructed it to produce the report within a year, Treasury did not submit it until 2011.[82]

The much-delayed Treasury Report was a victory lap for DAFs and their sponsors. It concluded that no further changes to the deductibility of contributions to DAFs was necessary, as they were not meaningfully different from contributions to other public charities. The Report acknowledged the exceptional appeal of contributing appreciated property to DAFs as opposed to a private foundation, given that associated deductions for a DAF contribution would be set at the property's fair market value. It was, however, unconcerned. All donations to public charities offer donors the same tax bargain and contributors to DAFs must part with more control over donated assets than those who fund private foundations.

Treasury was likewise unworried about the potential time lag between a contribution to a DAF and ultimate charitable use of contributed funds. It explained simply that the potential for delay was "no different" for DAFs than other charitable organizations.[83] Existing deductibility rules combined with new excise tax penalties under the PPA, it reassured Congress, would suffice to prevent abusive distributions from DAFs for noncharitable purposes or to donors themselves.

On the question of payout, Treasury supported the status quo. Data gleaned from sponsor disclosures mandated by the PPA showed an average payout of 9.3 percent of assets in 2006. Commercial funds paid out an average of over 5 percent more than the overall figure. All these payout rates far exceed that for private foundations, the average annual payout from which "tend[s] to hover just above five percent," the mandated payout rate required by law.[84] Although the Report noted that it had limited data on which to draw and recognized that aggregate payout rates can mask much lower or even zero distribution rates by individual DAFs, Treasury opined that a recommendation on payout rates would be "premature."[85]

Continued Calls for Reform

Despite Treasury's optimistic conclusions, DAFs' proper place in the charitable works remains contested and the concerns the PPA raised about them endure. Indeed, the staggering growth of these vehicles, particularly within commercially affiliated sponsors, has only intensified the alarm. The influential[86] 2014 tax reform proposal released by Representative Dave Camp, Chairman of the House Ways and Means Committee, advocated reforming many areas of charitable tax treatment, including a payout requirement for DAFs.[87] His plan would have required DAF sponsors to distribute DAF assets within five years of receipt or pay a penalty tax equal to 20 percent of undistributed funds. But it was not adopted.

Calls for DAF payout reform resurfaced during the debate over the 2017 tax legislation. Professors Ray Madoff and Roger Colinvaux wrote a letter to Senator Orrin Hatch arguing for adoption of a payout rule for DAFs because "the public value of DAFs does not occur until such time as funds come out of the DAF sponsor and make their way to active charities."[88] Their concerns about payout rates were supported by an IRS study showing a quarter of DAF sponsors had annual distribution rates below 1 percent.[89] The professors also noted the unsettling practice of DAF distributions being paid out to other DAFs, inflating reported distribution rates.[90] Focusing on donors rather than sponsors, Madoff and Colinvaux called for deductibility of contributions to DAFs to be conditioned on donors naming a default public charity to receive any undistributed funds after ten years.

Again, the calls for reform were rebuffed. The 2017 Tax Cut and Jobs Act included a few provisions relating to charitable entities, but none addressing DAFs made the final cut. In a revealing twist, during this tempestuous period, the IRS released a request for comments on changes to the DAF rules but said nothing about payout.[91]

Undeterred, Professor Madoff teamed up with billionaire philanthropist John Arnold (of Arnold Ventures, discussed in chapter 1) and a team of academics, foundations, and charity leaders to launch a new series of proposals in 2020.[92] Their Initiative to Accelerate Charitable Giving addresses DAF reform together with proposals to reform private foundation law and expand charitable tax benefits for nonitemizers. Its efforts soon spurred the introduction of the Accelerate Charitable Efforts Act, by Senators Angus King and Chuck Grassley.[93]

The ACE Act would replace current DAF structures with two options for donors: either a fifteen-year time-limited DAF, contributions to which would be entitled to immediate income tax deductions, or a fifty-year time limited DAF, for which income tax deductions would not be available until distributions were made to operating charities. Sponsoring organizations would face a fine of 50 percent of the undistributed assets of DAFs that failed to make timely payouts. Even for fifteen-year DAFs, deductions for contributions of appreciated property would be limited to the amount realized on sale. The bill would also prohibit private foundations from satisfying their payout obligations thorough contributions to DAFs.

A bill was also proposed in California in 2020 to require large DAF sponsors to submit fund-by-fund disclosures to the state. The reporting would have been anonymous and could have provided data to test the extent to which average DAF payout rates reflect a widespread norm, but it was opposed by industry on grounds it "would jeopardize donors' privacy, leading to a reduction in charitable giving."[94] The original bill was withdrawn from consideration and a replacement intended to spur regulatory action in the area stalled as well. The Supreme Court's recent ruling striking down an existing California donor disclosure requirement further diminishes the likelihood that this reform will be adopted.[95]

Industry's Response

As much of the appeal of DAFs lies in their endowment-like functions, the industry has been understandably resistant to calls for payout reform. A joint letter from four different philanthropic industry groups responding to the Madoff/Colinvaux proposals argued that a payout requirement was a solution in search of a problem, as DAF sponsors already paid out considerable average grant distributions each year, and that imposing such a rule would "severely restrict philanthropy, and would reduce overall charitable giving in communities across the country."[96] Although the response to the ACE Act has been more mixed, many have raised dire objections warning its provisions will dampen charitable giving.[97]

Perhaps anxious to preempt new government requirements, some sponsors have self-regulated on payout. Internal policies ensure DAF funds will be distributed after a period of inactivity, generally only if attempts to obtain recommendations from the fund's donor-advisor have been unsuccessful. Community foundations' operation of grantmaking funds of their own, as well as the variance power broadly allowing them to diverge from any of their donors' stated preferences, make such policies especially easy to implement. With the express intent of staving off unwanted regulation in this area,[98] the National Standards for US Community Foundations adopted a new standard in 2017 requiring accredited community foundations to have a "process to ensure that a fund remains active."[99]

Commercially affiliated sponsors too apply fund inactivity policies. For example, at Schwab Charitable, if no grant recommendation is made from an account for three and a half years, it will be treated as dormant, though even a grant of $50 from a DAF of any size will avoid this characterization.[100] The donor-advisor is asked for a recommendation, and if none is forthcoming, Schwab Charitable will issue a grant to a public charity based on the donor's prior grantmaking advice or future planning on record, or will grant out funds to the Philanthropy Fund, from which the sponsor organization makes its own charitable grants. Schwab Charitable will continue to reach out to the donor-advisor or successor donor-advisors of persistently dormant accounts, but they are subject to closure and transfer of assets according to a succession plan on file or to the Philanthropy Fund.

Some commercially affiliated sponsors have also voluntarily adopted mandatory payout rates on an aggregate basis. Fidelity Charitable and The Vanguard Charitable Endowment have pledged an annual payout of at least 5 percent of their average net assets since 1998.[101] Amalgamated Bank's affiliated DAF sponsor announced a plan in 2018 to differentiate its offerings by pushing donors to speed the payout of their funds.[102] Account holders who chose their "advance change funds" are asked to pledge to pay out 10 percent of contributed funds annually.[103] Operating for just a few years, it has already proven highly successful, with Amalgamated reporting a 50 percent payout rate.

Despite some concerns that the PPA and possible new regulation of DAFs would create obstacles for DAF sponsors and donors,[104] the industry has thrived. Statutory prohibitions on classes of grant recipients were easily translated into narrow limitations on distributions, like Fidelity's allowance of grants only to public charities and private operating foundations. Sponsors also designed offerings around the new rules, such as Vanguard's partnership with an "expert in global giving" to provide donor-advisors with the due diligence necessary to ensure that grants to international recipients will comply with legal requirements. "Additional fees may apply."[105]

Commercial sponsors, with their vast size, administrative capacity, and accounting expertise, are perhaps best equipped to assimilate antiabuse legislation into their business models. A combination of strategic self-regulation and skillful advocacy has thus far kept legislation imposing timing requirements for distribution at bay. If the ACE Act or similar efforts succeed, they would present a more profound challenge to the industry.

A Changing Climate

Donor-advised funds have come a very long way from their origins in community foundations conceived as experts on and advocates for the charities of their city, state, or region. Donor-advised fund sponsors are still aggregators, but now there are a few massive ones, whose huge influence comes tinged with the for-profit environment out of which they were created. These commercially affiliated sponsors' focus is very much on charitable donors rather than recipients or a specific charitable community. Institutions across the charitable spectrum are all responding to this tectonic shift.

Operating Charities Join the Party

Charitable organizations with major operating programs like Nature Conservancy as well as historic charitable fund aggregators like United Way have recognized the appeal of DAFs and jumped into the fray. Following their lead, a diverse range of operating charities now offer DAFs,[106] though religiously oriented charities, colleges, and universities are the most frequent adopters.[107]

Sometimes operating charities sponsoring DAFs require a minimum allocation of disbursements on their own behalf, using the funds to incentivize and smooth donations for their own programs. But many merely offer the vehicles as a service to any consumers who might be interested, impose no requirement of donations to the sponsor organization, and allow donors to deposit their funds with them and disburse them to any charities they like. For example, alumni or "friends"—read anyone willing to deposit the minimum $10,000 investment—of Ohio Wesleyan University can create a DAF there rather than at Goldman Sachs or Schwab.[108] The university operates indistinguishably from these commercial sponsors. It retains legal ownership of the funds and distributes grants from the accounts to 501(c)(3) public charities on donors' recommendations. While donors decide on their charitable priorities, contributed funds are invested for growth.

Few operating charities could handle the technical, legal, and administrative burdens of running DAFs on their own, but vendors now offer private-label DAF services to make the product accessible to charities of more modest scale. Who are these vendors? Surprise, surprise—commercial sponsors. Ohio Wesleyan might not be able to manage a DAF program in-house, but a relationship with Vanguard allows it to solicit donor-advisors with the promise of investment options in one of nine Vanguard funds.

Charities can secure even more help from commercial sponsors in setting up their DAF offerings. Those using Morgan Stanley's white label DAF product actually run their accounts through the commercially affiliated sponsor, which handles not only investment management but also investigations of grant recipients and ultimate distributions. It allows charity clients to offer donor-advisors an internet portal and investment statements "designed by Morgan Stanley GIFT, but [which] carry the participating charity's name and brand."[109] Other than an optional feature to require contributions to the sponsoring charity and the use of its branding, private label products are designed to be identical to those offered by commercially affiliated sponsors.

Community Foundations Compete

Community foundations have also been impacted by the rise of commercial sponsors. No longer virtual monopolies in their charitable communities, they now must operate in a highly competitive national market for donors. Their responses to this changing environment vary, but they are all feeling the pressure to respond and making the case for the special value community foundations offer as sponsors of DAFs. The Philadelphia Foundation asserts

> When you set up a Donor Advised Fund through the Philadelphia Foundation, you gain access to our extensive knowledge of the region and the thousands of effective nonprofits addressing its greatest needs. Our service is personal, not transactional. We'll help you research nonprofits addressing the causes you value and will accompany you on visits to see your dollars in action.[110]

In addition to this differentiation message, The Philadelphia Foundation is offering its donors innovative new products. For example, it co-launched a locally focused social impact fund as an investment option for its DAFs. This novel offering allows donors to generate locally focused social returns not only on grants they ultimately distribute but also during the time that DAF contributions are invested through the community foundation sponsor. Marketing materials touted the Foundation's history of "us[ing] its deep knowledge of the community to promote the Greater Philadelphia region's economic, civic, and social vitality."[111]

Some of community foundations' biggest boosters have, however, come in for harsh criticism for following the commercial sponsor model too closely. Emmett Carson, former CEO of the Silicon Valley Community Foundation (SVCF), opined in 2002 that "the convening and community building roles of traditional community foundations have enormous value—a value commercial gifts funds and donor-focused community foundations are incapable of replicating."[112] Despite this focus on community foundations' links to local institutions, the SVCF established an East Coast department, designed to court new and serve existing donors 3,000 miles away from the community whose name it bears. It also—like most community foundations—does not limit grants geographically.[113] Donors can and do recommend charitable recipients around the country and across the globe.

The SVCF is the nation's largest community foundation by a significant margin,[114] due to contributions that have tracked the enormous accumulation of wealth in Silicon Valley's tech community and the increase in value of many of its donated assets. Indeed, in 2017, SVCF's assets outstripped that of the eighty-two-year-old Ford Foundation.[115] Although it distributed nearly a billion dollars in grants that year, critics challenge whether the SVCF is as concerned with distributing grants as it is with generating new donors. A *New York Times* investigation found virtually no grants had been made in the four years since Nicholas Woodman set up a $500 million DAF after his company, GoPro, went public.[116] Scandal also rocked SVCF when its top fundraiser was accused of sexual harassment and abuse of her subordinates, charges that were allegedly ignored by senior management due to her skill in attracting large donors.[117] The revelations led to the exit of three executives, including Carson, and touched off a storm of criticism about the foundation's misguided culture.[118]

Although few community foundations will become embroiled in situations like these, none can escape the donor-focused environment commercially affiliated sponsors have created. Sponsors affiliated with for-profit investment companies have access to resources and expertise quite unlike that possessed by community foundations and other early DAF adopters. They have developed easily accessible giving tools, offered donors a wide array of investment choices, and provided them with considerable flexibility around both the assets they can donate and the recipients to whom they can distribute donated funds. They also can do all of this with relatively low or even zero minimum account requirements and investment and administrative fees generally of 1 percent or less.[119]

Their appeal has fueled the huge growth in DAFs both within commercially affiliated sponsors and beyond. A new breed of upstart DAF sponsors that in many ways resemble fintech firms, are also entering and expanding the space.[120]

These new entrants are growing rapidly and offer innovations in realms as diverse as algorithms to determine giving types, opportunities to target grants to enhance diversity equity and inclusion, and convenient liquidation of noncash gifts. To remain viable sponsors, community foundations will continue to face pressure to match those attractive terms and offerings of their growing field of competitors.

The mix of low cost and easy access offered by DAFs is often lauded as democratizing philanthropy, and they may offer real value to middle-class donors seeking to smooth their giving or donate appreciated property. These vehicles are most prized (and used), however, by society's elite. Commercially affiliated sponsors' willingness to accept—indeed their active efforts to draw out—contributions of appreciated property are designed with big-ticket donor advisers in mind. An IRS error exposed Goldman Sachs' affiliated sponsor's incredible talent in obtaining such contributions. Three famously private tech billionaires made gifts valued from more than $100 million to nearly $2 billion to their DAFs held there. Two of the names are familiar ones from chapter 1's review of philanthropy LLCs. Steve Ballmer contributed $1.9 billion to his Goldman DAF in 2016, much of it in appreciated stock; Laurene Powell Jobs contributed $526 million.[121]

Available philanthropy LLC disclosures suggest they are not alone. The Chan Zuckerberg Initiative website describes its affiliated DAF at SVCF as "one of its three funding entities," and Zuckerberg and Priscilla Chan donated more than $160 million in Facebook stock to it in 2017.[122] In his study using the IRS Statistics of Income, economist James Andreoni sums it up in this way: "Donor Advised Funds are clearly a financial instrument that, when measured by dollars that pass through them, are used primarily by people at the very tops of the wealth and income distributions."[123]

Private Foundations Jump on the Bandwagon

Ironically, some of the largest donors that DAF sponsors are now courting are themselves private foundations. As private foundations are already endowments from which to make charitable grants, they would seem to have little use for the DAF model. But remember, private foundations are subject to the 5 percent annual payout requirement; sponsors of DAFs, which qualify as public charities, are not. Moreover, DAFs qualify as recipients of private foundations' mandated distributions. Therein lies the opportunity.

A private foundation can technically meet its payout requirement (completely or in part) through grants to one or more DAFs—even though the funds thus contributed will not necessarily be distributed to an operating charity for a very long time to come. Not all such practices are nefarious. A private foundation grant to a DAF at a community foundation can offer local expertise and a partner to ensure responsible giving.[124] For a private foundation that miscalculated its required distributions and finds itself short of the 5 percent payout with little time to investigate and make a full-fledged grant, this technique is a welcome workaround to avoid substantial penalty taxes.

Private foundation grants to DAFs can also keep controversial donations private. The foundation will need to report the distribution to the DAF on its public informational return. The DAF sponsor will include the distribution in its aggregate reporting on grants from its many funds. Neither the foundation's nor the sponsor's disclosures, however, will link the identity of the donor and the ultimate recipient.

Shielding the identity of foundation donors appears to fly in the face of the transparency and accountability the Grand Bargain traded for private foundations' tax advantages. Still, one's view of the technique's propriety may also vary with particular use cases. A desire to avoid public scrutiny of grants that might signal a particular foundation donor's health status is understandable. Less so foundation grants to DAFs designed to obscure contributions to charities that undermine a founding family's misleading public statements or those made to a charity connected to political figures. Reports of DAFs' distributions to hate groups, while obscuring the donor's identity, place the risks of DAFs' lack of transparency in stark relief.[125]

Highly aggressive uses of the technique, such as making all or much of a private foundation's required distributions to DAFs, retaining the donated assets in the fund indefinitely, or both, are harder to justify. And such uses do occur. A *Chronicle of Philanth*ropy study found "just six foundations [] distributed more than 95 percent of their grants to a national donor advised fund" but also identified 557 foundations "that made at least one grant to a DAF during the 2014 to 2016 fiscal years."[126] An Economist study found 10 percent of a randomly selected sample of private foundations made grants to the largest sponsors, and of these over a quarter gave DAFs over 90 percent of the funds they distributed.[127] Elon Musk's foundation distributed nearly $38 million to DAF sponsor Vanguard Charitable in 2016.[128] Such moves look less like careful grantmaking or a measured workaround for exceptional situations and more like a giant loophole.

The payout requirement forces private foundations to pay at least some tax-benefited assets out to operating charities so they can be used to benefit worthy causes currently, rather than invested for perpetuity. A foundation that complies with this mandate through distributions to DAFs that can themselves languish untouched makes a mockery of the rules carefully crafted in 1969. Yet when the IRS requested public comments on whether grants to DAFs should continue to count toward private foundation payout requirements,[129] fund sponsors and foundations predictably argued they should. Professors Madoff and Colinvaux called for a legislative fix in their 2017 letter to Senator Grassley[130] and a prohibition on the practice is included in the ACE Act.

The Form 990-PF does require foundations to report annually on whether they made any distributions to DAFs. For foundations that do so, the requirement to list grant recipients will make their actions transparent to those who go looking. It remains to be seen whether regulations or legislation to combat the practice more aggressively will be forthcoming.

Conclusion

The basic question of when tends to dominate when commercially affiliated DAFs come under scrutiny. In truth, they present the same broad array of concerns triggered by other illustrations of for-profit philanthropy considered in this part. The rise of philanthropy LLCs, the growth in strategic corporate giving, and the emergence of powerful new intermediaries transforming the way we donate as thoroughly as credit cards have remade the way we spend threaten the regulatory structure that targets billions of charitable dollars toward hospitals and relief organizations every year. Regulations do not feed the hungry, but for years a structure built on the Grand Bargain's legal framework has done just that.

The dominance of for-profit-affiliated sponsors has upended the charitable sector, reorienting it toward a more transactional approach to philanthropy and channeling contributions into vehicles beyond the reach of foundation regulation. It has also, of course, yielded immense transfers of assets that—absent intervention by some accommodating future Congress or perhaps further signal victories in the courts—will one day be put to charitable use. Attempts to rein in the growth of commercially affiliated DAFs have been limited. Concerns about their impact on the timing, transparency, and targeting of giving are mounting.

Since their inception DAFs have been creatures of tax law and their sponsors are highly responsive to tax policy. Congress could, as a result, have much more of an impact here than in the philanthropy LLC context. Fund-by-fund transparency requirements, mandatory payouts, or limited lifetimes would certainly shift the current practices of DAF sponsors but will not drive them out of business. Reduced deductibility or termination of DAFs' eligibility to receive private foundations' mandated grants would curtail demand for their services but not eliminate it.

Recharting the charitable regulatory map to create an appropriate place for these important institutions would involve a difficult tradeoff between incommensurables. Less red tape could increase philanthropy. Less accountability concentrates control in the hands of society's elites, all while obscuring their influence. But these trade-offs lie at the heart of for-profit philanthropy's rise.

The growth of commercially affiliated DAFs highlights the migration of traditionally for-profit norms, players, and practices into historically nonprofit arenas. All the for-profit philanthropy trends that this part highlights blur the line between charity and business, and as they do, each generates similar benefits and risks. The next chapter turns to a third example of this dynamic: the shift of corporate philanthropy ever closer to the core of company's business models. On the one hand, this phenomenon can deliver an infusion of resources to pursue social good at a time when society's problems desperately require investment. On the other hand, like the philanthropy LLCs and commercially affiliated DAFs already explored, it magnifies the influence of already powerful elites and shields their activities from regulation and public scrutiny.

3

Strategic Corporate Philanthropy

The rise of the philanthropy LLC and the growth of commercially affiliated donor-advised funds suggest that for-profit philanthropy represents a sharp break with the past. Chapter 2 reveals a more complex truth, tracing the origins of Vanguard Charitable to the creation of the 1969 Grand Bargain. This chapter uncovers the deep roots of the third aspect of the for-profit philanthropy phenomenon.

Strategic corporate philanthropy sidesteps the long controversial question of corporations' proper objectives by perceiving a connection between the fortunes of stakeholders and shareholders. Corporate philanthropy itself may represent nothing new. But today, a growing consensus among corporate America's leaders that doing good for employees and other constituencies reveals a clear path toward doing well for shareholders neatly resolves a century of conflict.[1]

Corporate giving has become a significant part of both business life and of the philanthropic landscape. A small but important portion of US charitable contributions each year comes not from individuals but from corporations. Companies tout contributions of cash, inventory, and employee time everywhere from advertising to annual corporate citizenship reports. In aggregate, corporate giving represented more than $21 billion in cash and in-kind donations either made directly by corporations or through their affiliated foundations in 2021, making up 4 percent of overall US giving, down slightly in the past few years from a fairly consistent norm of about 5 percent.[2]

Given those high levels of activity and lofty expectations, one might conclude that corporate philanthropy has never been controversial. As this chapter demonstrates, although it has always represented an important aspect of business, the practice has long been buffeted by dissent. Today, widespread agreement over why and how to give has displaced debate over whether corporations should give. Strategic corporate philanthropy, both a new face of corporate giving and another example of for-profit philanthropy, sees profit in serving the community.

Large multinational corporations increasingly align their charitable giving as closely as possible to their business models. The dismantling of separate corporate foundations and transfer of their former grantmaking activities to divisions within the sponsoring company casts that shift in stark terms. Google pioneered this effort a decade ago; Pearson and General Motors followed suit in 2014 and 2017, respectively. Like donors to LLCs and commercially affiliated donor-advised funds, rejecting conventional methods offers these corporations

For-Profit Philanthropy. Dana Brakman Reiser and Steven A. Dean, Oxford University Press. © Oxford University Press 2023. DOI: 10.1093/oso/9780190074500.003.0004

flexibility, privacy, and control. And as with those other instances of for-profit philanthropy, despite eschewing the foundation form, strategic corporate philanthropy sacrifices little of the tax advantage of giving.

Less dramatic than shuttering a corporate foundation, but far more widespread, the embrace of a strategic blueprint for corporate philanthropy reimagines charity not as a duty but as an opportunity. At our most prominent companies, philanthropy no longer represents a counterweight to the usual profit-maximizing modus operandi but instead becomes part of the core business strategy. Firms—eager to burnish their corporate social responsibility bona fides and to tap capital markets increasingly focused on the environmental and social impact of their investments—deploy philanthropic activity as a signal of their commitment to the needs of investors and other stakeholders.

In a business world saturated by win–win discourse, linking profit-making and social good generation has made corporate philanthropists simply writing checks to anodyne charities an anachronism. Today, sponsoring museum exhibits or nights at the ballet and calling it a day would seem like walking by a twenty-dollar bill lying on the sidewalk. Blending doing well and good, contemporary corporate charitable grants, product donations, and employee giving programs address environmental damage in regions where businesses operate, smooth corporate donors' supply chains, and increase satisfaction among their labor pools.

Rather than an exception to the traditional for-profit norm of shareholder primacy, this strategic approach to philanthropy has come to exemplify it. Inevitably, some examples of corporate philanthropy reenvisioned around this for-profit norm threaten to stretch the concept beyond recognition. When corporate contributions become a means to achieve greater profitability or market share, or to reduce risk, they share little with the conventional legal definition of a charitable gift.

This chapter sets the stage for Part II's (chapters 4 and 5) exploration of the risks of corporations' strategic integration of for-profit philanthropy within their core businesses by revealing the breadth and power of this for-profit philanthropy phenomenon. Alongside the rise of philanthropy LLCs and commercially affiliated donor-advised funds, strategic corporate philanthropy threatens the Grand Bargain that has preserved philanthropy law for half a century. Transforming corporate charitable contributions into an aspect of shareholder primacy might produce a kinder capitalism, but at what price?

Creating Corporate Philanthropy

The first corporations did not merely engage in charity. They were charitable and religious organizations. Even early business corporations pursued public purposes like transport and public safety.[3]

During the nineteenth century, many states removed requirements that corporations form for specific purposes. States also did away with the need to obtain the legislative charters that often limited corporations to public endeavors. The advent of general incorporation laws paved the way for the formation of business corporations for any lawful purpose. Over time, as public purposes yielded to private interests, corporations and corporate law became the province of profit.[4]

Corporations grew dramatically under this system, as did the fortunes of their founders. Some became part of the founding cohort of American philanthropists like Rockefeller and Carnegie. Closely identified with their founders, corporate motivations for giving in some respects anticipated those driving today's strategic corporate philanthropy practices.

Of course, the major philanthropic efforts of Rockefeller and Carnegie occurred outside the confines of the corporations they controlled. These philanthropists donated profits earned through their corporations' success but did so in their own names and on their own accounts. Once they extracted it from the corporate form, these influential American philanthropists donated wealth directly to charities (and sometimes municipalities). They also created foundations to receive and invest donated assets and undertake coordinated grantmaking programs. Corporate philanthropy, with corporate assets donated by the corporation itself, tended to be a smaller and more local affair, benefiting organizations pivotal to the communities in which businesses operated.[5]

Legitimizing Corporate Giving

Even such limited corporate giving practices could seem radical. After all, investors might prefer firms not give away their assets. The legal boundaries of corporate giving took shape over time as courts and legislatures grappled with the obligations managers owed to owners and their communities.

In *A.P. Smith Manufacturing* v. *Barlow*,[6] a New Jersey manufacturing concern sought judicial clarification of the legality of a corporate donation of $1,500 to Princeton University's annual fund. The New Jersey Supreme Court strongly affirmed the corporation's entitlement to donate.[7] It resolved the legal question expeditiously, drawing on state legislation common by that time (and universal today), which explicitly empowered firms to make reasonable charitable contributions.[8]

That legislative authority dovetailed with the court's belief that such contributions rested comfortably within a corporation's authority even without specific statutory clearance. It pointed to earlier cases from a variety of jurisdictions highlighting the firm-specific benefits corporate charitable contributions generate. A.P. Smith's president testified to the existence of these benefits. Corporate contributions, he noted, generated goodwill and a "favorable environment for their business operations."[9]

The *A.P. Smith* court did acknowledge limits on corporate contributions. They must be reasonable in amount, made to further corporate interests, and not be disguised compensation to managers or directors who might solicit for "pet" charities.[10] Other cases reviewing corporate contributions often mention these limitations, but they rarely invoke them to disqualify challenged contributions.

These constraints did not stop a court from upholding a consumer goods corporation's gift of stock worth more than half a million dollars to a charitable trust controlled by its majority shareholder.[11] Nor did they prevent court approval of a settlement allowing Occidental Petroleum to contribute at least $50 million to fund a museum to house its former CEO's art collection.[12] Even when quite sizable gifts go to causes or organizations with deep connections with corporate insiders, corporate charitable gifts tend to be sustained.

In part, this reflects courts' intuitions about the value of corporate charitable donations for donors and for society. The opinion in *A.P. Smith* lavished praise on the practice for precisely those reasons. It noted the importance of corporate philanthropy to meet public expectations of corporate citizenship. Going further, it cast contributions to higher education as a vital bulwark for the free enterprise system itself.

The court also noted approvingly that as corporations had taken over from individuals as the primary holders of wealth in American society, philanthropic causes naturally turned their attention and requests to corporate donors. These sentiments reflected carefully crafted testimony from business leaders. Corporate heavyweights Standard Oil and U.S. Steel Corporation worked with the Ford Foundation and others in order bring this impact litigation to further "develop corporate philanthropy"[13] and its legitimacy.

Their efforts proved wildly successful. The *A.P. Smith* opinion has been highly influential. Over time, it helped corporate philanthropy become not only mainstream but an expected part of corporate life.

Of course, tax benefits for corporate philanthropy don't hurt. When the federal income tax deduction for charitable contributions made by individual taxpayers was inaugurated in 1917, it did not apply to corporations. Extending the charitable deduction to corporations proved so controversial it took nearly two additional decades. Powerful opponents, including President Franklin D. Roosevelt, explained that "corporations should not be able to 'purchase' goodwill and . . . charitable contributions were properly the domain of shareholders."[14] F.D.R. finally relented in 1935 and signed Congress's proposed deduction for charitable contributions by corporations.[15]

Since then, like the individuals discussed in chapters 1 and 2, corporate donors have been able to deduct from their taxable income any "contribution or gift to or for the use of" a recognized charitable organization.[16] The corporate deduction was limited to no more than 5 percent of a firm's taxable income for decades,[17] but eventually it was doubled in 1981.[18] As part of the suite of federal enactments responding to the COVID-19 pandemic, the limit was raised to 25 percent for corporate charitable contributions made in cash to operating charities in 2020 and 2021.[19]

Basic principles of tax law establish the idea of a "gift" as a transfer of money or property without expectation of anything in return. In the words of a frequently invoked case, gifts must be made from "detached and disinterested generosity."[20] Justifications for allowing taxpayers to deduct such generosity abound. If the income tax is designed to apply to income available for personal consumption or some concept of net income in the corporate setting, gifts to charity can simply be understood as outside its scope.[21] Alternatively, the deduction can also be viewed as a subsidy for the public benefit provided by charitable organizations.[22] Rather than the government directly subsidizing individual charities, which might create thorny separation-of-powers problems and invite corruption, deductions allow taxable corporations to be the direct agents of support for charities. Their support can then be bolstered by tax benefits.

Corporate law cases addressing the permissibility of corporate philanthropy in general and reviewing specific transactions frequently cite its tax benefits. A few have even suggested the percentage limit on such deductions should serve as an outside limit on reasonable contributions, but this limit is not particularly salient to firms. Precious few companies ever come close to contributing 5 percent of their annual incomes to charity, let alone 10 or 25 percent.

Competing Explanations for Corporate Philanthropy

As tax law appears to contemplate only corporate charitable contributions divorced from the profit motive—gifts state statutes and case law clearly permit—it remains unclear why an individual corporation would actually make them. For some, the moral imperative described in cases like *A.P. Smith* provides sufficient justification. Corporations, as holders of an ever-increasing share of national assets, have an obligation to give back to the broader society that supports them.

Such a moral rationale resonates with the managerialist view of corporations that prevailed at mid-century. From this perspective, corporations become social institutions and its managers an integral part of society's fabric. Those managers—in their dual roles as employees and citizens—must prioritize not only financial but also societal prosperity.[23]

The alternatives to that managerialist justification invite more skepticism of corporate generosity. The most cynical view sees corporate charitable contributions as a symptom of the pernicious principal-agent problem at the heart of corporations. Investors in an incorporated firm turn over their collective assets to secure the benefits of centralized management. They also, inevitably, suffer losses when managers—their agents—put those assets to their own uses rather than those of the corporation.

Corporate philanthropy may simply be disguised payments or perks for managers or directors, who guide corporate resources to charities these fiduciaries would otherwise support with their own dollars or to charitable efforts that elevate their individual reputations.[24] It would be easy to paint Occidental Petroleum's museum contribution with this brush.

Critics have offered the example of Morrison Knudsen Corporation's contribution to a charity established by its CEO's wife[25] and cited evidence executives use their authority over corporate contributions to ease their paths to prominent board seats.[26] When executives and managers can exploit their control over corporate giving to serve their own purposes, corporations and their stakeholders bear the costs. Those who perceive corporate philanthropy as this kind of fiduciary nest-feathering understandably oppose encouraging it through corporate and tax law.

A third take falls somewhere in the middle. It paints managers as neither angels nor devils but instead as faithful corporate servants. It treats corporate philanthropy as a signaling device, which can be used to communicate firm strength, workplace attractiveness, or product quality.[27] That view puts a contemporary spin on *A.P. Smith's* fairy tale of corporate generosity, reimagining selflessness as a subtle communications strategy. By choosing to make a significant charitable contribution, a firm can broadcast its robust financial position, which may reassure potential investors, employees, and consumers of unobservable facts about both current assets and projections for the future.

One might understand Texaco's more than half-century long sponsorship of the Metropolitan Opera's radio broadcasts as an example of corporate philanthropy used in this way. The sponsorship, which cost the company $7 million/year when finally discontinued in the early 2000s, involved a charitable good (opera) with no relationship to the company's products or industry (energy).[28] No details have emerged about particularly cozy relationships between Texaco executives and the Met program. The signaling explanation suggests some or all of the value of this very public contribution lies simply in demonstrating that Texaco had the resources and confidence to undertake it.[29]

When it began, the story of Texaco and the Met Opera looked quite different. The company initiated its contributions in 1940, when its reputation had been sullied by press accounts of its secret sales of oil to Nazi Germany prior to America's entry in the conflict.[30] Affiliation with an iconic cultural institution, and particularly its efforts to make its music widely available to the public, helped to rehabilitate its corporate image, allowing it to buy goodwill, just as F.D.R. feared.

The philanthropic world has long been replete with attempts by donors to burnish—or perhaps launder—their reputations. Charitable gifts made by Jeffrey Epstein to MIT and other institutions and the legions of gifts by the Sackler family serve only as the most recent and sordid examples.[31] Corporate philanthropy can function in this nefarious way as well.

Corporate philanthropy undertaken to signal prosperity or rehabilitate a firm's reputation hardly represents the selfless generosity of a corporate moral being. But it does at least parry criticisms of corporate charity as managerial theft. While falling short of the gauzy perfection corporate titans peddled in *A.P. Smith*, these explanations tie corporate philanthropy to corporate interests rather than individual vanity.

The last rationale for corporate charity effectively doubles down on that notion, suggesting that corporate philanthropy serves corporate interests directly. Rather than merely broadcasting corporate strength, it intimates, generosity augments it. Advocates for corporate social responsibility argue that corporate philanthropy can breed brand awareness, improve public and community relations, build generalized goodwill, and perhaps even generate value for the firm in the long run. Strategic corporate philanthropy as advocated by Michael Porter and Mark Kramer makes an even bolder claim.

Porter and Kramer dismiss the idea that corporate philanthropic efforts should aspire merely to generate publicity or generalized goodwill. They argue that corporate philanthropy can—and the best corporate philanthropy should—deliver real "competitive advantage" for its corporate donors.[32] This "true strategic giving . . . addresses important social and economic goals simultaneously, targeting areas of competitive context where the company and society both benefit because the firm brings unique assets and expertise"[33] to bear.

Countless examples of corporate philanthropy conform to these explanations, and, no matter how disparate, legal standards align with each. Empirical studies have sought to identify the proportion of each strain but have been inconclusive.[34] Increasingly, the value-enhancing, strategic vision dominates the way large corporations understand their own philanthropy. It has become the standard account they offer to stakeholders and the public. That stark shift, from mid-century altruism to modern strategic behavior, hints at the promise and peril for-profit philanthropy represents.

Corporate Social Responsibility

This contemporary account of corporate philanthropy is tied closely to the concept of corporate social responsibility (CSR). Rather than donating its financial, product, or human resources, this concept—also referred to as corporate social performance, corporate sustainability, and frequently simply as CSR—asks corporate leaders to acknowledge their firms' impacts on people and planet as they operate and expand. Unlike the conventional corporate philanthropy of *A.P. Smith*, CSR actions go beyond making contributions. They engage the full scope of corporations' manufacturing, labor, marketing, and operational decisions, both internally and through the firm's dealings with other entities in its supply chain or distribution network. Under the banner of corporate social responsibility, business leaders have reimagined an obligation to the public as an integral part of their business operations.

CSR's History

Arguments for corporate social responsibility first blossomed in the 1950s. Echoing the rhetoric of corporate charity, this early version of CSR acknowledged the growing power of corporations in society. Their privileged position demanded that corporations not only consider their impact but act ethically as good citizens.[35] Exhortations to corporate charity were interwoven with a broader obligation to "consider whether [corporate] action is likely to promote the public good, to advance the basic beliefs of our society, to contribute to its stability, strength, and harmony."[36] This social orientation clearly reflects the prevailing managerialist views of the era.

In the more than half-century since, the CSR concept has morphed into an inward-looking exercise, focused on the value of CSR for corporations themselves.[37] JP Morgan Chase CEO and Chairman Jamie Dimon captures this shift in the firm's 2018 Environmental Social & Governance Report on its efforts to address the needs of underserved communities, create economic opportunity, and enhance sustainability. "By addressing some of the world's biggest challenges, we are positioning our Firm and communities we serve to be successful today and over the long term."[38] Ford's leaders take a similar view, recognizing that "[i]f we are to become the world's most trusted company, designing and building smart vehicles for a smart world, we need to be part of the solution to [sustainability and climate change] challenges, not part of the problem."[39]

Both today and in the uncertain future, corporate social responsibility has come to be valued because it contributes to firms' profits, market share, and other indicia of success. Thanks to this transformation, CSR elides a long-standing and oftentimes bitter legal debate about a corporation's proper objectives.[40] Once viewed as a drain on corporate assets requiring justification, the contemporary vision of CSR as a source of firm value aligns the interests of shareholders and stakeholders.

The CSR Debate

Ubiquitous state legislation authorizing corporate charitable contributions leaves no doubt that managers have the power to make donations. With the blessing of legislatures, courts uphold corporate giving without needing to commit to any particular view on whether a corporation may sacrifice return for investors in order to achieve social aims. CSR activities can appeal to no analogous legal safe harbor. Over the years, whether a corporation's proper objectives can or should encompass CSR has engendered considerable controversy.

The argument against corporate social responsibility was framed most pithily by Milton Friedman in the title of his 1970 *New York Times Magazine* article, *The Social Responsibility of Business Is to Increase Its Profits*. The idea that a corporation's directors and managers must act to maximize value for shareholders rather than to improve the lot of other potential corporate constituencies has proven tenacious in the legal literature. In Friedman's words, "the manager is the agent of those who own the corporation." Corporate leaders who act to pursue social responsibility in a way that diminishes corporate profits are "spending [the shareholders'] money."[41]

Friedman was, of course, an economist, but prominent legal scholars have shared these views as well. A similar position was articulated in the pages of the *Harvard Law Review* as early as the 1930s by Professor Adolph Berle, who argued corporate power was "exercisable only for the ratable benefit of all the shareholders as their interest appears."[42] Leo E. Strine, Jr.—a former member and chief judge of Delaware's Chancery and Supreme Courts (highly expert trial and appellate courts that handle corporate cases in the state where nearly two-thirds of Fortune 500 companies are incorporated)—also strongly advocated this shareholder primacy view in scholarly papers.[43] Chief Justice Strine warned that to assume otherwise would blunt efforts to regulate against corporate excesses.

Few actual controversies have given courts the opportunity to opine on the question of whether CSR violates state corporate laws—and none using those precise terms. The most often cited case, a century-old chestnut involving Henry Ford's refusal to issue dividends in order to finance lower prices and increase wages, long preceded the emergence of the CSR movement. The 1919 Michigan Supreme Court chastised Ford: "a business corporation is organized and carried on primarily for the profit of the stockholders. The powers of the directors are to be employed for that end."[44] Similar statements can be found in two later cases decided by Delaware courts.

The first came at the height of the 1980s takeover frenzy. The Delaware Supreme Court held in *Revlon* v. *MacAndrews* that—at least when the board has given up defending a corporation's independence—its directors must focus single-mindedly on shareholder value.[45] A digital-era case revisited the questions confronted in *Ford*, pitting a profit-seeking minority craigslist shareholder (eBay) against its community-focused controlling shareholder founders. The Delaware Chancery Court concluded that however profoundly our notions of for-profit corporations might have changed, these entities are still "not an appropriate vehicle for purely philanthropic ends."[46]

Shareholders become especially vulnerable when control of their firm hangs in the balance. Courts—particularly Delaware courts—pay extra attention at those moments. Ordinarily deferential scrutiny of fiduciary behavior acquires a more skeptical edge in the change-of-control context. Concerns that corporate directors may throw shareholders overboard in an attempt to save their own positions trigger a protective judicial response. Militant statements of shareholder primacy in both *Revlon* and *eBay* must be understood as having been articulated in these extreme circumstances. Whether they apply more broadly remains hotly debated.

Ford and *eBay* also both turned on the fraught power dynamics of controlling shareholders in closely held corporations, which prompt particularly searching review from courts. Despite their small number and special circumstances, the language of *Ford*, *Revlon*, and *eBay*—frequently read not merely as elevating shareholders over other stakeholders but as completely dismissing stakeholder concerns—continues to exert considerable power.

Fierce and esteemed opponents of shareholder primacy read these authorities differently. One of the earliest to argue for the social obligations of business corporations to the broader community was Berle's interlocutor in the *Harvard Law Review* debate, Professor Merrick Dodd. In his words, a corporation's leaders can "employ its funds in a manner appropriate to a person practising a profession and imbued with a sense of social responsibility without thereby being guilty of a breach of trust" even if their actions do not maximize value for shareholders.[47]

Many modern scholars too advocate stakeholderism, rather than shareholder primacy. They argue that corporate fiduciaries owe their obligations to the corporation rather than to its owners, and therefore must take account of its impact on all of its stakeholders. Employees, creditors, community members, even the society or environment at large may—or even must—be considered alongside owners.

Stakeholder theory's proponents insist that shareholder primacy advocates overstate their case. After all, corporate statutes and case law entitle fiduciaries to enormous discretion as long as they do not act to enrich themselves.[48] In addition, stakeholder theory devotees can cite judicial and legislative chapter and verse to support their position. Indeed, *Revlon*'s stark language is employed to create an exception to the default rule for Delaware corporate fiduciaries defending takeover bids. This default, which applies whenever a *Revlon*-like endgame has not been triggered, allows corporate directors to respond proportionally to threats not only to shareholder interests but also those of "creditors, customers, employees, and perhaps even the community generally."[49] Stakeholder advocates can also point to the fact that more than half of US jurisdictions have adopted so-called constituency statutes to expressly permit corporate fiduciaries to consider and privilege interests of stakeholders other than shareholders.[50]

Some proponents go still further. They argue not only that shareholder primacy advocates mistake legal doctrine but that their focus on owners can be corrosive. The late UCLA and Cornell Professor Lynn Stout put it this way: "many and perhaps most of our corporate problems can be traced . . . to a flawed idea: that corporations are managed well when they are managed to maximize share price."[51]

The legal question remains contested, having stymied scholars and courts for a century. Berle and Dodd found the question so vexing they ultimately switched sides. Berle came to recognize the need for corporations to be run for constituencies beyond shareholders. He publicly retracted his earlier position in the 1950s, conceding the argument was decided "squarely in favor of Professor Dodd's contention."[52] For his part, Dodd came to fear the power of directors free to serve a range of constituencies.[53] Courts too have sent mixed signals. *Ford* and *eBay* speak of shareholder value maximization as "primarily"[54] the proper objective of corporate fiduciaries. Moreover, they insist it only becomes only dominant "when there are other stockholders interested in realizing a return on their investment."[55]

Practice Overcomes Theory

Whether for good or ill, CSR as practiced today neatly evades the knotty legal debate over shareholder primacy versus stakeholder theory. Rather than embracing calls from critics and scholars to prioritize shareholders or stakeholders, CSR practitioners have advanced the notion that stakeholderism is shareholder primacy. Corporate social responsibility has become a fully coopted component of business strategy.

Whether their CSR programs reduce a company's carbon footprint, improve labor conditions for its workforce, increase the diversity of its leadership team, or add safety features to its products, the increased value of its core operations justifies all of them. Companies approach social responsibility as a route to enhanced reputation, market share, profitability, and long-term financial sustainability. Corporate social responsibility in modern practice embraces a strategic imperative fully aligned with shareholder value maximization.

Corporate leaders need not dampen their devotion to the bottom line to diminish their firms' environmental impacts if doing so reduces costs as well. They can take any and all actions to reduce social inequality or improve public health that will also strengthen current and future labor and consumer pools. Aligning CSR with business value has allowed it to flourish.

Over the last half century, CSR has become a central part of how large corporations view themselves and of the image of value and values they project to the public. If they agree on nothing else, the nearly universally acceptance of CSR as part of doing business and firms' willingness publicize their CSR efforts to their shareholders and beyond confirms that business leaders believe that CSR delivers bottom-line results.[56] The 2019 "Statement on the Purpose of a Corporation" issued by the Business Roundtable, an association of top US corporate CEOs, explicitly expands its view of corporations' proper objectives beyond shareholder value. "Each of our stakeholders is essential," it declared, "[w]e commit to deliver value to all of them, for the future success of our companies, our communities and our country."[57]

At least some major investors agree; BlackRock CEO Larry Fink's recent letters to CEOs implored them to "embod[y] your company's purpose in your business model and corporate strategy"[58] and insisted that "[t]he more your company can show its purpose in delivering value to its customers, its employees, and its communities, the better able you will be to compete and deliver long-term, durable profits for shareholders."[59] Whether or not one believes that firms should practice corporate social responsibility, as a practical matter they already do.

Following CSR's Lead: Strategic Corporate Philanthropy

With surging acceptance of CSR, it comes as no surprise to see corporate philanthropy reimagined to align with the shareholder value story. Movement along this trajectory has been steady over many years. The Conference Board identified the trend in a 1999 report, finding that "corporations now embrace strategic philanthropy, which requires that every dollar given must mesh with the company's markets or employees,"[60] and that "corporations are increasingly integrating their contributions programs into their overall strategic plans."[61] These findings and others grounded its prediction that companies would only increase their demands for linking philanthropic spending and corporate bottom lines.[62]

A 2012 Council on Foundations report bore out this forecast. By that time, it categorized corporate philanthropy as a "field in transition" with "emerging paradigms" focused on values and value created, aligned, and integrated with underlying businesses.[63] The transition was not complete, but the tipping point had passed: "[m]ost corporate philanthropy professionals say they are under increasing pressure to align corporate philanthropy and giving with business objectives."[64]

The transformation continued through the decade. The 2017 and 2018 reports of the then-named Committee Encouraging Corporate Philanthropy, a CEO-led group of more than 200 top companies, noted increases in direct cash contributions relative to foundation and in-kind giving overall, explaining that a greater share of direct company contributions provide corporate donors opportunities to "leverage their brand and be more aligned with business strategies in terms of the causes they support."[65] A 2017 report by the international group Corporate Citizenship reported that "North American corporate foundations increasingly see the benefits of close strategic alignment with the parent company. Two-thirds agree that a foundation should 'harness the business acumen and networks of its parent company to guide foundation strategy.'"[66]

In a telling move, CECP dropped the reference to corporate philanthropy from its name entirely in 2019, adopting the moniker "Chief Executives for Corporate Purpose."[67] The move preserved its CECP abbreviation well known in philanthropy circles but allied the group with ascendant stakeholder-focused rhetoric about the corporation. CECP's reports still track cash grants directly from corporations and from corporate foundations, as well as in-kind gifts. After its rebranding, however, its language shifted from reporting statistics on "corporate giving and employee engagement" to measuring "corporate social investments."[68] This view perceives philanthropy as fully subsumed within the corporation's core purpose.

Holdouts only underscore the speed and scale of this transformation. Some corporations, often neither the largest nor the wealthiest, lag and continue to pursue more traditional philanthropic ventures. Integrating corporate philanthropy fully within corporate business models can also be seen not as innovation but its opposite, a return to earliest models of corporate charity, providing benefits to the community and employees in compliance with legal rules requiring a tight link between contributions and business gains.[69] Still, the shift from the *A.P. Smith* vision of corporate philanthropy to that embraced by corporate America's leaders today remains formidable. The largest firms overwhelmingly project a strategic view of their philanthropy and operationalize that view in the structure and practice of their philanthropic programs.

The Structure of Corporate Philanthropy

Large corporations deliver corporate philanthropy in two ways. Some embed their philanthropy directly in one or more corporate departments. Others create and staff a separate corporate foundation. Many do both. Whichever route a corporation takes, "having a formal office directing philanthropic activities is associated with higher levels of giving."[70]

Companies that embed corporate philanthropy internally distribute philanthropic staff across a wide range of business functions. In its 2021 study of 230 of the world's largest companies, CECP found just 2 percent of full-time employees focused on corporate giving or volunteering were located entirely or in part within a Giving, Foundation or Philanthropy department. The rest served as part of Communications/Marketing (28 percent of respondents); External/Public/Corporate Affairs (17 percent of respondents); Human Resources (14 percent of respondents); Community Affairs/Relations (13 percent of respondents); Admin/Finance/Legal (8 percent of respondents); Corporate Social Responsibility (CSR)/Citizenship/Sustainability; (7 percent of respondents); the Executive Office (5 percent of respondents); or Strategy (3 percent of respondents) teams.[71]

Maintaining a separate entity will nearly always increase costs, so a separate corporate foundation remains a realistic option for only the largest firms.[72] Even those corporations with foundations do not operate them like the independent and family foundations discussed in chapter 1, using income earned on a substantial, permanent endowment to fund their grants. Instead, corporate foundations typically operate on a pass-through basis, whereby the funds their donor companies provide to them are spent and replenished annually.[73] Cash donations made to a foundation under such arrangements immediately flow out as grants over the course of the following year, at which time the corporation refills the foundation's coffers to start the cycle anew. A pass-through structure can, of course, be combined with a small endowment in reserve.

Some of the advantages of a corporate foundation may be obvious. Creating a separate entity entirely devoted to charitable activity that shares the corporation's name can offer a branding advantage reminiscent of that sought by Carnegie and Rockefeller. Corporate executives weary of being pressured for donations by community groups and business contacts also benefit from the ability to shunt these requests to a separate body over which they (at least purportedly) lack control.

Others will be less apparent. A corporate foundation can, for example, sometimes offer reputational benefits over embedding corporate philanthropy internally. In the words of one corporate philanthropy professional "we think [the corporate foundation] is the only safe haven. . . . [T]he foundation has such a halo around its worth."[74] Corporate foundations also allow for staff specialization, capacity building, and organizational learning. They provide a space for companies to develop the muscle of philanthropic giving by engaging with grantees and others in the philanthropic community.

Ordinarily, the tax benefits of corporate charitable giving do not differ whether or not a company employs a corporate foundation. The same charitable deduction is available to a company that makes a $50,000 charitable contribution to an operating charity directly from its marketing or HR department and one that makes a $50,000 contribution to its corporate foundation (which will ultimately grant out the funds). In each case, the corporation may take a $50,000 deduction against its taxable income. Amounts in excess of the relevant percentage ceiling can be carried over to generate future deductions for a limited time,[75] and, unlike for individuals, the percentage cap is the same whether the recipient is a public charity or private foundation.[76]

Corporate foundations, however, can provide a tax-related benefit to funders in particular circumstances. When a company has a different appetite for corporate giving than for spending those contributions, using a foundation allows a corporate donor to deduct contributions when set aside for charitable use at the foundation, rather than when ultimately put to work by grant recipients.

Consider a company that finds itself wanting to donate far more than it has in typical years due to anomalously high profits on which it would prefer not to pay tax, or a precipitous rise in taxes it wishes to avoid. Making significantly larger donations—perhaps two, three, or even ten times its previous contributions—could raise numerous concerns. Prior recipients might be swamped by donations many times more than they have previously accepted. A one-time jump in donation amount can also prompt a corporate donor to think on a larger scale or about different issues or geographies to address. If publicized, it will also likely provoke scrutiny from shareholders, other stakeholders, and the press.

In such circumstances, a corporate foundation gives corporate donors breathing room. The foundation can accept the donations at any time, generating an immediate tax deduction for the company on receipt. Yet the donor corporation enjoys the luxury of time to conduct any necessary analysis to make larger contributions effective and to prepare recipients to take them on board. As long as it meets the 5 percent annual payout requirement, the foundation's staff can take the time and resources necessary to wisely parcel out the contribution over years to come.

The few permanently endowed corporate foundations take this kind of smoothing to its ultimate degree. The far more typical corporate foundation operating on a pass-through basis, however, can also hold some of its funds from unusually good years to ensure effective and consistent support of philanthropic projects, including in leaner times. In the recessionary 1970s, corporate foundations functioned in just this way. "[T]he rate of increase in corporate contributions outpaced inflation,"[77] sustaining the level of contributions from more profitable periods.

Sometimes the shocks that create fluctuations in corporate donations come from changes in law. The extremely high corporate tax rates of the early 1950s, for example, led to a spike in corporate contributions that were used to grow or establish several large corporate foundation endowments.[78] More recently, the 2017 Tax Cuts and Jobs Act (TCJA) prompted a few companies to publicize plans to increase charitable contributions. The legislation's dramatic rate cut and other elements[79] combined with a strong economy to significantly boost corporate profits in its first year of effect, freeing up potential funds for philanthropy. Wells Fargo announced the 2017 tax law changes would prompt it to make $400 million in corporate charitable donations the following year, a 40 percent increase over the prior year's giving, and to begin to target spending 2 percent of after-tax profits on philanthropy beginning in 2019.[80] Wells Fargo was experiencing its own reputational challenges at this time, but it did make the promised increase.[81]

Wells Fargo and a few other examples aside, though, the TCJA did not prompt a swell of corporate philanthropy. Many more corporations took other actions with their increased after-tax profits, like increasing dividends, making capital investments, and issuing much-discussed stock buybacks. This is not surprising as, unlike the high 1950s rates that prompted giving, the 2017 legislation made corporate tax burdens lighter and opened other avenues to obtain valuable tax deductions. As in the case of the TCJA's tax changes for individuals discussed in chapters 1 and 2, its corporate tax changes could easily suppress corporate giving.

It is too soon to tell precisely how the numbers on either score will shake out. Corporate giving remained strong in the early years following the law's implementation, rising slightly in 2018 and 2019.[82] A slight downtick was observed in 2020, but it is difficult to disentangle the impact of tax law changes from the massive shocks companies and charities faced that year, and 2021 saw giving rise.

The global COVID-19 pandemic and the outcry following the murder of George Floyd upended corporate giving in a variety of ways. Corporate donors often increased their levels of funding, particularly in the early days of the pandemic. One study found 72 percent had increased their giving in the first few months after COVID-19 outbreaks began in the United States.[83] Even with the economic challenges many firms experienced, another 20 percent kept giving constant. "Corporate foundations accounted for only 14 percent ($1.1 billion) of all corporate funding for COVID-19; the remainder was attributed to corporations themselves and their direct giving programs" at the end of the first six months of 2020.[84] By the one-year mark, corporations and corporate foundations had contributed 44 percent of the $20.2 billion in global COVID-19 giving.[85] Like the individual philanthropists discussed in chapter 1, many corporate donors also changed outstanding grant terms to remove restrictions and empower charitable recipients to take whatever actions they deemed most important.

As the country's reckoning with structural racism intensified, many corporate donors also shifted their practices to prioritize grantees and communities of color. Indeed, they were early leaders in these efforts. A July 2020 review revealed that while "[b]efore 2020, 6 percent of grants awarded for racial equity came from corporate foundations or corporate giving programs[, s]o far in 2020, these corporate funders account for 79 percent of the dollars [nonprofit research organization] Candid has tracked." Although the report noted that corporate donations may be more quickly reported in the press and easily tracked, the "sudden shift" was striking."[86] Corporate COVID relief targeted to BIPOC communities, however, was limited to only 11 percent of total corporate COVID giving.[87]

Time will tell whether these giving patterns will prove durable. Pressing new needs will continue to emerge, as the humanitarian crisis prompted by the invasion of Ukraine vividly demonstrates. As the pandemic recedes, corporate donors with available funds and assets may view new emergencies as equally pressing or may find their urgency to push funding out the door diminished. Some typically generous firms thrust into financial exigency by COVID-19 will weather the storm and return to a smooth trajectory of giving; others may never recover. Firms that expanded their funding and outreach on racial equity in response to consumer and employee pressure will need to continue to satisfy these important stakeholders. Heightening giving in response to the Black Lives Matter movement may forge new relationships between corporations and Black-led charities and communities. Other relationships may prove to be transitory.

The Corporate Foundation Question

Corporate foundations can help donors realize whatever ambitions they may espouse, but the question of whether to utilize a foundation can be a thorny one. Concentrating giving decisions in a legally distinct entity organized as a tax-exempt private foundation can ease concerns about potential abuses. All tax-exempt charitable entities must abide by a ban on "inurement," which consists of distributing net earnings to substantial donors or insiders with organizational control.[88] Operating a private foundation—including a corporate foundation—also triggers the Grand Bargain's panoply of rules intended to constrain elite philanthropy.[89] These regulatory restraints offer no guarantee that corporate giving will not be coopted by powerful corporate actors and establishing a foundation subject to them will increase the costs of corporate giving. But by embracing those limits, foundations can help corporations achieve their philanthropic aspirations by insulating corporate philanthropy from business pressures.

Firms also sometimes change their minds. For example, General Motors announced in 2017 that it dissolved the GM Foundation after thirty years in operation. In its stead, the firm embedded its philanthropic activities in its internal corporate giving department. The move responded in part to efficiency concerns, but also to a desire to align its giving more closely with GM's business goals.

As Jackie Parker, director of GM global philanthropy and corporate giving explained, "What we're more interested in funding is programs so that we can measure societal impact and have a deliverable back to our shareholders and the folks that are interested, investors, potential consumers, potential employees."[90] In GM's case, that meant moving away from many gifts to small, often local, nonprofits and toward a "focus on high-tech education, safety and economic sustainability," both globally and in its home city of Detroit.

The rebranding of GM's corporate philanthropy efforts has continued, with corporate giving becoming the principal focus of the "social investment" aspect of the company's website, and then appearing as part of its "social impact" commitment to communities.[91] GM appears to still fund only nonprofit, tax-exempt organizations through grants. Would-be grantees must access this site to seek funding.

Despite its emphasis on grants, one need not look hard to find connections between GM's philanthropic focus and its business as a transportation and technology company. The site describes a focus on STEM education with the pipeline of future workers in mind, sustainable solutions for transport, and vehicle and road safety. It also leans heavily on the role of social investment as community relations—highlighting its many programs dedicated to Detroit.

Google offers another fascinating example of the shift away from the foundation model. The company formed a corporate foundation around the time it went public in 2004 but announced the formation of an internal division it called Google.org (or DotOrg) soon after. This embedded unit is tasked with managing all of Google's philanthropic activities. For many years, this included oversight of the Google Foundation, until the foundation officially dissolved in 2017.[92]

DotOrg began with an eclectic mix of programs. It analyzed data from a fleet of plug-in electric cars used by its employees. It seeded an investment fund for small- and medium-size businesses in India and other developing economies. It also developed a global flu tracker. Considering the fate of even these few programs suggests the early Google.org resembled a kind of high-risk research and development program.

The rechargeable car program evolved into another project managed elsewhere in the company, but Google remains heavily involved in electric—and now self-driving—cars.[93] Google.org eventually placed its small and medium-size business initiative on the backburner, but Google itself continued courting Indian SME owners as users.[94] The Google.org flu-tracker did not survive, ultimately shelved after a decidedly mixed performance. Still, researchers at Google and beyond learned from this experiment in real-time health modeling and forecasting.

At its inception, Google.org also aimed, like philanthropy LLCs, to combine philanthropically motivated investment activity and political advocacy together with corporate giving. Its early initiatives involved investments in for-profit firms as well as grants and collaboration with nonprofits. It even stated its intent to "lobby for policies that support our philanthropic goals."[95]

Google today no longer appears to engage in investment or political activity through the DotOrg division, although of course Google at large (and its parent Alphabet) remains an active investor and political voice. The current website for Google.org describes activities concentrated solely on support for nonprofits and sponsorship of Google Fellows. These employees "leave their day jobs at Google [for six months] to work alongside the organization's staff to build scalable solutions, working as a team to ensure that the work has a sustained and lasting impact."[96] DotOrg's goals have expanded from addressing specific issue areas—"climate change, poverty and emerging disease"[97]—at its inception to its broader contemporary vision of "bring[ing] the best of Google to help solve some of humanity's biggest challenges."[98] COVID-19's enormous impact prompted it to pledge $100 million and 50,000 hours of pro bono support.

Through its various iterations, Google.org has continued to provide social innovators not only with funds but also with Google products, services, and expertise. That fluid interchange between DotOrg and the other parts of Google's business made possible by its place embedded within the company would be nearly impossible to replicate with an external corporate foundation.[99] A standalone foundation so enmeshed with the business activities of Google proper might cross the line into being a commercial entity, ineligible for state law nonprofit status and unqualified as a tax-exempt private foundation. Resource-sharing arrangements with a foundation would also demand constant scrutiny to ensure the foundation did not violate the self-dealing rules.

The experience of Pearson Inc., the self-described "world's leading learning company," demonstrates that the IRS is not the only potential challenger to corporate foundation behavior. The New York Attorney General launched an investigation of the firm's foundation, which unusually ran its own charitable programs, over concerns about its close ties with its parent company. The parties ultimately agreed to a more than $7 million settlement,[100] after which the firm opted to close its foundation. It explained the move would "integrate all of its corporate responsibility activities and functions into its business as a way to maximise social impact."[101]

Shuttering a corporate foundation also frees a corporate donor from the cost and complexity of compliance with the federal tax disclosure regimes described in the last two chapters. A corporate foundation must not only contend with tax regulations on investment, political activity, and resource-sharing but also must file annual Form 990-PF informational returns on the foundation's activity with the IRS. Like all Forms 990—but unlike every other tax return—a corporate foundation's filings must be made publicly available.

Companies do often widely publicize their corporate charitable contributions to gain PR and marketing benefits, recruit and retain employees, and project a positive corporate image. But as the (mostly individual) donors decried as insensitive to long-standing inequality and suffering quickly learned after pledging millions to support the reconstruction of Notre Dame cathedral,[102] not all news of charitable giving will be well received. Public criticism followed exposure of Walmart's massively increased giving in markets it was trying to penetrate.[103] Berkshire Hathaway terminated its one-of-a-kind system, allowing shareholders to select recipients of corporate philanthropic dollars based on negative responses to revelations that Planned Parenthood received some of its donations.[104] Both Oxford and ExxonMobil were embarrassed by revelations the energy giant had made corporate donations to the university after Oxford had committed to divesting fossil fuel holdings from its endowment. The gifts were not included in required foundation reporting or selective reporting of direct company gifts but unearthed by activist students.[105] Embedding philanthropic activity within the corporation itself allows a company to decide which contributions to make quietly and which to trumpet.

Shifting away from a foundation model casts the allure of aligning corporate philanthropy with a firm's business model into stark relief. Substituting corporate and shareholder value maximization for traditional objects of charity makes it possible for corporate philanthropic efforts to enhance both business and social goals.[106] But removing corporate philanthropy operations from the private foundation's regulatory regime reduces the public's ability to target those charitable objects it deems worthy and impose a timeline for these expenditures. Embedded corporate philanthropy also diminishes the transparency that compliance with foundation regulations promotes.

Corporate foundation closures are difficult to track—and simply deemphasizing corporate foundation activities in favor of internal corporate philanthropy will have much the same effect—so the penetration of these trends remains unknown. The 2018 CECP Study's finding that the share of direct cash giving compared with other types of corporate philanthropy increased over the prior five years and "was mostly shifted from foundation cash" suggested significant changes might be afoot.[107] By the 2021 Study, however, there was a rise in noncash giving and product donations, with direct cash giving decreasing and foundation cash giving rebounding.[108] It is too soon to offer firm conclusions about a trend one way or the other, but each shift demonstrates the nimbleness with which corporations deploy their largesse.

It would certainly be premature to read too much into a few prominent examples. Corporate philanthropy through internal giving departments has always outpaced foundation giving, and relatively few corporations have announced they are taking this dramatic step. Moreover, just as some corporations close their foundations, new foundations are being formed, and at a clip that suggests overall number of such entities could stay constant or even rise.[109]

Flexibility, privacy, and control make embedded corporate giving programs attractive for firms—whether or not they choose to found or continue to fund a foundation. That GM could terminate its foundation virtually without comment puts an exclamation mark on a for-profit philanthropic trend that tends to operate in the background. Increasingly, the practice of corporate philanthropy—whether undertaken by a foundation or an internal division—differs in ways both more subtle and pervasive, embracing the pursuit of business goals and objectives.

The Practice of Strategic Corporate Philanthropy

A strategic vision of corporate philanthropy not only alters the form corporate philanthropy programs take but also transforms their substance: from grantee selection to program design to staffing. Once corporate philanthropy becomes viewed as an aspect of the business model, it becomes integrated into corporate operations in a whole host of ways.[110] As the examples that follow demonstrate, the practice of strategic corporate philanthropy can take hold in internal corporate departments whether or not the corporation also operates an affiliated foundation. These programs can be developed in coordination with a corporate foundation—if one exists. But they do not need that formal structure to support them.

Strategic Corporate Philanthropy within CSR Teams

At the largest companies, strategic corporate philanthropy can be found operating within a broader CSR, citizenship, or ESG umbrella. For example, Citibank's 2018 Global Citizenship report described organizing its various CSR functions along with corporate philanthropy together under its Head of Corporate Citizenship and President of its Citi Foundation.[111] This senior executive also managed the Corporate Sustainability team and reported annually to the Board's Committee on Nomination, Governance and Public Affairs. By 2020, the rechristened Global ESG Report explained:

> Through our core business and philanthropy, we address some of society's greatest challenges—an imperative stated in our mission and an idea that shapes our decisions every day. Our ESG commitments are an essential part of our firm-wide strategy, deeply integrated into our business and long-term priorities, yet nimble to adjust and respond to the ever-changing realities around the globe.[112]

The report touched on topics ranging from COVID-19 philanthropy initiatives to sustainable finance efforts to executive compensation incentives tied to ESG goals.

ExxonMobil's combined description of its philanthropic contributions and other "community investments" is likewise instructive. Together, these

> community investments seek to address strategic local priorities where we do business around the world. We partner with governments, other private sector companies and nongovernmental organizations to help enhance quality of life. We help address community and business needs such as health care, education and economic development.[113]

Rather than siloed corporate giving or foundation activities, strategic corporate philanthropy is an integral part of CSR practice.

ArcelorMittal's conservation efforts in the Great Lakes region also illustrate how a strategic philanthropic initiative can fit within a broadly conceived CSR umbrella. The firm is a major multinational mining and steel manufacturing concern, operating industrial sites in nineteen countries. In North America, the company has a substantial presence surrounding the Great Lakes region. To conserve, protect, and maintain these vital water sources, it joined with the National Fish and Wildlife Foundation and several government agencies to fund the Save Our Great Lakes program, contributing $8.4 million to the cause since its creation in 2008.[114] This program aligns closely to at least two of the company-wide "sustainable development outcomes" outlined in its CSR commitments. ArcelorMittal aspires to be a "trusted user of air, land and water" and an "active and welcomed member of the communit[ies]" in which it operates, maintaining the trust and support of local governments and community members to retain its "social license to operate."[115] Its Great Lakes program uses grantmaking as one tool in pursuing its overarching sustainability goals, and ArcelorMittal touts its utility in enhancing government relations.

Strategic Corporate Philanthropy as Supply Chain Management

The apparel industry exemplifies the ways that strategic corporate philanthropy has become intertwined in companies' efforts to address working conditions across their supply chains. Concerns about sweatshop conditions and unfair business practices in apparel factories have repeatedly roiled the industry, from Nike's scandal in the 1990s to the Rana Plaza fire in 2013 and allegations of wage theft during the pandemic. Apparel companies have taken many steps to improve working conditions, including CSR programs that roll out safety and sustainability assessments and codes of vendor conduct that upgrade manufacturing conditions and procurement practices. Philanthropy plays a crucial supporting role.

Philanthropic initiatives within individual apparel brands often focus on education, capacity-building, and community improvement in locations where they and their suppliers operate. The Nike Foundation's "Girl Effect" effort included foundation "invest[ments of] $130 million through 150 partners across 90 countries in support of the principle that investing in a girl is the best way to break the cycle of intergenerational poverty" before spinning off the program into an independent nonprofit in 2015.[116] From its origins in education and job training, Girl Effect has expanded to a diverse portfolio of activities, including mobile skills development apps, as well as media and other brands targeting developing world youth with messages of empowerment.[117]

Gap, Inc. also focuses on girls. Its "Personal Advancement & Career Enhancement (P.A.C.E.) program was initially created to support women in the global apparel industry" working in Gap vendor facilities with education, life skills, and technical training.[118] Over its decade-plus of existence, the program has evolved to be deployed on a community basis beyond vendor sites. These programs do not directly confront problematic working conditions in supplier communities but instead focus on a broader vision of individual empowerment, particularly for women and girls. The effectiveness and propriety of these efforts have not gone unchallenged,[119] but they demonstrate well how philanthropic activities complement operational initiatives to together present an overall picture of a responsible firm.

Coalitions to address working conditions, worker safety, training, and more recently sustainability are also funded with the support of leading apparel and fashion brands. The large-scale corporate manufacturer members of the Sustainable Apparel Coalition provided critical funding and knowledge to this effort to develop "tools [to] measure environmental and social labor impacts across the value chain."[120] Its membership list reads like a who's who of the apparel industry. The UK Ellen MacArthur Foundation has developed several collaborative programs to develop a "circular economy" in which waste and pollution are designed out of production processes.[121] Players from across the apparel industry—from fast fashion giant H&M to design house Ralph Lauren—have joined as funding partners, together with leading firms and government entities from around the world.

Strategic Corporate Philanthropy as Marketing

Strategic corporate philanthropy also permeates firms' marketing and sales functions. Cause-related marketing, in which sellers promise to donate to charity some portion of the price consumers pay for a promoted product, is a tried-and-true example of the synergy between corporate philanthropy, marketing, and sales. American Express was an early and wildly successful adopter of the technique. For a limited time in the early 1980s, it pledged to link Amex activity to donations to the project restoring the Statue of Liberty. For each transaction current cardholders executed, the company would donate a penny; for each new card account opened, it would donate a dollar. The campaign not only raised $1.7 million for the Statute of Liberty project but generated staggering returns for the company. American Express saw a 28 percent rise in card use and a 17 percent increase in applications for new cards during the promotional period.[122]

Cause-related marketing is now so commonplace as to be unremarkable, with supermarkets and drug stores teeming with items linked to dozens of causes. Critics of the practice challenge whether it really generates gains for charities[123] and whether its focus on consumption has potentially toxic effects.[124] Nonetheless, it remains pervasive.

A newer variation on the tied purchase strategy links consumer decisions even more closely with philanthropic action. The one-for-one model was popularized on a mass scale by TOMS Shoes. As originally conceived, the company would match a free, donated pair of shoes in the developing world for each pair of shoes purchased by consumers. Critics challenged the company on whether shoes were really the item most needed by the low-income individuals to whom they were donated and on how its manufacturing practices impacted their communities.[125] Over time, TOMS evolved its corporate philanthropy practices away from the one-for-one approach, but the die was cast. Countless other firms now employ similar programs, either as general operating practice or for specific, time- and/or product-limited campaigns across the apparel, shoe, home goods, sports equipment, and myriad other consumer product categories.[126]

Strategic Corporate Philanthropy as Business Development

Where corporate giving that enhances brand image or loyalty with existing customers is marketing, seeding new markets with philanthropic investments might be better classified as business development. As noted earlier, some of Google.org's philanthropic activities functioned to develop new markets the firm would access over time. The Verizon Foundation's donation of $1.5 million to the American Foundation for the Blind (AFB) to fund expansion of the AFB website for older users and others with low vision functioned this way as well. The contribution coincided with the company's launch of products and services targeting these underpenetrated demographics. Verizon used input from AFB in designing a highly successful special phone for low-vision users, and also developed a new service plan targeting older individuals. The latter "brought in 100,000 new customers."[127]

In a program highlighted by Porter and Kramer, Cisco Systems used its philanthropy to address a block on its growth. They explain: "[A]s Internet use expanded, customers around the world encountered a chronic shortage of qualified network administrators, which became a limiting factor in Cisco's—and the entire industry's—continued growth."[128] The company had donated networking equipment to schools in the region around its headquarters in the hope that school programs would provide the necessary training, but realized local schoolteachers lacked the necessary skills to manage the technology.

The company then allowed its engineers to provide the needed training on a volunteer basis, and soon recognized their valuable courses could be deployed on a far more widespread basis. Online course delivery ultimately enabled them to train a large cadre of the very network administrators the industry badly needed to facilitate growth. Its Cisco Networking Academy has trained and mentored 15 million students around the world in its 25 years in operation.[129] The availability of skilled network administrators across the globe also facilitated Cisco's increasing market penetration.

Strategic Corporate Philanthropy as Human Resource Development

Firms engage in strategic corporate philanthropy not only to develop new customers and motivate sales, but also to attract and retain talent. Quite distinct from the far-flung philanthropic efforts described above, some of the largest corporate philanthropy programs today operate much closer to home. Employee charitable gift matching programs—ubiquitous at large corporations—epitomize the idea of corporate philanthropy as an employee recruitment, engagement, and retention technique. The 2021 CECP Study found that among its 230 survey participants 93% offered at least one matching-gift program and 40% offered more than two.[130]

Matching gift programs promise to contribute company funds to the charity of the employee's choice, in an amount determined by the employee's own contribution, either throughout the year or during specified campaign periods. Matching rates tend to be 1:1, though some especially generous firms contribute two or even three times the employee gift amount.[131] A ceiling typically limits the amount the employer will match any individual employee's giving per year. Some firms also limit the types of charitable recipient for which they will match employee gifts, either by category or by identifying a list of approved charitable recipients. The trend, however, is toward open matching programs, under which the company will match an employee's gift made to any §501(c)(3) organization.[132] COVID-19 spurred many additional firms to become multiple matchers and to inaugurate new or higher employee matching commitments, sometimes with a requirement that employees donate to local or pandemic relief charities to participate.[133]

Modern corporate philanthropy programs also extend far beyond the donation of money, whether company funds, employee funds, or both. Alongside employee matching gift programs, corporate programs to encourage employee volunteer work are also proliferating. These contributions include hours donated at events that combine employee volunteer time with team-building or bonding experiences, as well as programs where employees themselves play a role in structuring contributions of their work time. Pandemic constraints made employee-led programs particularly popular, but they were already on the rise.[134] These programs take various forms, including paid time off and flexible scheduling for volunteer work, as well as pro bono service programs in which trained employees deliver professional services they use in their jobs to a recipient nonprofit organization, free of charge. In "Dollars for Doers" programs, matching financial grants are paired with volunteer services. If an employee contributes the required number of volunteer hours to an eligible charity, the corporation will make a financial gift as well.[135]

The Unique Value Proposition of In-Kind Corporate Giving

Along with company funds and employee time, donations of products and services form the third leg of the modern corporate philanthropy stool. As companies stepped up to respond to the COVID-19 pandemic, in-kind gifts of every conceivable description were rolled out.[136] Individuals, organizations, and communities in need received food, medical supplies, and technological support. Emergency workers were provided with personal protective equipment, lodging, and transportation. Creativity abounds in these donations even in ordinary times, with charitable organizations receiving a wide variety of in-kind gifts.

Sometimes these programs tie directly to marketing campaigns. Anheuser Busch's canned water is one well-known example, thanks to the company's feature of this effort in a 2018 Superbowl advertisement.[137] Procter & Gamble's Loads of Hope program, which provides free laundry services in disaster zones, has also featured in several company commercials and promotions and is run by its marketing department.[138] Tide also used a Loads of Hope cause-related marketing tie-in: allowing consumers to purchase a special detergent bottle and have a portion of the purchase price used to fund the program.[139] Publicity allows product donations to improve company reputation not only with recipients, who may become grateful and loyal customers after receiving donated goods and services, but with the public more broadly.

When contributed products constitute unusable surplus inventory, donations can also reduce a firm's operational costs.[140] Consider the alternatives. Inventory can be marked down to lower and lower prices. Unusable inventory might be returned to suppliers for reuse; for low-value items; however, the costs of transport, refurbishment, and storage will often overwhelm the value of returning them. Liquidators might purchase unusable inventory, but at steeply discounted prices that will be passed on to bargain-hunting consumers and can damage brand value. In today's overtaxed waste management context, even disposal can be expensive, and dumping valuable products rather than finding some good use for them can have reputational costs as well. Identifying appropriate recipients of unusable inventory is not without logistical challenges, but an industry of product donation intermediaries has sprung up to help smooth the process for corporate donors.

The benefits of in-kind contributions can be enhanced by especially generous tax treatment of such gifts. While gifts of inventory are generally deductible, the amount of the deduction can often be quite low for producers. Corporations qualify for higher levels of deductibility, however, if they donate inventory property to be used to care for "the ill, the needy, or infants"[141] or donate "scientific equipment or apparatus substantially all of the use of which by the donee is for research or experimentation . . . or for research training, in the United States in physical or biological sciences."[142] The enhanced deduction is designed to ensure that a greater tax benefit results from the donation of these types of property rather than either disposal or donation of the equivalent value in cash.[143] Pharmaceutical companies, virtually all of whose products easily fit these special rules, have long been high-profile devotees of in-kind donations.[144] Unsurprisingly, in 2020, pharmaceutical and other healthcare firms again lead the list of donors heavily tilted toward product donations.[145]

Healthcare firms also provide an instructive example of the drawbacks of the enhanced deductibility incentive. The COVID-19 pandemic has vividly demonstrated that donated drugs and medical devices can be literal lifesavers, but they won't always be. Medicines donated to needy communities may or may not be the drugs most useful for these populations. Often what is most needed will not be drugs at all, but food, shelter, clean water or energy sources, or political stability. Even when the cure of an in-kind donation fits the ills of a recipient community, it will only rarely be the most efficient approach. Cash donations, which can be used to procure whatever interventions are most required, provide recipient communities and individuals with far greater flexibility—and autonomy.[146] They also do not depend on a fortuitous match between the needs of a particular community and the products of a generous firm.

The same concerns about in-kind donations can arise when other industries engage in this practice, which cuts across all types of firms. Along with the healthcare sector, consumer staples and communications firms also made more than 40 percent of their annual donations in-kind in 2020 and seven of ten of firms surveyed had made at least one form of in-kind gift.[147]

A subset of firms combines contributions of company funds, their products or services, and employee time. One of the most well-known is Salesforce, a leading provider of customer relations management software. The company has been committed to donating one percent of its employees' time, one percent its profits, and one percent its services since its beginnings in 1999. It now coordinates these efforts through Salesforce.org, which appears similar to Google.org. This separate website also showcases Salesforce offerings for nonprofits and educational institutions.[148]

Marc Benioff, who serves as both Salesforce co-CEO and Salesforce.org chairman, has been vocal about the value the company ascribes to this approach. He champions Pledge 1%, an effort to recruit other companies to sign a public pledge to contribute any combination of product, equity, profit, or time to their communities.[149] Although such pledges will not create legally enforceable commitments, they require committing companies to define giving as one of their values and to put at least some reputational capital at risk.

Strategic Corporate Philanthropy's Dark Side

The examples above—just a few of many one could glean from the ever-growing mass of corporate philanthropy and CSR websites—portray the strategic vision of corporate philanthropy and shareholder value in a relentlessly upbeat light. They become a parade of philanthropic needs met and—seamlessly and simultaneously—corporate reputations burnished, customer bases expanded, and human resources engaged. Less rose-colored stories, of course, can also be told about attempts to achieve business and philanthropic synergy.

The tales of unscrupulous collaborations between tobacco companies and academic researchers have become so legion that they have spawned not only journalistic exposes but popular books and movies recounting the associated intrigue. The industry's use of its philanthropic assets to push its strategic business agenda has given it an unenviable reputation. Indeed, when Philip Morris established its "Foundation for a Smoke-Free" world, the World Health Organization issued a public refusal to work with the ostensibly independent group.[150] Reports suggest other potential beneficiaries and collaborators followed suit.[151]

Pharmaceutical companies seem determined to push those same boundaries. They too may have ventured over the line between strategic corporate philanthropy and abuse in their support of so-called copay charities. A copay charity does precisely what you might imagine in our world of sky-high prescription medication prices: covering copayments for insured patients who cannot afford them. Some copay charities are independent, but many receive support from pharmaceutical companies, for whom charitable contributions become doubly strategic investments.

Making medications more accessible for insured patients can reduce pressure to lower drug prices. But funding copayments by patients can also translate into billions of dollars in revenue from insurance companies, who pay the lion's share of the drug's costs. This strategic philanthropy has generated just the wrong kind of publicity for drug companies' philanthropy programs. Some have even been ensnared in government investigations; California imposed restrictions.[152]

Pearson's experience facing the wrath of regulators for entangling its business and foundation arms did not sour Pearson on aligning its philanthropic and business goals. Instead, it seems to have doubled down. After closing the foundation and switching to an in-house philanthropy mode, it "ask[ed] its corporate-responsibility arm to make grants that more closely link giving with its global network and expertise."[153] Without the operational restrictions and transparency requirements imposed by foundation law, activities like those questioned in the attorney general's investigation are much less likely to violate legal mandates. They will certainly be much harder to uncover.

A pair of studies by overlapping groups of economists suggests this dark side of strategic philanthropy extends beyond a handful of alarming line-crossing stories. In the first study, researchers created company-legislator pairings that linked individual firms with particular legislators, such as those who sat on committees powerful in setting policy that would impact that firm's profitability. They then compared contributions from the foundation associated with each firm in a pairing to charities in the paired legislator's district or on the board of which the paired legislator served. The comparisons yielded a robust correlation between the incidence of contributions associated with a legislator and their political utility to the firm. For example, the researchers found "a non-profit is more than four times more likely to receive grants from a corporate foundation if a politician sits on its board" and "a [corporate] foundation is more likely to give to a politician-connected non-profit if the politician sits on committees lobbied by the firm."[154]

The second study also linked corporate philanthropy with political influence-seeking. Following several news stories reporting on seemingly unrelated charities that submitted comments on federal regulations favoring the outcomes preferred by their corporate donors, the authors set out to conduct a more comprehensive inquiry. After assembling a data set spanning hundreds of companies and more than a decade, the researchers found

> that nonprofits are more likely to comment on the same regulation as their donors, and that this "co-commentary" is most strongly associated with donations in the year immediately preceding the comments . . . The effect is large: a donation in the preceding year is associated with a 76% increase in the likelihood of co-commentary. It should be noted that co-commentary is not a rare event: about 10% of the average firm's comments have a co-comment by grantees they recently supported.[155]

With strategic corporate philanthropy's ascendance, the boundary demarcating the line between charitable acts and business decisions is disappearing. Staffing of philanthropic initiatives and internal business units overlaps, while corporate foundations are selectively sidelined or even shut. Staffers feel "increasing pressure to align corporate philanthropy and giving with business objectives."[156] It comes as no surprise that the appeal of the dark side beckons, and that our philanthropic legal framework is ill-equipped to stop future forays across the line.

Corporate Strategic Philanthropy as For-Profit Philanthropy

The rise of strategic corporate philanthropy first observed decades ago now moves at a fever pitch. It offers corporate donors an array of benefits familiar as the hallmarks of for-profit philanthropy. Tying philanthropic initiatives and operations to business goals and departments gives corporations flexibility over when, to whom, and what they give. Embedding philanthropy within a firm also affords corporate donors more privacy: the freedom to choose which details about their philanthropy to disclose and when to disclose them. It allows them to control their philanthropic destinies, and carefully limit how much their philanthropy will detract from their bottom lines—if at all.

Likewise, the shift to strategic corporate philanthropy raises recognizable concerns for the legal system and society at large. The decrease in accountability becomes obvious when a corporate foundation closes. Without federal tax law's disclosure demands, payout requirements, and limitations on grant recipients, society loses influence over who will receive corporate largesse and when it will reach them. It will learn about these programs only what their corporate sponsors choose to divulge. The limits on timing, targeting, and transparency at the heart of the Grand Bargain simply fall away.

Even when a firm keeps its foundation alive, allowing the traditional corporate philanthropy *A.P. Smith* legitimized to be set adrift in a wide-ranging vision of corporate responsibility has much the same effect. Corporate philanthropy folded into a CSR mandate to serve a host of constituencies—while generating the same tax and business benefits for the firm as a corporate private foundation—replicates the accountability deficits (timing, transparency, and targeting) fueled by the rise of commercially affiliated DAFs and the philanthropy LLC. Each revives the perennial question that the Grand Bargain sought to put to rest: *cui bono* (who benefits)?

Backlash remains an ever-present risk. When strategic philanthropy veers too far toward the dark side, corporate reputations may not be the only ones endangered. Charities keen to trumpet the names and contributions of their benefactors have been caught flat-footed when donors' reputations dim. Just ask the many charities scrambling to distance themselves from contributions by Sackler family members as investigations uncovered the role in the opioid crisis of the family controlled company Purdue Pharma.[157] The Sackler scandal involves individual, rather than corporate donations, but this is only by happenstance. Vaunted corporations—just like esteemed individuals—can become tainted by bad behavior. Corporate donors perceived as losing their way may not only imperil their beneficiaries but the charitable sector at large.

Conclusion

As in chapters 1 and 2, this chapter presents a picture of for-profit philanthropy's gains and losses putting donors on the winning side at the expense of broader societal interests. The Grand Bargain promotes balance when corporate philanthropy remains within a foundation's bounds and apart from a firm's core profit-making apparatus. But in both form and substance, corporate philanthropy has moved in a different direction.

With strategic corporate philanthropy, the boundary between charity and business becomes permeable, and the legal rules regulating it lose their purchase. As with philanthropy LLCs and commercially affiliated donor-advised funds, corporate philanthropic practice has outgrown its regulatory framework, leaving only corporations themselves to reassure that their "giving" serves the public. The next chapter explains how the law established boundaries before players, practices, and norms native to the for-profit sector began migrating into philanthropy. This history will set the stage for exploring the risks dismantling the Grand Bargain poses and for our proposed interventions to expose, countervail, and guide for-profit philanthropic power in the corporate context and beyond.

PART II

PROTECTING THE PARTNERSHIP BETWEEN ELITES AND THE PUBLIC

4
The Grand Bargain

For-profit philanthropy, like the phenomena of social enterprise and environmental, social, and governance (ESG) investing described in chapter 5, embodies the creative destruction that fuels so much of our economic life. Reflecting a tension between elite philanthropists and the public they claim to serve through their giving, the cycle of philanthropic innovation and regulation for-profit philanthropy heralds would be familiar in almost any place and time. To highlight the pivotal role government can play in replacing skepticism with trust, this chapter looks back half a century to the last major US effort to broker a truce between elites and the public: the 1969 Grand Bargain.

Gilded-age industrialists like Rockefeller and Carnegie pioneered the concept of a philanthropic foundation, designed to manage and give away capital as a charitable antithesis of a hedge fund. Newly minted moguls followed suit in the ensuing decades. By mid-century, public skepticism ran high, fueled by perceived abuses within these organizations. High-profile inquiries by administrative agencies and congressional committees paved the way to major reform legislation in 1969.

This chapter describes the regulatory regime that emerged from that Grand Bargain, detailing the tools it deploys to channel foundation activity toward public-regarding activities and at least some significant current spending and away from entanglements with business interests and politics. Demanding heightened accountability through unyielding prophylactic rules barring noncharitable distributions and transactions between foundations and their donors and managers prevents the worst abuses. Enhanced disclosure allows both regulators and the public to track compliance with this augmented regulatory framework. Much that follows will trace the development of the private foundation as a legal concept. To do so, it will also chronicle foundations' resounding half-century of achievement.

The Grand Bargain the 1969 reforms embodied did not punish elite philanthropy or impose direct public oversight. Instead, it offered wealthy donors an opportunity to make robust commitments with respect to the targeting, timing, and transparency of their voluntary and tax-subsidized philanthropic efforts.[1] Officially dubbed "private foundations," these philanthropic funds retained an extraordinary degree of freedom and the privilege of perpetual life along with

For-Profit Philanthropy. Dana Brakman Reiser and Steven A. Dean, Oxford University Press. © Oxford University Press 2023. DOI: 10.1093/oso/9780190074500.003.0005

valuable promises of tax forbearance in exchange for government regulation and transparency.

The unraveling of this truce between elites and the public can be observed in the rise of the philanthropy LLC, the growing dominance of commercially affiliated donor-advised funds, and the ascendance of strategic corporate philanthropy. Through each of these innovations, for-profit philanthropy frees donors from the transparency, timing, and targeting demands embedded in the private foundation model. This chapter reviews the terms and context of the Grand Bargain not as a playbook for responding to for-profit philanthropy's disruption but to highlight the nature and magnitude of the threat it represents.

Foundations' Antecedents

The human impulse toward altruism, of course, predates any sort of organized philanthropy. Inherently social beings, people have been providing assistance, comfort, and fellowship to one another for as long as they have built clans and communities. Whether the desire to do so stems from survival instinct, evolutionary imperative, or some spark of what constitutes humanity, its existence constantly surprises but should not.

Charitable organizations, too, have a lengthy pedigree. The faithful have organized mosques, temples, and churches for millennia. Sick houses and homes for foundlings and professional and civic entities like guilds and social clubs claim an only slightly more recent vintage.

Philanthropy has not only a long-standing but a global history. In China, kinship organizations tied closely to wealthy families provided public services to the poor for centuries before the nationalization of its economy.[2] Perpetual endowments for charitable purposes called *waqfs* have likewise existed in the Islamic world for more than a thousand years.[3] European charitable organizations, too, have flourished for hundreds of years, sometimes in collaboration with the church or the state or both, and sometimes in competition with these institutions.[4]

The history of US charity must necessarily be shorter than in some other societies but boasts a vigor equal to that anywhere. On his tour of Jacksonian America in the early 1830s, Alexis de Tocqueville found charitable entities—"associations," as he termed them—both ubiquitous and pivotal to democracy. "Wherever, at the head of some new undertaking you see the government in France, or a man of rank in England, in the United States you will be sure to find an association."[5] This fertile ground set the stage for a philanthropic flourishing in the early twentieth century.

The Rise of US Foundations

The foundation can seem a Rorschach test. Foundations' power and ubiquity often seems reassuring. But the origins of modern foundations do not present what everyone would consider a flattering picture of America.

As the US population and its economy grew dramatically in the late nineteenth and early twentieth centuries, it spawned both unparalleled wealth and extraordinary need. Rather than elites inevitably being those with inherited wealth, self-made industrialists also built massive businesses and fortunes. Often, monopolistic power catapulted them and their families to levels of wealth unimaginable in prior generations.

Historian Olivier Zunz recounts that the number of American millionaires rose from only one hundred in the 1870s to just over four thousand in 1892 to more than forty thousand in 1916.[6] At the other extreme, cities swelled with a growing class of manufacturing workers, new immigrants, and former farm dwellers. In both the largest cities and shrinking rural areas, many endured crushing poverty.

Scores of gilded-age robber barons and their successor elites in the early twentieth century donated much of their wealth rather than keeping it within their own families. These donations created educational and research institutions as well as massive general-purpose foundations with broad philanthropic visions and national or even global ambitions.[7] Smaller foundations with specific purposes had existed as early as the post-Revolutionary period,[8] but the scale of late nineteenth and early twentieth century foundations had no precedent. Exceedingly rich and often reviled industrialists creating new types of institutions with unparalleled scope did not sit well with many critics and the public at large.[9]

Foundations Raise Alarms

No foundation launch generated more debate than that of the wealthiest of the elites of the time: John D. Rockefeller. In 1909, Rockefeller settled a charitable trust funded by shares of his Standard Oil Company worth $50 million. This already enormous endowment by standards of the time—its value would be $1.5 billion in today's dollars—was intended to be doubled in short order.[10] Rather than continuing the entity's life as a private trust with specific purposes, however, Rockefeller wanted to incorporate as a general purpose foundation.

Nonprofit corporations were then, as now, creatures of state law. Rockefeller could have sought approval for his foundation from his home state of New York.

But state charters for foundations often capped endowment sizes in the low single millions and frequently still resisted general statements of purpose.

Rockefeller and his advisors decided instead to pursue a national charter.[11] They brought their request to Congress, where a bill to nationally charter the Rockefeller Foundation was introduced in 1910. Their efforts spanned several years and generated sharp criticism. Surprisingly given Rockefeller's influence, they ultimately proved unsuccessful.

Some detractors feared the foundation would extend the power of Standard Oil. The company already represented a sprawling giant generating both unimaginable wealth and ceaseless condemnation for its founder. In what many viewed as suspect timing, the charter push coincided with the Justice Department's antitrust prosecution against the firm.

Today, it would be easy to see the foundation as an attempt to distract. Even at the time, it would have been difficult not to see it as a ploy to generate support for the company from potential beneficiaries otherwise disposed against its excesses. The broad charitable mandate Rockefeller sought amplified these fears. "Many newspapers saw the vagueness . . . as a gauzy curtain behind which the evil wizard of Standard Oil could work his mischief."[12] Both former President Theodore Roosevelt and then-President Taft opposed it, the former of whom quipped "no amount of charities in spending such fortunes can compensate in any way for the misconduct in acquiring them."[13]

Other critics focused less on the foundation's potential for extending the reach and influence of Standard Oil. Instead they feared the antidemocratic nature of such a potent philanthropic force.[14] Foundations' entirely private governance and their perpetual existence came across as particularly threatening.

Fostered by an ability to accumulate ever greater fortunes through investment rather than expenditure of funds nominally dedicated to charity, foundations seemed poised to grow beyond the power of regulators to control them. Without public input into the philanthropic visions of such institutions, their size and duration would give already privileged individuals, families, and corporations unmatched social power. Once created and endowed with perpetual life, there would be little government could do to restrain them. A 1915 article decrying not only the (by then established) Rockefeller Foundation but the foundation concept more generally, Chairman of the Industrial Relations Commission Frank P. Walsh made the point vividly: "huge philanthropic trusts, known as foundations, appear to be a menace to the welfare of society."[15]

Rockefeller and his advisors tried to appease their opponents by offering Congress a revised national charter bill with concessions.[16] The new bill capped the assets of the foundation at $100 million and limit its lifetime. Moreover, it allowed public input on foundation governance at the highest level; a combination of government officials would be granted a veto over new members of the foundation's board. The new bill made progress and was passed by the House of Representatives but ultimately died when the Senate session ended without a vote. Rockefeller and his advisors quickly shifted their attention back to New York State,[17] which in the interim had demonstrated its willingness to incorporate foundations with vast endowments and broad missions by chartering the Carnegie Corporation. The state legislature swiftly granted the Rockefeller charter and the governor approved.

The Rockefeller Foundation's state charter contained none of the concessions from the revised federal bill. Some commentators laud this outcome as avoiding increased government oversight and regulation and the politicization of philanthropy.[18] To others, it represents a lost opportunity to strike a better "balance between plutocratic voice and democratic voice in the operation of American foundations."[19] Whatever one's view, it was not the last time foundations would face public scrutiny.

The anticommunist fervor of the 1950s spawned two congressional investigations and reports, which reached polar opposite conclusions. The Cox Committee's unanimous and quite favorable report in 1953 recommended improvements to foundations' transparency but ultimately "characteriz[ed] them as a 'vital and essential factor in our progress.' "[20] It even supported tax changes to encourage more contributions to foundations.

In contrast, the majority report of the following year's Reece Commission warned of the looming power and subversive tendencies of foundations.[21] The Reece Commission—anticipating the accountability measures that would serve as the core of the Grand Bargain—recommended limitations on foundation lifetimes, a mandatory income distribution rule, and restrictions on political activity and involvement with businesses. Congress had already, in changes enacted in 1950, imposed reporting obligations on foundations—albeit without penalties for noncompliance. Perhaps in part viewing this new disclosure regime as sufficient, Congress acted on neither report.

No voice decrying foundations was louder than Congressman Wright Patman, a fiery populist from the state of Texas. Patman ran studies and hearings investigating foundations, employing a congressionally funded staff for this purpose, and issued a series of stinging reports starting in 1961.[22] The reports depicted foundations as corrupt, anticompetitive forces undermining small business, serving the narrow interests of their wealthy patrons.

In Patman's view, foundations represented a drain on public funds unworthy of the tax advantages they possessed. He warned of the increasing power they amassed outside public view. His reports recommended limitations on foundation lifetimes and of their control over business entities.[23] He also advocated greater government supervision and fewer tax advantages for foundation donors. Patman's efforts garnered interest from the press and continued to stoke public suspicion regarding foundation power and practices. He won over some important allies in the process, but the poor esteem in which many of his congressional colleagues held Representative Patman limited the impact his work could generate directly.[24]

The handful of foundations playing key roles in the civil rights movement also drew the ire of segregationists in Congress. The Carnegie Corporation as well as several smaller family foundations fought to enforce civil rights and create opportunity and security for Black Americans in the early 1960s.[25] None of these efforts made headlines—or enemies—quite like the Ford Foundation's interventions.

Ford had been established with a grant of just $25,000 in 1936 and grew into the largest US foundation through bequests from Henry and Edsel Ford sufficient to control a substantial majority of Ford Motor Company's shares.[26] In 1965, it reported a net worth of nearly $2.5 billion.[27] Soon after, Ford made some of its most controversial grants.

The Ford Foundation gave to the Congress on Racial Equality (CORE) to fund voter registration during a Cleveland mayoral race. And it supported school desegregation activists in a pitched battle with the New York City teacher's union.[28] For public officials keen to maintain the racist policies of segregated America and those concerned about how left-leaning elites might jeopardize their political fortunes, foundation interference rankled. When combined with foundations' perceived anticompetitive activity and tax avoidance—or worse, tax subsidies—the appetite for reform became insatiable.

Tax Enters the Picture

Over the course of the twentieth century, the use of foundations spread to wealthy individuals and families quite a few rungs down the wealth ladder. No longer a vehicle utilized by only the super-rich, foundation numbers trended upward. This growth was especially significant once the income and estate tax advantages of foundations began to be widely marketed in the post-World War II period.[29]

Recall again the two key types of tax benefits in this context. First, charitable organizations themselves benefit from a tax exemption on the income they generate. Second, donors to charitable organizations may deduct their contributions in calculating their income, gift, and estate tax liabilities.

Although the details have been revised and refined many times, tax exemption for charitable entities has always been a part of federal tax law.[30] Exemption for charitable entities was included in the ultimately doomed corporate income tax of 1894 (held unconstitutional by the Supreme Court just a year later).[31] Navigating around the constitutional shoals revealed there, a 1909 tax on corporations was structured as an excise tax on the privilege of incorporated status.[32] It, too, contained an exemption for charitable entities. After ratification of the Sixteenth Amendment in 1913 removed constitutional obstacles, Congress imposed an income tax on corporations, again including an exemption for charities. The outlines of this original approach remain evident in today's charitable income tax exemption found in Internal Revenue Code §501(c)(3).

The story of charitable deductions reaches back almost as far. The modern income and estate taxes were effectively born in 1913 with the ratification of the Sixteenth Amendment. In each case, a deduction for charitable contributions followed quickly on the heels of the tax's adoption.[33] In broad strokes, the similarities and differences between the two deductions have been present since their creations. Qualifying recipient organizations largely mirror each other. Both allow a taxpayer to remove contributed amounts from the total against which tax rates will be applied.

They differ, however, in one key respect. The estate tax charitable deduction promises the possibility of a much larger benefit for taxpayers because it is unlimited. That can result in even the largest estates paying a tax bill of zero.[34] In contrast, as noted in previous chapters, for most of its recent history the income tax deduction has been applicable only up to a percentage ceiling set well below a taxpayer's full income.

The period from 1924 to 1964 was notably different. During these years, the percentage limitation did not apply to taxpayers who regularly (for more than a decade) donated nearly all their income (over 90 percent) to charity.[35] This exception was of little moment to most taxpayers, who would not be able to consistently devote nearly all their income to charity. For the very wealthiest individuals and families, though, the exception held out the possibility of doing what no other taxpayers had been permitted before or since.

During those years, these very wealthiest Americans could fund a foundation pursuing their own vision of the public good and thereby avoid any responsibility to shoulder public efforts toward a broader vision.[36] This combination of freedom for donors and lost revenue for Treasury made the unlimited charitable deduction a particularly glaring target for reformers. It was phased out for contributions to foundations as part of the lead-up to the Grand Bargain[37] and repealed entirely in 1969. Apart from time-limited exceptions for contributions to public charities in times of national crisis, percentage limitations have remained in effect ever since.[38]

Most early adopters of general-purpose foundations at the turn of the twentieth century undertook their efforts before tax considerations became relevant. Following the adoption of the income and estate tax regimes, however, the tax benefits of charitable giving generally and foundation use specifically became highly salient. When top marginal rates rose over 50 and sometimes 70 or 90 percent, the appeal of exemption and deductions grew stronger.[39] Thanks in no small part to its favorable tax treatment, the general-purpose foundation model found itself both widely adopted and chronically decried.

Foundations endured withering critiques for acting as abusive tax shelters for the wealthy. Families could "donate" assets but continue controlling them. Unchecked by strong regulatory guardrails, such power over foundations' assets and investments created opportunities for donors and managers to enrich themselves. That absence also allowed foundations and their leaders to become heavily entangled in operating businesses—often ones in which foundation donors played significant roles as well. More broadly, critics continued to worry that the hoards of wealth represented by foundations were also "dangerous concentrations of economic and social power."[40]

Congress imposed prohibitions on unreasonable accumulations of income and foundation transactions with insiders other than at arm's length in 1950.[41] After nearly fifteen years of legislative silence, it removed the unlimited charitable deduction for donations to private foundations in 1964. But legislators declined to impose particularized limits on foundation spending, investment, and management, deferring instead to Treasury to study the issues. Treasury acted quickly, publishing an extensive report the following year.

The Treasury Report proved, on the whole, very positive.[42] Rather than unearthing a sector rife with exploitation, its study found the allegations of foundation abuses largely overstated and amenable to solution by relatively modest measures. Treasury proposed reforms designed to encourage foundations to distribute assets rather than amass them. It recommended curbing foundation involvement with business entities and transactions between foundations and their donors and managers. The report also offered proposals to improve overall foundation management.

The Treasury's report found that only a minority of foundations engaged in serious abuses. That conclusion did little to quell public and congressional suspicion of these entities. Pressure to impose boundaries and oversight for philanthropic organizations controlled by wealthy individuals, families, and corporations persisted until Congress took action four years later.[43]

The Grand Bargain

The 1969 Tax Reform Act[44] was a watershed event for philanthropy. It remade the regulatory landscape by brokering the Grand Bargain. Although not the product of formal negotiations, the contours of the Act indicate clear victories and concessions for both elite donors and the public at large.

Foundations secured their perpetual existence. Funders ensured their ability to retain control of their foundations. Efforts by congressional committees and the Treasury department to limit foundation lifetimes and require board independence failed. In return, foundations made significant concessions on tax and yielded to extensive regulatory intervention.

The first three chapters introduced aspects of this legislation, still in force and largely unchanged today. This chapter presents a comprehensive overview of the 1969 Act's Grand Bargain, as the culmination of decades of critique and repeated regulatory attempts to bring foundations to heel. Half a century on, philanthropy LLCs, commercially affiliated donor-advised funds, and strategic corporate philanthropy all subvert the Grand Bargain's power over the targeting, timing, and transparency of elite philanthropy. As a result, for-profit philanthropy provides a glimpse not only into a poorly understood past but into a discomfiting future, each defined by an absence of trust.

Perpetuity Persists

Foundations' one unqualified triumph under the 1969 Act cannot be found in its text. Advocates staved off attempts to require foundations to spend themselves out of existence. Regardless of their life spans, foundations harness the power and influence attendant to the great wealth of their donors and their families. Granting them perpetual life transfigures that power. It animates the dead hands of individuals from prior generations, allowing them to guide social welfare and policy for generations to come.

For this reason, foundation lifetime limits had been a mainstay of efforts to curtail foundation power for decades leading up the Grand Bargain. The revised Rockefeller plan offered fifty- or one hundred-year limits to satisfy its critics. The Reece and Patman reports recommended considerably shorter lifetime limits to restrain foundations' power. It should be no surprise that perpetuity reform remained on the table in 1969.

Some philanthropists had long embraced a vision of foundations with limited lives. Julius Rosenwald, who earned his fortune building the Sears, Roebuck Company, created his foundation in 1917 and endowed it with $25 million.[45] Although the foundation was established with a general-purpose mission, its signature accomplishment was funding construction and operation of more than five thousand schools for Black children in the segregated South.

Rosenwald directed the foundation's trustees to spend down its assets entirely in the twenty-five years after his death and they did just that, exhausting the foundation's endowment and shuttering in 1948. Other early twentieth-century philanthropists also experimented with limited-life vehicles. Stymied by the rapid expansions of their fortunes, however, Rockefeller and Carnegie found their spending could not keep pace with their growing wealth and turned to the perpetual model.[46]

By 1969, foundation perpetuity had become deeply ingrained. Unsurprisingly, the Treasury Report viewed perpetual foundation life as a problem. In its words, "Many foundations continue in existence year after year without achieving any of the external indicia of unique advancement of philanthropy."[47]

Despite that scathing critique, Treasury differed from other would-be reformers by eschewing a direct limit on foundation lifetimes. Instead, it pursued an indirect approach. Its proposal targeted not perpetuity itself but the risks of donor influence and insular management it bred.

Under Treasury's proposal, perpetuity survived, but a wealthy donor could maintain control over a foundation for only a limited period. After twenty-five years of existence, the foundation need not terminate, but no more than 25 percent of its board could be comprised of donors and related parties. Had this vision been adopted, the independent judgment of these boards—rather than the influence of founders or their relatives—would have determined when and whether to wind down a foundation.

The 1969 Act's original House version failed to address the perpetuity issue, containing neither direct nor indirect limitations. But Senator Albert Gore, Sr. took up the charge to curb foundation lifetimes in the Senate Finance Committee.[48] He was able to insert a limit, compromising upward from his desired twenty-five-year maximum to forty years. His efforts would prove to be for naught. On the Senate floor, Senator Walter Mondale pushed hard against the cap and his side won the day. Despite years of effort, when the moment for comprehensive foundation reform arrived, the final legislation imposed no limit on foundation lifetimes.

Congress's embrace of perpetuity represented a great victory for foundations. This decisive 1969 win silenced long-standing concerns about the dangers of permitting elite philanthropists to exert dead hand control.[49] Although there continue to be founders who follow Rosenwald's model and create foundations with expressly limited lifetimes, in the blueprint the Grand Bargain created for modern foundations, perpetuity became the accepted norm.[50]

Charitable Compromise

It would be easy to misinterpret that victory as an unqualified embrace of elite philanthropy. The tax treatment of private foundations under the Grand Bargain highlights the law's ambivalence toward giving by the wealthiest Americans.

Where foundations won on the question of perpetuity, on taxation both sides gave up ground.

The Grand Bargain preserves, but limits, foundation tax benefits. Those reduced benefits—along with the complex regulatory system aimed at foundations alone—rely on the 1969 Act's division of the universe of charitable tax-exempt entities into two distinct categories. On one side stands private foundations and on the other, public charities.

Organizations that can gain entry to the favored public charity category obtain greater tax benefits, both for themselves and their donors. They also shoulder less intense regulation and public exposure. Those unable to make the required showings become private foundations by default.

The 1969 Act could have, but did not, adopt an openly hostile stance toward private foundations. To forge the Grand Bargain between elites and the public, Congress instead approached elite philanthropy with a wary openness. Private foundations receive pointedly less generous tax benefits for themselves and their donors, but they do receive them. Private foundations must comply with a panoply of spending, investment, and management restrictions. They also bear greater public scrutiny under heightened transparency requirements. Yet on the fundamental question of whether elites should be permitted to shield their wealth from public control, Congress held its fire.

The private foundation and public charity represent mutually exclusive and collectively exhaustive categories.[51] Legally, a tax-exempt charitable organization must be one or the other. An organization qualifies for public charity status by demonstrating the existence of constituencies that will hold it accountable. If an organization cannot make such a proffer, it is consigned to the private foundation category.

An organization can secure public charity status by detailing its broad public financial support or by demonstrating significant earnings from a deep pool of consumers (rather than from investment income). Alternatively, it can establish its close connection with another organization that has achieved public charity status. Each path emerges from a set of parameters detailed in statutory and regulatory tests.[52]

Many organizations will fail to secure public charity status under any of these tests. Foundations surely will. Foundations endowed by an individual, a family, or a corporation have a small number of funders. That will cause them to fail the tests for broad public support.

Foundations also typically maintain and invest an endowment. They primarily engage in charitable activity through grantmaking rather than operating their own programs. Their investment income will therefore eclipse revenues from other sources.

Finally, foundations operate independently. They support a wide range of grantees rather than being intimately connected with a single public charity. The public charity tests screen out foundations not accidentally but deliberately.

The Grand Bargain created the separate private foundation category for these elite philanthropic vehicles. Congress relied on that distinction to constrain the freedom of elite philanthropy, but it could have gone much further. The 1969 Act could easily have embraced proposals to limit foundations' life span and independence.

In a posthumous win of sorts for Rockefeller, the Grand Bargain offered formal federal recognition of foundations, granting them perpetual life and sparing them direct public oversight. Of course, that victory was a partial one and private foundations face an array of structural safeguards designed to provide accountability. Less generous tax treatment paired with a host of regulatory requirements hint at the contours of the Grand Bargain's compromise.

Reduced Tax Benefits

When it comes to income taxation, private foundations do not enjoy the same exempt status as public charities. Private foundation donors qualify for tax deductions, but deductions not quite as generous as those offered to public charity donors. Each of these differences serves to throttle the flow of capital from wealthy donors to private foundations, establishing the private foundation as a sort of second-class charitable entity. By design, everyone involved with foundations will feel the pinch of the Grand Bargain's skepticism—the organizations themselves, their donors, and their leaders.

Foundations Pay Income Tax

One might see the fact that federal tax applies to their investment income as the Grand Bargain's harshest blow against foundations. But this obligation has always weighed lightly. The applicable tax rate has fluctuated over time but has steadfastly remained in the low single digits,[53] an order of magnitude lower than income taxes borne by other corporations and trusts.

When the private foundation regime went into effect in 1969, the rate was set at 4 percent. Corporate tax rates stood at over 50 percent and, of course, applied to income from investments as well as all other sources. The foundation investment income tax was reduced to just 2 percent in 1978.

In the mid-1980s, foundations gained the ability to replace half of this tax burden with additional charitable distributions. Changes in late 2019 eliminated that option. But they also reduced the tax rate on all foundation investment income to just 1.39 percent.[54]

Even when compared with the historic low 21 percent corporate tax rate adopted at the end of 2017,[55] these rates still offer foundations tremendous savings over their taxable peers. And, of course, this tax applies only to investment income. Foundations' income from any other sources remains fully tax-exempt.

Cumulatively, the investment income tax imposes meaningful costs on the foundations subject to it. In 2017, the tax generated roughly $875 million in revenue for the US Treasury.[56] Private foundations made all these payments. The contribution by public charities: $0.

Foundation Donors' Receive Less Valuable Income Tax Deductions

Federal income tax benefits for donors to private foundations likewise compare unfavorably to those available to public charity donors. As noted in chapter 2, donations of appreciated property to public charities benefit from a double benefit. Donors need not recognize the gains on donated property. They can also deduct its (appreciated) fair market value.

Private foundation donors receive the double benefit only for contributions of up to 10 percent of the appreciated stock of a public company.[57] For contributions of shares beyond this limit, stakes in private companies, real estate, and many other types of property, gains go untaxed, but a private foundation donor's deduction becomes much smaller. The amount of the tax break matches the historic cost of the contributed property rather than its current value.

The percentage limitations on charitable deductions reveal the same ambivalence toward private foundations. Recall that charitable donors typically may not deduct all their charitable contributions but instead face a limit beyond which these donations will be ignored for tax purposes.[58] As of 2017, the percentage limits allowed individual donors to offset up to 60 percent of their income with cash contributions to public charities. Cash contributions to private foundations faced a 30 percent limit (and counted toward the overall 60 percent limit). Contributions of appreciated property were further constrained by 30 percent and 20 percent limitations, respectively. Corporate contributions face a 10 percent limit regardless of type of charitable recipient. As noted in prior chapters, Congress significantly loosened the percentage limits on charitable deductions to encourage contributions during the COVID pandemic in 2020 and 2021, but these time-limited changes specifically excepted donations to private foundations (and DAFs).

Transfer Tax Deductions

For the elites most likely to feel their bite, the income tax's percentage limits telegraph skepticism of donations to private foundations. That makes the exceedingly generous treatment of charitable contributions under the federal estate and gift tax—which impose top marginal rates of 40 percent—all the more remarkable. Here, unlike in the income tax context, no percentage limitations apply at all.[59]

Charitable contribution deductions under the federal estate tax regime matter solely to the most affluent. Estates of individuals under $12.06 million (and twice that for married couples) will not be subject to today's estate tax.[60] Only the very largest estates will surpass these dizzying levels. And only they have anything to gain from the estate tax charitable deduction.

It may seem counterintuitive that the estate tax neither imposes limits nor makes any distinction between private foundations and public charities with its deduction. Anyone funding a private foundation and claiming an estate tax deduction for their contributions would be at the outer limits of wealth and privilege. The estate tax charitable deduction would provide a perfect opportunity to constrain elite giving.

Despite concerns over the charitability of private foundations and their links to wealthy and powerful families, the estate tax remains one area in which private foundations operate on equal footing with public charities. Contributions to either qualify for an unlimited deduction.

The charitable deduction under the federal gift tax likewise has no limit regardless of the type of charitable recipient a donor selects.[61] Most taxpayers will never have cause to take an estate tax charitable deduction, but federal gift tax applies to any gift over the annual exclusion amount, currently $16,000 per gift recipient for individual donors.[62] While a $16,000 gift lies well out of reach for millions of taxpayers, more donors make gifts of this size than give 30 percent or 60 percent of their income to charity in a single year or leave estates valued over $12,060,000.

The $16,000 limit, however, can be stretched. Married couples can each make untaxed gifts of up to $16,000 to each recipient, gift tax exclusions can carry over five future tax years, and gifts over the exclusion amount can ultimately be counted toward the lifetime estate tax limit. If these workarounds prove insufficient, the unlimited gift tax charitable deduction—allowing gifts of any size to pass to either private foundations or public charities without tax to donor or donee—offers welcome relief.

Only the wealthiest Americans will ever need to rely on transfer tax charitable deductions. Yet the Grand Bargain left them largely untouched. It included provisions "designed to apply. . . the new private foundation provisions[] to trusts with [both] charitable [and private] interests in situations in which there is the potential for tax avoidance" but otherwise maintained the unlimited deductions intact.[63] It imposed no upper limit on their value to taxpayers and made no distinction between contributions to public charities and private foundations. Half a century after playing hardball with Rockefeller, Congress all but sent an engraved invitation to wealthy donors to transfer their wealth to private foundations.

Greater Regulation

Private foundation status may seem a punishment. But from an income and transfer tax perspective, the Grand Bargain imposes surprisingly gentle treatment on private foundations and their wealthy donors. Put simply, these taxes play the role of the carrot rather than the stick.

But Congress's Grand Bargain also imposed an array of regulatory requirements on private foundations, enforced through financial (excise tax) penalties. These regulations insert federal law into virtually every component of foundation operations. They restrain the real and potential excesses of these powerful institutions and the people behind them.

They tell foundations how to spend the money they distribute, how to invest the money they retain, and how to manage their relationships with fiduciaries, employees, and donors. This regulatory regime brings the terms of the Grand Bargain into sharp relief. Compliance with its demands ensures access to the reward of a permanent exemption from virtually all tax for a philanthropic venture and considerable tax benefits for donors. The price for this access remains public regulation of the timing, targeting, and transparency of philanthropists' largesse.

Spending Rules: When, How Much, to Whom, and for What?

Federal law regulates foundation spending on virtually all possible dimensions. Its payout requirement addresses both the timing and the amount of foundation spending by penalizing foundations that fail to distribute at least 5 percent of their assets each year for charitable purposes. Through excise taxes imposed on certain types of expenditures, it also targets favored recipients of foundations' resources and purposes for which they may be distributed. Working together, this suite of spending rules channels foundation spending on the timeline and in the direction Congress prefers.

When and How Much to Spend

The potential for a time lag between a donor's contribution to a tax-favored entity and the use of the donated resources to provide charitable services raises both tax and managerial concerns. On the tax side, as deductions accrue immediately upon contribution, a substantial time lag enables donors to enjoy tax advantages years or even decades before the associated donation funds any societally beneficial programs or services. Such mismatched timing creates the risk of oversubsidization. If a deduction underwrites taxpayer support of activities beneficial to the public in today's dollars in return for purchases of those activities far into the future, the public may pay too much.[64]

On the managerial side, retention and growth of donated (or even earned) assets can lead to distraction. As organizational wealth grows, charitable leaders can be sidetracked from obligations to their charitable missions. They may instead concentrate on investment strategy or even empire-building, either for the foundation's sake or to enhance their private reputations.

This temporal disconnect between donation and charitable use can occur in any charitable organization. But the risk is particularly salient for perpetual private foundations. If foundations were treated as qualifying recipients for tax-deductible contributions without additional regulation, a donor might receive an immediate tax deduction upon transferring assets to the foundation regardless of when—and perhaps even whether—the funds flow to any charitable programs.

This concern tends to be muted in the context of operating charities. Their need to fund their activities will typically demand that they draw down a considerable portion of donated funds for current use. By contrast, a core part of the foundation concept rests with the idea of an endowment, a critical mass of assets kept within its possession and control as principal to be invested to create income for current and future use.

Private foundations appear especially vulnerable to the managerial risks of nondistribution. Without some payout requirement, foundations would pose the risk not only of perpetual existence, which the Grand Bargain accepts, but of perpetual growth. They could hoard donated funds, investing and reinvesting them endlessly for some hypothetical eventual charitable use. Since endowment size often serves as a proxy for influence, the temptations of such a continued growth strategy would be manifold. The reputation of a foundation named for its donors could easily be conflated with their own, even more so when donors or their family members comprise its board.

Foundation leaders whose fortunes fuel a venture (and their families or their associates) also may have more experience and expertise with the readily quantifiable task of making money than the murkier proposition of doing good. Without outside contributors and or consumers to monitor or discipline management, foundations can employ tools to counteract the pull of investment's distraction. Large foundations typically recruit separate investment and grantmaking staffs, and some foundations seat independent directors. But both tools remain voluntary, and neither offers any guarantees.

Of course, the threat of empire-building hangs over all sorts of organizations. As discussed in chapter 2, these very issues of premature deductions and managerial distraction have been identified by critics of donor-advised funds. Predictably, those critics have called for Congress to establish a payout rule or other incentives to encourage early distribution.

Ballooning university endowments pose the same dangers. Educational endowments can be justified as tools to smooth spending over periods of market boom and bust. They can also promote equity between spending on today's students and those who will matriculate in future years.[65] As long as endowment sizes bear some relation to these educational purposes, allowing the tax-free accumulation of the investment income they generate can be defended within the broader rationale for educational tax exemptions. At some point, however, endowments outstrip these justifications.

For Congress, by 2017, that point had been reached if not long passed. For a mixture of purposes including encouraging tuition decreases and raising revenue, it enacted a 1.4 percent tax on investment income of the most richly endowed colleges and universities.[66] Notably, this number is (likely not coincidentally) a mere 0.01 percent different from the current investment income tax rate for private foundations. Although the new college and university endowment tax was met with intense opposition from the higher education community, bills proposing to undo the tax have garnered little support.[67]

Treasury's 1965 report on foundations pointed to these same concerns about the delay in foundation spending as one of the major problems to which legislation should be addressed. Although prior tax reform legislation in 1950 denied exemption to foundations with "unreasonable" accumulations of income, Treasury's "[f]ourteen years of experience ha[d] indicated that in this context standards such as 'unreasonable' . . . are inadequate as well as difficult and expensive to administer."[68] It recommended instead that private foundations be mandated to distribute the entirety of their net income to charities on an annual basis. Although initially sympathetic to this approach, Congress eventually settled instead on a payout requirement. The mandate initially required foundations to distribute their adjusted net income or at least 6 percent of the value of their assets each year; the payout rule was simplified to 5 percent a few years later, where it remains to this day.[69]

Not quite a mandate in form but certainly one in practice, the current provisions impose a two-tiered penalty tax if a foundation fails to distribute 5 percent of the fair market value of its assets each year.[70] For every dollar below the 5 percent floor it falls, the foundation must pay an initial tax of 30 cents.[71] If a foundation fails to cure this error, the provision assesses an additional 100 percent tax on the undistributed amount.[72] The regime softens the application of the rule from a straight annual requirement to allow one year's expenditures beyond 5 percent to be carried over for the following five years. Still, the ultimate effect remains stark. The potentially confiscatory second-level tax ensures that no rational private foundation will intentionally distribute amounts below the floor.

In a potentially unanticipated but undoubtedly undesirable consequence, many quarters report that this floor has also become a practical ceiling.[73] Private foundation distributions fall in the 5 percent range far more often than mere chance would predict. Even in the context of extraordinary need created by the global COVID-19 pandemic, many foundations have stuck staunchly to the 5 percent number. As noted in chapter 1, a few even took the extraordinary step of taking on debt to fund additional distributions, rather than spend down their endowments at a time of significant investment losses.[74]

Whether it functions only as a floor or also a ceiling, the significance of the payout rule depends on what counts toward the 5 percent. The statute and regulations term those expenditures "qualifying distributions."[75] The list of potential qualifying distributions includes three types of expenditures that qualify far more easily than others.

First and foremost, distributions to domestic public charities to pursue the foundation's purposes will nearly always meet the criteria. Only if the recipient organization happens to be controlled by the foundation, its leaders, or its substantial contributors will it fail to do so.[76] Second, reasonable and necessary administrative expenses related to such expenditures will also count.[77] Although critics continue to argue that foundations pad these expenses, the regulatory standard remains generous.[78] Third, a foundation can count the amount it pays under the investment income tax against its required distributions.[79] This credit against the 5 percent rule will depend on the returns to the foundation's portfolio and the tax rate in place at any given time. To make up the rest, foundations concentrate on straightforwardly compliant grants to public charities and associated administrative expenses.[80]

Foundations need to put in additional effort for other types of expenditures to count against the required 5 percent payout. Grants to foreign charities may qualify, if the private foundation issuing them determines in good faith their equivalency to a US public charity.[81] Program-related investments, when a foundation undertakes a debt, equity, or other investment rather than a grant, to achieve its charitable objectives (discussed in more detail below), may also qualify. But extraordinary measures can be necessary. When compared with simply confirming that a recipient organization qualifies as a public charity and will use the grant funds for the private foundation's exempt purposes, the diligence required to ensure grants to foreign charities or program-related investments will be qualifying distributions predictably steers foundations away from them.

What Not to Spend

The list of qualifying distributions targets modes of foundation spending favored under the Grand Bargain. Another part of the 1969 Act broadcasts distaste for other ways foundations might deploy their resources. Under the umbrella category "taxable expenditures," a catchall provision penalizes several categories of foundation spending.[82] Notably, these penalties apply not only to offending foundations but also to their managers.

Any taxable expenditure triggers an initial tax of 20 percent of the amount expended, assessed against the foundation, and 5 percent of this amount assessed against "any foundation manager who agreed to" making it.[83] If the foundation fails to correct, both foundations and managers are subject to onerous second-tier taxes of 100 percent and 50 percent of the expenditure, respectively.

Political spending carries a special stigma under the Grand Bargain. Any spending "to carry on propaganda, or . . . influence legislation," "to influence the outcome of any specific public election," even (with limited exceptions) to fund voter registration drives, will be a violation.[84] All charitable tax-exempt entities face extensive restrictions on political activities, and transgressions can result in a revocation of tax-exempt status. The Grand Bargain's strictures for private foundations go well beyond those applicable generally and its taxable expenditure penalties on political spending apply only to them.

Concerns about cozy relationships between foundations and politics also fueled restrictions on grants to individuals. Many were incensed to learn the Ford Foundation awarded travel grants to eight members of Senator Robert F. Kennedy's staff following his assassination. Ford Foundation President McGeorge Bundy, who had been both a friend and National Security Advisor to President Kennedy, explained his view that the grants fell within the foundation's educational purposes in the 1969 House Ways and Means Committee hearings.[85] For many, however, his testimony was perceived to suggest grants to these highly credentialed and well-connected individuals were instead "a suitable expression of sympathy" paid for with taxpayer-subsidized funds.[86]

The assembled representatives remained unconvinced, and the Grand Bargain restricted foundations' ability to make similar grants in the future. Grants to individuals "for travel, study, or other similar purposes" are subject to penalties as taxable expenditures unless awarded through a process preapproved by the IRS.[87] Preapproval vets such grantmaking to ensure it will operate to serve the foundation's charitable purposes, rather than to funnel foundation money to favored persons for their individual enjoyment.

Grants to organizations other than public charities—ranging from other private foundations to taxable entities—also trigger these two-tiered taxes on organizations and managers unless the foundation undertakes additional diligence. For such recipient entities, foundations must exercise "expenditure responsibility"[88] to ensure the money achieves its intended purpose. Specifically, they must obtain grantee reporting about the use of funds and provide detailed reports to the government. Foundations making these types of grants can avoid penalties by exercising the required pre- and post-grant diligence. But many instead take the hint and simply confine their spending to the grants to public charities the Grand Bargain targets.

Taken together, the foundation spending rules send wealthy donors clear messages on timing and targeting. To avoid further scuffles like those that threatened their existence more than fifty years ago, they should spend at least (and perhaps at most) 5 percent of their assets annually. Those expenditures should be devoted to serving their charitable purposes mostly through grants to public charities, a group that Congress identified as proper targets of foundation largesse. And they should absolutely stay out of politics.

Investment Rules: Imperatives on Risk, Return, and Control

As foundations' ability to meet the Grand Bargain's timing and targeting goals depends on their financial viability, the private foundation rules also have a great deal to say about how foundations invest. The jeopardy investment rules warn foundation leaders away from speculation that might endanger their charitable purposes. The excess business holdings rules limit the stake foundations may take in the investments their fiduciaries select, subjecting stakes greater than the cap to penalty taxes.

The law also directs attention—and suspicion—toward relationships between foundation leaders and donors and the investments they make. Much the same way the payout rules impose timing restrictions and the taxable expenditure rules target foundation spending, the foundation investment rules help hold foundations to their end of the Grand Bargain. To remain focused on their charitable missions, they must avoid functioning (or appearing to function) as vehicles to benefit their donors or managers.

Keeping Foundation Assets Safe

By now it should be abundantly clear that the Grand Bargain can trace its roots to Treasury's influential 1965 report. Treasury raised alarms about foundations engaging in active trading and speculation that introduced volatility into foundation investment portfolios. Intriguingly, high-risk strategies worried its authors whether they succeeded or failed.

The danger of foundations losing their shirts on failed arbitrage attempts or speculating in risky ventures requires no imagination. Depleting their assets would result in fewer resources for charitable grants and programs. But big financial wins from trading and speculation also worried the report's authors. They pointed to the possibility of "financial empire building and the severance of a foundation from dependence upon contributors."[89]

For Treasury, forgoing the high returns that high risk investments might generate was a cost worth bearing.[90] It fretted that discretion would encourage foundation leaders to spend too much time tending to the heady world of trading and speculation and to devote too little energy to identifying and supporting valuable charitable programs. Big wins might generate more assets for charitable use but without constituencies like independent donors or customers who might be counted on to exert the necessary discipline on management.

Existing law in 1969 imposed a prohibition on investment of accumulated income "in such a manner as to jeopardize the carrying out of the charitable, educational, or other purpose or function constituting the basis for [charitable tax] exemption,"[91] but Treasury wanted stronger medicine. It proposed to extend this prohibition on jeopardy investment to all foundation assets as well as a "specific interdiction of devices ordinarily deemed inherently speculative—as, for example, the purchase of 'puts,' 'calls,' 'straddles, 'spreads,' 'strips,' 'straps,' and 'special options,' selling short, and trading in commodity futures."[92]

Congress shared Treasury's concerns about foundation investment practices but did not go quite so far. It imposed penalty taxes when a foundation "invest[s] any amount in such a manner as to jeopardize the carrying out of any of its exempt purposes."[93] Treasury then promulgated regulations providing investments become "jeopardizing" when not undertaken with ordinary care and prudence.[94] Although each investment must be considered individually, its place within a foundation's overall portfolio remains relevant. The regulations also demand special scrutiny for "trading in securities on margin, trading in commodity futures, investments in working interests in oil and gas wells, the purchase of 'puts,' 'calls,' and 'straddles,' the purchase of warrants, and selling short."[95]

Foundations that violate the rule pay a penalty tax equal to 10 percent of the jeopardizing investment. An additional 25 percent tax may be imposed if the "investment is not removed from jeopardy."[96] Foundation managers who make jeopardizing investments knowingly may find themselves subject to penalty taxes of 10 percent of the investment initially and an additional 5 percent should the violation not be cured.[97]

One striking exception to the jeopardy investment rule's mandate for prudence does exist. Foundations may make an investment without regard to its financial risk if its "primary purpose . . . is to accomplish one or more [charitable purposes]."[98] Indeed, to fit within this program-related investment (PRI) category, the investment's purpose must not be to generate financial gains for the foundation.

The jeopardy investment rule and its penalties simply do not apply, even though PRIs necessarily pose significant financial risks to a foundation. PRIs neither seek nor expect an economic return. Instead, their objective is to accomplish the foundation's charitable goals. Consistent with that requirement, PRI expenditures also count toward the 5 percent payout requirement, one for one with grants.[99]

Properly understood, the PRI exception does not undercut the message of prudent investing that the jeopardy investment rule transmits. A PRI's equivalence to a grant offers the key to understanding the apparent anomaly of its regulatory treatment.[100] While PRIs are investments in form, foundations undertake PRIs because they will yield charitable returns rather than financial gains. Grants, of course, generate a negative 100 percent return and they represent the bread and butter of foundation expenditures.

Some of the very first PRIs, made by the Ford Foundation and actually predating the 1969 Act, took the form of business loans extended in undercapitalized urban communities and were designed to stimulate economic growth.[101] Despite legal uncertainty, Ford extended the loans with the goals of stimulating additional capital infusions for the communities and recycling the funds from those borrowers who were able to repay. The PRI exception in the 1969 Act blessed this practice, though it remains relatively little used.[102]

Despite its breadth and its threat of both sanctions on organizations and personal liability for managers, the jeopardy investment rule has done relatively little to limit the investment activities of private foundations. Litigation has been infrequent and the penalties under the rule have rarely been applied.[103] Those few foundations undertaking PRIs may engage in greater diligence,[104] but for the most part foundations can essentially eliminate the risk of violations by constructing and fully documenting diversified portfolios with expert assistance.

Not all foundations have access to this advice, of course, and some foundation investment practices may continue to be chilled by the rule's broad mandate and ominous penalties (assuming uncounseled foundations become aware of the rule at all). Professor Richard Schmalbeck opined nearly two decades ago that the rule's "provisions are close to being deadwood, but not quite; and, as such, they continue to impose compliance costs, and may chill investment strategies that would be beneficial for foundations as a whole."[105] Unsurprisingly given this assessment, he advocated repealing the rule altogether. Even without it, state law would limit the investment practices of private foundations to only those consistent with their fiduciaries' duty to prudently manage their assets.[106]

For private foundations, penalties for failures to carefully steward their assets could be levied by states. By contrast, the other set of investment rules imposed by federal tax law—limiting the stake private foundations may hold in any business in which they invest—has no state law counterpart. Linked directly to concerns about foundations' entanglement with business interests, the excess business holding concept can be directly traced to the Treasury Report.

Keeping Foundations Away from Business

A fair amount of suspected private foundation wrongdoing was revealed by the Treasury Report as unfounded. But it validated the fear that they were heavily involved in business. Of the 1,300 foundations the report reviewed, approximately 180 held a 10 percent or larger stake in a corporation.[107] Many held larger interests, including forty that wholly owned one or more companies.[108] More foundations operated businesses directly.

Treasury identified three important concerns arising from this entanglement between foundations and businesses. First, it worried that private foundations' tax exemption and freedom from shareholder demands would provide businesses controlled by foundations with an undue advantage over their competitors.[109] A special unrelated business income tax (UBIT) adopted in 1950 taxed exempt organizations' income from businesses unconnected to their charitable purposes. Still, the report suspected that businesses controlled by foundations would have greater capacity to accumulate untaxed capital for use in operations, for capital investments, and for acquisitions.[110] In support of these concerns, it cited the "remarkable number of foundation-owned enterprises [that] proceed from year to year realizing substantial profits, but making negligible or no distributions to their parent organizations."[111]

The Treasury Report also raised the specter of mission drift. It feared that substantial business holdings were distracting foundations and their management from their proper focus on charitable activity. In a remarkable paean to the foundation ideal, it spoke of foundations' exceptional suitability for "development of individual insights, the testing of new approaches, the exploration of uncharted areas."[112] The authors fretted that these crucial functions could not be optimally pursued by a foundation enmeshed in overseeing an operating business—or, in numerous cases, many of them. Boards of such foundations would find their time dominated by business issues, "charity, an insufficiently considered and mechanically accomplished afterthought."[113] In addition, the report argued that business involvement by foundations tended to dovetail with or exacerbate the problems of delayed charitable benefit and self-dealing endemic to private foundations.[114]

To combat these problems, the report recommended a strict cap on foundation business holdings. It floated the idea of a 20 percent maximum, choosing this number as a rough estimate of the ownership stake required to ensure control.[115] This idea eventually formed a key part of the Grand Bargain.

Treasury also sought a remedy against donors who used foundation business ownership to extend control of their own private businesses.[116] Data collected from its study of private foundations showed that among those with substantial business holdings, holdings of related family businesses predominated. This strategy, which allowed donors to enjoy both continued practical control and the tax benefits of contributing (sometimes highly appreciated) stock, had become fodder as well for the popular press.

Perhaps even more important, these assets proved strikingly unproductive. The report gives example after example of foundation holdings of family businesses where no or negligible dividends were issued, sometimes for years at a time, which declined in value, and yet the foundation retained the assets.[117] In a follow-up report, Treasury found that among over two hundred foundations holding 20 percent of more of a business, "almost precisely half had no current yield whatever in the surveyed year."[118] Retention of these assets had more to do with donor preference than any investment value for the foundation—and unproductive assets meant fewer resources for grants, which meant less money for operating charitable programs.

In response, Treasury recommended that donated interests in a business not be deductible until the foundation disposed of the asset or used it in its charitable operations, or the donor's control ceased.[119] Disallowing deductions proved a bridge too far for Congress, but the Act did strictly limit foundation holdings. As noted in chapter 1, foundations may retain only "permitted holdings" of up to 20 percent of a company's voting stock.[120]

The percentage of foundation holdings is calculated by combining its direct holdings with those of the foundation's managers, substantial contributors, members of their families, and related parties (including related foundations) in determining whether the ceiling has been met.[121] A detailed statute and accompanying regulations provide additional refinements on the cap,[122] but the message comes through unmistakably. Foundations should not have large stakes in businesses, particularly when major donors, managers, and related parties own stakes themselves.

Violations incur sizable penalties. A ten percent tax applies to the value of any holdings over the statutory cap and a second level 200 percent confiscatory tax applies to recalcitrant foundations that refuse to divest.[123] Even in instances when divestment will be a costly loss, the second-level tax is designed to motivate sale—paying 200 percent of its value to the government will surely be worse. The findings of the Treasury Report made evident that, if applied immediately, many foundations would be in violation of the excess business holdings rule and would be pushed by its penalties to divest at a swift clip. To ease the transition, the Act applied prospectively and with generous extensions and phase-in schedules.[124]

Over time, the foundation community came into compliance and the excess business holdings rules have remained largely intact for decades. Indeed, chapter 2 related that Congress extended a similar cap to donor-advised funds in 2006.[125] As chapter 1 described, the one notable divergence came online quite recently, in large part due to the persistent efforts of the Newman's Own Foundation[126] whose structure and holdings fit its terms precisely. Provisions enacted in 2018 except certain foundation holdings of 100 percent ownership stakes from the excess business holdings rules.[127] The exception applies only to stakes in business enterprises the foundation obtains other than by purchase (presumably by gift or bequest) and only if the wholly controlled business operates independently of the foundation and donates all profits to charity. Though a victory for Newman's Own, these narrow provisions will be relevant for few other foundations.

In the same way the foundation spending rules target how foundations deploy their assets, the investment rules guide how they steward them. Again, the Grand Bargain can be seen directing foundations to stay in their proper sphere, focused on investing purely in service of enabling a long-term (likely perpetual) charitable mission. The bright-line excess business holdings rule makes its imperatives to avoid controlling businesses—whether related or unrelated—potent. The ambiguous standards and limited enforcement that characterize the jeopardy investment rule dilute its impact on well-counseled foundations, but its meaning and message remain consonant. Foundation investment generates the resources required to further charitable missions over time. Allowing the investment tail to wag the charitable mission dog risks at best distraction and, at worst, impropriety.

Management Rules: Deterring and Uncovering Impropriety

The foundation management rules pursue impropriety more directly. The self-dealing rules prophylactically penalize a wide range of transactions between foundations and their contributors and managers. As earlier chapters have noted, those rules can prohibit even transactions that might benefit both parties.

Together with the spending rules discussed above, the management rules target foundations in a public-regarding, congressionally endorsed charitable direction and away from benefiting their donors and leaders. The disclosure regime developed to track and enforce the entire suite of foundation rules makes foundation management vulnerable to both regulatory and public scrutiny. Within the universe of tax-benefited charitable organizations, foundations must embrace the highest level of transparency.

Preventing Self-Dealing

The nature of private foundations makes them particularly vulnerable to abuse. Funded by a single donor—or relatively small group of donors—a foundation may need to reckon with powerful people harboring feelings of entitlement to continued access and control over donated assets, even after the foundation takes legal title.[128] Often well-positioned to gain entrée through board positions or employment with the foundation, either directly or through family members, funders can exert power over its actions.

Even when a foundation enjoys professional management by unrelated parties, the ties between the foundation and a donor family could understandably breed deference to generous benefactors.[129] That combination of entitlement, access, and management deference creates a greater likelihood of transactions between a foundation and its donors. If such transactions become commonplace, managers themselves could begin to see them as the normal course of business, access to which they too should be granted.[130]

Charitable entities qualify for a federal tax exemption only if "no part of the[ir] net income . . . inures to the benefit of any private stockholder or individual."[131] Distributing a foundation's assets directly to its managers or donors would qualify as a breach and endanger the organization's exempt status. But self-dealing transactions differ from direct distributions. Deals between a foundation and its insiders may benefit or harm the foundation, depending on their terms.

Consider a foundation donor who leases office space to the foundation or a foundation that employs the spouse of one of its directors as a consultant. Whether such transactions represent bargains for the foundation or abuses of the insider's position will depend on the rent or the compensation arrangement and perhaps how the transactions were conducted. Federal tax law provided little guidance on the subject until 1950, when it prohibited only donor-foundation transactions and only if concluded on non-arm's-length terms.

For foundation managers that serve as state law fiduciaries, nonprofit corporate and charitable trust law also imposes limits on permissible transactions with foundations. Both regimes hold fiduciaries liable for self-dealing transactions that are unfair to the charitable entity. Charitable trust law can void even those undertaken on market terms.[132] State fiduciary law thus imposes discipline on some categories of foundation managers. But in practice, these transactions can be difficult to uncover, and nonprofit fiduciary law remains notoriously underenforced. Moreover, donors who do not serve as directors, trustees, or officers will not be fiduciaries. In such cases, state law imposes no restrictions on their transactions with their associated foundations.

The Treasury Report identified the lack of comprehensive regulation of self-dealing transactions as one of the foundation sector's "major problems," generating "undesirable consequences" for foundations and the public.[133] The authors tied permission for self-dealing to suboptimal levels of current spending, reasoning that those donors, aware they might transact with the foundation's assets in the future, would be reticent to distribute them to charities. Similarly, they feared access to self-dealing transactions would color investment decisions donors would make for their foundations in an official capacity. Whereas a closed-end fund or real estate investment might be an attractive addition to the foundation's portfolio, a donor seeking ready access to the foundation's assets for self-dealing transactions would prefer more liquid alternatives. The report also argued that even in transactions on arm's-length terms, donor-foundation transactions would likely confer subtle advantages to donors—to the detriment of their foundation counterparties.

In addition, the Treasury report raised broader policy problems with allowing self-dealing between donors and foundations. Such transactions, the authors worried, gave foundation donors an advantage over other taxpayers. One example they offered imagined foundation donors might "donate" assets to the foundation but then cause the foundation to loan those assets to themselves or their businesses, securing valuable deductions while retaining use and control over assets that taxpayers without a foundation at their disposal could not access. More generally, they feared that self-dealing transactions contributed to taxpayer skepticism about the fairness of the tax system, noting "[t]he belief is becoming more widespread that the creation of a private foundation is a *tax dodge* used by some taxpayers to obtain tax advantages."[134]

In Treasury's view, the 1950 arm's-length restriction not only represented weak tea but also required case-by-case examination and arduous line-drawing that made enforcement a struggle. Looking to state charitable trust law which, at the time, also imposed a flat prohibition on trustee self-dealing, the report's authors favored a similarly straightforward ban. When concluded between a foundation and its donors, loans, compensation, agreements for the purchase or sale of services, property sales, and leases should all be prohibited. The report also recommended clarifying that donors' family members and related business entities would be treated as equivalent to a donor, and it contemplated only extremely limited exceptions, such as for interest-free loans from donors to their foundations. Recall as well that its authors advocated a new rule limiting donors and their associates to a minority of foundation boards after twenty-five years.

On these issues, Congress proved largely, though not entirely, persuaded. It did not require foundations to shift to independent management on a federally mandated timeline. But the self-dealing proscriptions it enacted—that remain in force today—follow Treasury's recommendations closely.

As noted in chapters 1 and 3, the law defines self-dealing to include transactions in which substantial donors, foundation managers, their family members, and their related business entities participate directly or indirectly in a "sale or exchange, or leasing, of property," "lending of money or other extension of credit," "furnishing of goods, services or facilities."[135] Other transfers of foundation assets to or for the benefit of such parties are also self-dealing and subject to penalty. In line with the other private foundation rules, the penalties now impose a moderate (10 percent of the transaction amount) first-tier penalty on the self-dealer followed by a confiscatory (200 percent) second tier. Similar two-tiered penalties (5 percent/50 percent but with caps of $20,000 per transaction) apply to foundation managers who participate in such transactions knowing them to be self-dealing, "unless such participation is not willful and is due to reasonable cause."[136]

Congress has continued to perceive self-dealing infractions as particularly egregious. Statutory language added in 1984 permits abatement of the initial taxes for violations of the other private foundation rules if "due to reasonable cause and not to willful neglect" and promptly corrected.[137] Initial penalty taxes for self-dealing transactions do not qualify for such abatement.[138]

The 1969 Act countenances a somewhat broader range of exceptions than Treasury advocated, most notably allowing reasonable, nonexcessive compensation when "necessary to carrying out the exempt purposes of the private foundation."[139] Overall, though, it firmly rejects the idea that arm's-length transactions pose no threat. This approach forgoes potential benefits. In the absence of the self-dealing rules, donors, related parties, or foundation managers could transact with their foundations on generous terms. Congress accepted this sacrifice in the foundation context. Interestingly, when it returned to the topic of self-dealing three decades later to enact an enforcement regime for public charities, it opted instead for an arm's-length approach.[140]

Congress also added to its version of the self-dealing rules a final disfavored transaction that fits less easily with the overall theme of management objectivity but rather hearkens back to concerns about targeting foundation spending. It tags as self-dealing any "agreement by a private foundation to make any payment of money or other property to a government official," unless for employment after the official's government service will end.[141] In theory, the political power of government officials might well enable them to persuade foundations to transact with them in ways analogous to the foundation's own donors and managers. Deeming such transactions self-dealing and subject to penalty taxes certainly bolsters foundations' ability to decline such arrangements. But this category of "self-dealing" still seems more a type of disfavored spending than an insider transaction.

Pragmatic considerations better explain the designation of payments to political officials as self-dealing, rather than merely disapproved (and taxable) expenditures like lobbying or individual grants. The self-dealing provisions are unique among the private foundation rules in that their excise taxes do not apply to foundations at all. Only the foundation's self-dealing counterparties pay the penalty. Designating payments to political officials as self-dealing ensures that those officials (and foundation managers) involved will pay the price, rather than foundations themselves.

As with any precautionary rule, it can be difficult to know how much deterrence the self-dealing rules generate. The IRS has few resources to investigate exempt organizations' compliance with their federal tax obligations.[142] Professor Ellen Aprill's statistical analysis suggests less than one-quarter of one percent of private foundations reported self-dealing penalty taxes in the most recent year for which statistics are available.[143] But, as she recognizes, these numbers may not tell the whole story. On the one hand, they may reflect the self-dealing rules exerting a significant chilling effect. On the other hand, if those who seek to violate them with relative impunity need only go the small further step of declining to report self-dealing transactions on their annual informational returns, these rules may accomplish little.

Enhancing Transparency

The same insularity that makes foundations ripe for self-dealing also makes transgressions difficult to detect. When the same or related individuals create or fund an organization, serve as its fiduciaries, and run its day-to-day affairs, few outside this tight circle will ever learn about the transactions it undertakes. For the suite of new private foundation rules to be effective, enhancing transparency was essential.

The 1960s Treasury Department and IRS faced a profound informational deficit with respect to foundations. Existing law required foundations to file basic annual informational returns with the IRS, but it lacked effective penalties for failures to do so. The Treasury Report requested a remedy for the situation, relating that "its efforts have been hampered by the absence of an effective sanction for non-compliance."[144] The 1969 Act not only included new penalties but also deepened the level of transparency required of foundations.

The new law increased disclosure requirements for all exempt organizations but imposed more extensive burdens on private foundations. Where a general statement of income, receipts, and disbursements suffices for public charities, private foundations must provide a balance sheet, "itemized" statements of assets, and lists of grants and contributions made, as well as the names and addresses of its managers and contributors indicating which individuals play both roles.[145] The Act also required foundations to make their annual informational returns available for public inspection, a mandate not extended to public charities until nearly twenty years later.[146]

Exempt organizations' disclosure mandates have been updated several times since 1969, and some of these changes have narrowed the gap between the disclosure obligations of public charities and private foundations. Today, all exempt organizations' publicly available required filings can be accessed with a click on Guidestar.org. Still, private foundations remain subject to greater transparency than other exempt organizations, including a requirement to make public the names of their donors.[147] The recent Supreme Court decision in *Americans for Prosperity Foundation* v. *Bonta* raises questions about whether this foundation donor disclosure mandate will withstand First Amendment scrutiny should it be challenged.[148] The case struck down state attorney general donor disclosure mandates but specifically reserved judgment on whether a challenge to IRS donor disclosure obligations would pass constitutional muster.

The 1969 Act also took the first steps toward improving enforcement of exempt organizations' disclosure obligations. Provisions enacted then meant failures to file required disclosures or make them available for public inspection triggered monetary penalties.[149] Over time, these fines have been augmented and now repeated failure to file required informational returns can even result in revocation of exemption.[150]

By calling out self-dealing transactions as illegitimate and generally letting sunlight shine into foundation operations, the foundation management rules reinforce the recurring message found throughout the 1969 Act's provisions. The self-dealing rules remind foundations to stay centered on their charitable targets. They must not let the interests of donors who found or fund them eclipse their proper public-regarding, not private-regarding, missions. The disclosure obligations and penalties enhance the transparency of foundations to ensure that deviations from required targeting and timing will have consequences.

Accountability

The 1969 Act allowed private foundations to exist in perpetuity. But it exacted a price for that concession and for the generous—albeit slightly less so than for public charities—tax benefits the law continued to offer foundations and their donors. Responding to both broad fears and specific concerns, Congress offered elites a vehicle for giving that limited philanthropic power and curbed its most dangerous excesses.

Congress's Grand Bargain targeted foundations toward activities society found unthreatening (at least as they understood its preoccupations). The spending rules shaped the timing of giving by constraining the ability of elites to stockpile wealth while discouraging political activity and encouraging support of public charities. The investment rules limited their entanglement with business and discouraged speculation. Its focus on managers built guardrails against abuses while demanding transparency in exchange for forbearance.

This Grand Bargain made the immense private power of elite philanthropy inoffensive by staking out boundaries for its conduct. Only foundations that confine their activities within this publicly palatable sphere remained safe from the lingering threat of taxation. Even isolated violations could expose great fortunes to stinging penalty taxes and the possibility of vast payments to the fisc.

But the Grand Bargain should not be mistaken for an effort to impose public control over elite wealth. Observing the timing, targeting, and transparency demands of the Grand Bargain offered wealthy philanthropists a way to ease public anxieties about foundation accountability that had persisted for decades. Replacing public skepticism with trust—and perhaps even admiration—freed foundations to accomplish extraordinary feats.

Foundations' Growth and Impact

After a brief dip in interest in creating new private foundations immediately after the 1969 reforms, philanthropists and their advisors adapted, and the form resurged by the 1980s.[151] Data compiled by Professor James Fishman reveal a foundation sector at the turn of the twenty-first century marked by sustained growth. In each five-year period from 1995 to 2015, the number of foundations grew considerably—in all but one of these periods by more than 15 percent and in the period from 1995 to 2000 by nearly 40 percent.[152]

Much of the growth in the number of foundations resulted from the formation of small family foundations.[153] Still, measured by assets, the overall size of the foundation sector has been growing by leaps and bounds. In 2002, foundations held just under $432 billion in assets.[154] By 2017, they controlled more than $1 trillion.[155] In April 2020, despite COVID's impact on the market, Candid.org estimates pegged corporate and independent foundation assets together at roughly $997 billion, supporting $71 billion in grants.[156]

Some of today's largest foundations—venerable institutions like Rockefeller, Carnegie, and Ford as well as others endowed by early industrial giants like Getty and Lilly—boast a long history of giving. In recent decades, these legacy foundations have been joined by new entrants, many funded with riches amassed in technology and finance.[157] The Bill and Melinda Gates Foundation, whose endowment merges contributions from both its eponymous founders and Warren Buffett, has a $53.3 billion war chest far larger than any other US foundation.[158]

Other important new entrants include George Soros's Open Society Foundations, the Robert Wood Johnson Foundation, the Bloomberg Philanthropies, and foundations endowed by both William and Flora Hewlett and David and Lucile Packard. The combination of their founders' splashy business success and high-profile philanthropic pursuits have made these foundations household names. Leading corporations of all stripes, as described in chapter 3, have also established foundations to distribute their largesse.

Since the first general-purpose foundations were created at the turn of the twentieth century, foundations have made grants of countless billions of dollars to organizations pursuing all manner of charitable activity. They flourish across every state and region of the United States. Canvassing the breadth and scale of their accomplishments would require a much longer book than this one. A few examples particularly salient in our own time, though, provide a taste of some of the most dizzying of elite foundations' achievements.

From their earliest days, general-purpose foundations have dedicated considerable resources to medical care and research. The outpouring of billions of dollars in foundation grants to fund research, manufacture, and distribution of a coronavirus vaccine represents only the latest example.[159]

Rockefeller's history of funding health initiatives stretches back over a century. Prior to the creation of the general-purpose Rockefeller Foundation, John D. Rockefeller funded a special-purpose philanthropic institution: the Rockefeller Sanitary Commission for the Eradication of Hookworm Disease.[160] It was sufficiently successful that it closed its doors just five years later. One of the Rockefeller Foundation's first initiatives created an international health program that spread its hookworm program globally. It later funded research leading to the successful development and deployment of a yellow fever vaccine.[161] In the 1980s, the foundation collaborated with the World Health Organization to ramp up vaccination among children worldwide.[162]

These efforts were bolstered by an infusion of interest and funding from the Gates Foundation in the 1990s, forming the Global Alliance for Vaccines and Immunization (Gavi). Gates's most recent grant to Gavi is a five-year $1.5 billion commitment to providing those in the poorest countries in the world both routine immunizations and coronavirus vaccines.[163] Although the foundation's initial stance on intellectual property protection for vaccine developers generated criticism, it eventually backed down and as of September 2022 reported having "committed more than $2 billion to support the global response to COVID-19."[164]

Foundations have also played a key role in supporting the development of public services, providing policy support or proof of concept for innovations that government would ultimately adopt and fund. For example, foundation backing was pivotal to the growth of public radio and television broadcasting in its infancy. The Ford Foundation and the Carnegie Corporation provided early support for developing nationwide broadcasting capacity and funded a series of commissions and reports that proved essential to ultimate federal approval.[165] Ever since, foundation grants have sustained these vital but chronically underfunded public institutions.

In the mid-1970s, the Robert Wood Johnson Foundation tackled a very different sort of challenge. It provided critical grant funding to develop and implement an emergency response system in forty-four regions in the United States. The program's success spurred federal funding for the development of 911 capacity nationwide.[166]

Notwithstanding such far-flung achievements, nowhere has the impact of foundations been more indelible than in the field of education. Chapter 1 recounted one prominent recent example; hundreds of millions in Gates Foundation funding for research and advocacy around the Common Core curriculum helped spur a sea change in state education policy in just a couple of years.[167] Gates grants funded academics to develop the standards, advocacy groups across the political spectrum to evaluate them and often offer their viewpoints to policymakers, and ultimately states to assist with implementation. The reform was widely and decisively adopted, becoming a mainstay of American public schools.

The extraordinary success of this effort highlights both the power and the frailty of the Grand Bargain. Common Core—and Gates's involvement with it—has attracted withering criticism from all sides.[168] Republican governors and others on the political right have decried Common Core as unwanted federal usurpation. Teachers' unions and others on the left questioned whether Gates's immense funding push marginalized voices challenging Common Core's value and offering alternative solutions. When Microsoft entered the Common Core digital education business, some even suggested the initiative had ulterior motives.

The reaction to Gates's Common Core support offers a particularly vivid example of the fears the Grand Bargain went a long way toward allaying. Wielding political influence while seeming to blend business interests and philanthropic pursuits trips the same alarm bells Treasury and others sounded in the years leading up to the 1969 Act. Magnified by its immense scale, its intersection with high-profile policy issues, and its overlap with its founder's business interests, the controversy over Common Core suggests what might be commonplace in a world without the Grand Bargain.

Criticism of foundation efforts comes with the territory of elite philanthropy. Despite their growing influence, thanks in no small part to the Grand Bargain, foundations have been insulated from such concerns. Worries about foundations' ideological and policy commitments permeated the climate that ultimately led to major reform in 1969. That the Common Core controversy seems at all remarkable testifies to the success of the Grand Bargain in putting those fears to rest.

The Grand Bargain cemented by the 1969 Tax Reform Act channels foundations' tremendous power while providing benchmarks for determining whether their efforts should be praised or scorned. The investment and self-dealing rules set limits on how the innovations they seed can benefit their donors. The spending rules require foundations to come off the sidelines and the disclosure regime brings the resulting funding decisions into the light. Without such clearly defined boundaries, elite philanthropy may once again find itself mired in questions about its motives and methods.

Conclusion

For-profit philanthropy does not present a new challenge. The same threat to democratic ideals that philanthropy LLCs, commercially affiliated donor-advised funds, and strategic corporate philanthropy pose once forged the private foundation, the lynchpin of the 1969 Tax Reform Act. For-profit philanthropy reveals the limits of the Grand Bargain's ability to contain those pressures.

As for-profit philanthropy tools allow wealthy elites to elide the Grand Bargain's regulatory architecture, the wheel turns full circle. The concerns Treasury detailed half a century ago have reemerged as the private foundation's power over philanthropic targeting, timing, and transparency has waned. For generations, elites have been spared the powerlessness Rockefeller experienced when his bid for a nationally chartered foundation died in Congress. With for-profit philanthropy, elites increasingly court the public skepticism that frustrated him. Part III (chapters 6, 7, and 8) explores potential remedies for this resurgence of distrust.

The next chapter highlights the risks of inaction. The Grand Bargain brokered a truce grounded on trust. Its accountability measures allowed the public to trust elite philanthropists. They, in turn, adopted the vehicle to forestall more intrusive regulation and to burnish their own reputations. By turning away from the Grand Bargain's vehicle of choice, for-profit philanthropy risks undermining trust, and all it has gained for elite philanthropists in the process. Turning to two adjacent spaces where innovators are blurring the boundaries between doing business and doing social good, chapter 5 explores two disturbing visions of how a loss of trust in elite philanthropy might play out. Both the noble failure of the creation of specialized legal forms for social enterprise and the extraordinary success of ESG investing show how keenly felt the absence of trust can be.

5
In Search of Lost Trust

Philanthropy has always relied on trust. The public must believe that elites will deliver the benefits they promise. And elites must believe that their sincere efforts will not be disrupted by heavy-handed regulation and burdensome taxes. A half-century ago the Grand Bargain reassured policymakers and the public that elite philanthropy could be trusted. Elites deployed capital—wealth that could have been taxed away—according to their own private visions of the public good, subject to laws limiting the targets of their largesse, setting a timeline for their spending, and making their actions more transparently observable. This compact fueled decades of philanthropic achievement.

Yet the rise of for-profit philanthropy testifies to its diminished power. As the Grand Bargain's appeal to donors wanes, the accountability it generates will struggle to sustain public trust in elite philanthropy. Each of the for-profit philanthropic innovations surveyed in Part I (chapters 1, 2, and 3) unconstrained by legal limitations on the targeting, timing, and transparency of their giving documented in chapter 4, take the public's trust for granted.

For-profit philanthropists can be forgiven for viewing 1969's Grand Bargain as reflecting a narrow vision of philanthropy. That does not change the fact that eschewing the lightly regulated safe spaces created by foundations has increasingly become just another form of privilege. Elites might reasonably believe that once they decide to gamble their vast fortunes to benefit the public, they have nothing to lose. But undermining public trust in philanthropy could prove a grave error.

This chapter begins by identifying the combination of features the Grand Bargain employed to bolster public trust in philanthropy and the reasons its constraints were palatable to elites for five decades. The advent of for-profit philanthropy risks undermining this delicate truce. By way of warning, it also offers a glimpse into two potential futures in which trust has been lost. Venturing into two adjacent spaces, social enterprise and ESG investing, this chapter reveals the harm for-profit philanthropic "slacktivism" does by undermining trust, no matter whether it produces a feast of activity or a famine.

Like for-profit philanthropy, both these phenomena reject tradition to blend private profit and the pursuit of social good. Social enterprises are "for-profit ventures dedicated to generating both social good and financial returns."[1] ESG investing emphasizes environmental (E), social (S) and governance (G) concerns

For-Profit Philanthropy. Dana Brakman Reiser and Steven A. Dean, Oxford University Press. © Oxford University Press 2023. DOI: 10.1093/oso/9780190074500.003.0006

in composing and managing portfolios. Each has experienced a surge in interest mirroring the rise of for-profit philanthropy. They both show how easy it would be to allow the trust long supplied by the Grand Bargain to unravel and illustrate best- and worst-case scenarios for pursuing social returns without trust.

Investors—and other constituencies as well—rightly fear trusting that a social enterprise or ESG investment fund prioritizes environmental or social good when in fact it may not. A desire to constrain such insincere virtue signaling fueled the creation of specialized legal forms for social enterprises. More than two-thirds of US states have developed new legal forms to house social enterprises, which explicitly empower for-profit firms to serve a double bottom line. Just a few have adopted the low-profit limited liability company (L3C), but dozens more now offer firms a benefit corporation form, and Delaware—corporate law's behemoth—came on board with the public benefit corporation (PBC) in 2013.[2] Unfortunately, although these forms' new governance rules endeavored to persuade investors to trust double bottom-line firms, their feeble assurances of accountability have fallen flat thus far, generating underwhelming uptake of these new hybrid forms.

In ESG investing, the risk that slacktivism will devolve into insincere virtue signaling can be seen flaring each time a supposed ESG fund proves to invest in high-carbon impact firms or a study shows ESG funds invest and vote their shares much like their non-ESG-branded counterparts.[3] Regulators at the Securities and Exchange Commission and the US Department of Labor have taken notice and indicated skepticism about the unconventional dual missions of these funds (and their portfolio companies). Yet ESG funds are growing by leaps and bounds, drawing over $51 billion in assets in 2021 alone.

For-profit philanthropy too can fall prey to virtue signaling. The tepid embrace of social enterprise forms and the wariness critics and regulators have displayed toward ESG's claims remind us there are limits to the public's willingness to take the powerful at their word. When philanthropy LLCs, commercially affiliated DAFs, or strategic corporate philanthropists exaggerate their impact, or even conflate self-interest with the public interest, the blowback may not be limited to these innovative players. The halo of the entire philanthropic sector has been put in jeopardy by their cavalier attitude toward trust.

The explosive growth of ESG, however, shows how the Grand Bargain's golden age of philanthropy could end not with the bang of scandal but with the whimper of greed. Investors may believe they can trust claims of devotion to environmental and social impact made by ESG funds. More likely, those flooding into ESG funds believe that trust in their virtue simply does not matter. ESG funds do not ask investors to sacrifice financial returns to achieve environmental or social progress. Instead, they offer investment opportunities that align ESG with financial return. With ESG serving as a focal point at which social return and financial return converge, trust becomes superfluous.

That raises the specter of crowding out. Steering companies and funds to sustainable and responsible business approaches that also enrich investors would represent a remarkable contribution by capital markets. Indeed, true ESG victory would be achieved if dedicated ESG funds outcompete more conventional firms that refuse to take into account stakeholder concerns at all. That victory would be tainted if ESG also outcompetes ventures placing a heavier emphasis on public benefit as compared to private profit.

Should for-profit philanthropy follow ESG's trajectory of growth—unhindered by the fact that its promises seem as "meaningless [a]s wind in dry grass"[4]—the risk that it will displace other forms of philanthropy likewise increases. Philanthropic funds drawn to the natural focal point at the convergence of financial and social returns might pour into these new vehicles, serving only the slice of charitable purpose where business methods and philanthropic goals conveniently overlap. Leaving a dearth of capital to combat unmarketable societal ills unsuited to business-inflected solutions, such a philanthropic monoculture may be one neither the public nor policymakers would be inclined to preserve.

Trust forms the cornerstone of the Grand Bargain, binding even the most powerful elites to their promises. Public trust diluted by for-profit philanthropy's accommodation of donors' business interests and personal preferences leaves conventional philanthropy in a precarious spot. Without adequate accountability, public trust may yield to public skepticism, testing the public's resolve to refrain from asserting more direct control over elite wealth.

The loss of trust triggered by blurring the lines between profit and purpose can produce feast as well famine. This chapter shows why both outcomes represent a threat to philanthropy. A future in which for-profit philanthropy thrives without trust jeopardizes not just the public's support of its leaders and their innovative techniques but public confidence in the entire enterprise of elite philanthropy.

Trust within the Grand Bargain

The Grand Bargain reinforced a fragile public trust in elite philanthropy by allowing even the wealthiest and most powerful individuals and businesses to credibly commit to serving the public. The foundation form it designed combined state law's nondistribution constraint with a series of accountability safeguards to make philanthropy—and the philanthropists who practice it—worthy of trust. It transformed the derision the masses might display toward elite individuals, families, and firms claiming to act in the greater good—with resources the public might rightly claim—into admiration for their generosity.

This unlikely alchemy begins at the core of nonprofit law, with the nondistribution constraint.[5] Foundations, like all tax-exempt nonprofit organizations, are asset-locked entities. Once donated to them, funds cannot be retrieved by the donor.[6] Nor can this capital, or the profits earned deploying it, be distributed to individuals who control the organization. There are no foundation stockholders; directors cannot receive options or equity distributions; officers and employees cannot take a cut of its profits.

This arrangement imposes efficiency costs but provides an elegant solution to increasing trust in organizations producing public goods and services whose quality would otherwise be difficult to safeguard. Prohibiting those forming and leading a nonprofit from increasing their own rewards by skimping on the quality of goods or services they supply to beneficiaries vastly reduces their incentive to do so. We can worry less about foundations and other nonprofits serving the private interests of their founders and managers as they treat our maladies, educate our children, and protect our vulnerable environment. Foundation founders' commitments to pursue their philanthropy within asset-locked, distribution-constrained vehicles represented a first step toward securing the public's trust.

The public's belief that the nondistribution constraint's prohibition and the asset lock's directive would be followed remained critical. After decades of skirmishes, it became clear by 1969 that more was required to shore up trust that foundations would serve public rather than private ends. Operating charities like schools, soup kitchens, or animal welfare groups pursue their charitable goals directly, very much out in the open, led by volunteers and employees unrelated to each other beyond a shared commitment to their cause.

Foundations look quite different, engaging in charitable activity only by the indirect means of doling out funds, at the discretion of small groups with close ties to their founders and their families and related firms. Whereas operating charities must often solicit infusions of funding, foundations sit on endowments of assets they assure us they will use their acumen to grow and distribute for the benefit of society in perpetuity. Trust in another's good intentions comes more easily when verification becomes possible and when they have little to gain from deception, especially when they must continually prove themselves worthy to secure future funding.

The promise of philanthropy lies in using great wealth in the service of society, of others. But great wealth can also be used to finance a lavish lifestyle, to enhance one's own influence, and to secure a legacy of power into the future. To permit elite wealth to be retained (rather than taxed away) and deployed privately (rather than publicly) requires a leap of faith that foundations could be trusted to pursue altruistic purposes rather than self-serving ones. Given foundations' insularity, vast resources, and control by America's most powerful families and firms, this leap required more reassurance than a generic promise of locked-in assets or nondistribution. The Grand Bargain delivered this reassurance through its tripartite accountability regime of targeting, timing, and transparency.

Although retaining the broad and pluralistic vision of charity espoused by Section 501(c)(3), targeting rules mark potentially self-serving behavior as off limits. Transactions between a foundation and its substantial donors or managers might serve charitable objectives but also might line founders' and leaders' pockets. The self-dealing rules penalize this activity, clarifying boundaries. Foundation lobbying activity might further charitable goals but also might buy influence for its donor families and firms. The taxable expenditure rules impose strict sanctions on such efforts, warning foundations to stay well away from the blurry edges between altruism and self-interest. Even foundation investments must maintain a careful separation from founder influence. The excess business holding rules prohibit foundations from holding substantial stakes in for-profit companies not only to ensure diversification but also to avoid such stakes being used to mask advantages to their donors or leaders. The Grand Bargain's targeting provisions create bright-line rules and impose prophylactic sanctions on foundations skating too close to the nondistribution constraint, enhancing the public's ability to trust their good intentions.

Timing rules bolster this reassurance. Although the Grand Bargain lets foundations live forever, its payout rules ensure foundations must serve others. Foundations cannot simply stockpile the wealth of their donors on empty promises to serve society in some eventual future. Actual expenditures of 5 percent of their assets must go out the door each year. While from our modern perspective the degree of payout demanded may seem worth revisiting and increasing, a mandate for action itself represents a radical departure from the proscriptions the asset lock and nondistribution constraint impose. Forcing their hands—and their funds—into action likewise bolsters public trust that foundations will be active, not passive, serving others and not just themselves.

Without transparency rules, though, all these reassurances would ring hollow. Thanks to the Grand Bargain's disclosure rules, enhanced over the ensuing decades, the public need not blindly trust, it can verify. Foundations must share detailed information about their activities, their leaders—and even their donors—with not only regulators but with everyone. Forms 990-PF—accessible online in just a few clicks—allow the media and even casual observers to investigate whether a foundation deserves continued trust. Self-reported disclosures—particularly in a world in which funding for enforcement remains scarce—will not always ensure that if a foundation or its leaders seek to dissemble, they will attract attention and redress. Still, the presumption of openness and access the Grand Bargain's disclosure rules generate provides a powerful boost to the public trust in foundations.

A Commitment Device for Philanthropists

None of the Grand Bargain's careful interventions would have worked, of course, had the elite philanthropists of the time rebuffed them. As chapter 4 showed, the strategic deal at its heart provided key benefits to the wealthy individuals, families, and firms it invited to adopt the private foundation. On the surface, it offered tax advantages and perpetuity to adopters. On a deeper level, the 1969 reforms constructed a commitment device that elites badly needed. By embracing a narrower range of activities, a stricter timeline, and greater disclosure, elites broadcast a reliable signal of commitment to a wary public. Channeling contributions through purpose-built foundation forms allowed philanthropists to keep more burdensome regulations—or even wholesale tax reform—at bay.

For charities supported by the public, nonprofit law reassures potential donors that their contributions will always serve their interests. For a private foundation, commitment matters just as much, but for a different reason. Choosing a foundation allows some of society's most powerful actors to bind themselves to the proverbial mast—making "a unilateral promise" as "an inducement to the other player to make a choice in the mutual interest"[7]—not in order to persuade the public to give but to urge it not to take.

Creators of foundations work hard to deploy capital rather than to attract it. The bulk of the rules governing foundations put specific behaviors out of bounds. Rather than delivering active scrutiny of foundations—and the extent to which they deliver on their philanthropic promises—regulators punish failures linked to their insular natures. Designed to accommodate philanthropists free to opt out, the private foundation envisions an organization controlled by a private individual, family, or firm yet designed to reassure the public that the interests of the many will win out over those of a favored few.

The private foundation form not only allows a supplier of capital to make an enforceable promise, it helps deliver that signal to the public by providing "*evidence* that a commitment exists."[8] The foundation constitutes and broadcasts an enduring commitment to pursuing public ends with a clearly defined portion of a private fortune. Opting for a foundation serves as both a wealthy patron's pledge and a "delegation"[9] to state attorneys general and federal tax authorities to enforce it.

That robust commitment solves a problem described by one of the wealthiest Americans of any era. Andrew Carnegie once wrote that anyone "who dies . . . rich dies disgraced."[10] This may seem a strange sentiment for one so adept at acquiring wealth. But, of course, he did not object to accumulating fortunes. Quite the opposite, Carnegie believed that parting ordinary Americans from their earnings represented virtue rather than vice.

For Carnegie, though, accumulating wealth served only as a first act. Having thrived in business, a self-made man like Carnegie proved himself worthy of the power his wealth granted him. Carnegie imagined himself "but a trustee for the poor; intrusted for a season with a great part of the increased wealth of the community"—generated through his acumen and ruthlessness—and "administering it for the community."[11]

Putting that wealth to work on behalf of those less prosperous saved him from disgrace. Donations to charities controlled by others, of course, might have served equally well. Doing so openly might even offer a philanthropist absolution in the eyes of the public. But from Carnegie's point of view, donations of cash or property would still fall short.

Simply writing a check would deny the community the benefit of his proven genius. The Carnegies and Zuckerbergs of the world provide—he suggests—not only capital but leadership. As Carnegie concedes, the wealth they wield belongs to the community, merely entrusted to them "for a season" for the betterment of all. A tycoon generates wealth, then keeps both their share and the public's for a time before returning the latter to the community in a "far better" manner "than it could or would have done for itself."[12]

From Carnegie's perspective, both a heavily taxed magnate left with only their acumen and a skeptical public controlling its rightful share of their wealth would miss out on the benefits of their lost collaboration. Alone, Carnegie insists, they could not achieve what they could accomplish together. With no means of verifying their trustworthiness, however, ordinary Americans would be fools to so empower even the most talented individuals or firms. The Grand Bargain's private foundation plays a critical role in delivering that trust. A foundation allows a donor to retain control even after giving their wealth away but imposes an array of limits to reassure the public that their trust in its founders is warranted. In so doing, it elegantly enables elite ventures to be trusted to embody the public/private partnership Carnegie envisioned.

Redeeming Reputation

As daunting as the threat of more direct public control over their giving may be for the for-profit philanthropists steering clear of even lightly regulated philanthropy, another danger of losing the public's trust looms even larger. The public could challenge the very business practices that allow them to become extraordinarily wealthy and powerful. Carnegie was neither the first nor the last ruthless competitor to trade the title of monopolist for that of philanthropist in search of redemption.

For Bill Gates, philanthropy has served as precisely the sort of second act Carnegie urged. In his rise to digital domination as the head of Microsoft, Gates became the world's richest—and quite possibly most hated—man. Fortunately, the Bill and Melinda Gates Foundation redeemed him. Whatever surprises fate delivers, embracing the rigid constraints of the Grand Bargain allows him the freedom to deploy the public's share of the wealth "intrusted" to him.[13]

Despite Warren Buffet's resignation and his very public split with Melinda French Gates, Bill Gates remains free—within the clear bounds of the Grand Bargain—to lead his foundation with the same uncompromising vision he used to create what was, for a time, the world's most feared firm. For those who only know Bill Gates through his philanthropic work, it may be difficult to imagine the man at the height of Microsoft's power. Today, a handful of global digital giants tower above their rivals. In the 1990s, Microsoft stood alone and wielded its tremendous power to crushing effect.

In one sense, the Gates Foundation presents no mystery. It embodies the encore performance Carnegie predicted, with Bill Gates leaving the world better off in ways that would be difficult for a dispersed group—here, the millions of Microsoft customers that would have been marginally better off had its monopoly power been better contained—to replicate.[14] Gates focused on education and public health rather than on parks and libraries as Carnegie did, but he nevertheless followed in the footsteps of other profoundly wealthy men who did very well before doing good.[15] Decidedly conventional, Bill Gates's philanthropic path seems at once inevitable and impossible.

Viewed as leverage to force a ruthless magnate to embrace public service, the power of the Grand Bargain's tax breaks over someone like Gates seems modest at best. How do you bribe the richest man in the world? Keep in mind that, as recent ProPublica disclosures underscore, Gates had little need for charitable deductions to avoid paying tax.[16]

Charitable contributions generate valuable tax benefits for high-income professionals. But like other tech moguls, Gates earns the vast majority of his "wages" in the form of appreciation in the value of his Microsoft shares. Current income tax law ignores these accumulations. As a result, despite enjoying an enormous income on paper, the income tax represents little more than a nuisance for men such as Gates. Economists in the Biden administration paint a clear picture of why, estimating that the wealthiest Americans face a true tax rate of 8.2 percent on their income.[17] Given Gates's long history of fiercely preserving his independence it would be foolish to imagine a 10-percent-off coupon on philanthropy making a compelling case for embracing the Grand Bargain's wide-ranging demands and prohibitions.

Tax benefits tend to be seen as drawing those who could easily afford a bespoke approach into the world of regulated philanthropy, yet funding the Gates

Foundation did not represent an urgent tax planning necessity for its founder. Even the estate tax Carnegie envisioned as a goad to philanthropy, for a man in his forties, represented only a distant threat.[18] Nevertheless, by the end of 2000, the Gates Foundation had an endowment worth more than $20 billion.[19] For Gates, embracing tradition in the form of a private foundation represented a strategic decision, an end as well as a means. Before the Gates Foundation spent a single one of its billions of dollars, thanks to the Grand Bargain, the public could confidently gauge the broad sweep of its ambitions.

When viewed as a costly sacrifice made by—rather than a generous subsidy delivered to—philanthropists, the difference between the choices made by Bill Gates to embrace the Grand Bargain and by Mark Zuckerberg to reject it becomes clear. Gates's reputation meant he needed philanthropy law to broadcast evidence of a commitment to the public interest. In 2015, Zuckerberg did not.

In Facebook, Zuckerberg held the power to tell its story and that of the Chan Zuckerberg Initiative on his terms. Rather than a foundation, Chan and Zuckerberg designed a philanthropic vehicle carefully suited to their needs. Bill and Melinda Gates could have chosen a similar approach to philanthropy. The LLC form was available and $20 billion could buy a great deal of legal tailoring. Instead, they followed in the footsteps of countless others before them. The juxtaposition of the radically different paths followed by Gates and Zuckerberg in the face of apparently similar circumstances crystalizes the challenge of for-profit philanthropy.

For all the parallels between the men, Gates and Zuckerberg inhabited starkly different eras. Microsoft, like Rockefeller's Standard Oil—but unlike Facebook—faced an existential threat in the form of an antitrust suit when his foundation took shape. A breakup of the company seemed a distinct possibility.[20] In the years since, Facebook and others have come under increased scrutiny,[21] but at the time of CZI's founding Zuckerberg faced a regulatory tide falling along every dimension. With the threat of more intrusive regulation not just of his philanthropy but of his prosperous business seemingly safely off in the distance, the temporal flexibility, privacy, and control an LLC offers became that much more tempting. But tides shift and reputations falter.[22]

However strategically appealing the Grand Bargain's loose regulatory framework has been for the last half-century, for-profit philanthropists find its rules nettlesome. So CZI cavalierly dispenses with the foundation's political restrictions, the excess business holding rules designed to limit entanglement between donor firms and philanthropies, and the self-dealing rules designed to prevent sweetheart deals for insiders. Envisioning synergistic relationships fueled by technology and know-how developed in the donors' related for-profit venture, these half-century-old targeting rules begin to seem not quaint but dangerous.

Avoiding the Grand Bargain's timing rules allows CZI to set its own pace; sidestepping its transparency rules lets it curate its image. Without regard to what represents baby and what represents bath water, embracing the philanthropy LLC allows funders to rid themselves of the Grand Bargain. Stripped of the foundation's redemptive power, though, hard-fought philanthropic reputations could unravel along with ambitious philanthropic plans. Carnegie's ominous "disgrace" looms large.

For each philanthropist, whether to emulate Gates or Zuckerberg depends on the unique set of circumstances they face. Most will not face the extremity of being simultaneously the world's richest man and the villain in an epic antitrust lawsuit. Nor will they control the world's most influential media company.

The next Gates or Zuckerberg will face a more difficult decision. They will have the opportunity to either follow the well-worn byways of the Grand Bargain or the uncharted paths of for-profit philanthropy, but not both. In becoming a trustee for the community, blending their proven entrepreneurial talent and whatever wealth the public's restraint leaves at their disposal, they must decide what tools will best serve their objectives. If they choose for-profit philanthropy, they will face fewer restrictions but risk forever closing an avenue for redemption for themselves and those to follow.

Social Enterprise Hybrid Forms and Underutilization

The recent history of social enterprise law reveals how failures of trust can drain the life out of potentially valuable tools. The social enterprise hybrid form saga represents only the most recent chapter in a story tracing back to the rise of the limited liability company or perhaps even to the birth of the corporation itself. The former showed that new legal forms could swiftly become dominant, with LLCs far outpacing all other business firms within a few decades of its introduction. The latter, of course, showed how easy it can be for investors and entrepreneurs to collaborate to create successful business ventures. The rise of legislation enabling specialized forms for social enterprise reflected a confidence that the novelty of the LLC could be married to the power of the corporation to provide fuel for a new breed of business venture.

Social enterprises do not closely conform to a single ideal. Indeed, examples of every conceivable variation of blended business model have risen to prominence. The One World Play Project became known for its one-for-one strategy of donating ultra-durable soccer balls to underprivileged children with every purchase. Today, it pledges a percentage of its sales to support "play and sport" in communities across the globe.[23] TOMS Shoes, another early one-for-one social enterprise famous for donating a pair of shoes for each pair purchased, likewise now pledges it will give away one dollar for every three it makes.[24]

Other social enterprises demonstrate their commitments beyond profit through their employment practices. Greyston Bakery adopted an open hiring model in 1982. The for-profit bakery emphasized employee interests by pledging to hire workers with "no interviews, no background checks, and no resumes [] required to get a job."[25] The additional expenses it incurs through the need to train employees reflect a commitment to leavening profit-seeking with other goals, in this instance serving employees who might otherwise be unemployable.

Still other social enterprises' products themselves incorporate their social missions. Embrace Innovations got its start designing infant warmers for babies born in developing countries and rural communities without access to hospitals. With products marketed at a tiny fraction of the price of traditional incubators, Embrace's warmers have touched the lives of more than 350,000 premature infants around the globe.[26] Expansions from its core product target healthy sleeping more generally, donating part of the proceeds toward the original mission.

Interstitial by nature, social enterprises blend private profit and public benefit according to varied formulas. Accessing conventional capital markets might be anathema to social enterprises of one stripe, while tapping such a rich vein might be eminently sensible to others. Disruptive in ways both large and small, social entrepreneurs embrace contradiction by commandeering the tools of private enterprise to pursue public benefits. Inspired by that disregard for convention, policymakers created a collection of vehicles, each custom-designed to house ventures with more than one bottom line. The specialized legal forms for social enterprise they created promised to connect social entrepreneurs with mission-driven investors. That—or perhaps why—they have not offers a crucial lesson for for-profit philanthropy.

Despite the compelling vision of capitalism offered by social enterprise, these dozens of hybrid legal forms sit largely unused on the statute books of jurisdictions across the United States.[27] These forms are hard to find in the wild because they do little to assure investors and entrepreneurs they can trust one another. If for-profit philanthropy innovations sufficiently undermine trust, they might fall into similar disuse—and could take more conventional philanthropic approaches down with them.

The LLC Model

The L3C and the corporate social enterprise hybrids that followed share the DNA of an earlier entity. The LLC, designed not to build trust but to deliver tax breaks, freed entrepreneurs from the burdens of complexity and the corporate tax. Unknown in the United States until Wyoming enacted the first statute enabling firms to form as LLCs in 1977, the LLC is now available in every American jurisdiction and new businesses are far more likely to take this form than any other.[28] The runaway success of the LLC form was not immediate, however, and was tied specifically to a key development: the change in its tax treatment.

The LLC's staggering growth occurred because it forged for entrepreneurs an easy path to a nirvana of both limited liability and advantageous tax treatment. Since the advent of the modern income tax, the limited liability coveted by entrepreneurs generally came paired with a hefty tax bill. Unlike partnerships, which risk investors' personal liability for the debts of the business but whose profits are taxed but once, incorporated firms pay tax on each dollar of profit at the firm level, with only the remainder distributed to—and taxed again in the hands of—shareholders. Business owners long faced a choice between a second tax bill on a venture's profits and the risk of exposure to its liabilities.

The history of the tax law's rules for classifying entities as partnerships or corporations took a fateful turn in 1960. A Dr. Kintner aimed for corporate treatment and prevailed in court against tax authorities attempting to impose the partnership treatment that would ordinarily be desirable. "Kintner" tax regulations reversed that loss in 1960, in what would prove to be a short-sighted attempt to withhold corporate treatment from Dr. Kintner and his ilk. Those regulations made partnership tax treatment available, but only for well-advised and deep-pocketed taxpayers whose lawyers could wade through the regulations successfully.[29]

The LLC eventually changed that, but it took time and very specific circumstances. Indeed, in 1980, proposed regulations responded to the emergence of the LLC with considerable skepticism.[30] Under those proposed regulations, the absence of liability for all members—precisely what made them desirable—would have triggered corporate treatment for LLCs, but history went in a different direction. A decade and a half later, the LLC would make combining limited liability for all owners with a single level of tax as easy as checking a box.

The "tax nothing"—an LLC with a single owner—proved one of the "major breakthroughs" of the 1996 Al Gore-led effort to reinvent government.[31] The single-member LLC does not receive formal tax-exempt status, but each item of income or expense of this "disregarded entity" becomes an item on the owner's tax return. Unlike the 1980 proposal that would have made limited liability for all fatal to any effort to avoid the corporate tax, the arrival of the "check-the-box" era paved the way for the Chan Zuckerberg Initiative structured as an LLC—a philanthropic nothing.

Tax Breaks, Not Trust

As chapter 4 detailed, the tax rules governing foundations detail both what they must and what they may not do. Foundations must distribute 5 percent of their assets each year. They may not make risky investments or hold controlling stakes in businesses. The treatment of program-related investments implicates all three directives.[32] Although structured as an investment, a PRI must focus on mission, furthering the philanthropic objectives of a foundation rather than generating income.

A successful program-related investment not only allows a foundation to take on risk and control, it also helps satisfy a foundation's distribution requirement. Foundations can make program-related investments to satisfy the Grand Bargain's mandate that they open their pocketbooks each year to spend a portion of their assets. Satisfying this spending requirement by making PRIs rather than outright grants to charities tends to be an expensive, bespoke affair. Costly legal advice, government preapproval, or both have become table stakes in a complicated, potentially risky game. As a result, PRIs remain the exception rather than the rule.

The L3C—the first of many social enterprise hybrid entities—aimed to strip away red tape just as the LLC before it had. The L3C's creators hoped to deliver a trouble-free route to program-related investments, emulating the LLC's success in providing ready access to preferred regulatory treatment. Adding a few features drawn from the program-related investment rules to the standard LLC framework, the L3C form is available to entities that "significantly further the accomplishment of one or more charitable or educational purposes," and "would not have been formed but for the company's relationship to the accomplishment of charitable or educational purposes."[33]

The L3C never achieved the regulatory breakthrough its creators sought. Adopters face no scrutiny of their social mission bona fides at the entity's inception; they merely file with the secretary of state. Moreover, the form comes with no assurances an adopting entity will remain devoted to its social mission. It can throw off the L3C mantle and transform into an ordinary LLC without any notice to investors, regulators, or the public at large merely by changing its operations such that it "ceases to satisfy any one of the [statute's purpose] requirements."[34] As a result, federal tax rule makers have shown no interest in promulgating check-the-box approval for L3Cs to receive program-related investments, and multiple bills put forward in Congress to do the same have gone nowhere.

That reluctance can be understood as an effort to prevent foundations from abusing program-related investments, virtue signaling by camouflaging conventional investments as charity. Had an L3C-linked PRI pre-clearance regime taken root, regulators would have lost the ability to vet specific investments without any reliable assurances they would conform or continue to conform to program-related investment requirements, undermining the foundation payout requirement in the process. Today, making a program-related investment remains as burdensome as ever and early progress by the L3C in state legislatures has stalled.

Corporate Hybrids without Concessions

The L3C failed to replicate the success of the LLC. But its demise did not dampen interest in hybrid legal entities. Drawing on the lessons of the LLC's achievements and the L3C's disappointments, corporate variants emerged, pivoting from pursuing program-related investments from foundations to chasing the private and public capital markets. State legislatures widely adopted the benefit corporation form and Delaware created its public benefit corporation with hopes of recapturing the magic of the LLC, but without repeating the L3C's mistakes.

At first glance, the swift uptake of the benefit corporation form by state legislatures appeared to accomplish this feat, thanks to the tireless efforts of a social enterprise entrepreneur. B Lab[35] brought legislatures flocking to these new legal forms. Organized as a traditional charity, B Lab offers its imprimatur to eligible businesses. Ventures that implement governance requirements to consider stakeholder interests and achieve a sufficiently high score on B Lab's self-assessment tool earn the right to license the B Corp mark and display it on their websites and products.[36] B Lab drafted model benefit corporation legislation, adding a number of features to the standard corporate form to broadcast the blended value espoused by social enterprises. Within ten years, more than thirty states had adopted statutes roughly following this model legislation. Companies could embrace the new form at inception or, with shareholder approval, by conversion.

Benefit corporation statutes expand required corporate purposes to include a general public benefit, defined as a "material positive impact on society and the environment, taken as a whole, from the business and operations of a benefit corporation assessed taking into account the impacts of the benefit corporation as reported against a third-party standard."[37] A benefit corporation must use a standard developed by a third party—either B Lab's standard or another's. Only the adopting firm need find itself to have a material positive impact, however. No approval from B Lab or any other outside third-party certifier is required.

In addition, the benefit corporation form requires fiduciaries to consider nonshareholder constituencies as they make their decisions. Fiduciaries must consider these other constituencies but need not prioritize nonshareholder interests, and there can be no monetary liability under the statutes even if fiduciaries ignore them completely. Benefit corporation statutes also impose disclosure requirements demanding annual reporting to shareholders and the public, although (unsurprisingly given the absence of penalties for failures to make the mandated disclosures) noncompliance is rampant.[38]

Delaware's enactment of its public benefit corporation statute, distinct from but not dissimilar to the benefit corporation statutes springing up across the country, cemented the corporate social enterprise hybrid as a standard offering on the menu of legal forms. By that time, the appearance of new forms for social enterprise had become almost routine. But Delaware's public benefit corporation represented something different. For nearly a century, Delaware has been the preferred legal home for US public companies. An accommodating legal regime and a dedicated court have made the tiny state a giant in the corporate world.

When Delaware embraces a new legal entity, the results can be seismic. Delaware has more than one million LLCs registered in the state.[39] Many hoped its public benefit corporation might gain similar prominence. Delaware law provides that public benefit corporations are firms "intended to produce a public benefit or public benefits and to operate in a responsible and sustainable manner" and imposes fiduciary directives to "balance" "stockholders' pecuniary interests, the best interests of those materially affected by the corporation's conduct, and [a] public benefit" it must identify in its charter.[40] Shareholders can track a public benefit corporation's progress through its required disclosures and hold fiduciaries accountable through derivative litigation. But the statute specifically noted that a failure to balance those interests will not ordinarily constitute a fiduciary failure.[41]

Although Delaware lagged in enacting legislation to create a social enterprise hybrid corporation, the same was once true when the state paved the way for its first LLC. Despite the late start, it remains possible that the Delaware public benefit company might replicate the LLC's achievement, this time blending the social returns of a charity with the capital market curb appeal of the corporation. But it will need to solve a daunting trust problem to do so.

Allowing Defection

Alas, although legislative adoptions are thriving, thus far adoption of specialized corporate forms by actual entities has not followed the sharp upward trajectory of LLCs.[42] The new hybrids have not provided social entrepreneurs the capital market access the corporate form promises. Whereas Delaware's LLC flourished, thus far, its PBC has not.

To understand why requires attention to features of the corporation that no longer seem remarkable. When the Dutch East India Company barred owners from withdrawing their investments, some investors undoubtedly thought it radical. Yet that innovation allowed investors to credibly commit to ambitious ventures, in turn allowing the ventures themselves to take a longer view. Secure in the knowledge that they need not forgo richly rewarding voyages in order to keep cash on hand to mollify skittish investors, managers could pursue bold visions.

Without adequate accountability, investors intent on social impact have not flocked to the hybrid corporation as for-profit investors embraced its conventional counterpart. Merely by purchasing stock, investors irrevocably commit their capital to a corporation. Corporate social enterprise hybrids promise to allow investors to do the same with respect to a social enterprise's mission. But the reality of social enterprise hybrids looks quite different.

In theory, buying shares in a Delaware public benefit corporation allows investors to demonstrate their resolve to support the hybrid's social mission. Even if that investor later decides that, for example, abandoning an open-hiring model would boost profits, management need not fear. As long as the venture remains subject to the Delaware public benefit corporation statute, that shareholder has no power to challenge its balance of doing well and doing good.

Viewed generously, the public benefit corporation and its counterparts represent a simple variation on the corporate form, calving social entrepreneurs and like-minded investors off from the capital market iceberg.[43] And, in theory, since no individual shareholder can withdraw their commitment to social mission, it could work. Social enterprise hybrids hoped they had mastered the Dutch East India Company's long-ago trick. Unfortunately, on closer inspection, the mission "lock-in" provided by the hybrid social enterprise corporation falls apart.

Hybrid forms allow entrepreneurs determined to combine mission and profit to safely raise capital just as easily as a conventional corporation. But although founders using these forms may have nothing to fear from any individual shareholder, they have everything to fear from shareholders as a group. When they neither know nor control those shareholders, any apparent lock-in becomes illusory. The shareholders of a benefit corporation have the collective power to strip away its public benefit mission and convert the organization into a conventional corporate form, though doing so often requires a supermajority vote.[44] Imagine the Dutch East India Company trying to set sail if all of its shareholders could collectively withdraw their capital whenever conditions seemed unfavorable for the voyage!

Delaware's public benefit corporation began by gating entry to the form with a 90 percent shareholder vote requirement and exit with a two-thirds majority.[45] But amendments in 2015 and 2020 reduced that 90 percent threshold to two-thirds and then eliminated the supermajority requirement entirely.[46] These legal forms may have been created to facilitate trust between shareholders and entrepreneurs but—lacking adequate protections against investor defection—they emphatically do not.[47]

The L3C failed to provide social enterprises with easy access to one heavily regulated source of capital. If the Delaware public benefit corporation delivered even a sliver of the investment captured by conventional Delaware corporations to double-bottom-line ventures, the L3C's failure would be a forgotten chapter in the larger story of the social enterprise hybrid's rise. Unfortunately, in the years since Delaware's much-anticipated embrace of the social enterprise hybrid corporation, few hints of that success have materialized.[48]

Permanently locking in investor capital allowed the Dutch East India Company to plan long, risky voyages. Unfortunately, social enterprise hybrid corporations do not tie shareholders to serving the public good. If the shareholders of the Dutch East India Company could have collectively walked away at any time, those voyages would never have happened. Unlike conventional charities—which may not shed their mission or enrich insiders no matter how profitable they might become—a public benefit corporation stands only a shareholder vote away from becoming an ordinary for-profit corporation.

Serving Many Masters

Even short of conversion, hybrid corporate statutes require merely that firm decision makers "consider" or "balance" interests beyond shareholder wealth maximization. Directors of a Delaware public benefit corporation not only may, but in fact must, pursue a second bottom line but face no consequences should they fail to do so.[49] These provisions mark only a modest departure from older "constituency statutes" that offer corporate directors the discretion to, should they choose, affirmatively consider interests beyond those of shareholders.

Constituency statutes protect directors but do not demand anything of them. Social enterprise hybrid corporate forms, by contrast, purport to do precisely that. Where constituency statutes grant permission, allowing directors to consider the factors they wish, hybrid corporate forms require that directors look beyond the interests of shareholders.[50] They must consider their interests. They must balance them. But hybrid forms do not prioritize social mission, nor do they instruct directors on how to they should navigate serving their many masters.

Without such direction, enforcement becomes exceedingly difficult. Even if a motivated benefit corporation shareholder brought an action challenging its fiduciaries' consideration of the interests of nonshareholder constituencies, a defendant director could be absolved by corporate minutes documenting a discussion of those interests and a decision to elevate shareholder interests above them. In a case against a Delaware public benefit corporation alleging that a directorial decision harmed the public benefit its charter dedicated it to promote, it could likewise defend this particular decision as balancing the public interest with the financial well-being of its stockholders. As has long been the critique of constituency statutes, he who serves too many masters may be accountable to none.[51]

Liability limitations and weak disclosure mandates only exacerbate the structural accountability problems of benefit corporations and Delaware public benefit corporations. The model benefit corporation legislation specifically abjures personal liability for directors based on "failure of the benefit corporation to pursue or create general public benefit."[52] As noted earlier, the Delaware statute likewise eliminates personal liability for failures in balancing under the duty of loyalty or requirement of good faith.[53]

Both types of regimes do also provide for disclosure—the benefit corporation to the public and the public benefit corporation to shareholders—but neither punishes failures to disclose, and studies of compliance thus far generally show rates in the single digits.[54] Without any potential penalty for failing to meet even the anemic demands they place on directors and little reason to expect organizational transparency, investors have no reason to trust these forms to discipline directors.

With help from legal forms such as Delaware's public benefit corporation, private actors gained a new vocabulary to express their commitment to a double bottom line. But accountability and transparency for social enterprises have proven elusive. The forms' governance rules provide no assurance that entrepreneurs and investors can trust each other. The lack of clear priorities makes enforcement difficult and the absence of sanctions for betrayals renders the statutes toothless. The fewer than ten thousand adoptions of these forms in the last ten years[55] offers powerful evidence that they failed to solve the trust problem at the core of social enterprise's attempts to raise capital.

For-Profit Philanthropy's Lessons from Underutilized Social Enterprise Forms

Social enterprise defies the rigid boundary that once separated nonprofit and for-profit ventures. US law has embraced social enterprises by creating a suite of legal forms designed specifically to allow entrepreneurs to showcase their intention to pursue a double-bottom line. For centuries, the corporate form has provided traditional entrepreneurs with access to capital markets. For a time, the social enterprise hybrid corporation seemed poised to do the same for these unconventional ventures.

The story of the social enterprise hybrid form's underutilization reveals what can happen—or more accurately, not happen—when sufficient trust does not exist. Regulators did not trust the L3C enough to endow it with automatic program-related investment status. The years that followed saw many more social enterprise hybrid forms emerge but few real breakthroughs.

In addition to the traditional focus on generating profits for owners, these blended ventures also identified other core constituencies. Entrepreneurs gained the power to signal aspirations beyond maximizing shareholder wealth. But without trust, the use of social enterprise hybrid forms has been limited.

The Dutch East India Company used lock-in to ensure it could trust investors to support its boom-or-bust voyages. The Delaware PBC will not fulfill its potential until it and the other social enterprise hybrid corporations lock in their social missions. If a benefit corporation's or public benefit corporation's shareholders lose their nerve, they can convert and leave burdensome social mission and stakeholders behind. Without more, adopting a social enterprise hybrid form offers investors little assurance that a firm and its leaders will—even in their day-to-day efforts—pursue the public benefits their charters advertise. Without lock-in or robust enforcement regimes, social entrepreneurs cannot safely set sail.

Social enterprise offers one vision of for-profit philanthropy's future. Innovation is exploding. Thanks to the rise of the philanthropy LLC and the donor-advised fund, the wealthiest Americans have never enjoyed more modes of giving. Strategic corporate philanthropy thrives as means to drive shareholder return.

But, by design, these new tools reduce regulatory control over elite philanthropy. By turning its back on the Grand Bargain, for-profit philanthropy curtails public oversight. In truth, even wealthy funders may not know whether a philanthropy LLC will remain committed to a cause or when—or perhaps whether—commercially affiliated donor-advised funds will make contributions to charities. The public must take corporate donors' words that their giving represents philanthropy rather than virtue signaling.

Without commitments to sustain public trust, for-profit philanthropy risks the same fate that swallowed the L3C and that now looms over corporate hybrid forms for social enterprise. And that irrelevance may actually be a relatively benign outcome. If for-profit philanthropy taints traditional philanthropy, the public may find the prospect of allowing the wealthy to control vast flows of philanthropic capital no longer holds the appeal it did half a century ago.

Elite philanthropy needs trust, not to *attract* capital but to *retain* it. The Grand Bargain represented a truce, not a capitulation by the public to the preferences of wealthy donors. Should for-profit philanthropic innovations raise sufficient doubt, voters hold the power to strip this capital away. Steeply progressive taxation would put the public firmly in control of capital that for decades has flowed through a vanishingly small number of private hands. For-profit philanthropy's trust gap runs the risk that the public may decide that they can no longer trust the elites that grew wealthy at their expense to save them.

The public has largely chosen not to invest in social enterprise, despite an extraordinary outpouring of legal innovation designed to persuade them to do so. Without trust, investors and entrepreneurs have found themselves hunting for small game alone when cooperation would have allowed them to bring home a much bigger prize. Trapped in what economists call a stag hunt—a variation on the well-known prisoner's dilemma in which trust brings rich rewards rather than simply minimizing punishment—they have received little help from much-ballyhooed social enterprise hybrid forms. Should they discover that elite philanthropists have unilaterally abandoned the Grand Bargain, the public may decide to withdraw their support as well, putting the philanthropic stag forever out of reach.

ESG and the Risks of Victory

Despite more than a decade of efforts by state legislators to build a hybrid social enterprise legal form to generate a virtuous circle of private investment and public benefits, the statutes they have rushed to enact have increasingly fallen flat. Identifying trust as the culprit suggests these statutes do not do enough to prevent virtue signaling. Their lack of lock-in and weak governance fan fears that social enterprises will prioritize financial returns over social good. Founders and ventures seeking to legitimize claims that they embrace a double bottom line will need to look elsewhere.

The peril of virtue signaling, of course, exists beyond social enterprise. It lurks everywhere individuals and firms assert they will "do well by doing good." The next example of slacktivism shows how virtue signaling can sometimes seem not a bug but a feature.

Social good will at times overlap quite considerably with financial wisdom. For their own safety, employees, customers, and community members would prefer products not be made with dangerous chemicals. Given the specter of lawsuits, a corporation's stockholders—even if concerned only with financial return—will frequently share that preference. As chapter 3 noted, shareholder and stakeholder interests can converge.

But although possibilities do exist for financial and social return to coincide, doing good often requires economic sacrifice. To avoid this pain but still claim the mantle of blended value, social benefits can be overstated (a phenomenon so common in the environmental context that it has earned the epithet "greenwashing"). Managers can surreptitiously hide the real costs of the social agendas they adopt. They may even shunt them off onto vulnerable constituencies.

Even with the best of intentions, in the realm of social good, values will inevitably be disputed, and metrics contested. The risk of virtue signaling masquerading as impact hangs over any claim to serve a double bottom line. Yet if social enterprise hybrids languish on the shelves like the 1980s ill-fated "new Coke," America's demand for ESG investments recalls its thirst for bottled water. That success reveals both how virtue signaling has come to play a key role in ESG's rise and a troubling truth about for-profit philanthropy.

Just as corporate America and Main Street embraced a healthy and profitable—albeit environmentally costly—alternative, both investors and money managers have enthusiastically embraced ESG's blend of public and private benefits. In 2021, mutual fund companies launched one hundred twenty-one sustainable mutual funds and ETFs and the sustainable fund category as a whole received inflows of $69.2 billion.[56] That capped a decade of extraordinary growth in ESG investing, appearing to deliver the successful blend of virtue and commerce that hybrid legal forms have not. Unfortunately, ESG may merely illustrate the commercial power of virtue signaling.

The differing fortunes of legal forms for social enterprise and ESG investing present a puzzle. Trust seems essential to one but not the other. The absence of any regulatory framework—even the weak safeguards provided by social enterprise hybrid forms—to provide accountability to investors regarding industry claims has done nothing to frighten off either retail or institutional investors. Whatever shared suspicions keep social entrepreneurs and investors from joining forces, confidence in ESG seems to come easily.

The secret to this astonishing victory may lie in a cagey shift of goalposts. Rather than persuading would-be investors that they will resist the lure of greenwashing, ESG instead embraces virtue signaling as a means of improving the bottom line. Like the modern business case for corporate social responsibility described in chapter 3, the theory and practice of ESG today rests predominantly on a view that environmental and social sustainability and good governance drive profit rather than detract from it. If choosing ESG top performers will, particularly over the long run, yield high returns for investors, the growing crop of ESG funds can maintain a quest in pursuit of conscience quite compatible with investor returns.

ESG Investing for Market Returns

The roots of ESG investing, of course, lie in appeals to sacrifice. Negative screens,[57] the simplest mechanisms in ethical forms of investing, can be traced to religious practices forswearing investments opposed to their core tenets. Once focused on "sins" like tobacco, guns, alcohol, and gambling, negative screening can be applied in a fund with virtually any focus, simply by refraining from purchasing shares in companies operating in the industries it believes investors will have an appetite to avoid. Although some investors embraced such ethical investments, the field was decidedly niche for decades.

Over time, however, funds with negative screens operating in the real world demonstrated that forgoing profitable investments incompatible with one's values need not make a portfolio uncompetitive. Some studies do show that negative screening can reduce yields.[58] Others, however, suggest that excluding specific categories of businesses tends to have no impact on investment returns.[59] That negative screening need not drive down returns might seem surprising, but at least in some cases doing well and doing good have proven to be compatible.

In truth, if presented with the holdings of such a modern negatively screened fund, a casual observer might not even suspect it represents anything out of the ordinary. Funds such as the Vanguard FTSE Social Index Fund, launched in 2000, avoid adult entertainment, alcohol, tobacco, cannabis, arms, and fossil fuels but still manage to count household names such as Apple and Tesla among their largest holdings.[60] Ethical perhaps, but a hair shirt such funds are not.

The dramatic rise in ESG investing has occurred along with a sea change in the investment practices on which it relies. Since 2000, when that Vanguard negative-screened fund represented the cutting edge of ethical investing, the range of strategies employed by investment funds claiming to prioritize values beyond financial gains has evolved. Negative screening remains popular. But more ambitious approaches have gone beyond exclusion to embrace a variety of affirmative means of combining the goals of pursuing profits and sustainability.

The broad umbrella of ESG funds today uses diverse techniques and granular approaches to identify investees. Portfolio investments might be selected, for example, by applying minimum criteria on key ESG measures[61] or based on firms outperforming their peers on ESG matters relevant to their industry.[62] Or a fund might identify particularly environmentally or socially focused companies and weight them more heavily in its portfolio.[63]

Mutual fund families have the resources to search for investments that suit a variety of financial and nonfinancial goals.[64] They also have the power to drive change in laggards. That influence becomes particularly important for the index funds that now dominate the market.[65]

Passive strategies like that used to compose an S&P 500 index fund preclude picking winners to add and losers to remove from their portfolios, whether on grounds of financial return, ESG performance, or both. But share ownership grants even passive funds the right to vote those shares on behalf of their investors. Increasingly, they are touting their engagement—through both voting and informal influence—as well-suited to nudge management toward stronger ESG commitments.[66]

The election in 2021 to ExxonMobil's board of three candidates put forward by a hedge fund with an environmental agenda offers one of the most striking examples of this influence to date.[67] The tiny Engine No. 1 hedge fund controlled an incredibly small minority of the firm's shares. Its success relied on persuading the Big Three investment fund companies (Vanguard, BlackRock, and State Street) as well as major pension funds like the California public employees and teacher's union and the New York's Common Retirement Fund to join their cause. The advocacy behind this effort did not, however, call upon mutual fund operators and pension fiduciaries to cast their votes based on environmental conscience. It argued that ExxonMobil would miss a critical market opportunity on the scale of bottled water—and risk a future of stranded assets—unless it picked up efforts to explore and exploit non-fossil fuel–based energy.

In these efforts by branded ESG funds—as well as the conventional funds now increasingly adding ESG factors into their decisions on portfolio composition and engagement—ESG serves not merely as an indicator of good corporate citizenship. It has become a factor in predicting long-term return, a way to minimize systemic risk, or even as a proxy for good management. A 2020 McKinsey study highlights the shift in perceptions about ESG impact on shareholder value. Its authors found that "83 percent of C-suite leaders and investment professionals say they expect that ESG programs will contribute more shareholder value in five years than today" and "just 3 percent of respondents believe such programs reduce shareholder value."[68]

Among ESG funds focused more narrowly on particular industries, recent counts of fund launches and flows are also concentrated in sectors like clean energy, which also generate large returns.[69] The vast number of funds in existence means that one can find an ESG fund to suit almost any taste. And as no less an investment authority than Morningstar put it: "as more sustainable funds build competitive performance records, lingering doubts about underperformance have diminished."[70]

Regulators Sound Conflicting Cautionary Notes

The regulatory response to ESG suggests no clear explanation for an ESG premium. An array of regulators remains vigilant to threats posed by ESG, but they seem unable to agree on whether virtue signaling represents a feature or a bug. The Securities and Exchange Commission monitors capital markets to ensure that individual investors have the access they need to make informed decisions. Together with the Department of Labor, they protect the nest eggs of countless savers invested through intermediaries who might fail to faithfully safeguard their clients' assets.

ESG and Markets

Most Americans do not hold shares directly. Although more than half of families have a stake in the stock market, in 2019 only about 15 percent owned the shares of individual companies.[71] For most people, investment and pension funds allow them to participate in the equity markets without purchasing a single share of stock. In defined-benefit pension funds, future beneficiaries will not even select the investment vehicles tasked with generating the returns on which their retirements rely.

In their role as antifraud watchdogs, securities regulators have good reason to worry about issuers or fund creators peddling virtue signaling alone. They care particularly about ensuring that ESG alternatives do not charge higher prices than their conventional alternatives without good reason. If ESG investments offer nothing different than conventional funds, branding them as unconventional would be as problematic as labeling ordinary apples "organic"—especially if they were then sold at a premium price.

In a 2020 request for comments, securities regulators articulated these concerns directly.[72] The Securities and Exchange Commission's Names Rule strives to prevent fund creators from misleading investors, knowing how important names can be to investor decision-making. It deems a fund name misleading if it suggests its investments are in certain asset types, industries, countries, or geographies when the fund fails to invest at least 80 percent of its value accordingly.[73] Thus, for example, if a mutual fund changed nothing about its investment strategy while rebranding itself a "pan-African" investment opportunity, they may intervene.

Yet funds can use terms like "growth" and "value" to refer to a range of investment strategies without attracting scrutiny under the Names Rule.[74] Securities regulators discount such descriptions as the financial equivalent of a grocer's boast that their apples taste delicious, exempting them from its requirement that the name of each fund accurately describes its contents.[75] Such claims remain subject to the blanket securities law protection against fraud and deceit,[76] but purchasers must judge for themselves how tasty the fruit—or impressive a fund's returns—will be.

Whether ESG designations implicate that rigid 80 percent rule (think organic) or the fraud standard ("these apples are delicious!") depends on whether they qualify for the investment strategy safe harbor. Regulators have noted "confusion" on that particular question, and in 2022 issued a proposed rule clarifying how to treat ESG names.[77] Under it, a fund using ESG factors as a significant or primary consideration for investment decisions or articulating stated ESG impact goals would be subject to the 80 percent rule and the general antifraud regime, as well as enhanced disclosure obligations. For a fund merely invoking ESG as part of a more conventional strategy, using the term in its name would be impermissibly misleading.

The proposed expansion of the Names Rule to funds signaling a particular investment focus would affect funds outside the ESG landscape. Still, the SEC highlighted "potential investor protection issues . . . with names that suggest an investment focus in companies that meet certain ESG standards" and its desire to "prevent potential greenwashing."[78] Regardless of the outcome of the debate over the Names Rule, ESG will remain a source of controversy as long as uncertainty remains over what it means to investors.

Cutting-edge research highlights the potential for confusion created by inconsistent use of the term "ESG." A small 2019 study comparing ESG and non-ESG offerings in the mutual fund and ETF space found substantial convergence between their holdings and voting practices, though ESG funds tended to have higher fees.[79] A larger empirical study in 2021 found more robust differentiation between ESG and non-ESG funds.[80]

Its review of fund voting on shareholder proposals, for example, concluded that their ESG claims were meaningful, representing more than mere virtue signaling at the same time that "investors in [ESG] funds might do a bit better, on average, than investors in non-ESG funds."[81] Yet another study found the reverse, observing that conventional funds held portfolio firms with fewer labor and environmental law violations and lower fines as well as lower carbon emissions than ESG-branded funds managed by the same financial institutions.[82] Regulators' growing impatience reflects real confusion over the proper metrics for ESG, which remain hotly contested and often proprietary.

ESG and Pensions

Whereas the Securities and Exchange Commission focuses on the threat of virtue signaling, the evolving position of the Department of Labor on ESG investing over a quarter-century reveals the opposite concern. As the regulator tasked with oversight of pension funds governed by the Employee Retirement Income Security Act of 1974, it wrestles with whether pension fiduciaries making ESG investments might focus too enthusiastically on environmental or sustainability gains. Failure to adequately prioritize financial returns risks impoverishing pension funds, precisely what the law guards against.

The Department's guidance on the subject has shifted dramatically from administration to administration. In 1994, it expressed an openness to managers taking ESG into account by treating stakeholder benefits as a tiebreaker between otherwise equivalent investments.[83] In October 2008, new guidance took a decidedly more skeptical tone, indicating its view that "fiduciaries who rely on factors outside the economic interests of the plan . . . will rarely be able to demonstrate compliance with ERISA."[84]

In 2015, the Department issued a new interpretive bulletin clarifying that its 2008 guidance should not unduly dissuade retirement plan fiduciaries from ESG investing. Then the Trump administration revised that stance again. While noting that in some circumstances, "ESG issues present material business risk or opportunities," it warned that "[f]iduciaries must not too readily treat ESG factors as economically relevant to the particular investment choices at issue when making a decision."[85] It followed this guidance with a new regulation stating explicitly that "[a] fiduciary's evaluation of an investment or investment course of action must be based only on pecuniary factors."[86] Shortly after President Biden took office, the Department indicated its intention not to enforce this rule and to review the question once again.[87] A similar back and forth has occurred over the issue of fiduciary voting on ESG shareholder proposals, and ESG investing by pension fiduciaries has become a political football.

A Focal Point

A simple through line emerges from this tangle of conflicting claims, conclusions, and regulatory mandates. If ESG and financial returns converge, regulators could ensure that investors receive a meaningful ESG benefit and at the same time prevent pension fiduciaries from sacrificing yield in favor of ESG gains. When it does not water down financial returns but bolsters them, neither virtue signaling nor financial underperformance alarm bells sound when an investment prioritizes ESG.

Viewed this way, ESG reveals itself to serve as a focal point, allowing investment managers and investors to find their way. With fund managers and their clients naturally drawn to a spot where the ESG premium allows profit and purpose to coexist, regulators can rest easy regarding the safety of all those nest eggs. For the same reason, ESG should elicit equanimity from securities regulators. ESG investments that meet or beat their non-ESG comparators can satisfy both the mandate that investors receive a meaningful ESG benefit and the requirement that they not sacrifice yield.

When Larry Fink first wrote in his annual letter to CEOs to rally them toward ESG, he adopted precisely this focal point perspective. Companies that failed to gravitate toward ESG would, over the long term, Fink warned, be left behind.[88] As would be expected when the head of the world's largest money management firm turns conventional devotion to shareholder value maximization on its head, the world took notice.[89]

Collapsing the Categories

Fink's optimistic vision suggests that rather than overweighting financial returns as compared to social gains as market regulators fear or, vice versa, as troubles pension watchdogs, ESG investing neatly collapses those categories. Meta-studies support that view, indicating that ESG funds either match or outperform their conventional counterparts, though temporary shocks can be disruptive for either variety. That even ordinary funds often rely on ESG factors in making portfolio management decisions suggests broad consensus that ESG does not demand sacrifices on the part of investors but enriches them.

All of which suggests that investors need no special regulations, restrictions, or disclosures to trust in a fund or manager's ESG commitments. If their social returns boost financial yield rather than competing with it, the simple law of supply and demand will suffice. Standard investment market dynamics would persuade managers to seek out investments and strategies where they coexist.

Although not universally accepted, the convergence of financial and ESG performance does not lack for explanations. One particularly tempting account after the outsized returns ESG funds posted during 2020 is that ESG strategies offer risk protection—especially from systemic risk that cannot be diversified away.[90] Environmental stewardship generally and climate change readiness in particular offer a particularly vivid example. Losses due to a lack of preparedness for a warming planet may be most obvious in industries like fossil fuels and casualty insurance, yet all businesses will suffer if life on Earth becomes markedly more difficult. And the blistering 2022 performance of fossil fuel producers underscores that one should expect surprises.

It may be hard to predict which companies and industries will benefit from a warming planet. But, inevitably, some will. The impact of COVID-19 did boost some firms' performance (Zoom comes immediately to mind). Investors and the business press noted frequently that ESG funds fared better through the early days of the comprehensive global economic disruption the pandemic produced.[91] This could be explained simply by the underrepresentation of traditional energy firms in ESG fund portfolios, as well as their frequent overrepresentation of tech firms. ESG performance may also be making firms more resilient, notwithstanding their more recent fall to earth as oil stocks boomed.

An even broader view suggests ESG acts simply as a proxy for good management—especially management focused on long-term value. Attending to a wider range of concerns requires broad and sustained focus and information-gathering on multiple fronts. Perhaps firm leaders managing across the dimensions of financial return, environmental sustainability, social value, and good governance are simply excellent managers. This argument that ESG performance offers an unconventional method of predicting management success could also explain the significant growth in active funds using ESG in portfolio selection and management and even in passive funds emphasizing ESG engagement.

A Zero-Sum Game

However much truth lies in each of these explanations for ESG's success, another simpler possibility exists. Virtue signaling might actually be the key after all, with ESG broadcasting a focal point to companies, fund managers, and investors. This phenomenon could be described in terms of the cost of capital. Although Fink does not put it in precisely these terms, Blackrock's influential role in capital markets allows his firm's pursuit of ESG to directly increase the cost of capital for firms that refuse to take ESG seriously. Being blacklisted by Blackrock might not be a fatal blow but could be costly in a financial sense.

As ESG companies became attractive enough to influential investors relative to their conventional counterparts—whatever the reason—increased supply would reduce their cost of capital. These lower capital costs for ESG firms translate into higher returns for ESG fund investors. Blackrock's embrace of ESG would have precisely that impact.

This tidy resolution leaves one problem behind—the failure to explain why ESG performance tends to positively impact financial bottom lines—only to suggest a disturbing possibility. At some level, contributions toward socially valuable projects represent a zero-sum game. The flood of assets pouring into ESG funds promising to meet or exceed conventional competitors' returns becomes a self-fulfilling prophecy, increasing profits by reducing capital costs.

That focal point dynamic takes on a different cast depending on the alternative asset uses these investments might be crowding out. If the explosion of ESG factors in investment merely siphons assets away from funds (and the portfolio firms they hold) that pursue the most brutish vision of capitalism, it would be hard to object. Companies and investors have long been decried for failing to internalize the costs that preoccupation with shareholder value alone pushes off onto workers, consumers, and communities.[92] Quite a rosy crowding-out story emerges if ESG's gain represents a loss only to firms that continue to harm people and planet in search of profit.

Another possibility traces some of the dollars flowing into sustainable investing from ventures more committed to environmental, social, and governance goals rather than less. Economic and social value can be blended in endlessly variable proportions, but ESG investments that provide environmental, social, and governance performance along with market-rate financial returns will be particularly attractive offerings for firms that earn their own profits based on fund yields. And that description just happens to match those firms sprinting to meet demand for ESG investments.

The surfeit of such market-rate funds now being created and promoted might displace not—or not only—conventional investing but investment vehicles adopting an impact-first approach. Those investments demand a willingness to concede financial returns in exchange for creating social value. "Impact" or concessionary investments combine the opportunity to generate profit while creating social value but willingly trade economic gains for social ones.[93]

The program-related investments described earlier provide an illustrative example of this approach. The Ford Foundation pioneered this concept by making loans in economically depressed communities to small businesses with high-risk profiles.[94] The interest rates they charged did not fully account for these risks, precisely because Ford was primarily seeking the social benefits of economic development and empowerment, not a market-rate return.

Mainstream ESG funds pursue a very different combination of financial and social returns. Their success inevitably means higher capital costs for others. Drawing capital away from investments that seek financial return even when they create social harms may not be worrisome but steering would-be impact investors to vehicles providing more modest social value would increase the cost of capital for the most deserving.

Or perhaps not. Sustainable investing is, after all, investing. The types of investors who will—or should—embrace concessionary returns may be limited to quite a small range. Foundation endowments must be given away. They occupy a highly unusual space where concessionary financial returns could actually be an economic win over their reasonable alternatives. Together with very wealthy individuals and families with greater assets than they will ever require to maintain even lavish lifestyles, they can form a niche market for true impact investments willing to trade economic returns for social value. But for legions of unsophisticated mutual fund customers and retirement savers, thinning the herd of investment options to only those providing market-rate returns seems precisely the right outcome.

If ESG investing draws dollars away from actual charities, that focal point dynamic becomes more sinister.[95] It is easy to understand how an ESG investment might appeal to erstwhile charitable contributors. ESG—like impact investing—boasts financial return profiles far more attractive than the 100 percent pretax loss guaranteed when one donates funds to charity to pursue environmental or social gains. The scale of the interventions promised by ESG investments can also compare favorably to those a charity or even an impact investee can tackle. The footprint of multinational firms held by ESG funds would be nearly impossible for charities or impact fund investees to match.

But it would be foolish to think ESG or even impact investing will be sufficient to combat the mounting environmental or social crises we face. Siphoning cash away from businesses with poor ESG profiles and toward those with better ones describes a virtuous circle, with capital markets rewarding socially beneficial commitments. If ESG begins shortchanging charity to provide cheap cash for businesses, even those with ESG bona fides, elements of a vicious alternative emerge.

Thanks to the rise of commercially affiliated donor-advised funds, resources that a foundation might have been compelled to give to charities today might instead remain invested in ESG funds indefinitely. Capital that might otherwise have funded impact-first or charitable ventures may instead be harvested by for-profit companies, reducing the price they pay to fund operations and growth. The resulting higher capital costs for charities would impede efforts toward progress on climate, inequality, hunger, and so many more serious fronts.

For-Profit Philanthropy Lessons from ESG Investing's Success

The for-profit philanthropic innovations described in this book collapse the categories of economic and social value in ways reminiscent of the blend of "doing well by doing good" promised by the growing array of ESG funds. Wealthy donors have replaced traditional forms of giving with philanthropy LLCs. Powerful financial institutions created affiliated donor-advised funds sponsors to hold and invest wealth for eventual charitable use. Major corporations' shift to strategic corporate philanthropy integrates charitable giving seamlessly into their business models and operations. As practices, players, and norms migrate from the business to the philanthropic sphere, they too blur the boundaries of business and charity.

Indeed, the marriage of business methods and social goals lies at the crux of for-profit philanthropy's value proposition. Philanthropy LLCs pursue their lofty social missions aided by the tailwinds of regulatory and operational freedom provided by business law's most flexible tool. Commercially affiliated donor-advised funds leverage the investment acumen of blue-chip financial institutions to grow assets a donor will one day direct to charitable uses. Strategic corporate philanthropy envisions corporate giving as a fully integrated part of a firm's strategy, employed to support shareholder value. These innovations rely on leaders and lessons from business to fuel charitable success.

The pairing of for-profit philanthropy's two core concepts creates a powerful focal point that could allow it to mirror ESG investing's rise. Sidestepping questions of trust and accountability with promises of win–win solutions could propel these techniques into a new philanthropic mainstream. If DAFs, philanthropy LLCs, and strategic corporate philanthropy can boast public benefits on par with conventional philanthropic alternatives and private benefits to boot, old-fashioned ideas like sacrifice might not matter anymore. Yet dollars deployed through for-profit philanthropic innovation must come from somewhere and the risk of crowding out looms large.

As with ESG, a rosy story can be easily told. The resources pledged to CZI might once have been devoted to distinctly noncharitable endeavors. A philanthropic LLC's promises of flexibility, control, and privacy may convince high-net-worth individuals to dedicate assets to charity that they would otherwise spend on themselves or keep in their collective pockets. Vanguard's convenience may replace wealth generation for oneself with charitable giving (eventually) to others. Or liberated from a spending floor too often treated as a ceiling, commercially affiliated donor-advised funds may deploy capital faster than foundations. Strategic corporate philanthropy may convince Citigroup, GM, and Google to spend more on serving their communities and sustaining the environment than they otherwise would have.

But a darker version exists as well. Just as mainstream ESG pursues the slice of environmental, social, and governance performance that aligns with healthy financial returns, for-profit philanthropic innovations will emphasize those parts of the charitable universe that can be harmonized with the business tools and tropes they adopt. GM may be spending more of its money on serving the Detroit community through direct giving because its human resources and government relations departments understand how doing so will improve employee retention and lower regulatory costs. But a focus on giving that increases shareholder value will devote little attention to other communities the firm leaves behind.

Philanthropy LLCs seeking to deploy the resources of their founder's firm in service of social good likewise contract the range of causes and solutions they pursue, as CZI's overabundance of educational technology investments vividly illustrates. For-profit philanthropists' shared notion of the value of business approaches creates risks of a philanthropic monoculture that would starve charitable needs not amenable to these solutions. With all of philanthropy's vast resources focused in one direction, many of the public's priorities would go unaddressed.

In this sense, for-profit philanthropy represents a sharp divergence from conventional philanthropic practice. Philanthropic institutions have, of course, always aligned their objectives with donor's desires. Indeed, donor intent is the fundamental value of the charitable trust. The pluralism the resulting diversity of viewpoint lends to the charitable sector tends to be considered one of philanthropy's chief virtues. If for-profit philanthropy drives a convergence around the focal point of profit, however, the public's willingness to tolerate its antidemocratic distribution of power will wear thin.

Conventional philanthropy's vision of the good can already be critiqued as narrow and heavily influenced by the privilege of its benefactors. For-profit philanthropy's focal point amplifies these long-standing concerns by displacing the Grand Bargain's architecture of trust. Shrinking private aims replacing expansive public goals will do nothing to preserve a collective confidence in the value proposition elite philanthropy represents.

Whatever one's view on whether a significant shift toward for-profit philanthropy would seed a charitable monoculture, it would supplant conventional philanthropic vehicles. It is hard to imagine that some portion of the funds streaming into for-profit philanthropic innovations would not otherwise have been routed to and through private foundations and operating public charities. Eliding the accountability mechanisms enshrined in the Grand Bargain empowers private benefactors and erodes public input and transparency.

For-profit philanthropy appears poised to replicate the growth trajectory of ESG investing. If it does, it would soon swallow traditional philanthropy and cast aside the brakes the Grand Bargain applies to the inherently undemocratic nature of philanthropy. Allowing elites to design and implement a social agenda free of even the modest constraints imposed a half-century ago represents no bargain at all for the public. They may one day decide to walk away as well, taking their capital with them.

Conclusion

Social enterprise and ESG investing exist far beyond the Grand Bargain. Neither makes any claim to be engaged in philanthropy. Still, their successes and failures highlight important risks presented by for-profit philanthropy's rise and its blend of business and charity.

Traditionally, charities have been fueled by gifts while for-profit firms raise money from capital markets. Donors and investors know what to expect on both sides of that divide, allowing each individual venture to focus on showing what sets them apart rather than on what makes them familiar. Without that advantage and with few reliable tools to generate trust, legal forms for social enterprises remain widely available but rarely used. Without strong governance tools to persuade investors and social entrepreneurs the social enterprises they fund and found will remain committed to producing their desired blend of financial and social returns, contractual tools like certification and creative financing fill the gap.

The ubiquity of private foundations makes it easy to take the accomplishment they represent for granted. Philanthropists could long ago have rejected the burdens the Grand Bargain imposed. That the private foundation did not languish, doomed to become the benefit corporation of its day, suggests that Congress succeeded in building trust where dozens of state legislatures have not.

For-profit philanthropy's cavalier rejection of tools designed to allay the concerns everyday Americans reasonably have with antidemocratic social agenda-setting by the most wealthy and powerful may soon leave foundations by the wayside. The potent appeal of for-profit philanthropy's focal point for donors—aligning their most private interests and practices with their public facing ones—suggests it is unlikely to fade into obscurity. Should for-profit philanthropy's forms become dominant, they would invite difficult questions from the public that may jeopardize support for the philanthropic enterprise.

ESG investing's blockbuster success sounds a very different cautionary note for for-profit philanthropy than social enterprise's failure to launch. Early ESG funds offered proof of concept for the notion that investors need not choose between doing well and doing good (or, more precisely, not doing bad). Today's ESG has evolved, embracing an extraordinarily broad array of strategies, ranging from simple negative screens to proprietary algorithms. Attractive market returns often—though not invariably—flow from these guilt-free investments delivering quantifiable ESG benefits. The neat trick of transforming ESG performance from a potential rival into an ally of financial gain can mollify even skeptical regulators worried that ESG may not be all that its advocates hope.

Collapsing categories of profit and social good allows assets once kept apart to flow across an increasingly porous border. In both the ESG investing and for-profit philanthropy contexts, competing accounts of crowding out clash. Reallocating funds away from firms prone to pollution or unfair labor practices and toward those blending profit and environmental stewardship makes ESG appealing. Likewise, directing a greater share of the wealth in affluent families and powerful corporations away from purely private uses and toward public ones seems an unvarnished good.

By contrast, transforming potential charitable donations and impact investments into ESG investments should give us pause. Even more so when for-profit philanthropy's focal point favors endeavors generating a narrow range of business benefits. Still more when for-profit philanthropy offers few opportunities for public input and scrutiny. Commercially affiliated donor-advised funds do precisely this when they draw resources away from charities and into investments. Philanthropy LLCs and strategic corporate philanthropy do the same by rejecting regulated philanthropy altogether.

Without the Grand Bargain's guardrails, for-profit philanthropy's innovations come at great risk whether they shrivel on the vine or flourish abundantly. Both underutilization and crowding out jeopardize the philanthropic ecosystem and risk disturbing the delicate balance between public and private control of elite wealth. Part III (chapters 6, 7, and 8) charts alternative responses to these threats, focusing on providing new forms of accountability. Rather than insisting on a return to 1969 or any single comprehensive solution, the remaining chapters imagine an array of tools to rebuild the trust that provided the foundation—pun intended—for its long success.

The balance of the book offers three distinct visions of how to provide the trust and accountability needed to ensure that the emergence of for-profit philanthropy represents a net benefit to the public. Interventions could be granular, as chapter 6 envisions, triggering minor course corrections to deliver shared benefits. They might not be interventions at all, but individual or sectoral commitments made through private ordering strong enough to build trust between philanthropists and the public as described in chapter 7. Finally, as chapter 8 shows, they could form part of a comprehensive More Perfect Bargain, crafting broad legal reforms to restrain elite influence.

The speed of social enterprise forms' legislative adoption and of ESG investing's rise to prominence highlights the urgency of understanding and responding to the risks generated by an ascendant for-profit philanthropy paradigm. Some would not mourn the end of an era in which the United States relied so heavily on elite philanthropy to address society's needs should the Grand Bargain's demise hasten it. The next part imagines what might replace the Grand Bargain and whether it might transform a potential loss into an opportunity to catapult philanthropy forward, empowering new voices and elevating values too long ignored.

PART III

RESTORING THE PUBLIC'S VOICE

6
Tailored Regulatory Interventions

The growing popularity of for-profit philanthropy offers no guarantee that it does not represent a poisoned chalice. Without the trust long supplied by the Grand Bargain, philanthropy LLCs, commercially affiliated DAFs, and strategic corporate philanthropy could easily return elites to the world in which suspicion doomed Rockefeller's bid for a federal charter. Those cutting-edge creations invite the same skepticism that inspired the 1969 Act.

A contemporary observer might have casually dismissed Rockefeller's philanthropic ambitions as so much virtue signaling. Today's public, having looked on as social enterprises like Etsy made bold promises to stakeholders only to watch it succumb to "The Barbarians" at its "Hand- Hewn, Responsibly Sourced Gates"[1] can be forgiven for keeping their expectations low. Chapter 8 underscores why a rekindled skepticism of elite "slacktivism" should make for-profit philanthropists wary of losing public trust. This chapter offers concrete examples of modest regulatory interventions that could help for-profit philanthropy avoid that fate.

A half-century ago, secrecy, tax benefits without public benefits, and cozy relationships between charity and business prompted Congress to intervene on a grand scale. The Grand Bargain offered philanthropists a lavish suite of tools to reassure the public that elite philanthropy meant more than idle vanity. Today, the wealthiest and most powerful increasingly set those safeguards aside. The striking parallels between for-profit philanthropy and practices Treasury described in the 1960s reveal a Grand Bargain drifting toward irrelevance. Recent efforts by legislators to increase the tax burden on the wealthiest Americans suggest the high price elites might pay for walking away from the Grand Bargain.

This chapter envisions responses that may appear less ambitious than those Congress offered a half-century ago, but in truth they represent a radical leap beyond the Grand Bargain. Describing tailored regulatory interventions that see for-profit philanthropy as equal parts opportunity and threat, it identifies pinpoint openings for impact. Requiring donor-advised funds to clearly and publicly name recipients of dormant assets, carefully easing strictures targeted at "self-dealing" by foundations, and making benefit reports mainstream could allow lawmakers to shrink the gap between what the public expects of for-profit philanthropy and what the powerful individuals and organizations leading the charge ultimately deliver. On their own, none of these narrow proposals would rebuild the trust between elites and the public the Grand Bargain once provided.

For-Profit Philanthropy. Dana Brakman Reiser and Steven A. Dean, Oxford University Press. © Oxford University Press 2023. DOI: 10.1093/oso/9780190074500.003.0007

But—even without chapter 8's More Perfect Bargain, a new compact to restore a balance of power that time has shifted in favor of elites—targeted measures could allow the public to ensure that for-profit philanthropy addresses urgent problems of today, rather than merely burnishing the images of the wealthiest Americans.

One of the many challenges presented by for-profit philanthropy lies in sheer scale. Towering wealth, vast social challenges, and yawning inequality can overwhelm our perceptions. As a result, it can be easy to lose sight not only of the granular benefits of the Grand Bargain that have been lost but of new small victories that could be won. This chapter zooms in to reimagine the Grand Bargain's lumbering approach to accountability for the more nimble age of for-profit philanthropy.

Focusing on particular aspects of for-profit philanthropy helps to underscore the unequal distribution of the benefits and burdens of both the Grand Bargain and its decline. Considering gender and race, for example, can reveal how the Grand Bargain's rise and fall helps or hurts distinct groups. Reacting to a world in which Fidelity and Vanguard realize their ambition of becoming the Visa and MasterCard of charity urges bold responses. Chapters 7 and 8 provide them, but this chapter operates at a more human scale.

Inevitably, for-profit philanthropy's disruptive arrival affects different groups in distinct ways, muffling some voices while offering a bullhorn to others. Spotlighting three for-profit philanthropy phenomena in turn helps show the many meaningful ways in which regulation could address philanthropic flaws. Challenging common assumptions about how philanthropy—and philanthropists—should look, for-profit philanthropy creates an opportunity to address today's problems rather than yesterday's, improving upon, rather returning to, the Grand Bargain.

Race, Gender, and Generation

Philanthropy LLCs, commercially affiliated donor-advised funds, and strategic corporate philanthropy implicate the distribution of power between the public and private spheres. Embedded within that perennial debate over control of the growing share of society's resources held by elites lie more acute tensions that could be all too easily overlooked.[2] Anchoring the search for solutions to for-profit philanthropy's displacement of the Grand Bargain in particularized discussions of identity helpfully problematizes common assumptions about philanthropy.[3]

Strategic corporate philanthropy, for example, offers us a reminder that philanthropy need not be the prerogative of individuals who look like Andrew

Carnegie or Mark Zuckerberg and a warning that for-profit philanthropy can reinforce gender disparities. Corporate America remains an overwhelmingly male-dominated field. In 2020, the number of women CEOs of Fortune 500 companies hit an all-time high.[4] Yet only thirty-seven of the country's largest businesses were led by women (proportionately far fewer than even a notoriously gender-imbalanced US Senate). Shielding corporate giving from the accountability the corporate foundation delivers—in part by providing detailed philanthropic information to a collection of stakeholders more diverse than any executive suite—seems a poor punishment for corporate America's mixed record on inclusion. Making benefit reports—already required for many social enterprise hybrids to document how they serve stakeholders—mandatory for all large corporations could more than compensate for that loss.

The philanthropy LLC invites reflection on the moment in their lives when individuals give. Today's most generous philanthropists have much in common with their predecessors. But one difference stands out. Chan and Zuckerberg created CZI as they entered their thirties. When he wrote the Gospel of Wealth, Andrew Carnegie was well into his fifties, a ripe old age for his day. When Chan and Zuckerberg chose an LLC over a foundation, their relative youth may have made all the difference.

Consistent with Carnegie's long-ago vision, the Grand Bargain's design temporally situates accumulation and giving at distinct points in a philanthropic life cycle. CZI's rejection of the Grand Bargain can be seen as an implicit dismissal of the notion that philanthropy belongs to those over fifty. The law governing foundations could be modified in one particular way, relaxing its self-dealing prohibition, to accommodate that.

Finally, commercially affiliated DAFs have been praised for democratizing giving.[5] Their reduced barriers to entry represent good news for a field not known for diversity. Yet making a meaningful contribution to racial equity requires far more than granting equal access. Given the depth of the racial wealth gap, merely making the pool of donors more diverse will not be enough to provide Black-led charities with the financial support they need.[6] Commercially affiliated donor-advised funds could transform the fates of Black charities overnight. Lawmakers could make great strides toward that goal simply by mandating publication of an annual list of recipients of dormant funds; they could also go even further.

This chapter offers targeted reforms designed to shape for-profit philanthropy's impact without changing its broad contours. Collectively, these innovations hint at the uncharted power of for-profit philanthropy and the vulnerability of the Grand Bargain's dated minimum standards. At a time when systemic racism, gender equity, and an emerging generation of advocates demands our attention, creating opportunities to amplify rather than diminish the voices of diverse stakeholders takes on new urgency.

The Human Impact of For-Profit Philanthropy

Forcing for-profit philanthropists to supply benefit reports like those demanded of the hybrid firms described in chapter 5 and to publicly commit to directing dormant donor-advised funds to organizations aligned with the values corporate sponsors espouse, while allowing them to engage in transactions that would have offended the sensibilities of long-ago lawmakers, could create a better world if not a perfect one. This is true because for-profit philanthropy, like its conventional counterpart, matters not because of the billions of dollars it consumes, but because of the billions of lives it affects. The Grand Bargain struck a balance between public and private power with profound implications for all Americans. But 1969 was a long time ago.

Binding philanthropy LLCs, commercially affiliated donor-advised funds, and strategic corporate philanthropy to the dated terms of the Grand Bargain could do more harm than good. Responding to the decline of the Grand Bargain and the rise of for-profit philanthropy offers an opportunity to set new priorities. Remaking a philanthropic landscape to reflect contemporary values represents a complex task. To put a fine point on those concerns, one might ask how to ensure that the values that inform giving do not simply reflect those of older, whiter, disproportionately male CEOs rather than their younger and more diverse workers and customers.

Gender and Strategic Corporate Philanthropy

Corporate America has long fallen short in its efforts to ensure that it mirrors the diversity we take for granted in many parts of our lives. In both its workforce and its leadership, women and minorities have struggled to achieve sustained success. During and after the 2020 Black Lives Matter protests, "Fortune 500 firms . . . boast[ed] about their commitments to diversity" but "firm industrywide assurances to bolster the hiring of black employees at the corporate or board levels, let alone among the rank and file," lagged.[7] No less striking than the lack of racial diversity in corporate America, the number of women in the top ranks of the largest companies remains remarkably low.[8]

Mary Barra became the first female CEO of one of the major US automakers less than a decade ago. Since taking control in 2014, Barra has made it clear that she feels quite comfortable challenging the conventional wisdom. In 2021, well before Biden embraced ambitious goals to reduce carbon emissions, she made headlines by announcing that General Motors would end production of gasoline and diesel cars by 2035.[9]

Those surprised by that initiative might have been equally unprepared for her decision, several years before, to eliminate the General Motors Foundation.[10] Whatever connections one might draw between her gender and her bold vision for the future of the auto industry and of her company's philanthropy, Barra represents a striking exception that highlights long-standing inequities. Power matters, and in corporate America, power has both a race and a gender.

Strategic corporate philanthropy embraces an insular vision that shifts power toward corporate insiders and away from other stakeholders. Thanks to transparency requirements imposed through the Grand Bargain (detailed in chapter 4), private foundations offer opportunities for employees, customers, and community members to monitor the choices their corporate sponsors make. Despite its name, the design of the private foundation reveals multiple points at which the public's voice can be heard on its priorities.

Not inconsequentially, elected representatives crafted the Grand Bargain that governs private foundations. State attorneys general speak for the public through their enforcement efforts.[11] But the most important tool available to the public to keep tabs on private foundations can be easy to take for granted. The Form 990 each charity must file once a year offers the public important insights about the funding and activities of private foundations. Corporations—even those that are publicly traded—keep their tax returns private.[12] Their private foundations must share their Forms 990-PF with us all. Even though few citizens will linger over their details, these disclosures are available for the media to scrutinize and publicize.

Revealing the information contained on those returns to the public allows stakeholders to ensure that private foundations deliver on their promises. Dissolving its foundation brought a long-standing flow of information to a swift end for General Motors. More incremental shifts of corporate giving operations to internal departments have similarly obscuring effects. Strategic corporate philanthropy interrupts precisely these opportunities—delivered by the Grand Bargain—for the public to monitor the philanthropic activities of the world's largest businesses.

If corporate America's leadership mirrored the diversity of the nation overall, the consequence of that shift would not be as troubling. Replacing corporate foundations with strategic corporate philanthropy moves charitable giving further from a diverse public's reach. Half a century ago, that fact might not have mattered. But today it represents an anachronism. Sometimes, as in GM's case, a shift to for-profit philanthropy will empower women or minorities. But more often, it will reinscribe the failures of the corporate sector to put women and other underrepresented groups in positions of leadership onto philanthropic giving by consolidating control of charity in the hands of what remains an overwhelmingly white, male group.

Age and Philanthropy LLCs

Chan and Zuckerberg launched their philanthropic efforts far earlier than most. Barely thirty, they announced CZI along with their first child.[13] Traditionally, philanthropy becomes a priority only after children are grown. But Chan and Zuckerberg explained that the decision to begin much sooner reflected a sense of urgency many young people share. In their announcement, styled as a letter to their child, Zuckerberg pledged to "continue to serve as Facebook's CEO for many, many years to come" while explaining that they planned to prioritize "issues . . . too important to wait until you or we are older to begin this work."[14]

Given their age, the choice of an LLC over a foundation offered a particular advantage. Any donor might prefer more choice over less and in light of the 2010—temporary—repeal of the estate tax a more flexible approach would have much to recommend it. But unlike many others in their privileged position, Chan and Zuckerberg could expect to enjoy the freedom afforded by an LLC over many decades as their personal circumstances and priorities evolved. At any point they might choose to go the more conventional route by transforming CZI into a private foundation. Had they chosen a foundation at the start, they could not later decide to turn that foundation into a tax nothing.

All else equal, a stock option that expires tomorrow sells for far less than one that expires in a year. The same would be true many times over for the founders of CZI and their LLC. The value of Chan and Zuckerberg's option—along with all the other choices they preserved by forming an LLC—is magnified by their youth. Younger by almost half a century than Warren Buffet when he pledged a $30 billion gift to the Gates Foundation, the value of remaining free of the requirements and prohibitions that come with the private foundation grows correspondingly larger. With little to fear in near-term tax obligations, millennial elites pay surprisingly little to secure that option.[15]

Race and Commercially Affiliated Donor-Advised Funds

Philanthropy has a race problem. Under the terms of the 1969 Grand Bargain, private foundations have no obligation to employ formal diversity, equity, and inclusion strategies to shape their giving. And most do not. Too slowly, this has begun to change.[16] Remedying a half-century-old oversight, the handful of commercial sponsors that dominate the donor-advised fund industry controlling more than $100 billion in assets could transform the fortunes of Black-led charities overnight.

Despite all this, the equity that first comes to mind when thinking of commercially affiliated donor-advised funds probably would mean publicly traded shares not inclusion. Advocates for these funds often tout their power to make philanthropy more accessible. Just as Visa and MasterCard have made credit widely available to consumers, financial powerhouses like Fidelity aim to emulate their success by making donating through "giving accounts" every bit as effortless as spending with a credit card.

By reducing long-standing barriers, innovations like commercially affiliated donor-advised funds could encourage participation from donors long excluded from the clubby world of philanthropy. Thus far, however, "when measured by dollars that pass through them, [donor-advised funds] are used primarily by people at the very tops of the wealth and income distributions."[17] But commercially affiliated sponsors certainly have the right incentives to expand their customer base. Changing the face of philanthropy to look and act more like the country as a whole would take a vast effort, but tools like donor-advised funds could easily help bridge the gap.

Even if philanthropic giving were transformed so that donors perfectly reflected America's diversity, a larger problem would remain. If philanthropy seeks to prioritize racial equity, it must reach beyond greater inclusion.[18] Given the huge disparity in wealth that exists between Blacks and other groups, simply removing obstacles to Black giving would still leave Black-led charities and those serving Black communities woefully underfunded.[19] Although comprehensive data are lacking, the information that does exist demonstrates that

> minority-led and serving nonprofit organizations are underfunded, smaller in terms of staff and volunteers, disproportionately likely to have higher amounts of restricted assets from government grants, more dependent on government grants, and more likely to be impacted by economic downturns in comparison to organizations with white individuals at the helm.[20]

"Overcoming the racial bias in philanthropic funding" so that philanthropy remedies rather than reinforces inequality requires more than an expanded customer base for DAFs.[21]

The anonymity offered by donor-advised funds may, in fact, make them particularly attractive for donors seeking to fund organizations with racist policies. Reports in 2019 and 2020 accused donor-advised funds at both community foundations and commercial sponsors of transferring donor contributions to hate groups—at the donors' requests.[22] Critics called for sponsors to tamp down on these practices, but the response from sponsors was muted, noting that they dutifully pass on contributed funds according to donor advice to any tax-exempt organization recognized by the IRS.[23]

No amount of growth in Black philanthropy on its own could overcome the extraordinary shortfalls in funding received by Black-led charities or the pernicious uses of donor-advised funds.[24] But the rise of commercially affiliated donor-advised funds just might. Critics have already called for sponsors to adopt hate policies limiting the ability of donor advisors to channel their funds to hate groups using their platforms. In addition, the technological sophistication that allows commercial sponsors to seamlessly serve their investment clients' philanthropic needs and would enable them to reach a new, broader swath of donors could, as described below, also be harnessed to help their clients support underserved causes.[25]

Targeted Regulatory Reforms

For-profit philanthropy embodies a contemporary reality that must not be ignored. Certainly, it represents a potent threat to the Grand Bargain. But viewing for-profit philanthropy only through the lens of the Grand Bargain would be no less a mistake than simply pretending it does not exist. For-profit philanthropy also represents an opportunity.

In the 1960s, the creation of the private foundation responded to documented abuses and perceived vulnerabilities, striking a balance between private autonomy and public control that lasted decades. But today, so much has changed. Individuals and corporate donors have begun to turn away from the Grand Bargain. And in some ways, that might prove to be a blessing in disguise.

A regulatory response to for-profit philanthropy could be comprehensive, such as the More Perfect Bargain described in chapter 8. But the likelihood of Washington rising to that challenge seems modest at best. Any legislative responses to for-profit philanthropy would almost certainly be narrowly targeted to address particularly compelling concerns.

The three reforms described in this section make no attempt to put the for-profit philanthropy genie back in the bottle. They do, however, seize opportunities for-profit philanthropy presents. Amplifying rather than silencing the voices of those underrepresented in corporate boardrooms, tackling the structural challenges posed by the emergence of younger philanthropists, and advancing racial equity would represent worthwhile achievements, although hardly on the epic scale of the Grand Bargain.

Stakeholder Oversight

That strategic corporate philanthropy results in fewer opportunities for women and minorities to exercise influence than conventional corporate giving may seem counterintuitive. The absence of diversity in corporate leadership largely mirrors a similar dearth in the philanthropic sphere.[26] But the shift toward for-profit philanthropy matters more than that simple comparison suggests.

Although their name suggests exclusivity, the design of private foundations delivers accountability. By demanding transparency, they empower stakeholders. In the United States, workers, suppliers, and customers generally have very little say in corporate decision-making. A corporate foundation creates a rare opportunity for outsiders to observe, and perhaps influence, the decisions corporate leaders make in their names.

Other jurisdictions take a very different approach. Arguably, none more so than Germany. Mitbestimmung, the German law of co-determination, empowers workers of all but the smallest companies to appoint members of their boards of directors.[27] The United States offers nothing of the kind.[28] The decline of unions over the course of the twentieth century underscores that absence.

A private foundation does not grant explicit authority to stakeholders. But it does create avenues for public control. A foundation must embrace objectives within the scope of activities federal tax law defines as charitable. It must regularly deploy a meaningful portion of its assets in pursuit of those goals each year and it must avoid a panoply of activities and expenditures that smack of insider interests. It must also disclose to the public information about both the sources from which its income is derived and how it spends those funds.

Strategic corporate philanthropy eliminates even the hint of co-determination provided by the Grand Bargain's invitation to stakeholders to scrutinize corporate giving. With a foundation, stakeholders have an ability to observe the choices insiders make with the aim of affecting outsiders. When no corporate foundation exists—or when that formal structure is used selectively—the window it provides onto a corporation's philanthropic choices slams closed.

Restoring that lost opportunity for stakeholder engagement could be accomplished in a variety of ways. Large corporations, particularly those organized in states that have adopted benefit corporation form, might, for example, be required to prepare and publish a benefit report. Many states require benefit corporations both to commit to generating a public benefit and to detailing their efforts to do so. Conventional corporations could be called on to do the same.

Although not a perfect solution, widespread acceptance of benefit reports by mainstream companies would only improve them. To remedy the shortcomings of benefit reports highlighted in chapter 5, they could be augmented in a variety of ways. Any constituency a firm claims to serve could also have to be consulted in meaningful ways and their views reflected in that report.[29] In addition, both the publication and consultation requirements could be made conditions of claiming charitable tax deductions.

For corporate donors, charitable deductions matter far less than they might for an individual.[30] Companies will often be able to deduct the same expenses as "ordinary and necessary" costs, which need not be justified by a burdensome reporting requirement.[31] Requiring those firms that adopt this workaround to divulge this fact to explain the absence of a benefit report would flag such avoidance.

Compelling or incentivizing corporations to complete benefit reports could provide a replacement for—and in some ways an improvement over—a corporate foundation's Form 990-PF. Benefit reports can directly capture information about corporate philanthropy, measuring impact against governmentally imposed criteria or third-party standards analogous to those benefit corporations invoke.[32] Precisely what those benefit reports would include should be informed, but not limited, by the demands of the Grand Bargain.

Transparently illuminating the targets of a corporation's philanthropy and the timeline on which it operates will reveal potential trouble spots for stakeholders to address. Consistency—notably absent in the ESG reports highlighted in chapter 3—will be key to ensure comparability, but the perfect uniformity of the Form 990 need not be replicated. Allowing for some variation in format and features will enable an iterative learning process for both companies and regulators.

As chapter 5 details, social enterprise hybrid forms such as the benefit corporation have seen limited uptake. That need not mean these innovative entities do not offer important lessons. Benefit reports have come to be defined by their absence.[33] But while many benefit corporations, often startups, lack the resources necessary to successfully produce them, GM and other corporate giants would not.

The result would be a far cry from Mitbestimmung. Workers and any other stakeholders would not have the right to control corporate actions. But preventing—or even just discouraging—corporations from claiming to engage in philanthropy in their name without transparency and consultation would represent a meaningful improvement. Facilitating reporting with consultation could not only replace what gets lost in a shift to for-profit philanthropy but surpass it.

Unleashing Co-creation

The Grand Bargain relies on assumptions about the behavior of philanthropists that, though not unreasonable at the time, have proven increasingly unreliable. Fueled by vast wealth earned early in technology giants, philanthropists such as Pierre and Pamela Omidyar did precisely as Carnegie suggested. eBay made them billionaires by their early thirties, spurring the Omidyars to begin working diligently to avoid the shame of dying rich.

Capitalizing on the options afforded by emergence of for-profit philanthropy, their Omidyar Network relies on amalgam of entities to accomplish its ambitious aims. Pairing a traditional private foundation with a philanthropy LLC, the Omidyar Network makes grants to operating charities alongside investments in startups and advocacy efforts.[34] That complex structure underscores how poorly the Grand Bargain's private foundation aligns with the Omidyars' omnivorous approach to philanthropy.

Central to the Grand Bargain's structure was Carnegie's now-dated presumption that a season of giving away riches predictably follows a season of acquiring them. Although once true, the Omidyar Network reveals a more complex contemporary reality. The neat life cycle of a several decades of industry punctuated by a grand act of philanthropy has been replaced by a complex tapestry of overlapping investments and grants.

The Grand Bargain makes earning wealth and deploying it concurrently surprisingly difficult. Yet that is no accident. As chapter 4 details, transactions between private foundations and their funders or related entities—even when demonstrably favorable for the foundation—can violate rigid prohibitions. Steep financial penalties designed to ensure that foundations enter into no such transactions and that they quickly rescind any they do leave no doubt that under the Grand Bargain business and philanthropy must not mix.

When philanthropy followed a predictable life cycle, such boundaries between philanthropy and business could easily be justified. Structurally, such combinations would be rare. Wealth accumulated in business over the first half of a lifetime became a store of philanthropic value given away during the latter. Co-creation by funders' firms and foundations simply would not—could not—exist. If transactions of this style did occur, their very rarity would make them suspect.

The philanthropy LLC highlights the limits of both assumptions. The old model of stockpiling cash and then writing checks has become increasingly anachronistic. Today's challenge becomes deciding not whether any such transactions should be permitted, but which. Embracing a post-life cycle regulatory vision that acknowledges the ties produced by overlapping business and philanthropic operations would require rolling back many of the constraints imposed on private foundations.

The self-dealing rules currently constrain transactions between private foundations and their funders, managers, and relatives. The ability to engage in such transactions unhindered represents a key advantage of the philanthropy LLC alternative. Permitting private foundations to engage in at least some of these transactions would create an opportunity to replace prohibition with disclosure. An experimental moratorium on the application of the foundation self-dealing rules could be conditioned on foundations disclosing details of any transactions with their funders and managers on the Form 990-PF. Such disclosures would need to reveal the existence, parties to, and terms of any such transactions, as well as the perceived benefit to the foundation.

While a striking—albeit temporary—reversal of the Grand Bargain's prophylaxis, a moratorium combined with a disclosure mandate could shift the calculus of philanthropy LLC adoption. The philanthropy LLC would still represent a more flexible, less regulated, and more private option. For some would-be adopters, however, the freedom to co-create might be enough to shift the balance in favor of regulated philanthropy. It would also provide opportunities for learning. Regulators and philanthropists alike could use the disclosures to determine what sorts of transactions provide valuable public benefits and which simply enrich wealthy donors. In time, those insights could shape prudential rulemaking.

If true reversal proved too radical, Congress could also turn to the rules that enable public charities to transact more freely with their donors and fiduciaries as a backstop. Unlike the 1969 Act's prohibitory approach to self-dealing in private foundations, public charities' transactions with their leaders or contributors trigger penalties only if they generate "excess benefit" for the latter.[35] "If the value of the economic benefit provided exceeds the value of the consideration (including the performance of services) received for providing such benefit," it crosses over into excessive territory.[36] Familiar two-tiered initial and confiscatory second-level penalty taxes are imposed on the recipient of the excess benefit and knowing managers. The regime also includes a procedural safe harbor for compensation transactions. A rebuttable presumption that a compensation arrangement does not create excess benefits arises if the transaction was approved in advance by an independent board, using comparability data, and with full documentation.[37]

Whether combined with application of the excess benefit regime or a pure moratorium, the addition of a disclosure regime would embrace the shift away from the life cycle model of philanthropy evident in the rise of philanthropy LLCs. Over the short term, making information available about what transactions and investments exist would represent an improvement over the haphazard reporting for-profit philanthropists currently provide. In the long run, a more nuanced self-dealing regime could be tailor-made for foundations—based on real-world examples.

Donor-Advised Fund Diversity, Equity, and Inclusion

Commercially affiliated donor-advised funds represent a sharp break with decades of philanthropic tradition. Given philanthropy's decidedly mixed track record on diversity, equity, and inclusion,[38] that might be good news. Yet—even if DAFs materially affect both the overall level of giving and the diversity of givers—their emergence seems unlikely to have a significant impact on efforts to create greater racial equality in philanthropic funding.

In the half-century since the Grand Bargain was struck, the world has changed. A regulatory architecture designed for 1969 has not. The private foundation has watched not only the fall of the Soviet Union and the rise of the internet but the long struggle to operationalize the principles articulated during the Civil Rights struggle of the 1950s and 1960s. However much philanthropy has nurtured that process, it could do far more.

The United States has come far as a nation since the Grand Bargain was struck. Yet the events of 2020 and 2021, from the murder of George Floyd and the global Black Lives Matter protests to the differing law enforcement responses to those peaceful demonstrations and the Capitol Riot, underscore that it falls far short on countless measures of racial equity. In philanthropy, those racial inequities can be striking.[39] The lack of meaningful progress toward creating a philanthropic landscape that both resembles the nation and adequately reflects its values in terms of race creates opportunities.

Giving Gap, an organization created to "showcase the diversity of causes that Black-founded nonprofits organize around, and to make it easy for you and your organization to connect with them" reports that "Americans give $450 billion to charity each year, but only a tiny fraction of that goes to Black organizations."[40] Donors unsure of how to direct funds they seek to donate to advance racial equality can navigate to the Giving Gap website and find descriptions of hundreds of Black nonprofits, along with links to each organization's website. The list continues to grow and includes groups operating in fields as diverse as arts, food security, and criminal justice.

The sobering reality that the creation of Giving Gap in the fall of 2020 attracted national media attention serves as an indictment of the charitable sector generally and of commercially affiliated donor-advised funds in particular.[41] After a spring in which a pandemic revealed the deadly consequences of systemic racism in our healthcare system and a summer which saw a broad embrace by corporate America of the need to address persistent anti-Black racism, Giving Gap launched in October.

A month after George Floyd's murder and at least three months after the racially disparate impact of COVID-19 had become plain,[42] Fidelity Charitable had published a report of its own. It "examined Fidelity Charitable donor grantmaking activity from January to April 2020, [] zoom[ing] in to understand how donors in different geographic areas responded to the crisis—the ways they united behind a common purpose and the ways that their unique experiences with the virus created more location-specific giving patterns."[43] That report would later be featured in the same *New York Times* story describing the Giving Gap (then referred to as "Give Blck") launch. Remarkably, its forty pages do not contain a single mention the words race, racism, Black, or Latinx.

Grass-roots efforts such as Giving Gap fill a void left not just by entrenched players in the philanthropic world but also by relative upstarts like commercially affiliated donor-advised funds. But one can easily imagine commercially affiliated DAFs becoming agents of change, willingly or otherwise. Unlike private foundations, commercially affiliated DAFs face no annual payout requirement. As a result, reform efforts targeting these funds have emphasized extending Grand Bargain-like timing requirements to ensure that operating charities do not find themselves philanthropic Vladimirs and Estragons, endlessly waiting for their donor-advised fund Godots.[44]

The debate over imposing a payout rule or another goad to giving overshadows opportunities for reforms based on targeting. Giving Gap suggests what we might demand of commercially affiliated donor-advised funds to ensure the arrival of a charitable final act that is not merely timely but targeted and transparent. Critics urge reimposing the Grand Bargain's restraints on donor-advised funds by putting an expiration date—or imposing mandatory payout rate—on them. Dormant funds could instead flow to underserved charities like those highlighted by Giving Gap.

In an ideal world, a balance between the present and the future might be reflected in a perfectly calibrated payout rate that would apply both to private foundations and commercially affiliated donor-advised funds. In this instance, our flawed reality offers an opportunity to right a striking wrong. The June 2020 Fidelity Charitable report would have looked quite different had it announced the launch of a Giving Gap-style mechanism paired with thoughtful measures to spur giving to the charities it highlighted.

Corporate America has been widely criticized for failing to match its aspirational language on racial equity with action, and DAFs have been complicit in funding hate. Along with these failures, though, come opportunities. Commercially affiliated donor-advised funds have the power to shrink that gap in concrete ways. Commercial sponsors qualify as exempt based on their charitable purposes, a concept that encompasses a broad range of prosocial objectives, notably including "to eliminate prejudice and discrimination."[45] As outright owners of donor-advised fund assets once contributed, they are clearly empowered to act when donor-advisers fail to do so. To maintain their status as tax-exempt public charities, commercially affiliated sponsors could be required to publish a short list of priorities to receive a share of any dormant funds.

Some commercially affiliated donor-advised funds already maintain dormant funds policies.[46] But the public knows little about how they work and less about what they accomplish. Imposing clear standards requiring publication of those policies along with recipients of dormant funds would allow the public to assess not only how seriously players like Fidelity and Goldman Sachs engage with the questions at the heart of the Grand Bargain's accountability mechanism but whether they can transcend them.

Such a dormant funds mandate could take on challenges of racial inequity that went unaddressed by 1969's Grand Bargain. Sponsors could be required by regulators not merely to identify some public charity or charities as recipients of dormant assets but to name recipient charities for dormant funds led by and serving historically underserved communities. Shifting real money to these organizations could start to erode philanthropy's race gap. It would also incentivize commercial sponsors to devote some of their considerable time and energy to identifying worthy charitable recipients. Publicizing their choices would guide donors who want to contribute to the struggle for racial equality but remain uncertain about where to begin.

Three Principles for Tailored Regulatory Interventions

An absence of trust could mean boom or bust for for-profit philanthropy. Neither outcome will deliver the results the public expects nor secure the autonomy elites have long enjoyed. Yet rebuilding the trust for-profit philanthropy has eroded demands more than a return to the past.

Our society may not be more diverse than it was fifty years ago, but its commitment to embracing our differences has certainly changed. Today, merely devising tools that channel the most private resources to public ends while leaving the most vulnerable among us to suffer—exacerbating racial or gender inequity for example—would not be enough. This chapter does not argue that the most salient risk of DAFs lies in any harm they cause Blacks or that strategic corporate philanthropy should be curbed because it silences women's voices. But it shows that such risks lurk beneath the glossy surface of for-profit philanthropy and suggests that even a reinvigorated Grand Bargain would do little better by these measures.

Whereas the Grand Bargain once provided accountability, its strategies represent only one possible solution to the growing trust deficit. One could neatly match the three aspects of for-profit philanthropy to the Grand Bargain's transparency (chapter 1), timing (chapter 2), and targeting (chapter 3), but that would let a unique possibility pass us by. Critics of commercially affiliated donor-advised funds highlight their impact on the timing of philanthropy, for example. This chapter shows that responding to for-profit philanthropy need not—and perhaps should not—rigidly adhere to that rote formula, attempting to impose timing requirements on donor-advised funds, improved targeting on strategic corporate philanthropy, and heightened transparency on philanthropy LLCs.

The Grand Bargain, born in an era of Apollo missions and Vietnam protests, might not just be vulnerable to modern legal technologies but incompatible with today's values. Improving the targeting and transparency of commercially affiliated donor-advised funds with a well-crafted dormant funds policy would not renew the 1969 compromise on private foundation spending, but it would still represent worthwhile change. That observation underscores the fact that for-profit philanthropy presents an opportunity not simply to return to the Grand Bargain but to surpass it. Each innovation explored in Part I could be shaped by interventions designed to shore up any of the dimensions of accountability the Grand Bargain highlights or to pursue ambitions its architects never considered. Approaching the design of incremental regulation from this perspective offers opportunities to win meaningful victories even if it does not reclaim lost territory or deliver a comprehensive truce in the long war for control between elites and the public.

Strategic Corporate Philanthropy: Transparency and Targeting

The transformation strategic corporate philanthropy brings to corporate giving represents both risk and opportunity. Leveraging an organization's core strengths to pursue benefits for stakeholders as well as shareholders could have a far greater impact than simply writing a check. But those potential synergies come with a cost.

Corporate giving through private foundations creates an avenue through which each organization can publicly identify those stakeholders it prioritizes. And a private foundation allows those stakeholders to judge for themselves how successfully targeted those efforts have been. Unlike its countless other tax filings, reports filed by a corporation's private foundation must be made available to the public.

As remains true for all charities, the information they provide shapes "[h]ow the public perceives" both the foundation and its funder.[47] Strategic corporate philanthropy reduces that opportunity for stakeholder engagement. A benefit report would provide a different opportunity for the public to take the measure of corporate philanthropy. Participation by stakeholders in its preparation suggests how such reforms could not merely recreate but improve upon aspects of the Grand Bargain. Ventures may claim to be balancing doing well and doing good, but when corporate America's leadership does not mirror the composition of its workers, customers, and suppliers, how can those stakeholders trust that leaders will pursue their interests alongside those of shareholders?

Opportunities for stakeholders to add diverse voices to shaping corporate commitments to benefiting the public remain all too rare. Losing the transparency provided by the corporate foundation eliminates one way stakeholders can influence the targeting or the timing of corporate philanthropy. Without transparency, trust comes less easily, complicating the partnership strategic corporate philanthropy should represent. If stakeholders have no way to verify that apparently generous corporate behavior meets their expectations, virtue signaling becomes a distinct risk. It may make the temptation to present vice as virtue (or worse, to redeploy resources from virtue to vice) irresistible.

Any response to the rise of strategic corporate philanthropy must prioritize the role of stakeholders. Providing mechanisms for workers and other stakeholders to shape and respond to corporate claims to be acting in their interests would help hold corporate America accountable. No corporation must engage in philanthropy. And those that do need not form a private foundation to broadcast their intentions. But accountability—and the transparency that provides it—remains essential.

Providing stakeholders with the access necessary to police corporate philanthropic claims would allow workers and customers to hold corporations accountable. The central challenge posed by strategic corporate philanthropy lies in ensuring that what appears to serve the public interest does exactly that. Transparency does not offer a substitute for that targeting, but a tool for providing it. The Grand Bargain delivers transparency and targeting separately. Creating a universal benefit report mandate recognizes their inextricable connections and responds by melding the two.

Philanthropy LLCs: Timing and Targeting

Whether the timing of charity matters depends largely on your point of view. Donors, one might say, have a lower discount rate than those in need. Almost by definition, donors can afford to be more patient than most. The Grand Bargain did far less to encourage behavior reflecting the urgency of recipients than many policymakers hoped. As a result, the private foundation rules contemplate a long, possibly perpetual, life span for those philanthropic vehicles.

Aspects of for-profit philanthropy can similarly slow rather than speed the delivery of charity. By single-mindedly channeling the perspective of a patient donor, an LLC can put greater distance between the moment when charity leaves their hands and when it ultimately finds those in need. Any resulting delays will inevitably be felt more keenly by beneficiaries than by philanthropists.

For reasons that now seem quite dated, private foundations presume that the accumulation and the philanthropic distribution of wealth occur sequentially rather than concurrently. Revisiting assumptions that may needlessly delay giving, removing barriers to interweaving earning and giving, could further speed the receipt of charity. Such changes could provide help to those who need it today rather than tomorrow.

The rise of for-profit philanthropy has already begun to do just that. Allowing commerce and philanthropy to occur simultaneously with the aid of a philanthropy LLC means recipients do not need to wait until founders retire to benefit from their largesse. Removing Grand Bargain-era targeting measures that have long prevented private foundations from co-creating could accelerate the timing of philanthropic giving.

The Grand Bargain relegates philanthropic giving to a second act in the public life of wealthy donors. The philanthropy LLC allows considerably more overlap, potentially accelerating charitable giving ahead by decades. Revising the self-dealing rules would allow charities, funders, and regulators to adapt to a post-Grand Bargain reality in which commerce and philanthropy increasingly intersect, ensuring that philanthropy's benefits target those most in need, when they need it most. Thoughtfully easing the Grand Bargain's strict prohibitions against self dealing by private foundations could counterintuitively guard against virtue signaling by encouraging wealthy patrons to embrace those foundations once again.

Commercially Affiliated DAFs: Targeting, Timing and Transparency

Black Americans have shorter life spans[48]—and therefore higher charitable discount rates—than their white counterparts. That reality provides crucial context for the growing challenge posed by commercially affiliated donor-advised funds. As critics note, donors can employ them to delay and disguise their giving. For the wealthiest donors, commercially affiliated donor-advised funds make it easy to skirt the timing requirements of the Grand Bargain.

At the retail level, commercially affiliated donor-advised funds provide convenience. A simple change could help target charity to Black Americans, providing a counterweight to both the structural obstacles long faced by Black charities and the new challenges posed by for-profit philanthropy. Comprehensive reforms targeting commercially affiliated donor-advised funds might advance the cause of racial equity by limiting the life span of those funds in order to speed donated funds to those in need. But donor-advised funds, operating on a vast scale that allows financial giants to offer services other charities could not, could be compelled to take more direct action.

Such funds attract capital by promising to ease administrative burdens. For example, they readily accept all sorts of non-cash contributions, taking on the burden of liquidating those assets. The same resources that allow sponsors to supply liquidity to donors and charities could allow them to steer resources toward underserved organizations directly. Targeting even a small portion of the assets merely warehoused—rather than deployed toward charitable ends—toward racial justice might do little to address the broader question of how to regulate donor-advised funds. But it could nevertheless do a world of good.

Given the striking inequities in the funding available to Black-led charities "without active antiracist measures to ensure equity in funding for the entire social sector, philanthropists inadvertently contribute to inequities in society."[49] Vanguard and Fidelity could help to address that inequity. Simply requiring each to publicly identify a short list of funding priorities eligible to receive a portion of dormant funds would allow sponsors to make their commitments to racial equity much more than virtue signaling. Providing convenience to their clients while addressing long-standing shortfalls for Black-led charities would not silence critics but would give them food for thought.

Giving Gap might not exist if commercial sponsors had been compelled to highlight underserved charities in this way. In a better world, Vanguard or Fidelity might even have helped create it. At the height of the Black Lives Matter movement, corporate America embraced a commitment to challenging systemic racism. Translation of that allyship into direct action has been limited at best.

A dormant funds rule embracing the values of targeting and transparency would allow Vanguard and Fidelity to play to their proven strengths. They could advance the cause of racial equality with the same ruthless efficiency they have used to dominate the charitable sector. Publicizing their actions could then, in turn, enable and encourage their clients and others to support Black-led and Black-serving charities.

Commercially affiliated donor-advised funds threaten to slow the flow of funds from donors to charities. That dynamic poses a particular challenge for Black-led charities. Developing mechanisms that fill the gap revealed by efforts such as Giving Gap would allow sponsors to encourage their large and growing client base to counter the impact of that timing delay by targeting resources toward racial equality.

Conclusion

Some problems can be tackled incrementally, with many small victories building toward a larger objective. In other cases, pushing a proverbial boulder halfway up a hill may be no victory at all. This chapter suggests that piecemeal reforms aimed at commercially affiliated donor-advised funds, strategic corporate philanthropy, or philanthropy LLCs would curb the threat of virtue signaling—or of secret vice—those innovations pose. Its policies offer a stark contrast with the Grand Bargain's ambitious scope and with its hidebound approach to accountability.

This incremental approach creates unconventional opportunities to speed the flow of philanthropy, to target its impact to those in greatest need, and to provide outsiders with greater insight. It also reveals the importance of taking a fresh look at old questions. For-profit philanthropy pointedly rejects the terms of the Grand Bargain. The public might do the same if ordinary Americans understood how poorly its aging legal framework addresses contemporary concerns. In some respects, the Grand Bargain overreaches, whereas in others it ignores critical values simply because yesteryear's leaders did not share them.

Modest changes could fill gaps left by a half-century-old compromise but will not put a boulder atop a hill on their own. The next two chapters offer more ambitious responses to the disruptions caused by for-profit philanthropy. Given the outsized power held by a handful of for-profit philanthropy players, from Zuckerberg to Vanguard, chapter 7 considers how private actors might obviate the need for public intervention by undertaking timing, targeting, and transparency commitments on their own. Of course, enlightened self-interest might not be enough to persuade wealthy elites to police themselves.

The final chapter imagines what a new and lasting truce—a More Perfect Bargain—between elites and the public might require. A more sharply progressive income tax or a new wealth tax might provide an anvil strong enough to allow policymakers to fashion enduring accountability safeguards, much as the income and estate taxes once did for the Grand Bargain. But, as both this chapter and the next reveal, remaining fixated on tax simply because the Grand Bargain successfully relied on it would be as foolish as focusing only on the timing of commercially affiliated donor-advised fund distributions without considering their targeting or transparency.

Each of these three distinct responses to for-profit philanthropy shows why addressing its impact must not be a paint-by-numbers affair. Particularly when remedies take the form of tailored regulatory interventions, unorthodox strategies that focus directly on what matters most may prove essential. Merely attempting to impose the Grand Bargain on a new form of philanthropy and a new generation of philanthropists would squander an important opportunity to make today's values part of philanthropy's future.

7

Private Ordering Solutions

Chapter 6 showed how tailored regulatory interventions rebuild trust between elites and the public by nudging for-profit philanthropy toward closer alignment with today's values. Intervening at a more intimate scale than the Grand Bargain, it invites new solutions to old problems. This chapter and the next retain that unconventional perspective while broadening their focus. They turn to systemic solutions, recognizing that each aspect of for-profit philanthropy can be traced to the same unraveling.

The Grand Bargain offers strategic assurances as essential to seeding trust in elite philanthropy as state charity law has long been to charity writ large. Providing both wealthy benefactors and run-of-the-mill charities with a language in which they can reliably communicate their commitment to serving the public interest unlocks public support for both. Charities can proclaim to donors, beneficiaries, and the public that, once cash or property has been contributed to a charitable corporation or trust, its managers lack the power to divert those contributions to private uses. This core feature of state charity law—known as the nondistribution constraint—ensures that promises to serve the public interest will not be broken.

The regulatory guardrails of the Grand Bargain do the same and more for wealthy donors, ensuring that these philanthropists will be allowed to retain control over the capital they hold in trust for the public. By embracing a regulated form, philanthropists telegraph their intentions and point to a federal framework for holding them to their word. They will target their largesse to recipients Congress deems worthy and eschew unsavory entanglements with business and politics. They will give consistently over time, neither exhausting the supply of philanthropic capital capriciously nor hoarding it for future needs that may never materialize. They will be transparent to regulators and the public about the origins and destinations of the assets they command in service of the public good.

Coloring outside those lines represents a strategically destabilizing move that jeopardizes public trust and courts more forceful regulation. The public could join elites in rejecting the Grand Bargain to assert direct control over elite resources. That might come, for example, in the form of sharply higher taxes. Too much public control would bring an end to Carnegie's partnership—threatening

For-Profit Philanthropy. Dana Brakman Reiser and Steven A. Dean, Oxford University Press. © Oxford University Press 2023. DOI: 10.1093/oso/9780190074500.003.0008

a return to the philanthropic nadir of Rockefeller's congressional fiasco—a risk even for-profit philanthropists like Zuckerberg and Omidyar cannot ignore.

Chapter 8 will turn to the government for help, but this chapter rejects conventional regulation, asking instead whether wealthy elites can blaze their own path past these threats. The disruptive entrepreneurs embracing for-profit philanthropy can act strategically to reinforce the trust the Grand Bargain once secured, even in the absence of government enforcement. The private sector has, after all, fueled the innovation on display in the rise of philanthropy LLCs, commercially affiliated donor-advised funds, and strategic corporate philanthropy. Perhaps it can help tame those creations to build a more accountable for-profit philanthropy to forestall the risk that public skepticism will smother it.

Both elites and the public could gain much from the attempt. If they can devise an algorithm capable of maintaining the public's trust, for-profit philanthropists offer society vast resources and a compelling new paradigm to deploy them flexibly and efficiently. It would also allow elites to preempt regulatory action and enable them to retain control of the "great part of the increased wealth of the community"[1] the Grand Bargain long entrusted to them.

Much of charity law can be described as tools to demonstrate commitment. The nondistribution constraint that locks charitable assets in place in particular has proven a remarkably potent source of trust by helping insiders warrant they will resist the temptations of personal enrichment or other private benefit.[2] Rather than relying on policymakers to supply the trust for-profit philanthropy needs, careful private ordering could reveal corporate philanthropists, commercially affiliated donor-advised funds, and philanthropy LLCs to be quite capable of reversing the damage their innovation has already done.

A precisely tailored corporate governance scheme could impose targeting limitations on strategic corporate philanthropy conducted through a dedicated subsidiary. A commercially affiliated donor-advised fund could adopt a contractual dead man's switch to enforce timing restraints on their clients on their own, or as part of an industry-wide initiative. Philanthropy LLCs could build transparency obligations into their operating agreements, and even execute self-enforcing agreements to ensure compliance.

Before dismissing the possibility that powerful elites might be capable of successfully binding themselves to the proverbial mast—committing to accountability by embracing "fewer opportunities rather than more"[3]—consider the little remarked role corporate governance played in preserving the legacy of one of conscious consumerism's most iconic brands.[4] When Ben and Jerry sold their business to Unilever, the Vermont-based venture's social mission seemed certain to be stripped away in the name of financial profits. Both men "worried that Unilever would abandon the progressive aspects of the business and run it as a soulless subsidiary."[5] Today, one could say that the reverse has happened, with

Unilever embracing constituencies and stakeholders that once would have received little attention.[6] The key to the story: private ordering.

As a subsidiary of a global giant, Ben & Jerry's maintained its stance on social issues impacting its production and distribution through the careful design of its governance structure. An independent board at the subsidiary level was a key part of the agreement concluded when Unilever acquired control of Ben & Jerry's shares.[7] Nearly all the subsidiary board's members serve without any need for Unilever's blessing even though the subsidiary controls "the essential elements of the brand."[8] Private contract, not public regulation, insulates Ben & Jerry's from financial pressures that might draw it into a vicious circle of doing well at the expense of doing good.

Acquiring control of Ben & Jerry's stock without insisting on control of its board allowed Unilever to put its money—or more precisely its intellectual property—where its mouth is. Controlling the Ben & Jerry's brand gives its independent board immense sway over Ben & Jerry's fate. Their example has been a key influence in the prosocial shifts of its multinational parent, not all of which the markets approved. Indeed, the commitment forged at the time of Ben & Jerry's acquisition proved so powerful that in 2021, the Unilever parent was unable to stop its subsidiary from cutting ties with an Israeli affiliate, despite investor pressure.[9] Some suggest Unilever's early 2022 decision to separate its ice cream brands into a stand-alone division can be explained in part as a response to this conflict,[10] a kind of vindication for its independent board.

Endowed with limitless resources and spurred on by a fear of public humiliation of the sort once delivered to Rockefeller, elites could turn to private ordering to recapture the trust lost to for-profit philanthropy. Of course, skepticism about the capacity of private actors to adequately address societal risks has a pedigree as old as philanthropy itself.[11] Chapter 6 underscores why the public remains wary of the idea that private interests might willingly embrace sacrifice. After all, despite Ben & Jerry's success using easily imitated corporate governance tools, few social enterprises have replicated its achievement at scale.[12]

Yet Ben & Jerry's shows how for-profit philanthropy could succeed through private ordering where smaller players have not. When they negotiated the acquisition that defied expectations to help preserve their mission, Ben, Jerry, and their eponymous firm enjoyed a luxury for-profit philanthropists share: power. Like the formidable team of Ben and Jerry—but unlike capital-starved social enterprises, dependent on investors for the fuel their ventures need and on state legislatures' craftsmanship for their vehicles—for-profit philanthropists have the freedom to set their own priorities. CZI, Fidelity Charitable, and GM all have the power to chart their own path, precisely as the latter did when it announced its embrace of electric vehicles. All have the resources needed to erect the legal architecture necessary to balance the interests of a variety of stakeholders.

No less important, the members of the privileged circle of for-profit philanthropists also have reason to roll out a robust commitment to giving. Doing so may preempt tailored regulatory interventions of the types described in chapter 6, as well as more dramatic public interventions like the Grand Bargain or those envisioned in chapter 8. In addition to this ample incentive, adopting accountability devices through private ordering can protect their reputations along with the ambitious social agendas their for-profit philanthropic innovations embrace. For those with the means, designing a way to shield for-profit philanthropy's nimble new paradigm against a backlash powered by distrust and that threatens to prompt potentially intrusive regulation could prove a prudent investment.

As the Grand Bargain yields to for-profit philanthropy, trust has begun to give way along with it. Skepticism about elite commitment to the public interest may have fallen sharply since Rockefeller's day, but a renewed interest in wealth taxes reveals that the faith the 99 percent have found in the 1 percent has its limits.[13] If for-profit philanthropists could shore up that trust by embracing a commitment to accountable philanthropy—"a *strategic* move . . . that induces the other player to choose in one's favor"[14]—robust enough to tame even the risk of gold-plated doomsday scenarios like a billionaires tax they would be foolish not to try. This chapter offers three examples of how for-profit philanthropists might deploy private ordering to enhance accountability and to build trust without government intervention.

For-Profit Philanthropy's Compelling New Paradigm

The appeal of for-profit philanthropy's new paradigm mirrors that of the hybrids considered in chapter 5. Unlike charities, social enterprises can—at least in theory—draw on capital markets to fuel their missions. For their part, for-profit philanthropists deploy business tools the Grand Bargain forbids foundations. Powerful enough to build fortunes and empires, it seems reasonable to wonder whether they might also anchor successful responses to society's biggest challenges.

The Grand Bargain's rigid requirements can seem frustratingly arbitrary. Red tape presents its own challenges but placing potent weapons for pursuing philanthropic goals out of reach puts wealthy donors in an unfamiliar position. Enjoying the benefits of charitable status means accepting a host of obligations. Some appear more burdensome today than they once did.

Foundations, including those embedded within a corporate structure, must abide by extensive disclosure protocols.[15] And although a foundation might have no objection to detailing its contributions to museums, ballets, and concert halls,[16] for-profit philanthropy's integration of mission and profit-making changes that calculus. For all the reasons firms jealously guard their strategies and know-how, secrecy becomes more valuable when a firm shifts from conventional to strategic corporate philanthropy. Disclosure understandably becomes less appealing as philanthropy implicates core businesses and the interests of stakeholders—including employees and customers—rather than a safely distant group of charitable beneficiaries.

Such tensions inevitably grow as for-profit philanthropy's unconventional strategies clash with regulatory mechanisms crafted in a different era. A nimbler approach to providing transparency could help deliver a blend of doing well and doing good never contemplated by the Grand Bargain's architects. Just as easily, of course, it could open the door to self-aggrandizing virtue signaling with little basis in fact. Corporate greenwashing such as Volkswagen's "defeat devices" illustrates the threat of betrayal posed by strategic corporate philanthropy.[17] Without a reliable means of verifying assertions of public benefit—whether the Grand Bargain's extensive disclosure apparatus for foundations, the stakeholder-monitored benefit reports described in chapter 6, or some other transparency device—it would be impossible to distinguish between sham philanthropy and the real thing.

Another salient boundary for-profit philanthropy threatens comes in the form of the ban on political campaign activity. Charities, including foundations, intervening in a political campaign lose the privileged status that allows them to avoid taxes on their income and to receive tax-deductible contributions. Such a charity becomes an "action organization if it participates or intervenes, directly or indirectly, in any political campaign" and therefore ineligible for §501(c)(3) status.[18]

In 1954, Senator Lyndon Johnson sought to "deny[] tax-exempt status . . . to those who intervene in any political campaign on behalf of any candidate for any public office."[19] He proposed what would become known as the Johnson Amendment after learning that "two wealthy Texans had used tax-exempt organizations they headed . . . to support a young state senator who opposed Johnson in that year's primary election."[20] By folding that bright-line rule prohibiting overt campaigning into the Grand Bargain, Congress permitted even the wealthiest philanthropists to make a credible promise to keep their philanthropy separate from political campaigns. In a world in which money translates ever-more readily into political power, such a commitment delivers a potent message of restraint.

Unsurprisingly, among the many limitations charitable entities bear in order to obtain favorable tax treatment, the Johnson Amendment has long been one of the most polarizing. A simmering discontent over the limits it imposes periodically boils over. The most recent episode related to scrutiny by the Internal Revenue Service of organizations with politically evocative terms in their names.[21] Both liberal and conservative charities found themselves subject to heightened scrutiny as a result of efforts to police that line.[22] The ensuing conflagration became one of the biggest scandals of the Obama era, in part thanks to perceptions of bias on the part of the Internal Revenue Service.[23]

Although that incident involved politically focused organizations, the Johnson Amendment implicates any tax-exempt charity that strays into political campaigning. A church, for example, might violate it by expressing strong views on a candidate on the eve of an election.[24] However closely tied to its charitable purpose, it strikes squarely at Senator Johnson's worry that a tax break might influence the outcome of an election.

Criticisms of the Johnson Amendment tend to take two forms. The first reflects constitutional concerns. Although the Supreme Court has squarely rejected First Amendment claims,[25] conditioning tax benefits on pastors limiting what they say at the pulpit remains hard to square with strong visions of free speech.[26]

The second—more relevant here—reflects the Grand Bargain's narrow vision of permissible social returns. Insisting that charities remain apolitical, even when shaping political reform represents the best pathway to achieving a charity's aims, the Johnson Amendment binds elite philanthropists to the mast. The results are remarkable. Despite its power, the Gates Foundation must endure the same constraints on intervening in a political campaign as the humblest parish church.

An unwillingness to forswear what might provide the most bang for each philanthropic buck defines for-profit philanthropy. Choosing a tax-exempt charitable form for a venture allows a philanthropist to foreclose the use of political leverage. For a wealthy donor, escaping the strictures of the Johnson Amendment might on its own justify rejecting the Grand Bargain.

Embracing philanthropy LLCs or strategic corporate philanthropy spares those seeking to generate public benefits from these constraints and a host of others. CZI enjoys the freedom to one day decide that the best way to achieve its lofty aims would be to elect Max or August Zuckerberg to higher office. Whether or not it seems plausible today that CZI would do such a thing hardly matters. The Gates Foundation unequivocally took that possibility off the table. When Melinda French Gates shifted her philanthropy away from the Gates Foundation and toward Pivotal Ventures, she did so in part to "get more women . . . to run for public office."[27]

These examples represent only the tip of the philanthropic innovation iceberg. Commercially affiliated donor-advised funds secure charitable status while skirting the Grand Bargain. Thanks to their freedom from the constraints imposed on foundations they can market temporal flexibility to attract vast stores of charitably committed resources.

Collectively, these innovations raise urgent questions of accountability, but each departure from traditional modes of philanthropy also testifies to the relentless creativity of those seeking to do good. Google's Flu Trends appeared poised to harness the power of Google's search feature to produce a public benefit, by monitoring "searches that match terms for flu-related activity" to track outbreaks in real time.[28] For-profit philanthropic innovation like this promises to yield even greater prizes than a foundation could. Unfortunately, the effort suffered a serious and public disappointment in 2013 when it mispredicted flu outbreaks by a substantial margin.

Free of the transparency requirements of the Grand Bargain, had Google not chosen to boast about its hopes for the technology, the public may never have had the opportunity to judge. Only Google's eagerness to take credit for its ill-fated effort made it possible for analysts to dissect this failure, at least to the extent Google made its data and processes available to them. When a foundation's ambitious effort to cure a disease goes astray, the public might not know why but they will know that can safely rule out the possibility that the donor's greed doomed it. Given the inconsistent nature of for-profit philanthropic transparency, that will not be true for every such misstep. As a result, those failures could undermine the public's faith not just in CZI or Fidelity Charitable but in philanthropy writ large.

In the absence of accountability, the use of political leverage may be seen as the culprit. Or that failure might be perceived to be the result of combining charitable and profit-making aims into an obscure amalgam or of warehousing wealth. Any of the countless differences between for-profit philanthropy and its traditional counterpart might be blamed.

By taking each of those options off the table, the Grand Bargain reassures the public that conventional philanthropy's inevitable failings will be honest ones. The collective costs that commercially affiliated donor-advised funds, philanthropy LLCs, and strategic corporate philanthropy could impose by putting trust at risk might be measured in the philanthropy that may never arrive. Whether because elites lose the power to win over a skeptical public or because that frustrated public decides to assert direct control over elite wealth, the philanthropy easily taken for granted might one day simply disappear. The lost fruits of that giving—"benefits from having fewer opportunities rather than more"[29]—would be lost to heavy tax burdens and more intrusive regulation.

For-profit philanthropy promises massive capital infusions and the innovation needed to supercharge private and public returns. It also jeopardizes the trust that has long sustained the flow of philanthropic capital. Fortunately, neither piecemeal public regulation, such as that described in the last chapter, nor the new comprehensive truce outlined in the next represents the only paths to solving philanthropy's accountability problem.

Private ordering presents a viable alternative. The remainder of this chapter imagines three ways for-profit philanthropists themselves might voluntarily offer up the accountability long secured by the Grand Bargain. These solutions are ones for-profit philanthropists can implement on their own or in concert, and that they might well embrace—if only to ward off more intrusive interventions.

Private Ordering for For-Profit Philanthropy

Rejecting conventional philanthropic forms means leaving behind the Grand Bargain. With that freedom comes the challenge of designing other means of sustaining the public's trust in philanthropy and philanthropists. Meeting this challenge with private ordering requires a clear understanding of how a faltering Grand Bargain and burgeoning for-profit philanthropic innovation spawns distrust, as well as the motivation and resources to dispel it.

Fortunately, elite philanthropists have powerful incentives—not least the specter of an empowered public displacing philanthropists that haunted Carnegie—to undertake private ordering. And unlike social enterprises—dependent on the state for off-the-rack corporate governance craftsmanship—they need not shop retail. They have the wherewithal to enlist whatever tailoring talent might be needed to broadcast persuasive evidence of their idiosyncratic commitment to the public interest. A $45 billion bet such as CZI's provides ample opportunity for the careful design that could safeguard for-profit philanthropy's compelling new paradigm by keeping aggressive regulation at bay.

Fidelity, Vanguard, and the other dominant players that sponsor the leading commercially affiliated donor-advised funds can likewise easily afford the necessary legal architecture. Protecting their brands and business models from intrusive regulation would certainly be a worthwhile investment. Corporate donors most of all should understand the critical role trust plays in preserving brand value and how easily it can be lost. Paying to shield it alongside their new vision of strategic corporate philanthropy should be an easy choice.

Accountability—once delivered in timing, targeting, and transparency by the Grand Bargain—has become the first victim of philanthropic innovation. Private ordering solutions can allay this trio of concerns, both reestablishing boundaries and providing the means to patrol them. By now it should be clear that philanthropy LLCs, strategic corporate philanthropy, and commercially affiliated donor-advised funds implicate each of these dimensions of accountability. To sharpen our focus, the remainder of this chapter will highlight how each of these for-profit philanthropy innovations creates gaps in just one of these aspects of accountability and then offers a private ordering proposal to address it.

Strategic Corporate Philanthropy and Targeting

Corporate titans, like Carnegie in his day, understand the levers of power. Few may appreciate the challenges facing the many constituencies within their sphere of influence better. Strategic corporate philanthropy leans into Carnegie's view that managers can orchestrate public benefits just as effectively as they can shareholder benefits. With that in mind, rather than accept the Grand Bargain's half-century-old congressional criteria for philanthropic largesse, corporate actors increasingly find ways to define charity in terms that equate public good with the needs of constituencies from shareholders to employees to customers and suppliers.

A crucial challenge posed by strategic corporate philanthropy lies in how these ventures will respond when events test this assumption. If forced to choose among stakeholders, charitable beneficiaries and public benefit will predictably take a backseat to louder and more powerful constituencies. How much we should trust corporations to define the targets of their philanthropy becomes a function of how large the area of overlap between profit and purpose proves to be.

Corporate foundations outsource the task of defining the proper targets of their largesse. By contributing to a foundation, a corporation can commit "to doing good" simply by embracing the Grand Bargain's vision of philanthropy. Corporate foundations funded annually will, of course, be responsive to their donors. But even that power of the purse remains subject to the Grand Bargain. A corporation might go so far as to withhold future contributions but must do so openly, in full view of the public. However imperfectly, the foundation allows the most powerful corporate philanthropists to be held accountable to standards imposed by Congress.

The nondistribution constraint—imposed by state charity law rather than by the Grand Bargain—undergirds that commitment. Once a corporate donor contributes to its foundation, it may not claw that contribution back. The self-dealing rules—reinforced with respect to foundations by the Grand Bargain—go further, ensuring that a corporation does not divert those contributions in order to derive an indirect advantage through its dealings with a captive foundation. Such clear legal boundaries between doing well and doing good operationalize the Grand Bargain's targeting objective, ensuring that a corporate foundation's actions match its aspirations.

When General Motors did away with its foundation, the Grand Bargain's targeting protections went with it. Corporate donors' ability to pick and choose what to fund with in-house giving likewise removes targeting protections even in firms that retain their foundations. Without carefully crafted constraints, strategic corporate philanthropy risks becoming whatever its patron wishes. Any alternative private ordering mechanism will have to not only identify legitimate targets but also police corporate actors' pursuit of them.

Donor-Advised Funds and Timing

Mutual fund giants such as Fidelity and Vanguard might be financial powerhouses little different than the industrial giants of Carnegie's time. Yet their commercially affiliated donor-advised funds disrupt his vision of philanthropists as trustees for the public. These funds seek to crowdsource philanthropy, the opposite of Carnegie's centralized control.

Mutual fund giants such as Fidelity and Vanguard might be business behemoths implementing strategic corporate philanthropy. Yet their commercially affiliated donor-advised funds project an image of democratizing philanthropy. Fidelity Charitable and Vanguard Charitable serve as platforms for crowdsourced charitable giving, not tools to centralize control. By acting as an intermediary between a donor and the recipients of their beneficence, they transform direct relationships into more distant connections.[30] When philanthropists give to a donor-advised fund, they separate themselves from the objects of their charity both legally and temporally.[31] Once Fidelity Charitable or Vanguard Charitable receives a donation, no legal connection between a donor and a hypothetical future recipient exists.

The Grand Bargain mandates that foundations spend 5 percent of their assets annually. By remaining public charities—skirting the stricter private foundation rules of the Grand Bargain—donor-advised funds spare wealthy clients from that timing requirement. A commercially affiliated donor-advised fund client may choose never to close the philanthropic loop by advising their fund to deploy the capital they contributed. They may go so far as to name a future advisor for their fund, to continue the potential timing delay even after their death.

This donor has already received and consumed the tax benefits of charity and has no obligation to ensure that Fidelity or Vanguard ever parts with that contribution. Neither the commercial sponsor nor the donor has any financial imperative to ensure contributed assets ever leave the fund. And should they fail to deploy the particular charitable resources contained in an individual donor-advised fund, the public would never know. For private ordering to restore trust that philanthropic promises will be fulfilled, it must discipline the timing of donor-advised fund distributions.

Philanthropy LLCs and Transparency

Elite philanthropists establishing LLCs to manage their prosocial portfolios have good reasons to guard their privacy and well understand the value of selective disclosure. Wealthy and prominent people have always been targets of unwanted attention from regulators, competitors, and the public at large.[32] In today's digital world, threats to privacy lurk everywhere.

High-profile individuals and firms guard their ability to tell their own story because they understand the power of controlling the narrative. At the risk of stating the obvious, Mark Zuckerberg has built an empire on the desire of millions of users to carefully curate the images they present to the world. But trust suffers in the absence of transparency.

The regulatory framework for foundations recognizes these concerns and responds with a surprisingly powerful tool. The Form-990 PF represents more than a tax return, serving as an annual disclosure document available to the public. Private foundations use this form to provide a balance sheet, statements of assets, and lists of grants, as well as a list of managers and contributors indicating which individuals fall into both categories. The press and public can easily obtain this information through the GuideStar website.

While they hardly make foundation activities an open book, the transparency obligations imposed on foundations require rigorous public disclosure. These demands stand in stark contrast to the obligations imposed on other legal entities. Tax returns, once made public as a routine matter, have since been made private. For taxable entities and individuals today, nearly all tax information can be disclosed only rarely.[33]

Opting out of the Grand Bargain's disclosure obligations secures for philanthropy LLC founders far more private treatment. There can be no risk that an embarrassing Form 990-PF will be unearthed to plague a philanthropy LLC when none exists. A single-member LLC's "philanthropy nothing" status avoids tax reporting at the organizational level altogether. Congress could change all of that, of course. Private ordering could too, providing transparency by ensuring public access to information about philanthropy LLCs' donors and actions.

Privatizing Commitment

Individually, strategic corporate philanthropy, commercially affiliated donor-advised funds, and the philanthropy LLC highlight the potential of for-profit philanthropy. Harnessing the power of wealthy individuals and influential firms to fuel innovation in philanthropy could generate extraordinary benefits for the public. Disruptive philanthropic technologies could help transform countless lives.

Viewed together, though, these three distinct aspects of for-profit philanthropy bring a troubling pattern into focus. In pursuit of public benefits, they skirt regulatory frameworks designed to generate accountability. Collectively, they threaten the trust long preserved by the Grand Bargain.

Fortunately, the juxtaposition of Rockefeller's misplaced reliance on Congress to provide and communicate evidence of a commitment to the public interest and Ben & Jerry's shocking success in shielding its mission with private ordering suggests that for-profit philanthropy could rebuild that lost trust on its own. Even if the state delivers neither the targeted regulatory interventions of chapter 6 nor the More Perfect Bargain envisioned by chapter 8, the influential actors disdaining the Grand Bargain could succeed on their own.

Rockefeller's push for a federally chartered foundation fell short despite—or perhaps because of—his vast influence. Ben & Jerry's succeeded in charting its unconventional path armed only with a profitable business and ordinary corporate governance tools. The remainder of this chapter shows how the same private parties that have undermined the Grand Bargain could rebuild trust in philanthropy without state intervention. Zuckerberg's entrepreneurial acumen, Fidelity's money management expertise, and the vast supply chains and distribution networks of firms like GM and Google make them more than equal to that challenge. Put differently, if Jeff Bezos can build a rocket to take him into space (and to bring him home) he could easily equal Ben & Jerry's feat.

The man-bites-dog story of Ben & Jerry's takeover by—and, figuratively, of—Unilever shows what improbable victories can be won by empowered and motivated private parties using conventional legal mechanisms. The purchase of the small Vermont ice cream maker by a global behemoth refused to follow the standard script. Rather than preserving its folksy charm while stripping it of costly principles, Unilever has allowed Ben & Jerry's to balance other priorities alongside profits, at times to do so in spades. Control of the Ben & Jerry subsidiary's board, preserved through a carefully tailored corporate governance framework, ensures that the ice cream maker's dedication to a broad range of stakeholders remains intact.

The philanthropic subsidiary, the donor-advised fund dead-man's switch, and the self-executing transparency mechanisms for philanthropy LLCs reject the narrow vision of the Grand Bargain just as the targeted regulatory interventions described in chapter 6 do. But they shift focus from what legislators can do for for-profit philanthropy to what these talent- and resource-rich organizations can do for themselves. Relying on private ordering to deliver targeting, timing, and transparency safeguards would rebuild trust by limiting for-profit philanthropy's degree of freedom. Through careful application of these conventional private tools, for-profit philanthropy's champions could defend their ambitious philanthropic visions and stave off the threat of public intervention.

A Strategic Corporate Philanthropy Subsidiary

The corporate foundation imposes constraints consistent with one late-1960s vision of doing good. Firms' turn away from the Grand Bargain's model of foundation giving need not mean the end of corporate philanthropy. For-profit philanthropy could simply open the door to new approaches. Private ordering could allow new philanthropic technologies to take shape while ensuring that such innovation serves stakeholders and shareholders.

A wholly owned GM philanthropy subsidiary could preserve its strategic corporate philanthropic vision with an independent board. Ben & Jerry's success shows it can be done. Chapter 5 shows that state law social enterprise hybrid legal forms keep entrepreneurs and investors from making a robust commitment to a double bottom line. Yet a conventional corporation has done just that.

Whether conventional or hybrid, the makeup and structure of our hypothetical corporate philanthropic subsidiary's board would control its fate. Naming stakeholder representatives, outside issue experts, or community advocates to a majority of the board seats would prove a more powerful commitment than filling its ranks with employees and officers.

Providing these independent directors the power to nominate their successors and control over key decisions—such as changes to the subsidiary's grantmaking parameters or even veto power over particular grants—would go even further. The board's members could also ensure that the subsidiary—which could, but need not, be a social enterprise hybrid—completes and submits a benefit report each year. They could do much more besides, involving stakeholders through a consultation process and pushing the subsidiary to make its report an accurate account of environmental gains and losses and employee interests served and sidelined.

Corporate governance tools that help shield corporations from market forces can require sophisticated legal advice to create and to maintain. For a shoestring social enterprise, such an expense would be daunting. Recognizing that—and eager to help social entrepreneurs embrace a balance between doing well and doing good—state legislators have made dozens of attempts to provide a ready-made alternative with hybrid forms. But in each case, they have balked at the cost of enforcement, leaving ventures vulnerable to disruptive market forces.[34]

Fortunately, GM and other leading corporations that may eschew foundations have the financial capacity to design enforceable protections for their philanthropic missions. They have the resources to revisit the private foundation and determine which of its accountability measures remain relevant in today's business context. Creating and sustaining the necessary machinery will represent a cost worth bearing if it helps realize the promise of strategic corporate philanthropy.

Strategic corporate philanthropy need not represent mere virtue signaling on a grand scale, but without adequate safeguards an absence of trust could make the two impossible for the public to distinguish. Deploying private ordering to ensure that strategic corporate philanthropy embraces a commitment to targeting resources toward stakeholders—including the public—could transform what threatens to become a race to the bottom into a race to the top. Critically, it could accomplish that end without help from the state.

A Dead Man's Switch for Donor-Advised Funds

Giving represents a means rather than an end. But for commercially affiliated donor-advised funds, that critical distinction has been lost. Commercially affiliated DAFs make it easy to give. Unfortunately, they make it all too easy to do little more than that.

Fidelity Charitable exemplifies that pattern. Navigating to its homepage brings assurances that donating to your "Giving Account" provides a tax deduction. It goes on to say that while givers "advise us on how to grant the money out to your favorite charities," a contribution will be "invested based on your preferences, so it has the potential to grow, tax-free, while you're deciding which charities to support."[35] As with strategic corporate philanthropy and philanthropy LLCs, donors to Fidelity Charitable gain new freedom by decoupling giving from the demands of the Grand Bargain.

But as chapter 2 shows, such choice creates both opportunities and risks. *Consumer Reports* sums it up.

> The flexibility of donor-advised funds can also be a drawback, some critics say. There is no government regulation requiring that the money in a DAF be donated to charity within a specific time frame. In theory, donors could let those assets sit indefinitely.[36]

Again, private ordering could help. In this context, that would mean first articulating a clear vision of spending—rather than accumulating—gifts and then creating a robust framework to carry it out. The major players are already taking steps in this direction.

The three largest commercially affiliated donor-advised fund sponsors by contributions[37] now all publish minimum grantmaking policies. On paper,

Fidelity takes the most aggressive stance, providing that they will contact donors whose funds are dormant for even one year, seeking advice, and will grant out 5 percent of a fund's value if it makes no contributions in two years.[38] Schwab Charitable and Vanguard Charitable each give donor advisors substantially more time—about five years in each case. After this time, a contribution will be made from the account, to a charity or charities preselected either by the donor or via the sponsor's controlled grantmaking entity. Accounts that continue to fail to make grants will eventually be closed, with the funds dispersed in one of these two ways, though Schwab notes extensions are possible.[39] All these policies apply only to funds that make no distributions at all, so a small grant can avoid their application even to an enormous DAF. Goldman Sachs' policy looks not only to nongranting accounts but to those that fail to distribute 5 percent of their average assets over a five-year period and "reserves the right" to make grants or close accounts, but its policies do not suggest these actions will be automatic.[40]

Although dormant fund policies are individually undertaken through individual private ordering, commonalities across their approaches suggest more organized self-regulation could also operate here at the industry level. Each of these commercial sponsors also makes statements in its policies about its commitment to make aggregate distributions of at least 5 percent of its assets each year to charitable recipients.[41] The connection to the private foundation payout rule and the common critique that donor-advised funds should be subject to a similar requirement is obvious.

Critics of commercially affiliated DAFs aim to extend the Grand Bargain to bring them closer to the private foundation annual distribution requirements. But these private players might individually or collectively set their sights on goals beyond merely matching the private foundation timing rules. On the one hand, they might require donors to identify default recipients on day one or they might seek faster spending than the oft-criticized 5 percent per year. On the other hand, commercially affiliated donor-advised funds and their clients might prefer to enshrine more flexible timing requirements.[42] Imposing giving requirements over a multiyear period, for example, allows donors to respond to crises when they arise while ensuring that gifts do not sit idle indefinitely. Whether a sponsor acts on its own or together according to industry norms or best practices, when these players establish clear guidelines and enforcement mechanisms through private ordering, they can make a big impact on the timing of philanthropy processed through their platforms.

A commercial sponsor's interests in maximizing the pool of assets under management—either through its donor-advised funds or through its traditional investments—could delay the impact donors seek to have when they give. Balancing that powerful incentive to hoard wealth with a bold commitment to aggressive giving would allow commercially affiliated donor-advised funds to leverage the broad reach of their giving platforms to surpass the Grand Bargain. Setting policies that govern individual funds could speed giving, but thanks to their unique roles as giving platforms commercial sponsors could also take steps no individual philanthropist ever could.

Designing clear rules that make it easy for clients to commit to giving could speed rather than slow giving. Creating a transparent, comprehensive system prioritizing early payouts could accomplish that. For example, a dead man's switch triggered for an individual fund after a clearly specified period of advisor inaction would go further. A switch that would trigger payouts by *all* of a sponsor's funds if a sufficient number of them go dormant would create powerful incentives to prevent philanthropic hoarding. The minimum grantmaking policies published by the largest sponsors gesture toward this approach but appear to fall well short.

Such a mechanism would help to ensure sponsors enact policies designed to promote aggressive philanthropic spending. Leveraging the power of their giving platforms to address urgent needs could placate a restive public. A proactive approach could forestall public regulatory interventions certain to provide suboptimal outcomes for both sponsors and donors.

Sponsors also might pursue aims beyond timing alone. Such a dead man's switch could also prioritize objectives other than those articulated by the Grand Bargain. They could issue guidelines prioritizing contributions to underresourced groups. Failing to meet those thresholds could shift control of the DAFs under their care so that rather than managing dormant funds through closely controlled entities as currently practiced, sponsors empower the stakeholder representatives, outside issue experts, or community advocates discussed with respect to corporate philanthropy subsidiaries to set the rules for and to make grants out of dormant funds. In competing for donor accounts, each sponsor could offer its own unique vision of accountable giving.

The use of donor-advised funds by high-end donors highlights the need to draw a clear distinction between careful and reluctant giving. The inadvertent 2018 disclosure of donations that in some cases exceeded $1 billion to Goldman Sachs's affiliated sponsor shatters the illusion that commercially advised donor-advised fund adopters merely require education.[43] Contributors with pockets that deep do not need warnings from *Consumer Reports* about the fact that sponsors have an interest in delaying payouts. For these philanthropists, the appeal of commercially affiliated donor-advised funds lies in the power it lends them to do what the Grand Bargain forbids.

Whatever innocuous justifications sponsors like Vanguard and Fidelity might offer for its upside-down credit card service wear thin when contributions drift near the billion-dollar mark. For such donors, the commercially affiliated donor-advised fund appears little better than a tax shelter, relying on the letter of the law in order to violate the Grand Bargain's spirit. It may be that every one of the billion dollars Ballmer contributed addressed urgent public needs in 2016. Unfortunately, by embracing for-profit philanthropy, commercially affiliated donor-advised funds threaten the public's trust in all philanthropists—because we will never know.

Without the Grand Bargain's guardrails, the public needs some other reassurance that billion-dollar charitable contributions will not sit idle indefinitely. When they learn merely by chance that Steve Ballmer received a billion-dollar tax deduction for a charitable contribution to the charitable wing of a legendarily profitable investment bank, with no requirement that Goldman ever relinquish it, the public can be forgiven a certain amount of skepticism.

Commercially affiliated donor-advised funds have already begun building commitment frameworks to push their donor's resources out into the charitable sphere. They could also devise ways to embrace commitments themselves, using the power of their platforms to advance the organizational values they espouse. The stronger and swifter these private ordering mechanisms—the closer they come to a dead man's switch for giving—the more they can reassure the public that donated funds will find their way to worthy causes quickly.

Philanthropy LLC Transparency Commitments

Philanthropy LLCs pose a different set of risks and rewards. The extremely wealthy donors behind them must find a way to broadcast their commitment to serve as trustees for the community. Not all, of course, will possess the communication tools at Mark Zuckerberg's disposal. Fortunately, private ordering can ensure that their efforts align with the stated goals of their ambitious philanthropy to build trust between donors and the public.

The powerful appeal of these entities lies in their flexibility. Whether curing diseases or improving access to education, virtually any vision of doing good can be translated into the language of LLC governance, making philanthropy LLCs the vehicle of choice for an increasing number of wealthy donors. Once articulated, principles of transparency could be enshrined through LLC operating agreements, the frameworks for governance of philanthropic LLCs.

The same flexibility that makes LLCs hard to resist makes it all too easy for donors to alter or simply flout philanthropic commitments to the public good. As described in chapter 5, the L3C, the first social enterprise hybrid, underscores that risk. Forming an L3C permits a wealthy donor to prioritize social returns but imposes no obligation to follow through on promises. Turning an L3C into a conventional, profit-focused LLC requires no approvals from or notice to the state or anyone else. A simple change of heart and shift in emphasis automatically turns an L3C into an LLC.

Fortunately, LLC agreements can be tailored to curb that flexibility by providing the public with insights necessary to verify compliance. Managers could be granted the authority to devise and implement a comprehensive strategy to provide transparency with respect to an LLC's financial and in-kind philanthropy. The disclosure increasingly embraced by philanthropy LLCs like CZI, the Omidyar Network, and Start Small could, for example, be broadened to include information about their investments and the in-kind support they provide.

The Grand Bargain's disclosure obligations would offer a familiar starting point. Providing the same details regarding assets, income, and transactions that fill the Form 990-PFs of the Ford and Gates Foundations would allow the public to compare philanthropy LLCs to their conventional counterparts. The Grand Bargain's stifling prohibitions could be replaced with revealing insights regarding philanthropy LLCs' transactions and investments. Armed with information sufficient to permit them to judge for themselves whether philanthropy LLCs generate higher social yields than private foundations, the public could decide whether to roll back the Grand Bargain or reinforce it.

Social enterprise and ESG investing offer a different blueprint. As B Lab envisioned, private certification undergirds the claims of benefit corporations. A new charity—P Lab?—could create a private system of standardized self-reporting and auditing tailored to philanthropy LLCs. The proprietary ESG metrics developed by and for investment managers suggest a decentralized, competitive approach. Rating particular investments (or CZI's entire portfolio of educational technology investments) by one or more privately developed benchmarks could help to reveal whether—and how much—they serve the public interest.

A different kind of dead man's switch could provide the ultimate transparency commitment. A philanthropy LLC agreement could compel its managers to deliver a fully executed (but undated) tax election to become a corporation to a trusted third party. The third party would be contractually bound to file the election should the philanthropy LLC fail to comply with its self-imposed disclosure obligations, keep its private certification, or hit other metrics that would ensure that its promises matter.[44]

The resulting corporation would remain free to seek tax-exempt status to become a private foundation subject to all the safeguards imposed the Grand Bargain. Or it might instead embrace that new corporate identity, seeking out private or public capital. But it could not simply disavow its philanthropic mission without consequences.

Conclusion

Philanthropy relies on an improbable collaboration, with the market's victors teaming up with its victims to gamble on their shared future. The Grand Bargain created the private foundation to preserve the trust that makes that unlikely teamwork possible. Its regulatory guardrails ensure that—despite all their power—these philanthropists will be allowed to retain control over the capital they hold in trust for the public.

Utilizing the foundation form broadcasts philanthropists' intentions and locks them into a federal framework to hold them to account. They must limit relationships with businesses and avoid politics altogether, targeting their generosity instead to those public charities the tax laws identify as most deserving. They must respect a congressionally endorsed timeline for significant annual giving, rather than warehousing wealth to magnify their own power. They must disclose their donors and grantees transparently, so regulators and the public can draw their own conclusions about the derivation and use of their assets.

In undermining these controls on targeting, timing, and transparency, for-profit philanthropy combines a promise to generously capitalize socially valuable projects for future generations with a threat to undermine the trust that makes philanthropy work. Chapter 6 offered one unorthodox approach to bringing trust to for-profit philanthropy, embracing small-bore regulatory fixes that the architects of the Grand Bargain could never have brought to life. Those narrowly tailored regulatory responses could address the hazards of for-profit philanthropy one by one. Inaction would invite the public to assert control, perhaps through steeply progressive taxes.

This chapter offers another approach by showing that philanthropists need not sit passively waiting on either outcome. The privilege that fuels for-profit philanthropy could also make it accountable. Ulysses managed to hear the Sirens without dooming his ship and crew with nothing more than some rope and wax.[45] For-profit philanthropists could—if they chose—use the limitless resources at their disposal to strike a new balance between freedom and accountability. And fortunately for all of us, they also have the motivation to do so.

Although it would not come cheap, private ordering could ensure that strategic corporate philanthropy serves more than one bottom line, perhaps through the creation of a corporate philanthropy subsidiary. Private ordering could prevent commercially affiliated donor-advised funds from becoming warehouses for charity with a dead man's switch. And it could deliver the discipline necessary for even the most powerful philanthropy LLC founders to make credible commitments to disclose the details of their efforts to pursue the public interest by delivering a simple tax election to a trusted third party. But only if for-profit philanthropists go all in on private solutions. The next chapter considers alternatives if neither private ordering commitments nor targeted interventions suffice, imagining systemic reforms designed to combat the inequality at the heart of for-profit philanthropy's trust problem.

8
A More Perfect Bargain

Given their influence, ensuring that the wealthy give justly has presented a puzzle for thousands of years.[1] Commercially affiliated donor-advised funds, strategic corporate philanthropy, and philanthropy LLCs have shrugged off the admonition at the heart of the Grand Bargain in the name of higher social returns. Chapter 6 envisions tailored regulatory interventions to address the timing, targeting, and transparency deficits of the resulting for-profit philanthropic order while chapter 7 demonstrates how private actors could independently make robust commitments to allay public fears about how and when they deploy their largesse.

The scope and scale of the threat posed by for-profit philanthropy, however, would demand constant renewal of targeted antiabuse measures as innovators develop new arbitrage opportunities. Regulators have limited patience, energy, and political capital for such sustained vigilance. Attractive as that might make reliance on for-profit philanthropists to self-police, it would be naive to rely on foxes alone to guard henhouses. This chapter considers systemic public solutions—including a More Perfect Bargain, an innovative complement to the Grand Bargain—that could make today's private funding of public benefits accountable in ways alternately quite similar to and quite different than the compact Congress delivered half a century ago.

It begins by detailing two proposals to reinvigorate the Grand Bargain. Recognizing that elites no longer fear the strategic threat of public control at the Grand Bargain's heart, these reform ideas seek to restore philanthropic balance by turning up the heat on the wealthiest Americans. Higher tax rates, more potent policing, and even an entirely new form of taxation endeavor to turn the clock back to 1969.[2]

The Biden administration's effort to bolster tax enforcement and Senator Wyden's billionaires tax represent precisely that sort of attempt to bring elites to heel. By making the most privileged Americans uncomfortable, such policy changes could breathe new life into the Grand Bargain and into philanthropy. Like the Grand Bargain itself these proposals harness tax to serve as a strategic means rather than an end. Both target wealth that might entirely escape tax but then ensure that success does not depend on elites contributing to public coffers.

Tax would only be imposed if "the property"—the hoarded wealth in the Biden administration's cross-hairs—"is not donated to charity."[3] Simply put,

For-Profit Philanthropy. Dana Brakman Reiser and Steven A. Dean, Oxford University Press. © Oxford University Press 2023. DOI: 10.1093/oso/9780190074500.003.0009

making the income tax great again as Biden suggests could perhaps restore the Grand Bargain by increasing the opportunity cost of foregoing regulated philanthropy even if it failed to generate as much as a single additional dollar in tax revenues. But the reality is considerably more complicated.

A wealth tax could do more, serving as a visceral threat to elite fortunes. If a wealth tax can clear the many legal and political hurdles it faces, incentives for accountable giving could easily be embedded within it. Developing this uncharted tax territory would also create an opportunity to do more—incentivizing, for instance, philanthropic efforts that address the deep inequality at the heart of our nation's growing sense of crisis. Even if the Grand Bargain's magic could be recaptured, the results would be disappointing if they served only yesterday's priorities rather than today's.

Our final proposal turns in an entirely different direction. Leaving to one side the question of whether a weakened Grand Bargain—and the private foundations at its heart—should be preserved or dismantled, it looks elsewhere for a solution to the challenge of transforming private wealth into public benefits. Acknowledging the primarily strategic role tax plays in the Grand Bargain invites the possibility of unexpected alternatives.

A More Perfect Bargain could strike a very different compromise between elites and the public. It might not rely on tax law at all to shift incentives, instead targeting elite power directly. Corporate law reforms demanding participation by workers and other stakeholders in corporate governance could, for example, be made preconditions for corporate political spending. Without even a gesture toward taxation such a compromise could create a "democratic institutional design for the organization and regulation of private funding of public benefits"[4] not so different than those of ancient Athens.

Such an approach would lean in to for-profit philanthropy rather than attempting to recreate the imagined perfection of the Grand Bargain. Empowering a diverse array of stakeholders to wield political influence could turn the dubious promise of strategic corporate philanthropy to serve interests beyond those of shareholders into reality. A More Perfect Bargain crafted as part of broader changes in election law, campaign spending, or corporate governance could deliver the accountability lost in for-profit philanthropy's rise without reviving Grand Bargain-era tax rates or enforcement.

Philanthropy existed long before 1969 and will continue long after the private foundation has been forgotten. As long as the wealthiest Americans acquire far more than they can spend in many lifetimes, they will continue to give much of it away. After half a century of stability, the demise of the Grand Bargain represents a loss but also creates an opening. Novel approaches like our vision for a More Perfect Bargain have the added advantages of creating space for goals too often absent from contemporary philanthropic discourse such as diversity, equity, and inclusion and expanding the suite of philanthropic legal tools beyond tax.

The Grand Bargain could not possibly reflect the tapestry of economic, political, and social changes that have marked the half-century since its creation. This chapter offers three visions of what a reimagined compromise between the public and elite philanthropists might look like today. Whether refreshed as part of a more highly progressive income tax, reborn with a wealth tax at its heart, or reimagined using tools beyond tax as a More Perfect Bargain, philanthropy must embrace these new challenges. It must look forward rather than back.

The Value of Systemic Solutions

The innovations embraced by for-profit philanthropy undermine the accountability required to counterbalance philanthropy's inherently antidemocratic nature. They are also part and parcel of a greater crisis of inequality threatening our national stability. Acknowledging that the examples of for-profit philanthropy presented in Part I (chapters 1, 2, and 3) represent just a handful of fronts in this broader conflict, this chapter considers systemic solutions.

Business history brims with illustrations of the dangers private players unleash when pursuing particular goals while ignoring the systemic risks their actions generate. For example, before its spectacular demise in 1998, the hedge fund Long-Term Capital Management prospered mightily, to the great benefit of its managers and investors. Their model was simple; operate a hedge fund to protect against risks of currency volatility and finance it with copious amounts of debt.

Regulations prevented borrowing to purchase stock so—employing the same relentless ingenuity that has fueled for-profit philanthropy—Long-Term Capital borrowed to purchase equity derivatives instead.[5] Meeting the letter of the law while courting the very risks the law put out of bounds allowed Long-Term Capital to post unparalleled returns. But at least one skeptic cautioned that prosperity gained by "picking up nickels in front of bulldozers"[6] would not last.

Foreshadowing the fall of Lehman Brothers a decade later, Long-Term Capital ultimately succumbed under the weight of leverage. Eventually its managers' predictions missed the mark, the value of its investments fell precipitously, and it could not keep up with payments due to its lenders. The private rewards of Long-Term Capital's success for its investors and managers proved short-lived. Worse, the systemic dangers their actions courted demanded a billion-dollar bailout by many of Wall Street's leading financial institutions under the auspices of the Federal Reserve. A distressingly similar story can be told about the 2008 financial crisis. When innovators seek private rewards and ignore systemic risks, society eventually pays the price. It remains to be seen whether the same will be true of for-profit philanthropy's heedless pursuit of public benefits.

As these accounts and so many others reveal, the systemic costs of unregulated behavior can far outweigh those borne by individual players engaging in aggressive behavior. Neither the Fed nor the Wall Street titans it persuaded to rescue Long-Term Capital had a legal duty to intervene. The same was true with AIG in 2008. The firms involved had simply managed to become too interconnected to be allowed to fail. Of course, CZI, Fidelity Charitable, and General Motors did not create elite philanthropy any more than Long Term Capital Management invented leverage. But by setting aside the Grand Bargain, these philanthropically critical players serve as a microcosm of our nation's elites, all out hunting for nickels in front of bulldozers.

Three Visions for Systemic Reform

This chapter's three visions for systemic reform all combat the pervasive timing, transparency, and targeting threats posed by the rise of for-profit philanthropy. None offers a simple cure. They will not remedy every harm caused by the decline of the Grand Bargain. But each envisions a reckoning with inequality, the root of the distrust in elites that underlies the phenomena explored here. Rather than limiting the range of potential solutions, it embraces successively less orthodox tools and considers their likely impact on for-profit philanthropy and inequality more broadly.

First, we test the lens of income. A return to steeply progressive mid-century tax rates combined with tempering the myriad loopholes and structural deficits that favor wealthy taxpayers represents one path toward reining in elite influence. Higher real rates would translate into more valuable tax deductions, counterbalancing the regulatory costs of traditional philanthropic tools. The Biden administration embraced this approach in its fight against inequality with mixed success.[7]

The second systemic reform approach views inequality not as a function of income but of wealth. A wealth tax could fuel greater economic equality gains than an income tax could. It even promises to allow the United States to take a few meaningful first steps toward narrowing the racial wealth gap.[8] Proposals to advance a wealth tax vary along important dimensions and all face potential constitutional scrutiny.

Wealth certainly matters more to elites than income. Threatening that wealth with a new tax regime creates new opportunities to encourage accountable philanthropy. It would be foolish to assume that a wealth tax could actually extract significant amounts of revenue from the wealthy in the form of taxes. It could, however, nudge elites back toward regulated philanthropy—preferably with incentives improving on 1969's blueprint of targeting, timing, and transparency. A wealth tax paired with incentives for philanthropy that target inequality would not merely reinforce the crumbling Grand Bargain but build it back better.

Acknowledging that the Grand Bargain ultimately represented a strategic compromise with—rather than a tax on—elites, the final approach turns in an entirely new direction. Growing disparities across Americans of different races, genders, identities, and abilities cannot be adequately addressed by narrowing differences in income or chipping away at the vast wealth held by elites. Financial redistribution could never compensate for voting rules that disproportionately suppress Black votes, campaign finance law that amplifies elite voices, and the magnification of influence worked by incorporation, and the Grand Bargain made no attempt to deliver such a result. In truth, the vectors of elite influence range far beyond the reach of tax law and so too must remedies to the obstinate inequality that plagues American society.

Confronting elite influence directly would have concomitant impacts on for-profit philanthropy. Exploring but one of many possible examples, we consider the impact of requiring a dramatic uptick in accountability for corporate philanthropy programs. Ensuring that the corporate engines of elite wealth run more cleanly would help to rebalance the scales without boosting taxes or tax enforcement. Redistributing power rather than revenues could create a new partnership between elites and the public.

Reducing Income Inequality

Expanding the share of income top earners must yield to the government for redistribution represents an obvious approach to combatting our increasing societal inequality. Calls to restore greater progressivity to our income tax system have gathered force and adherents across the Democratic political spectrum. Congresswoman Ocasio-Cortez raised the possibility of top marginal rates as high as 70 percent.[9] President Biden proposed eliminating the lower rates imposed on capital gains transactions while boosting enforcement spending.

The "Progressive" Income Tax

Although many found the idea of a 70 percent marginal tax rate on income astonishing, this was precisely the top rate in effect when the Grand Bargain was negotiated. A century of history shows that the low rates in effect today might actually be the outliers. Indeed, the first modern US income tax had much in common with today's estate tax. It targeted solely the most affluent, with the vast majority of Americans paying no income tax at all.

The reach of the income tax has expanded far beyond these modest origins, evolving into a shared ritual now a part of nearly every American life.[10] Indeed, more Americans today file federal tax returns than vote. With negative taxes like the child tax credit and the earned income tax credit providing support to families in need, the modern income tax touches the lives of Americans from every background.[11]

How much each taxpayer pays is far more complicated. Fundamentally—in terms of the tax rates set by Congress—the burden of our progressive income tax grows as taxpayer income rises. Over time, the top rates have varied widely. In 1913, 7 cents would have been collected in tax on the last dollar earned by a prosperous taxpayer. By mid-century, the top marginal rate would rise tenfold—at least on paper—for the highest-earning taxpayers, where it remained through the end of the 1970s. The election of Ronald Reagan ushered in dramatic reform and half a century later prolonged pressure to reduce rates had resulted in a tax rate collecting a moderate 37 cents at the highest levels of income.

That complex history of top marginal rates tells only part of the story. The manner in which taxpayers earn income also matters. For individuals, the rate on earnings from wages and salaries, taxed as ordinary income, exceeds that on gains from capital. Technical changes applying these lower capital gains rates to most corporate dividends means that while corporate earnings distributed to shareholders were once taxed at more than 90 percent, they now face a maximum rate of only 20 percent. Warren Buffet's famous observation that he pays a lower rate of tax than his secretary illustrates how this differential treatment undercuts the system's overall progressivity.

Corporations, unlike individuals, do not enjoy lower capital gains rates. But corporate tax rates have experienced a similar slide. The 21 percent rate adopted in the 2017 Tax Cuts and Jobs Act sits at less than half that in effect when the Grand Bargain was concluded. That 1969 rate of 48 percent fell just short of its all-time high of over 50 percent in the 1950s.

An overarching pattern emerges in the burdens the income tax imposes—or, more often as the years pass, fails to impose—on elites. Its load settles more heavily on income earned from labor than from capital, for example. Such differences disproportionately favor the wealthy. They also contribute to the racial wealth gap.[12]

Recent critiques seize on this pattern to highlight the failure of the ostensibly progressive income tax to curb inequality and the corresponding opportunity reinvigorated income taxation presents for constraining elite influence. Yet enhancing income tax progressivity presents obvious and well-known challenges. The large and vocal group of lawmakers who vow never to raise taxes on anyone represents only the most obvious.

The overwhelming political influence of the very elite taxpayers who would be the "losers" in any reforms makes such changes daunting for any legislator open to the possibility. Moreover, this systemic solution requires more than assembling a congressional majority to raise statutory rates at the top. The income tax progressivity gambit will work only if nominal rates on the books reflect the real rates elite taxpayers confront.

Nominal Rates and Real Risk

Economists attempting to identify the "optimal" tax rates for high-income earners have concluded that doubling current tax rates could boost revenues without distorting behavior over the short run.[13] But they rely upon key assumptions which inject an important caveat. If taxpayers can avoid or evade the new rates' application, rates twice as high would translate into little increase in taxes paid. To make an impact on government revenue, higher rates must be paired with "base broadening and tax enforcement."[14] Taxpayers must have neither legal nor extralegal means of lowering their effective rates through self-help.

In practice, returning rates to levels not seen for decades and rearming federal tax authorities may be the easy part. True progressivity would also demand reversing technical changes, like those that result in dividends paid to stockholders being taxed at rates much lower than those paid on wages. Without such adjustments, doubling the top marginal rates might leave the tax treatment of elites undisturbed.

Wealthy individuals have little to fear from the income tax. Tax rates have fallen by half and increasingly generous design features like the treatment of capital gains blunt even these diminished obligations for those at the top. The drop-off in enforcement has been, if anything, even steeper.

Tax authorities can never be expected to detect or defeat every scheme for avoidance or evasion. A half-century ago, however, enforcement at least remained a realistic possibility. By the 2008, a typical taxpayer's audit risk had fallen dramatically—four times smaller than the rate in the 1960s.[15] Since that time, that low enforcement trend has only gained momentum.

Today, neither high nominal rates nor a viable threat of enforcement exists–at least for wealthy taxpayers. In 2019, the highest audit rates in the country targeted taxpayers in poor, predominantly Black counties in the American South, with Latinx and indigenous counties close behind.[16] A 2020 report by Treasury's Inspector General for Tax Administration revealed "high-income nonfilers owing billions of dollars"[17] went unchecked, while poor communities faced heavy scrutiny. Authorities have no choice but to audit poor taxpayers, since they lack the resources to tie up its agents with challenges and litigation. The systematic effort to reduce funding to the Internal Revenue Service has hobbled its ability to challenge aggressive behavior by elite taxpayers, exacerbating inequality from multiple directions.

Today's lower rates subject to larger loopholes and combined with weakened enforcement mean a systemic reform intended to sharply increase income tax progressivity cannot stop at simply doubling top marginal tax rates. Making real equality gains will require the painstaking work of eliminating workarounds and devoting serious resources to enforcement. The Biden administration has made tentative steps on both fronts, proposing the elimination of preferential rates for capital gains and securing an $80 billion increase in the Internal Revenue Service's enforcement budget.[18]

Income Tax Reform and For-Profit Philanthropy

The rise of for-profit philanthropy illustrates the difficulty of reestablishing the Grand Bargain simply by restoring income tax rates and enforcement to the levels of fifty years ago. Even true systemic reforms enhancing progressivity in real terms would not eliminate the appeal of some for-profit philanthropic innovations. It would actually make others more attractive.

The light tread of today's income tax on those at the highest levels of income and wealth undermines the appeal of foundations as compared to philanthropy LLCs. It can be tempting to believe that reining in their use could be as straightforward as recreating the tax rates that prevailed in 1969 and shifting enforcement resources away from vulnerable Black communities and toward the wealthiest Americans. But that nostalgic view of mid-century tax policy obscures a more nuanced reality. Raising top marginal income tax rates from 37 percent to 74 percent would seem, after all, to double the appeal of the tax breaks a foundation offers. That simple math misapprehends both the complexity of the income tax and the value proposition for-profit philanthropy represents.

Without changing structural features of the income tax that favor wealthy taxpayers, even vastly increased rates will make little headway with those at the very top. But a foundation's tax appeal would certainly grow alongside higher real rates by comparison with a philanthropy LLC. Elite donors subject to higher real rates would need to recalculate the value of an LLC's advantages in flexibility, control, and privacy, against more substantial foregone tax benefits.

Yet as the value of tax deductions increases in step with marginal tax rates, the tax advantages elites gain from using commercially affiliated donor-advised funds would be magnified by such changes. Commercial sponsors would undoubtedly tout the enhanced benefits their offerings would provide. They have already done just that with respect to the unparalleled access their donor-advised funds provide to tax benefits for donating appreciated property.[19] Similar marketing efforts likewise drove billions in new contributions at the advent of the increased standard deduction under the 2017 tax law changes.[20] Efforts to enhance income tax progressivity, if made without simultaneous adjustments to commercially affiliated donor-advised fund regulation, would bolster rather than blunt the appeal of for-profit philanthropy.

The same logic applies to corporate charitable contributions. If corporate tax rates rise, so too do the benefits of corporate foundations. But the same would be true for all deductions, including those for business expenses. Strategic corporate philanthropy's slippery amenability to characterization as either a charitable contribution or a business expense—whether donated through a foundation or directly by an in-house department—frustrates the ability of higher corporate tax rates to spur corporate philanthropic accountability.

Nothing to Fear from an Income Tax

In 1969, the US income tax system was already plagued by evasion and loopholes, with "high rates tempered by many avoidance possibilities."[21] Nominal rates may have been high, but well-advised taxpayers could dull their impact. As the influential tax scholar Stanley Surrey documented, tax planning and tax avoidance blossomed, leaving elites with ample means to manage their tax obligations.[22]

Surrey seemed particularly galled when tax planning masqueraded as philanthropy, highlighting one instance in which in "1955, Congressman Curtis of Missouri introduced a private bill for the relief of the Cannon Foundation, which had been established by Congressman Cannon of Missouri."[23] Surrey's objection was simple. Before the Grand Bargain was struck, philanthropy might cost philanthropists nothing at all.[24] A contribution of appreciated property could not only be completely paid for out of tax breaks, what to all appearances was a generous gift would result in a net after-tax payment to (not from) a donor.

Which brings us back to for-profit philanthropy. Higher real rates would not bring the Grand Bargain back to life. It would actually heighten the appeal of strategic corporate philanthropy and commercially affiliated donor-advised funds. When a wealthy individual makes a billion-dollar contribution to a commercially affiliated donor-advised fund, one can imagine Surrey stirring uneasily in his grave. In the days before the Grand Bargain imposed minimum standards of accountability on elite giving, philanthropic gifts routinely made a mockery of income tax rates above 70 percent. Thanks to donor-advised funds, much the same would occur today.

Raising effective income tax rates without changes far beyond those Biden proposed would recreate the world Surrey railed against, not the world he helped create. The Grand Bargain allowed elites to limit their tax burdens by being faithful to its timing, transparency, and targeting mandates. It allowed elites to continue to avoid taxes while "creat[ing] some democratic control over wealth while still preserving certain privileges for the wealthy, such as honor, gratitude, and status as a civic benefactor."[25]

The rise of for-profit philanthropy has made it possible for elites to return to the pre-Grand Bargain world in which tax planning can be disguised as philanthropy. Higher rates on top earners could be combined with robust enforcement and—crucially—base broadening including crackdowns on abuses. In theory, the income tax might once again become a force for reducing inequality.

Narrowing the Wealth Gap

Today, elites such as Bill Gates and Mark Zuckerberg need not rely on the Grand Bargain to limit their income tax burdens. As amply documented in recent disclosures by ProPublica,[26] their wealth—and the bulk of the income it generates—lies safely beyond public reach. No matter how much tax authorities bolster enforcement or how high Congress raises rates, the wealthiest Americans have nothing to fear from an income tax even if every reform Biden proposed were enacted.

That stark reality makes it easy to understand the appeal of a wealth tax. But to truly appreciate its allure, it may be helpful to think of museums. Long a favored target for philanthropic largesse, critics complain that elite philanthropy favors cultural institutions over less glamorous needs such as poverty relief. But even if philanthropy provided precisely the level of funding for museums the public deemed appropriate, the results would remain distinctly undemocratic. In her book, *Culture Strike: Art and Museums in an Age of Protest*, former museum director Laura Raicovich details the downsides of elite philanthropy for cultural institutions.

Like many others, Raicovich turns to the wealth tax for deliverance. She imagines that the switch from an income tax to a wealth tax will bulldoze the obstacles that have prevented the public from collecting the revenues that would put ordinary Americans in control of such cultural spaces in place of elite donors. Unfortunately, neither a Grand Bargain renewed by a revitalized income tax nor one remade through a wealth tax would deliver what Raicovich seeks. Those hoping a wealth tax will actually collect taxes from wealthy citizens to pay for public benefits should prepare for disappointment.

Ambitious wealth tax advocates would not only tax any assets in billionaires' hands and personal accounts—including those held in pass-through form like CZI—but would also tax Chan and Zuckerberg on assets of foundations and donor-advised funds that they control.[27] Such a robust effort might indeed curb "the disenfranchisement of artists or publics that may engage in debate within its walls because the institutions' very power structures, historically and operationally, nullify concepts of civics to maintain a neutral position."[28] Raicovich sees collecting tax revenues and delivering them to museums and other institutions free of elite control as an alternative to the plutocratic domination of cultural spaces fueled by contemporary philanthropy.

Unfortunately, even at the height of its power, the Grand Bargain never managed that feat. Any wealth tax that provides the favorable treatment the United States has always afforded to philanthropists would not attempt it. Instead, a wealth tax would be far more likely to provide philanthropic exemptions designed to elicit an "increase in charitable giving" that might only indirectly "reduce wealth concentration."[29] That would do precisely nothing to solve the problem Raicovich highlights. It would not provide stakeholders or the broader public with a voice in how and where philanthropic resources would be spent.

In the 1950s, Surrey showcased foundations to exemplify how the tax system stealthily favored elites. Popular and political critics had been making similar claims for decades. Today—with philanthropy LLCs and commercially affiliated donor-advised funds offering philanthropists routes to bypass the Grand Bargain's "balance between plutocratic voice and democratic voice"[30]—private foundations have taken on an entirely different meaning, spotlighting all that has been lost in for-profit philanthropy's rise. A wealth tax incentivizing philanthropy on the Grand Bargain's original terms might revive them, but more would be required to usher us toward greater economic equality (or even deliver control of cultural spaces to the public).

Wealth tax advocates recognize that economic inequality exists not merely because individuals earn different incomes. Through the exponential growth dynamic familiar to anyone who has calculated compound interest, wealth begets wealth begets massively more wealth, a point made persuasively by Piketty in *Capital in the 21st Century*. To understand the urgency of the growing focus on wealth, one need only contemplate America's startling racial wealth gap. The average Black American family holds only 15 percent of the wealth that an average white American family does.[31] Achieving parity in incomes without addressing wealth inequality could never produce true equality, but a wealth tax will not necessarily do so either.

A Surfeit of Wealth Tax Plans

Targeting wealth directly remains novel territory for our country and our tax system, but calls for a wealth tax are diverse and growing. The best known proposal came during Senator Elizabeth Warren's presidential campaign.[32] Her proposed 2 percent annual tax on wealth above $50 million might seem modest. Even its increase to 3 percent on holdings worth more than $1 billion does not seem particularly draconian. The wealthiest Americans would hold on to at least 97 percent of their assets each year, presumably only slowing the growth of their fortunes.

But compared to the current treatment of elites—we now know that, even as his wealth ballooned, Jeff Bezos sometimes paid no income tax at all—even a 2–3 percent tax would represent a dramatic change. The wealth tax's appeal—both technically and ethically—lies in the fact that it focuses on accumulations. By forgoing the income tax requirement of a wage or a sale of shares, a wealth tax could address inequality more effectively. After all, disparities grow as wealth quietly generates more wealth. Breaking that cycle requires targeting accumulations directly.

But, as the above discussion suggests, successfully imposing Warren's wealth tax requires answering two surprisingly difficult questions. The first is "2% of what?"[33] The second, "How do I pay the federal government 2% of the value of a Basquiat?"[34] Undaunted by such obstacles, Senator Bernie Sanders offered his own wealth tax proposal that went as high as an annual 8 percent tax on holdings above $10 billion.[35]

Senator Ron Wyden suggests a different route that shows why, in some respects, the appeal of wealth taxes has been overstated. Wyden's proposal would subject even the paper gains of the wealthiest Americans to income tax.[36] While not formally a wealth tax, by forgoing the requirement of a transaction before imposing tax, it would reach stores of wealth in a way today's income tax does not.

An Opportunity for Compromise

A wealth tax promises to revive the Grand Bargain by providing a more potent threat to elites' holdings than the income tax. Even if they never pay a penny of it, a wealth tax "could spur an increase in charitable giving among the extremely wealthy."[37] Unfortunately, the extremely wealthy understand all of this, or employ others who do. Which reveals daunting challenges for a wealth tax aiming to replicate the Grand Bargain's feat.

Today, the hidden spending Surrey decried has been thrust into the light. His tax expenditure budget counts the cost of tax breaks. In 1969, even Surrey could not have clearly understood the value of the concessions the Grand Bargain offered philanthropists. Both elites and the public could view tax breaks for charity as bets made with house money. As a result, the true cost of the Grand Bargain remained hidden from both sides.

This obscurity allowed both elites and the public to focus on their overlapping interests, rather than on price.[38] Finding areas in which their preferences align and enshrining them in a Grand Bargain would be far more difficult than it was half a century ago. Ignoring the cost—in tax revenues and tax liability—that an income-tax-based bargain would impose on both sides has become impossible in the zero-sum world Surrey fought to create. Whatever they believed then, neither actually gambled with house money. That would now be abundantly clear to both sides.

Fortunately, the wealth tax remains largely unmapped today. That allows for the possibility that each side will see its hopes rather than its fears reflected in it. Both cannot be right, but since no US wealth tax has ever been enacted, neither knows whether—or to what extent—each will prove to be wrong. If a wealth tax could replicate this Grand Bargain-era sleight of hand, it might succeed in breathing new life into it or even going farther toward transforming our society's gaping inequality.

The timing is fortuitous. Forging an agreement between elite donors and the public will never be easier than before we know the wealth tax's measure. The future is anyone's guess. Even very low wealth tax rates could profoundly impact elites. Elite resistance could mean no wealth tax at all. An idealized wealth tax with no exemptions for philanthropy might quickly be riddled with loopholes and saddled with inadequate enforcement, leaving the public with little to show for their efforts.

In this moment when we can no more discount the possibility that the strong version wealth tax advocates envision will materialize than we can dismiss the chance a weak version will come into effect, compromise is distinctly possible. Given the wide range of possible outcomes and the uncharted territory of a wealth tax, the moment to renegotiate the Grand Bargain founded on a wealth tax is upon us. There are both incentives and opportunities to find common ground.

Wealth Taxes and For-Profit Philanthropy

A revived Grand Bargain promises a return to simpler times. A clear-eyed look at the past suggests that such simplicity never actually existed. The Grand Bargain made tax reform possible by sparing the wealthiest Americans from the heavy toll of daunting tax rates. A wealth tax might frighten elites back to the negotiating table, but only if it puts the for-profit philanthropy genies of donor-advised funds, strategic corporate philanthropy, and philanthropy LLCs back in the bottle.

A wealth tax aims directly at the massive inequality roiling American society and politics. Harvesting elite wealth—under the Grand Bargain held in trust—for the public to put those resources directly in its hands would represent the total victory Raicovich envisions, not a compromise. The remainder of this chapter reaches much further back in history to find a model of cooperation between elites and the public that might meet today's moment of democratic crisis.

As Rob Reich describes, the Athenians developed a "system whereby wealthy citizens could make voluntary contributions to various state projects that were of benefit to the entire citizenry, or *demos*."[39] Such "[l]iturgies in democratic Athens became a system of public finance via private contribution, something akin to a system of taxation."[40] These liturgies transformed elite wealth into public goods thanks to a system crafted to ensure accountability.

Yet the result resembles a strategic bargain more than it does a tax. Athenians could avoid compulsion by performing a liturgy voluntarily. They might, for instance, fund the construction of and captain a trireme warship, thereby becoming exempt from future liturgies.

Even reluctant elites understood that they might be selected from the registers of wealthy people kept by the state to perform a liturgy. They also knew that they might be identified by a less wealthy neighbor seeking to shift their liturgical burden through a process known as antidosis.[41] Given the likelihood that their reluctance might be exposed by the state or a less wealthy neighbor, the wealthiest citizens would not wait to be forced into action.

The Athenian liturgical system accomplished the same strategic goal as the Grand Bargain without the threat of a tax. In both cases, rather than directly compelling elites, the state made "a *strategic* move, a move that induces the other player to choose in one's favor."[42] Prompted to a first move[43] by a threat[44] whose enforcement[45] the Athenian state delegated[46] to other wealthy citizens well-suited to the task, its liturgical system wisely "preserv[ed] certain privileges for the wealthy, such as honor, gratitude, and status as a civic benefactor."[47] The Grand Bargain used the threat of income tax. As its power has waned, the time for a new catalyst has arrived.

Designing a wealth tax to revive the Grand Bargain will require a level of ambition far greater than that of recent efforts like those of the Biden administration. Wealth dedicated to philanthropy, whether held by public charities or private foundations or by individuals or corporations, would be excluded from the wealth tax base only if compliant with detailed timing, targeting, and transparency requirements. This approach would rein in the worst excesses of philanthropy LLCs, donor-advised funds, and strategic corporate philanthropy, at a minimum by pushing elites back toward foundations.

A wealth tax solution could also go further. It could exempt funds dedicated to philanthropy only if subject to narrower targeting requirements, swifter timing mandates, and greater transparency or tailor its exemptions to stimulate not just accountable philanthropy but philanthropy designed to combat inequality. Designing an exemption to incentivize empowering now marginalized communities and amplifying voices now silenced would attack inequality far more directly than the Grand Bargain ever did.

Raicovich—like Warren, Sanders, and Wyden—would prefer that elites instead be forced to trade the privileges of philanthropy for the pain of writing ten-figure checks to the US Treasury. That would, of course, put the public in control of cultural institutions and much else besides. But even ancient Athens recognized the limits of its capacity to move its wealthiest citizens by compulsion. The most ambitious wealth tax would ultimately represent only a strategic threat to revive the Grand Bargain

Empowering Stakeholders and Shrinking Power Disparities

However attractive a reboot of the Grand Bargain might be, it emphatically illustrates a much broader point. A More Perfect Bargain could rely on an array of policy instruments to combat inequality. Income and wealth disparities matter, of course. But they matter in large part because of the power disparities they reflect and reinforce. If tax agents merely serve much the same strategic role covetous Athenian neighbors once did, tax could be replaced by any number of threats or rewards.

For-profit philanthropy shows that elites have broken the spell of the Grand Bargain's tax-based compulsions. New taxes might bring them to heel. But to the extent empowering a diverse public—rather than boosting tax revenues—remains the primary goal, a different sort of strategic compact might produce a more satisfying result. That elites have little reason to fear tax while the corporations that make them rich have embraced for-profit philanthropy in part to be responsive to customers, employees, and investors invites a very different strategy, an approach that empowers those diverse stakeholders. The world has changed in profound ways since 1969, although power remains overwhelmingly in the hands of white, male individuals who experience life in America sheltered within a privileged elite. The deference the public showed fifty years ago to the whims of that slim slice of America will be in shorter supply today as empowered women and racial and ethnic minorities demand an equal voice.

Steeply progressive taxes, either on income or on wealth, promise to put ordinary citizens in control of a meaningful share of elite resources or at least to reinforce the faltering accountability regime the Grand Bargain erected. But if they serve as a form of political theater rather than a source of revenue, other legal levers may serve as well as—or better than—tax law, particularly given the decades-long evolution of public attitudes toward taxation that has helped drive rates and enforcement down. Although many have been drawn to the promise of the wealth tax, its power to raise tax revenues from the richest Americans remains untested. That might not matter if a renewed Grand Bargain catalyzed by the strategic threat a wealth tax represents could somehow curb the disenfranchisement Raicovich describes with such particularity in the museum world. But putting our faith in a gambit a half-century old to return our massively unequal society to a past that no longer exists would be naive.

The balance of this chapter instead focuses directly on power. Redistributing power—not income or wealth—would shift the calculus of all kinds of economic and social policies, limiting elites' ability to control the political agenda. Perhaps such efforts would even clear the way for sweeping income tax changes or wealth taxation. Even if not, reducing the power differential in our highly unequal society might render such proxies for control less relevant. Or the result might be something we could not predict from our vantage point today. Whatever the outcome, an entirely different kind of strategic pact—premised on rectifying inequalities of power rather than income or wealth—would profoundly alter the face of philanthropy.

A new strategic bargain to amplify the voices of ordinary Americans in shaping our shared future need not rely on an income tax, a wealth tax, or any tax at all. The law offers no shortage of alternative mechanisms. It would be impossible to canvass here all the tools available to shrink our society's massive power disparities, so we focus on a set of examples at the intersection of election law and corporate power. High-net-worth families wielding generational fortunes, affluent members of the 1 percent, and massive multinational corporations steer social change through political access and the agency of the businesses they control. Illuminating how election and corporate law reform might empower citizens and stakeholders highlights just how many paths exist to that goal.

Election Law Reform

Elections matter. They represent critical social inflection points. Today, a growing sense of electoral urgency, fueled in no small part by inequality, has spawned dueling claims of voter fraud and voter suppression.

Election law reform could upend the power dynamics at work in our highly unequal society. Deciding who should vote and how they should do it has an obvious importance. As the Johnson Amendment shows, so do ancillary rules such as those that govern political spending.

Each state sets its own election laws—even for national races—so the rules can be surprisingly different. That has become more obvious as recent changes to some state voting laws have expanded access to the ballot. Restoring voting rights to formerly incarcerated men and women in 2018 allowed more than a million voters access to the ballot box in Florida.[48] In a presidential battleground state, a million new voters could easily alter the course of an election.

Other changes have narrowed access. In response to unfounded claims of fraud, a number of states have imposed new restrictions.[49] Requiring voters to present identification, restricting early voting and voting by mail, and imposing new penalties for voting errors make voting more difficult and more costly. In other countries, voting may be universal (Australia) or online (Estonia), but in the United States voting remains remarkably difficult.

Elites, though, possess unhindered access to the halls of power. Not only do their routes to the ballot box lie unobstructed, but their wealth and influence mean their concerns receive lavish attention. A fully egalitarian society may be beyond reach, but easy and equal access to voting does not seem too much to ask. Reforms seeking to remove voting limitations and enhance voter access lend a louder voice to the public just as changes to philanthropy law might. Proposals to block voters and voices—particularly those from disempowered communities—will silence them.

However difficult voting can be, campaign spending seems just the opposite. While states write the rules for conducting elections, federal law governs election spending. Since 2010, when *Citizens United* struck down long-standing rules limiting corporate political spending, those laws have become significantly less restrictive.[50] *Citizens United* remade the political landscape, making it easy for wealthy individuals and big corporations to spend with little or no oversight.[51] In its wake, efforts to control political spending have garnered great interest but met with limited success.

Legislators perennially try to repeal the Johnson Amendment's prohibition on political campaign activity by tax-exempt charitable organizations.[52] As chapter 4 explained, this rule applies to both public charities and private foundations. Since private foundations are also subject to additional excise tax penalties for a wide range of political activities, including campaigning, a simple repeal of the Johnson Amendment would free only public charities to support or oppose candidates for office.

Whether repeal would serve to reduce or reinforce power disparities remains hotly contested. Advocates for repeal argue that public charities like churches and schools should be permitted to undertake political action to express and represent the political views of their communities[53]–which might serve as a counterbalance to elite influence. Opponents warn repeal would embroil charitable entities in political squabbles, allow them to be coopted by political forces, and undermine political transparency[54]–which would not.

Initiatives to regulate corporate political spending have also gained prominence, though as yet have made little headway. Senator Warren's proposed Accountable Capitalism Act featured a requirement for 75 percent of shareholders and directors to approve any political spending in firms with more than $1 billion in tax receipts.[55] Despite being introduced in two successive sessions of Congress and garnering significant media attention, the bill made no legislative progress post-introduction. In the wake of the January 6 attack on the Capitol, Senator Menendez reintroduced a bill requiring not only shareholder approval, but enhanced disclosure of corporate political spending as well, to little fanfare.[56]

A petition urging the Securities and Exchange Commission to adopt disclosure requirements for corporate political spending attracted the highest number of comments on record.[57] A legislative block long prevented the agency from acting on the issue, but its new leadership under the Biden administration has indicated interest in doing so.[58] The Supreme Court's 2021 decision in *Americans for Prosperity Foundation v. Bonta*,[59] however, has been perceived by many as an invitation for new challenges to even those campaign spending disclosure rules upheld in *Citizens United*.[60] For a More Perfect Bargain to be forged through election law reform, advocates will need to find a way past political headwinds and constitutional hurdles alike.

Corporate Law Reform

After the Capitol Riot, a wide range of corporations pledged to halt political contributions. Some paused all spending while others suspended giving only to Republicans who opposed the certification of Biden's victory.[61] Viewed against the backdrop of the unfettered freedom political donors have enjoyed in recent years, that restraint seems all the more striking. It remains to be seen whether those changes represent an aberration or the start of a shift toward greater deference to stakeholders on the part of corporate donors. Corporate reforms empowering stakeholders could tip the scales, improving the balance between plutocratic voice and democratic voice in the process.

Policymakers might affirmatively require that corporate campaign spending take stakeholder views into account. Recent proposals to require shareholder preapproval suggest how that might be accomplished. Corporate campaign spending could be conditioned on possessing not merely a shareholder but a stakeholder mandate.

Even if formal control remains out of reach, heightened transparency and increased reliance on social return metrics could grant corporate political power to more than a privileged few. Disclosure rules modeled on Senator Menendez's proposal or the SEC petition would offer employees, customers, and other constituencies an opportunity to scrutinize political spending. Each could voice their approval or disapproval in their own way, demonstrating loyalty or dissatisfaction with their feet and their pocketbooks.

Stakeholders might also be empowered to influence corporate decision-making beyond campaign spending. For example, Warren's Accountable Capitalism Act would provide employees of large corporations with the power to elect 40 percent of the members of a corporate board.[62] Inspired by Germany's Mitbestimmung, similar measures designed to grant a voice to other stakeholders have been embraced by a variety of jurisdictions.[63]

Variations on these approaches could expand the range of stakeholders with access to power even further. Granting employees or others the right to elect board members would amplify nonelite and marginalized voices. If they chose, stakeholders could employ this new access to help set corporate policies beyond campaign spending, much as ExxonMobil's shareholders did in electing two independent board members in response to concerns over climate change.[64]

Corporations could also be offered a choice. Rather than becoming subject to the requirements of an Accountable Capitalism Act (or being required to file a benefit report) firms might be allowed to forswear political spending. Such an option could sort the largest US corporations into one group committed to the shareholder capitalism model and another embracing political engagement with both the public and policymakers. Corporations would be allowed to speak only if they demonstrate a commitment to listening, transforming corporate governance into a tool to shrink power disparities.

Shrinking Power Disparities and For-Profit Philanthropy

The Grand Bargain represented a striking strategic victory, harnessing elite wealth to produce public benefits that have saved countless lives and improved even more. A More Perfect Bargain might notch victories on an even grander scale, drawing on the vast pools of capital Delaware's public benefit company aims to unlock for social enterprises. Targeting corporate political power with a compelling strategic threat and delegating enforcement to stakeholders presents a more politically palatable path to advancing the ideal of equality than either remaking our election laws and campaign spending rules or crafting a new tax on elite wealth. It also has the potential to nudge for-profit philanthropy—particularly strategic corporate philanthropy—toward delivering the social returns it promises.

Strategic corporate philanthropy today allows our largest firms to claim prosocial values can be served—win-win—along with increasing value for shareholders. It does so without consulting these broader constituencies they claim to serve and while collecting a tax subsidy comparable to that provided by the Grand Bargain. Introducing stakeholder participation and disclosure into the process, either as part of a general mandate or in return for a valuable prize like the ability to seek influence through campaign spending, will not return us to the Grand Bargain. Instead, it opens new pathways for the public to assert their values in the corporate setting—including those around the targeting and timing of corporate philanthropy—and ensures the transparency necessary for this process to function.

Embracing stakeholder values in formulating business strategy with a More Perfect Bargain might even encourage powerful actors to prevent future crises rather than merely supporting those who suffer when they come to pass. A shareholder capitalism Purdue Pharma[65]—without the power to spend corporate resources on politics—would have enjoyed less influence. Its stakeholder capitalism counterpart might have been more likely to consider the impact of its opioids on communities.

The uncertain strategic value of taxes today suggests that other threats (or promises) might prove more fruitful levers to mitigate the systemic risks for-profit philanthropy poses. Corporate political spending may be a better alternative, or it may not. Forcing the largest corporations to listen to stakeholders before being allowed to speak represents just one of many ways to achieve a greater balance of plutocratic and democratic voice.

Conclusion

Over time, elites and the public have found countless ways to encourage "private funding by wealthy citizens of state services and activities."[66] The rise of for-profit philanthropy and the waning relevance of the Grand Bargain serves as an urgent call for new modes of collaboration. Chapters 6 and 7 underscored the value to be gained in abandoning orthodox goals and methods. This chapter offers three visions of how to make philanthropy more accountable, whether designed to recapture the Grand Bargain or radically depart from it.

Income tax law played a central role in the rise and fall of the Grand Bargain. Today, elites have mastered the art of devouring the worm while avoiding the Grand Bargain's hook. When they need the tax advantages they might once have sought from a private foundation, the commercially affiliated donor-advised fund delivers them with fewer barbs. A More Perfect Bargain might try to resurrect the original version's potency, but both the history and the realpolitik of the income tax dampen its prospects.

A wealth tax might fare better, but as with the income tax, not by filling public coffers. In theory, such a tax would allow the government to collect taxes on accumulations of wealth, even on shares of tech giants. In practice, it would be more likely to merely present a more plausible strategic threat, encouraging generosity rather than enforcing obligations. Even that much success would mean little without remaking its targeting, timing, and transparency rules to combat today's greatest crises and the particular risks of for-profit philanthropy.

Reaching beyond tax law opens a virtually limitless frontier on which to address the gulf between elites and the wider public—and for-profit philanthropy in the process—with a More Perfect Bargain. Overhauling election and campaign spending law to reduce elite influence and enhance participation by marginalized communities would attack political inequality head on. But more oblique measures could also have a real impact. Empowering stakeholders in corporate political spending decisions–or more broadly as a condition for engaging in campaigns at all–would amplify democratic voices currently muffled by plutocratic privilege. Granting stakeholder employees, customers, and community members agency to assert their values offers an entirely different route to making strategic corporate philanthropy more accountable.

Just as the Grand Bargain once shaped expectations regarding philanthropic activity, a More Perfect Bargain might deliver the trust for-profit philanthropy jeopardizes in unexpected ways. Either a remade Grand Bargain or a More Perfect Bargain could reduce the relative costs of embracing traditional philanthropy. They could weave enhanced visions of targeting, timing, and transparency along with other important public values into the incentives we provide for philanthropic endeavors. Harnessing policy instruments beyond tax would allow lawmakers to take on inequality directly and make for-profit philanthropy more accountable and less worrisome along the way. Crafted carefully, a More Perfect Bargain could benefit both elites and the demos by preserving a balance between their interests.

Conclusion

In response to revelations that more than one hundred extremely wealthy taxpayers paid no income tax at all (without breaking a single rule), the Tax Reform Act of 1969 created the alternative minimum tax. More than half a century later, the country seems genuinely surprised to find that while they may have traded yachts for spacecraft, the wealthiest Americans still often pay not even one dollar of tax. As was true decades ago, they need not break—or even bend—any laws to do so.

Perhaps doubting its wherewithal to directly turn private wealth into public resources through taxation, the 1969 tax reform attempted to tame elite power with a strategic Grand Bargain. And for a time, it seemed to have succeeded. Its private foundation regime demanded accountability, and a golden age of philanthropy unfolded. Extraordinary public benefits flowed from a partnership between the wealthiest Americans and the most vulnerable.

Although other legislative bulwarks of the 1960s have been sunk by devastating broadsides, the Grand Bargain's slow death has been one of a thousand small cuts. The Supreme Court eviscerated the 1965 Voting Rights Act's protections against discrimination, dismissing its worries about the disenfranchisement of voters as "based on 40-year-old facts having no logical relationship to the present day."[1] The unsettling consequences of a new wave of voting limits loom large in our nation's political discourse. The impact of for-profit philanthropy on the 1969 Grand Bargain could be as devastating for society.

The rise of the philanthropy LLC, commercially affiliated donor-advised funds, and strategic corporate philanthropy has hardly gone unnoticed. But because they have been viewed as distinct phenomena affecting—respectively—the transparency, timing, and targeting of philanthropy, their collective impact on an aging Grand Bargain has remained obscured. As a result, the urgent efforts to ensure that the public's voice not be silenced through voting restrictions have not been matched by a similar push to contain the unbridled power of elites on display in the emergence of for-profit philanthropy.

Part I (chapters 1, 2, and 3) detailed the scope of the threat posed by for-profit philanthropy. That many of the nation's largest charities—tied to financial giants like Fidelity and Vanguard, understandably committed to client service rather than public service—do no charitable work at all should on its own be enough to give anyone pause. Part II (chapters 4 and 5) drew the broad contours of an aging

For-Profit Philanthropy. Dana Brakman Reiser and Steven A. Dean, Oxford University Press. © Oxford University Press 2023. DOI: 10.1093/oso/9780190074500.003.0010

philanthropic regulatory regime and offered a troubling vision of a philanthropic future with trust in short supply. Finally, Part III (chapters 6, 7, and 8) offered a call to action that honors the values of today's America.

For-profit philanthropy embodies a deeply American drive to innovate. Yet experimenting with philanthropy poses real risks to all of us, not merely to those controlling a disproportionate share of society's resources. The Grand Bargain's strategic compromise paired a modest degree of public control with a broad grant of freedom to wealthy elites and their vision of the public good. Today, the pendulum has swung too far toward unfettered autonomy for the most privileged Americans.

Tailored regulatory interventions will not turn back the hands of time, but they present a valuable opportunity, nonetheless. Incremental changes to the Grand Bargain's historic regime can reduce risks by combatting known abuses. Perhaps more important, they can be designed to inject today's values and concerns into a philanthropic regulatory regime crafted a half-century ago.

Private ordering may not be a Wizard of Oz, with the power to grant courage to corporations, a heart to commercially affiliated donor-advised funds, and a brain to philanthropy LLCs. But, like the lion, the tin man, and the scarecrow, each may find that they have no need for magic. Carefully designed self-regulatory commitments could reveal each to be precisely what it aspires to become.

Whether using familiar mechanisms of philanthropy regulation or representing part of a broader reckoning with inequality, tomorrow might deliver a More Perfect Bargain able to translate private resources into public benefits as effortlessly as the Grand Bargain once did. But just as easily it could bring heavy-handed public control, either in the shape of burdensome regulation or confiscatory taxes. One need not work too hard to imagine still other, darker futures in which the nation's trust in its elites suffers for the hubris of a handful of misguided would-be benefactors.

For-profit philanthropists believe they risk little by turning their backs on the Grand Bargain. After all, they fear the threat of tax about as much as they worry that their global business empires will be disrupted by regulators. But they should be afraid, just as Carnegie was.[2] Eliot's hollow men were not always impotent and ashamed, but somehow found themselves worse than dead: disgraced.

Notes

Introduction

1. Giving USA, Giving USA 2022 Infographic, https://store.givingusa.org/a/downloads/-/3e65016bdaf93d22/00a07ad39869332d; *see also* Giving USA, Giving USA 2020: Charitable Giving Showed Solid Growth, Climbing to $449.64 Billion in 2019, One of the Highest Years for Giving on Record (June 16, 2020, 8:00 AM), https://givingusa.org/giving-usa-2020-charitable-giving-showed-solid-growth-climbing-to-449-64-billion-in-2019-one-of-the-highest-years-for-giving-on-record/.
2. Bureau of Labor Statistics, U.S. Department of Labor, *The Economics Daily: Nonprofits Account for 12.3 Million Jobs, 10.2 Percent of Private Sector Employment, in 2016*, https://www.bls.gov/opub/ted/2018/nonprofits-account-for-12-3-million-jobs-10-2-percent-of-private-sector-employment-in-2016.htm (visited July 21, *2021*).
3. IRS Statistics of Income, Domestic Private Foundations: Tax Year 2017, https://www.irs.gov/pub/irs-pdf/p5505.pdf.
4. *See* 2 Alexis de Tocqueville, Democracy in America, 106 (1993) ("Americans of all ages, all conditions, and all dispositions constantly form associations. . . . Wherever at the head of some new undertaking you see the government in France, or a man of rank in England, in the United States you will be sure to find an association.").
5. Fidelity Charitable, *2020–2021 Financial Summary* 5 (2021), https://www.fidelitycharitable.org/content/dam/fc-public/docs/annual-reports/2020-21-financial-summary.pdf.
6. Kirk Kristofferson et al., *The Nature of Slacktivism: How the Social Observability of an Initial Act of Token Support Affects Subsequent Prosocial Action*, 40 J. Consumer Res. 1149 (2014) (concluding that the more public the act of low-commitment prosocial action the less it predicts future charitable acts).
7. *See* Aaron Horvath & Walter W. Powell, *Seeing Like a Philanthropist: From the Business of Benevolence to the Benevolence of Business, in* The Nonprofit Sector: A Research Handbook (3d ed. 2021) (Walter W. Powell & Patricia Bromley eds.) ("When philanthropists look at social problems and needs, they see them through the business lenses that have led to their wealth.").
8. *See* Natasha Singer & Mike Isaac, *Mark Zuckerberg's Philanthropy Uses L.L.C. for More Control*, N.Y. Times (Dec. 2, 2015), https://www.nytimes.com/2015/12/03/technology/zuckerbergs-philanthropy-uses-llc-for-more-control.html.
9. Chan Zuckerberg Initiative, *About Us*, https://chanzuckerberg.com/about/our-approach/.

10. *See* Internal Revenue Service, *Private Foundations*, https://www.irs.gov/charities-non-profits/charitable-organizations/private-foundations (detailing the restrictions that constrain private foundation investment, spending and management).
11. Fidelity Charitable, https://www.fidelitycharitable.org.
12. I.R.C. § 4966(d)(2).
13. *See* I.R.C. § 4942.
14. *See* Internal Revenue Service, *Charities and Nonprofits: Is a Tax-Exempt Organization Required to Disclose the Names or Addresses of its Contributors?*, https://www.irs.gov/charities-non-profits/public-disclosure-and-availability-of-exempt-organizations-returns-and-applications-contributors-identities-not-subject-to-disclosure.
15. Citigroup, Environmental, Social, and Governance Report 60 (2020), https://www.citigroup.com/citi/about/esg/download/2020/Global-ESG-Report-2020.pdf?ieNocache=561.
16. Posting of Sheryl Sandberg, Vice President, Global Online Sales & Operations, Google.org, to The Official Google Blog, http://googleblog.blogspot.com/2005/10/about-googleorg.html (Oct. 11, 2005, 9:02 PM) (stating that Google does not "expect to make further donations to the Foundation for the foreseeable future").
17. *See* Google Foundation, Form 990-PF (2018), https://pdf.guidestar.org/PDF_Images/2018/201/548/2018-201548253-10481c3e-F.pdf (noting the termination of the foundation). For a comprehensive review of the early days of Google.org, *see* Dana Brakman Reiser, *For-Profit Philanthropy*, 77 Fordham L. Rev. 2437 (2009).
18. *See* Valerie Strauss, *Pearson Foundation Closing (After Paying Big Fines for Helping Corporate Parent)*, Wash. Post (Nov. 19, 2014), https://www.washingtonpost.com/news/answer-sheet/wp/2014/11/19/pearson-foundation-closing-after-paying-big-fines-for-helping-corporate-parent/; Melissa Burden, *GM to End Foundation, Redirect Its Charitable Giving*, Det. News, (June 12, 2017, 9:39 AM), https://www.detroitnews.com/story/business/autos/general-motors/2017/06/12/gm-giving/102764328/.
19. *See* Eric John Abrahamson, Sam Hurst, & Barbara S. Hubinski, Democracy & Philanthropy: The Rockefeller Foundation and the American Experiment 44 (2013).
20. *See* Tax Reform Act of 1969, Pub. L. No. 91-172, 83 Stat. 487 (1969); *see generally* James J. Fishman, *The Private Foundation Rules at Fifty: How Did We Get Them and Do They Meet Current Needs?*, 17 Pitt. Tax Rev. 247, 248–69 (2020) (describing decades of criticism and concern about foundations and elite philanthropy leading up to the 1969 Act).
21. *See* Roger Colinvaux, *Charity Law in the 21st Century: Trending Toward Decay*, 11 Fla. Tax Rev. 1, 12 (2011) ("Charities are divided into broad categories: public charities and private foundations").
22. *See id.*; *see also* I.R.C. § 509 (defining "private foundations;" public charities are § 501(c)(3) tax-exempt charities that can avoid this classification).
23. *See* I.R.C. § 4942 (requiring, broadly, that private foundations distribute 5 percent of their assets annually or face significant penalty taxes).

24. *See* I.R.C. § 4943 (restricting, broadly, the stakes private foundations may hold in businesses to 20 percent or less; greater holdings must be divested or are subject to confiscatory penalty taxes).
25. *See* I.R.C. § 4944 (imposing penalty taxes on private foundations and their managers for investments that "jeopardize the carrying out of any of its exempt purposes").
26. *See* Tax Policy Center, *Historical Highest Marginal Income Tax Rates: 1913 to 2020*, https://www.taxpolicycenter.org/statistics/historical-highest-marginal-income-tax-rates.
27. *See* Fishman, *supra* note 20, at 274–75.
28. *See* Bill and Melinda Gates Foundation, *Vaccine Development and Surveillance*, https://www.gatesfoundation.org/our-work/programs/global-health/vaccine-development-and-surveillance. *But see* Alexander Zaitchik, *How Bill Gates Impeded Global Access to Covid Vaccines*, New Republic (Apr. 12, 2021), https://newrepublic.com/article/162000/bill-gates-impeded-global-access-covid-vaccines (arguing before the foundation shifted to support lifting patent restrictions on COVID vaccines that Gates's focus on IP protection has impeded public health efforts).
29. *See* Bill and Melinda Gates Foundation, *Malaria*, https://www.gatesfoundation.org/our-work/programs/global-health/malaria.
30. *See* Bill and Melinda Gates Foundation, *HIV*, https://www.gatesfoundation.org/our-work/programs/global-health/hiv.
31. *See generally* Rob Reich, Just Giving: Why Philanthropy Is Failing Democracy and How It Can Do Better (2018).
32. *See* Bill and Melinda Gates Foundation, *Consolidated Financial Statements* (May 22, 2022), https://docs.gatesfoundation.org/documents/f_331060e-1a_billmelindagatesfoundation_fs.pdf. The Gateses' recent divorce announcement has created uncertainty about the future management of the foundation, but not its assets, which have been dedicated irretrievably to the Foundation's charitable purposes. *See* Nicholas Kulish, *A Marriage Is Ending, But a Foundation Isn't*, N.Y. Times, May 5, 2021, at B1, https://www.nytimes.com/2021/05/04/business/bill-melinda-gates-divorce-foundation.html.
33. *See* Eva Mathews & Jonathan Stempel, *Warren Buffett Resigns from Gates Foundation, Has Donated Half His Fortune*, Reuters (June 24, 2021), https://www.reuters.com/business/buffett-resigns-trustee-gates-foundation-2021-06-23/.
34. *See* Scott Kohler, *The Emergency Medical Services Program of the Robert Wood Johnson Foundation: Robert Wood Johnson Foundation, 1973*, Center for Strategic Philanthropy and Civ. Soc'y (2007), https://cspcs.sanford.duke.edu/sites/default/files/descriptive/emergency_medical_services_program.pdf.
35. *See* Chan Zuckerberg Initiative, *Grants*, https://chanzuckerberg.com/grants-ventures/grants/.
36. *See* Prop. Treas. Reg. § 301.7701-2, 45 Fed. Reg. 75,709 (Nov. 17, 1980).
37. *See* Donald F. Parsons, Jr., R. Jason Russell & Koah M. Doud, *Seventy-Five Years Covering the Rise of Alternative Entities*, 75 Bus. Law. 2467, 2468 (2020) ("in terms of numbers, at least, the LLC has become the preferred entity type for businesses").

38. *See* Social Enterprise Tracker, https://socentlawtracker.org/#/map (providing state-by-state information on adoption of hybrid forms of organization designed for social enterprises).
39. *See* DEL. GEN. CORP. LAW §§ 361–368.
40. *See* J. Haskell Murray, *The History and Hope of Social Enterprise Forms*, 22 TRANSACTIONS: TENN. J. BUS. L. 207, 207 (2021) (noting that hybrid forms for social enterprise "have not gained significant mainstream adoption"); Ellen Berrey, *Social Enterprise Law in Action: Organizational Characteristics of U.S. Benefit Corporations*, 20 TRANSACTIONS: TENN. J. BUS. L. 21, (2018) (detailing empirical study of benefit corporations finding just 7704 had been formed, noting this represented "an extremely small proportion of the nearly thirty million businesses in the United States. Only .026% of those businesses are benefit corporations."); *see generally* DANA BRAKMAN REISER & STEVEN A. DEAN: SOCIAL ENTERPRISE LAW: TRUST, PUBLIC BENEFIT, AND CAPITAL MARKETS (2017) (describing lack of utilization of hybrid forms for social enterprise).
41. T. S. ELIOT, THE HOLLOW MEN (1925).
42. Morningstar, Sustainable Funds U.S. Landscape Report 10 (2022), https://www.morningstar.com/lp/sustainable-funds-landscape-report. ("For the sixth consecutive calendar year, sustainable funds set an annual record for net flows in 2021.").
43. *See, e.g.*, R. Boffo & R. Patalano, *ESG Investing: Practices, Progress and Challenges*, OECD PARIS, www.oecd.org/finance/ESG-Investing-Practices-Progress-and-Challenges.pdf ("The growing investor interest in ESG factors reflects the view that environmental, social and corporate governance issues—including risks and opportunities—can affect the long-term performance of issuers and should therefore be given appropriate consideration in investment decisions."); THE FORUM FOR SUSTAINABLE AND RESPONSIBLE INVESTMENT, 2020 TRENDS REPORT: EXECUTIVE SUMMARY, v, https://www.ussif.org/files/US%20SIF%20Trends%20Report%202020%20Executive%20Summary.pdf (reporting "a continuation of the significant growth in money managers and institutional investors that consider ESG factors to identify responsible, well-managed companies that will be resilient over the long term.").
44. *See* Andrew Carnegie, *Wealth*, N. AM. REV. 659 (June 1889).
45. *See* Mark Zuckerberg & Priscilla Chan, Facebook Post, A Letter to Our Daughter (Dec. 1, 2015), https://www.facebook.com/notes/770757020443898/?fref=nf; John Cassidy, *Mark Zuckerberg and the Rise of Philanthrocapitalism*, N.Y. TIMES (Dec. 2, 2015), https://www.newyorker.com/news/john-cassidy/mark-zuckerberg-and-the-rise-of-philanthrocapitalism.

Chapter 1

1. *See* William J. Carney, *Limited Liability Companies: Origins and Antecedents*, 66 U. COLO. L. REV. 855, 857 (1995) ("An oil company first sought to obtain passage of

an LLC statute in Alaska in 1975 but was unsuccessful. The Hamilton Brothers Oil Company of Denver, familiar with Panamanian *limitadas*, sought passage of a statute authorizing similar entities in the United States, and chose Wyoming for its legislative efforts.").

2. In 2019–21, well over twice as many LLCs were formed in Delaware than all other forms combined. *See* Delaware Division of Corporations, *2021 Annual Report*, https://corpfiles.delaware.gov/Annual-Reports/Division-of-Corporations-2021-Annual-Report.pdf.
3. Michael L. Schler, *Initial Thoughts on the Proposed "Check-the-Box" Regulations*, 71 TAX NOTES 1679, 1682 (1996) (inaugurating use of the term tax "nothing" to refer to disregarded LLCs). The LLC's popularity grew in the late 1980s after administrative decisions granted them favorable tax treatment. Bradley T. Borden, *Residual-Risk Model for Classifying Business Arrangements*, 37 FLA. ST. U. L. REV. 245, 263 (2010) (noting the "explosive growth of limited liability company acts" that followed a pair of IRS pronouncements).
4. *See* Mark Zuckerberg, *A Letter to Our Daughter*, Facebook (Dec. 1, 2015), https://www.facebook.com/notes/770757020443898/; *see also* Natasha Singer and Mike Isaac, *Mark Zuckerberg's Philanthropy Uses L.L.C. for More Control*, N.Y. TIMES, Dec. 3, 2015, at B1, https://www.nytimes.com/2015/12/03/technology/zuckerbergs-philanthropy-uses-llc-for-more-control.html; Leslie Lenkowsky, *Ending Philanthropy as We Know It*, WALL ST. J., A15, Dec. 3, 2015, https://www.wsj.com/articles/ending-philanthropy-as-we-know-it-1449100975; Gillian B. White, *Assessing Mark Zuckerberg's Non-Charity Charity*, ATLANTIC (Dec. 3, 2015), https://www.theatlantic.com/business/archive/2015/12/assessing-mark-zuckerbergs-non-charity-charity/418719/.
5. Mark Zuckerberg, Facebook (Dec. 3, 2015, 5:24 PM), https://www.facebook.com/zuck/posts/10102507695055801?.
6. *See, e.g.*, I.R.C. §§ 4941 (imposing penalty taxes on "self-dealing" transactions between a foundation and its managers or substantial contributors), 4943 (imposing penalty taxes on foundations holding "excess[ive]" stakes in businesses), 4945 (imposing penalty taxes on lobbying and electioneering expenditures by foundations).
7. *See* LARRY E. RIBSTEIN & ROBERT R. KEATINGE, RIBSTEIN AND KEATINGE ON LIMITED LIABILITY COMPANIES §§ 4:2, 4:5 & app. 4–5 (2021).
8. *See* Internal Revenue Service (IRS), *Form 990—PF: Return of Private Foundation*, IRS (2020), https://www.irs.gov/pub/irs-pdf/f990pf.pdf.
9. *See* Guidestar, https://www.guidestar.org.
10. *See* Jesse Eisinger, Jeff Ernsthausen, & Paul Kiel, *The Secret IRS Files: Trove of Never-Before-Seen Records Reveal How the Wealthiest Avoid Income Tax*, PRO PUBLICA (June 8, 2021, 5:00 AM), https://www.propublica.org/article/the-secret-irs-files-trove-of-never-before-seen-records-reveal-how-the-wealthiest-avoid-income-tax.
11. *See* IRS, Estate Tax, https://www.irs.gov/businesses/small-businesses-self-employed/estate-tax.
12. *See* Emerson Collective, *Our Mission*, https://www.emersoncollective.com/about-us/.

13. *See* David Gelles, *Laurene Powell Jobs Is Putting Her Own Dent in the Universe*, N.Y. Times (Feb. 27, 2020), https://www.nytimes.com/2020/02/27/business/laurene-powell-jobs-corner-office.html.
14. Emerson Collective, *supra* note 12.
15. Omidyar Network, https://omidyar.com/.
16. Omidyar Network, *Omidyar Network's Journey*, https://omidyar.com/omidyar-networks-journey/.
17. Good Ventures, *Learn About Our Structure and Leadership*, https://www.goodventures.org/about-us/governance.
18. Good Ventures, *Our Vision & Values*, https://www.goodventures.org/about-us/vision-and-values.
19. The Ballmer Group, https://www.ballmergroup.org/work; *see also* Andrew Greif, *Steve Ballmer Is Putting His Billions Behind Bigger Causes in L.A. Than the Clippers*, L.A. Times (July 8, 2020), https://www.latimes.com/sports/clippers/story/2020-07-08/steve-ballmer-group-foundation-clippers-owner-billionaire (describing how the LLC structure allows Ballmer Group to "back advocacy groups who try to help shape state and national policies on criminal justice issues including bail reform and expunging criminal records. Ballmer Group also works from the other direction, regularly talking with lawmakers from legislators in the state of Washington to Rep. Karen Bass (D-Los Angeles), in D.C.").
20. Arnold Ventures, *Our Work*, https://www.arnoldventures.org/work.
21. Jack Dorsey (@jack), Twitter (Apr. 7, 2020, 4:04 PM), https://twitter.com/jack/status/1247616216274894848; *FAQs*, #Startsmall *List of Grantees*, #Start small, https://startsmall.llc/#faq.
22. *See* Breakthrough Energy, *Our Story*, https://www.breakthroughenergy.org/our-story/our-story; Pivotal Ventures, *About Pivotal*, https://www.pivotalventures.org/about-pivotal-ventures.
23. *See* Joshua Chaffin & Andrew Edgecliffe-Johnson, *The Political Awakening of Melinda French Gates*, Fin. Times (July 11, 2021) (pointing out that "[i]n keeping with her cautious style, it launched without a press release or fanfare, and only came to light because some tech reporters stumbled on its website"); Sophie Alexander & Ben Steverman, *Gates Divorce Speeds Divergence of Separate Investing Goals*, Moneyweb (July 3, 2021), https://www.moneyweb.co.za/news/international/gates-divorce-speeds-divergence-of-separate-investing-goals/ (noting the Gates divorce "highlights their individual private-investment arms, which they have been quietly building over the past five years").
24. Nicholas Kulish & David Gelles, *MacKenzie Scott Gives Away Another $2.74 Billion Even as Her Wealth Grows*, N.Y. Times (June 15, 2021), https://www.nytimes.com/2021/06/15/business/mackenzie-scott-philanthropy.html.
25. Mackenzie Scott, *116 Organizations Driving Change*, Medium (July 28, 2020), https://mackenzie-scott.medium.com/116-organizations-driving-change-67354c6d733d.
26. Mackenzie Scott, The Giving Pledge (May 25, 2019), https://givingpledge.org/Pledger.aspx?id=393.

27. *See, e.g.*, Leena Rao, *This Startup Wants to Modernize Public Finance*, FORTUNE (May 16, 2017), https://fortune.com/2017/05/16/neighborly-public-finance; Fintech Collective, *Neighborly Raised a Series A*, NEIGHBORLY (May 16, 2017), https://www.fintech.io/articles/neighborly-raises-series-a; Gillian B. White, *Emerson Collective Acquires Majority Stake in the Atlantic*, ATLANTIC (July 28, 2017), https://www.theatlantic.com/business/archive/2017/07/emersoncollective-atlantic-coalition/535215/.
28. Flourish Ventures, *Who We Are*, https://flourishventures.com/who-we-are/.
29. *See* Anne Field, *Omidyar Network Spins off Flourish, A Financial Inclusion Investment Firm*, FORBES (May 25, 2019), https://www.forbes.com/sites/annefield/2019/03/25/financial-inclusion-investment-firm-flourish-is-omidyar-networks-latest-spinoff/?.
30. Connie Ballmer & Steve Ballmer, *Why We're Investing $59 Million to Make It Easier for Social-Service Groups to Do More Good*, CHRON. PHILANTHROPY (Aug. 9, 2018), https://www.philanthropy.com/article/why-were-investing-59-million-to-make-it-easier-for-social-service-groups-to-do-more-good/?.
31. Mike Cronin, *How an Austin Software Company Is Using $59M Investment from Steve Ballmer*, AUSTIN BUS. JOURNALS (Nov. 20, 2018), https://www.bizjournals.com/austin/news/2018/11/20/how-an-austin-software-company-is-using-59m.html?.
32. *See* I.R.C. § 4943.
33. I.R.C. § 4944.
34. John Gertner, *Business; Newman's Own: Two Friends and a Canoe Paddle*, N.Y. TIMES (Nov. 16, 2003), https://www.nytimes.com/2003/11/16/business/business-newman-s-own-two-friends-and-a-canoe-paddle.html.
35. I.R.C. § 4943 (g).
36. *See* Andrew Westrope, *Gov Tech Startup Neighborly Runs Out of Money to Pay Workers*, GOV'T TECH. (Oct. 11, 2019), https://www.govtech.com/biz/gov-tech-startup-neighborly-runs-out-of-money-to-pay-workers.html.
37. Jeremy Johnson, *The Future of Andela*, ANDELA, https://andela.com/insights/the-future-of-andela/.
38. *See* Kathleen Chaykowski, *How Facebook Is Making Sure Zuckerberg Stays in Control Forever*, FORBES (Apr. 27, 2016), https://www.forbes.com/sites/kathleenchaykowski/2016/04/27/how-facebook-is-making-sure-zuckerberg-stays-in-control-forever/#2b4d3ac4e97c; Erin Griffith, *Mark Zuckerberg Controls Facebook and He Intends to Keep It That Way*, FORTUNE (Apr. 27, 2016), http://fortune.com/2016/04/27/zuckerberg-facebook-control/.
39. *See* Dana Brakman Reiser, *Disruptive Philanthropy: Chan Zuckerberg, the Limited Liability Company, and the Millionaire Next Door*, 70 FLA. L. REV. 921, 934–36 (2018).
40. Jack Dorsey (@jack), TWITTER (Apr. 7, 2020, 4:04 PM), https://twitter.com/jack/status/1247616217512198145.
41. *See* Summit Public Schools, *Our Schools*, https://summitps.org/our-schools/; Chan Zuckerberg Initiative, *Summit Learning Platform* (Mar. 13, 2017), https://chanzuckerberg.com/newsroom/summit-learning-platform/.

42. *See* Chan Zuckerberg Initiative, *Grants*, https://chanzuckerberg.com/grants-ventures/grants/ (reporting over $61 million grants to Summit Public Schools and the related entity Gradient Learning) [hereinafter *CZI Grants*].
43. Summit Learning, *Privacy and Security FAQs: Is There a Relationship between the Summit Learning Program and Facebook?*, https://help.summitlearning.org/hc/en-us/articles/360000892408-Is-there-a-relationship-between-the-Summit-Learning-Program-and-Facebook-.
44. *See* Faith Boninger, Alex Molnar, and Christopher Saldaña, Big Claims, Little Evidence, Lots of Money: The Reality behind the Summit Learning Program and the Push to Adopt Digital Personalized Learning Platform, National Education Policy Center, 17–18, (June 25, 2020), available for download: https://nepc.colorado.edu/sites/default/files/publications/RB%20Summit.pdf; *see also* Valerie Strauss, *New Concerns Raised about Digital Learning Platform*, Wash. Post (June 25, 2020), https://www.washingtonpost.com/education/2020/06/25/new-concerns-raised-about-well-known-digital-learning-platform/ (providing answers to follow-up questions on the report posed to its authors).
45. *See, e.g.*, Theodore Schleifer, *Working for Mark Zuckerberg's Philanthropy Isn't Always Easy Since It Means Working for Mark Zuckerberg*, Vox (June 26, 2020), https://www.vox.com/recode/2020/6/26/21303664/mark-zuckerberg-facebook-chan-zuckerberg-initiative-philanthropy-tension.
46. *See* I.R.C. § 4941.
47. For a discussion of using social welfare organizations organized under I.R.C. § 501(c)(4) as a vehicle for elite philanthropy, *see* David S. Miller, *Social Welfare Organizations as Grantmakers*, 21 N.Y.U. J. Leg. & Pub. Pol'y 413 (2018). Dana Brakman Reiser, Sharon C. Lincoln, and Ingrid Mittermaier, *Using Non-501(c)(3) Vehicles to Accomplish Philanthropic Objectives*, Taxes: The Magazine 45 (Dec. 2017), 51–52.
48. Omidyar Network, *Our Commitment to Transparency and Democracy* (Oct. 6, 2020), https://omidyar.com/our-commitment-to-transparency-and-democracy-omidyar-network/ (statement by Beth Kanter, Omidyar Network Chief Advocacy & Strategic Communications Officer explaining, "[t]his LLC also allows us to invest in not-for-profits beyond just public charities, such as 501(c)(4) social welfare organizations. Recently, we've been doing more of this . . . we have to do everything we can to support those on the frontlines of change, in the service of our stated social impact goals.").
49. For example, the Collective highlighted an effort featuring a Shepard Fairey print to promote awareness about the Dream Act and provided tools on its website to encourage visitors to "call your member of Congress and urge them to pass the Dream Act now." Emerson Collective: Immigration, *Shepard Fairey's New Print Demands a Dream Act Now* (Jan. 2018), https://www.emersoncollective.com/articles/2018/01/shepard-faireys-new-print-demands-a-dream-act-now/.
50. Jessica E. Lessin & Miriam Jordan, *Laurene Powell Jobs Goes Public to Promote Dream Act*, Wall St. J. ((May 16, 2013, 9:08 PM), https://www.wsj.com/articles/SB10001424127887323582904578487263583009532; *see also* Alexandra Robbins, *The Welcome Committee*, Marie Claire (Aug. 15, 2018), https://www.marieclaire.com/politics/a22716448/laurene-powell-jobs-emerson-collective-immigration-reform/

(describing Emerson Collective's immigration advocacy work and providing information about the activities of several immigration team members).

51. Federal Election Commission, *Who Can and Can't Contribute*, https://www.fec.gov/help-candidates-and-committees/candidate-taking-receipts/who-can-and-cant-contribute/ (explaining that "[i]f a single member LLC has not chosen corporate tax treatment, it may make contributions; the contributions will be attributed to the single member, not the LLC").
52. *See* Open Secrets.org, *Emerson Collective Summary*, https://www.opensecrets.org/orgs/emerson-collective/summary?id=D000068512 (reporting contributions of $146,704 to DNC Services Corp., $72,755 to the Democratic Senatorial Campaign Committee, and $34,158 to Joe Biden, among hundreds of contributions in the 2020 election cycle).
53. *See* Abby Schultz, *Houston's John and Laura Arnold Change Tacks on Philanthropy*, BARRON'S (Feb. 1, 2019), https://www.barrons.com/articles/houstons-john-and-laura-arnold-change-tacks-on-philanthropy-01549051799.
54. Press Release, A Letter from Our President, ARNOLD VENTURES (Jan. 28, 2019), https://www.arnoldventures.org/newsroom/a-letter-from-our-president.
55. *See* Michael Hardy, *Arnold Ventures' New Leader of Advocacy Sees a Way to Cut through the Partisan Gridlock*, ARNOLD VENTURES (Oct. 24, 2019), https://www.arnoldventures.org/stories/from-presidential-campaigns-to-problem-solving-new-advocacy-vp-looks-for-big-challenges.
56. Omidyar Network, *supra* note 48.
57. *See* Pierre Omidyar, *Disclosing for Democracy: Why We're Sharing Our Contributions*, OMIDYAR GROUP (Mar. 30, 2020), https://www.omidyargroup.com/pov/2020/03/30/disclosing-for-democracy-why-were-sharing-our-contributions/.
58. Arnold Ventures, *Advocacy*, https://www.arnoldventures.org/work/advocacy.
59. The Ballmer Group, *supra* note 19.
60. Benjamin Herold, *Ex-Microsoft CEO (No, Not That One) Giving Big to K-12*, EDUCATION WEEK (Mar. 24, 2019), https://www.edweek.org/leadership/ex-microsoft-ceo-no-not-that-one-giving-big-to-k-12/2019/03.
61. *See* I.R.C. § 501(c)(3) (allowing organizational income tax exemption for a charity "no substantial part of the activities of which is carrying on propaganda, or otherwise attempting, to influence legislation . . . and which does not participate in, or intervene in . . . any political campaign on behalf of (or in opposition to) any candidate"); *see also* Eric Amarante Franklin, *The Perils of Philanthrocapitalism*, 78 MD. L. REV. 1, 52–56 (2018)(contrasting philanthropy LLCs' relative freedom to engage in political advocacy with restrictions on foundations' ability to do the same and arguing the lack of such restrictions on philanthropy LLCs exacerbate elite philanthropy's inherently antidemocratic nature).
62. *See* I.R.C. § 4945 (penalizing foundation expenditures "to carry on propaganda, or otherwise to attempt, to influence legislation" and "to influence the outcome of any specific public election, or to carry on, directly or indirectly, any voter registration drive"). A third-tier penalty tax imposed on willful, repeated violations drives that point home even further. *See* I. R. C. § 6684.

63. *See* Lyndsey Layton, *How Bill Gates Pulled Off the Swift Common Core Revolution*, Wash. Post (June 7, 2014), https://www.washingtonpost.com/politics/how-bill-gates-pulled-off-the-swift-common-core-revolution/2014/06/07/a830e32e-ec34-11e3-9f5c-9075d5508f0a_story.html.
64. *See id.*; *see also generally* Megan E. Thompkins-Stange, Policy Patrons: Philanthropy, Education Reform, and the Politics of Influence 20–28, 113–25 (2016).
65. *See* Layton, *supra* note 63 ("[T]he idea found a major booster in President Obama, whose new administration was populated by former Gates Foundation staffers and associates. The administration designed a special contest using economic stimulus funds to reward states that accepted the standards.")
66. *Id.*
67. *See* Ribstein & Keatinge, *supra* note 7, § 5:1.
68. *See id.* § 4:6.
69. Amber Elliot, *Houston Billionaires Commit to Donating 5 Percent of Their Wealth Annually,* Houston Chron. (Apr. 12, 2021), https://www.houstonchronicle.com/lifestyle/article/Houston-billionaires-commit-to-donating-5-percent-16079682.php.
70. Global Citizen, *Give While You Live*, https://www.globalcitizen.org/en/connect/give-while-you-live/.
71. *See* Jennifer Wang, *The New Forbes Philanthropy Score: How We Ranked Each Forbes 400 Billionaire Based on Their Giving,* Forbes (Sept. 8, 2020), https://www.forbes.com/sites/jenniferwang/2020/09/08/the-new-forbes-philanthropy-score-how-we-ranked-each-forbes-400-billionaire-based-on-their-giving/?sh=4e33bf19eba9.
72. Scott, *supra* note 25.
73. *See* Tax Reform Act of 1969, Pub. L. No. 91-172, 83 Stat. 503 (1969).
74. *See* I.R.C. § 4942(e).
75. Astra Taylor, *Universities Are Becoming Billion-Dollar Hedge Funds With Schools Attached*, The Nation (Mar. 8, 2016), https://www.thenation.com/article/archive/universities-are-becoming-billion-dollar-hedge-funds-with-schools-attached.
76. *See* I.R.C. § 4968; *see also* Molly F. Sherlock, Jane G. Gravelle, Margot L. Crandall-Hollick, & Joseph S. Hughes, Congressional Research Service, *College and University Endowments: Overview and Tax Policy Options* (2018), https://fas.org/sgp/crs/misc/R44293.pdf (considering the policy alternatives including a tax on university endowments); Janet Loin, *Senate Matches House's 1.4% Tax Proposal for College Endowments,* Bloomberg (Nov. 10, 2017), https://www.bloomberg.com/news/articles/2017-11-10/senate-matches-house-s-1-4-tax-proposal-for-college-endowments (reporting on this development).
77. *See* I.R.C. §4940(a) (setting foundation endowment income tax at 1.39 percent).
78. *See* Ford Foundation, *Financial Snapshot 2018,* 5 (July 10, 2019), https://www.fordfoundation.org/about/library/financial-statements/financial-snapshot-2018/ (reporting" annualized returns of 7.3 percent and 6.6 percent, respectively, for the three- and five-years ending December 31, 2018").

79. *See* Ford Foundation, The Ford Foundation Amended and Restated Articles of Incorporation, art. V (Feb. 2019), https://www.fordfoundation.org/media/1466/amended-and-restated-articles-of-incorporation-to-reflect-change-in-agents-name.pdf ("This being a benevolent corporation, its term is unlimited and in perpetuity.")
80. *See, e.g.*, Uniform Prudent Management of Institutional Funds Act § 3 (instructing fiduciaries that their management of institutional funds is "[s]ubject to the intent of a donor expressed in a gift instrument); Uniform Trust Code § 804 (directing trustees to "administer the trust as a prudent person would, by considering the purposes, terms, distributional requirements, and other circumstances of the trust").
81. *See* Rockefeller Foundation, *The Rockefeller Foundation: A Digital History, Rockefeller Sanitary Commission*, https://rockfound.rockarch.org/rockefeller-sanitary-commission.
82. *See* Joel L. Fleishman, Putting Wealth to Work 119–25 (2017) (describing Olin's limited life foundation in a work critical of the approach); John J. Miller, A Gift of Freedom: How the John M. Olin Foundation Changed America 185–90 (2005); *see also* Duke Sanford Center for Strategic Philanthropy, *Time Limited Foundations*, https://cspcs.sanford.duke.edu/time-limited-foundations-sorted-spend-down-date (listing foundations with spend down commitments); Francie Ostrower, *Sunsetting: A Framework for Foundation Life as Well as Death* (Aspen Institute 2011), https://www.aspeninstitute.org/wp-content/uploads/files/content/docs/pubs/Sunsetting2.pdf (discussing four case studies of modern limited life foundations).
83. *See* Gates Foundation, *Foundation Trust*, https://www.gatesfoundation.org/about/financials/foundation-trust ("Because Bill, Melinda, and Warren believe the right approach is to focus the foundation's work in the 21st century, we will spend all of our resources within 20 years after Bill's and Melinda's deaths.")
84. *See* Andrew Edgecliffe-Johnson & Joshua Chaffin, *Bill & Melinda Gates Foundation Plans Massive Giving Expansion*, Fin. Times (Jan. 26, 2022), https://www.ft.com/content/45bb12a7-24ee-4f6e-b839-aafb9e46500d?; *see also* Emily Glazer, *Melinda French Gates No Longer Pledges Bulk of Her Wealth to Gates Foundation*, Wall St. J. (Feb. 2, 2022), https://www.wsj.com/articles/melinda-french-gates-no-longer-pledges-bulk-of-her-wealth-to-gates-foundation-11643808602 (reporting Melinda French Gates "is no longer pledging to give the bulk of her wealth to the Bill & Melinda Gates Foundation and instead plans to spread it among philanthropic endeavors, according to people familiar with the matter" and a close reading of her November 2021 Giving Pledge); Andrew Edgecliffe Johnson, *Bill Gates Donates Another $20bn to His Charitable Foundation*, Fin. Times (Jul. 13, 2022), https://www.ft.com/content/5e6808b1-3061-4af2-a54b-6c58cd6b8f74? (reporting Bill Gates had donated another $20 billion to the foundation and announced a plan to increase distributions considerably beyond pandemic levels).
85. James B. Stewart & Nicholas Kulish, *Leading Foundations Pledge to Give More, Hoping to Upend Philanthropy*, N.Y. Times (June 10, 2020), https://www.nytimes.com/2020/06/10/business/ford-foundation-bonds-coronavirus.html.

86. At least some of the bonds are not scheduled to be redeemed until the year 2070. Press Release, Ford Foundation, Ford Foundation Announces Sale and Pricing of Landmark $1 Billion Social Bonds (June 23, 2020), https://www.fordfoundation.org/the-latest/news/ford-foundation-announces-sale-and-pricing-of-landmark-1-billion-social-bonds/.
87. *See* Stewart & Kulish, *supra* note 85 (noting Ford's plans to use its bond issue to "increas[e] the percentage of its endowment that it pays out annually to about 10 percent from nearly 6 percent"); #startsmall Tracker, https://docs.google.com/spreadsheets/d/1-eGxq2mMoEGwgSpNVL5j2sa6ToojZUZ-Zun8h2oBAR4/edit#gid=0 (recording spending by #startsmall as roughly 10 percent of its total assets since its inception in 2020).
88. *See* I.R.C. § 4942(g)(2)(E); *see also* Amarante Franklin, *supra* note 61, at 47–52 (highlighting the antidemocratic effect of philanthropy LLCs' lack of payout requirements).
89. *See CZI Grants*, *supra* note 42.
90. *See* Zuckerberg, *supra* note 5 (approximating the value of assets devoted to CZI at $45 billion).
91. *See, e.g.*, Nicholas Kulish, *What the Gates Divorce Means for the Bill and Melinda Gates Foundation*, N.Y. Times (May 4, 2021, updated July 7, 2021), https://www.nytimes.com/2021/05/04/business/bill-melinda-gates-divorce-foundation.html); Haleluya Hadero & Glenn Gamboa, *Gates Divorce Raises Questions about the Future of Billions in Philanthropic Cash*, Chron. Philanthropy (May 5, 2021), https://www.philanthropy.com/article/bill-and-melinda-gates-divorce-could-shake-up-philanthropy.
92. *See* Chaffin & Edgecliffe-Johnson, *supra* note 23; Nicholas Kulish, *Bill Gates Can Remove Melinda French Gates from Foundation in Two Years*, N.Y. Times (July 7, 2021), https://www.nytimes.com/2021/07/07/business/bill-gates-melinda-gates-divorce-foundation.html.
93. *See* Michael J. de la Merced & Nicholas Kulish, *Warren Buffett's Exit from the Gates Foundation Clouds Its Future*, N.Y. Times (June 23, 2021), https://www.nytimes.com/2021/06/23/business/warren-buffett-gates-foundation.html.
94. *See* Ribstein & Keatinge, *supra* note 7, § 14.30 (describing the distribution of an LLC's assets on distribution).
95. *See* Delaware Division of Corporations, *supra* note 2 (reporting 247,003 LLC formations in the state in 2021).
96. *See* Nicholas Kulish, *Giving Billions Fast, MacKenzie Scott Upends Philanthropy*, N.Y. Times (Dec. 20, 2020, updated June 15, 2021) https://www.nytimes.com/2020/12/20/business/mackenzie-scott-philanthropy.html.
97. *See* Nicholas Kulish, *MacKenzie Scott Gave Away Billions. The Scam Artists Followed.*, N.Y. Times (Apr. 24, 2021), https://www.nytimes.com/2021/04/24/business/mackenzie-scott-giving-scams.html.
98. *See* Sarah McBride & Jerry Smith, *Billionaire Laurene Powell Jobs Turned Her LLC Into a VC Machine*, Bloomberg (Apr. 25, 2019), https://www.bloomberg.com/news/articles/2019-04-25/billionaire-laurene-powell-jobs-turned-her-llc-into-a-vc-machine.
99. *See* Omidyar Network, *supra* note 48.

100. *See, e.g.*, Omidyar Network, *Responsible Technology Partners*, https://omidyar.com/responsible-technology-partners/ (listing the partner, amount, geographic area, and type of organizational structure for each recipient of ON funds directed toward its responsible technology area of focus).
101. Good Ventures, *Grant Making Approach: How Do We Decide What to Fund?*, https://www.goodventures.org/our-portfolio/grantmaking-approach#footnote-ref-1.
102. *See CZI Grants*, *supra* note 42.
103. *See* Chan Zuckerberg Initiative, *Ventures*, https://chanzuckerberg.com/grants-ventures/ventures/.
104. *See id.*; *but see also* Chan Zuckerberg Initiative, *2021 CZI Ventures: Investing in Progress*, (Dec 3, 2021), https://chanzuckerberg.com/newsroom/2021-czi-ventures-investing-in-progress/ (reporting CZI's 2021 move into investments outside EdTech with its participation in a $10 million Series A funding round for CarbonBuilt, which markets a green technological solution to concrete manufacturing).
105. *See* #startsmall Tracker, *supra* note 87.
106. Jack Dorsey, (@jack), TWITTER (Apr. 7, 2020, 4:04 PM), https://twitter.com/jack/status/1247616216887255042.
107. *See* I.R.C. § 6033(a)(3)(A).
108. The form 990-EZ is available to charities with gross receipts below $200,000 and assets of less than $500,000. For organizations with gross receipts of $50,000 or less, the even simpler 990-N is available. *See* IRS, *Form 990 Series: Which Forms Do Exempt Organizations File*, https://www.irs.gov/charities-non-profits/form-990-series-which-forms-do-exempt-organizations-file-filing-phase-in.
109. *See* IRS, Form 990-PF, https://www.irs.gov/pub/irs-pdf/f990pf.pdf; *see also* Amarante Franklin, *supra* note 61, at 56–60 (detailing these disclosure requirements and arguing the opacity of philanthropy LLCs intensifies philanthropy's tendencies toward paternalism and amateurism).
110. IRS, Instructions for Form 990-EZ Return of Organization Exempt from Income Tax (2020), https://www.irs.gov/pub/irs-pdf/i990.pdf (also noting that "some members of the public rely on Form 990 or 990-EZ as the primary or sole source of information about a particular organization").
111. Americans for Prosperity Foundation v. Bonta, 141 S. Ct. 2373 (2021).
112. *See* I.R.C. § 4940(a).
113. *See* I.R.C. § 170(c).
114. *See* Vada Waters Lindsey, *The Charitable Contribution Deduction: A Historical Review and a Look to the Future*, 81 NEB. L. REV. 1056, 1082–83 & n. 162 (explaining this "upside down" effect and collecting criticisms of it).
115. *See* Tax Cuts and Jobs Act of 2017, Pub. L. No. 115-97, 31 Stat. 2054 § 11021 (2017) (increasing the standard deduction to $12,000 for individuals and $24,000 for married couples filing jointly and allowing for inflation-based indexing).
116. *See* Coronavirus Aid, Relief, and Economic Security (CARES) Act, Pub. L. No. 116-136, 134 Stat. 281 § 2204 (2020); Consolidated Appropriations Act of 2020, Pub. L. No. 116-260, Div. EE, § 212 (2020).

117. *See* IRS, PUBLICATION 3402: TAXATION OF LIMITED LIABILITY COMPANIES 2 (2016), https://www.irs.gov/pub/irs-pdf/p3402.pdf.
118. *See, e.g.*, Alan Rappeport, *Biden Banks on $3.6 Trillion Tax Hike on the Rich and Corporations*, N.Y. TIMES (May 28, 2021, updated June 8, 2021), https://www.nytimes.com/2021/05/28/us/politics/tax-rising-on-rich-corporations.html (describing the Biden Administration proposal to tax capital gains of taxpayers earning over $1 million as ordinary income, subject to tax rate of 39.6 percent, rather than as capital gains eligible for a 20 percent rate).
119. *See* Roger Colinvaux, *Charitable Contributions of Property: A Broken System Reimagined*, 50 HARV. J. LEG. 263, 270 (2013).
120. *See, e.g.*, M. Todd Henderson & Anup Malani, *Corporate Philanthropy and The Market for* Altruism, 109 COLUM. L. REV. 571, 611 (2009) ("Without an efficiency justification for preferring donations of stock over cash, these rules distort private choices in ways that may be socially undesirable."); Daniel Halperin, *A Charitable Contribution of Appreciated Property and the Realization of Built-In Gains*, 56 TAX L. REV. 1, 36 (2002) ("the donation of low-basis property to charity enables [the donor] unfairly to substitute cash or new diversified investments for the donated property without paying tax on accrued gains").
121. *See* I.R.C. § 170.
122. *See* Colinvaux, *supra* note 119, at 266–67, 273–74 & nn. 57–58.
123. *See* I.R.C. §§ 1011, 1012 (defining "basis").
124. *See* #startsmall Tracker, *supra* note 87 (reporting a $250,000 grant to Aim High on May 10, 2021); Aim High for High School, https://aimhigh.org/ (describing Aim High's programs and its status as a tax-exempt public charity).
125. *See* Eisinger et al., *supra* note 10.
126. *See* I.R.C. §§ 2001, 2501.
127. *See* I.R.C. §§ 2055(a)(2), 2522(a)(2).
128. For comprehensive discussion of the estate and gift tax ramifications of philanthropy LLCs, see Brakman Reiser, *supra* note 39, at 952–56, and Benjamin M. Leff, *What Is Lost When Philanthropy Avoids Philanthropy Law?*, 70 FLA. L. REV. FORUM, 155, 157–58 (2019).
129. *See* I.R.C. § 2056.
130. *See* Press Release, The Royal Swedish Academy of Sciences (Oct. 14, 1997), https://www.nobelprize.org/prizes/economic-sciences/1997/press-release/ (announcing the Nobel Prize in Economic Sciences to be awarded to Merton and Scholes, for their option work "in collaboration with the late Fischer Block").

Chapter 2

1. *See* Peter Olsen-Phillips & Brian O'Leary, *How Much America's Biggest Charities Raise: 27 Years of Data*, CHRON. PHILANTHROPY (Oct. 31, 2017), https://www.philanthropy.com/article/how-much-americas-biggest-charities-raise-27-years-of-data.

2. *See* National Philanthropic Fund, 2021 DAF Report (citing this figure for the assets held by national charities defined to "include independent organizations, such as National Philanthropic Trust, and charitable organizations affiliated with financial institutions"), https://www.nptrust.org/reports/daf-report/; *see also* Michael Theis, *Donor-Advised Funds Saw Rapid Growth in 2020*, Chron. Philanthropy (Nov. 9, 2021), https://www.philanthropy.com/article/donor-advised-funds-saw-rapid-growth-in-2020 ("Only a few donor-advised funds account for the majority of 2020's contributions. The five largest donor-advised fund sponsors—Fidelity Charitable, National Philanthropic Trust, Schwab Charitable Fund, Vanguard Charitable Endowment, and the Silicon Valley Community Foundation—raised roughly $24.5 billion in 2020, more than half of the total amount contributed to such funds last year.").
3. *See* National Philanthropic Fund, *supra* note 2; *see also* James Andreoni, *The Benefits and Costs of Donor—Advised Funds*, 32 Tax Policy and the Economy 1, 6 (Robert A. Moffitt, ed. 2018)(reporting earlier statistics on DAF size and growth).
4. *See* Tom Metcalf, *A Peek into Goldman's Black Box Charity Reveals Tech Billionaires*, Bloomberg (Mar. 14, 2018), https://www.bloomberg.com/news/articles/2018-03-14/peek-into-goldman-s-black-box-charity-reveals-tech-billionaires.
5. *See* Andreoni, *supra* note 3, at 25 (reporting Fidelity's findings of its customer study).
6. *See* Aaron Horvath & Walter W. Powell, *Seeing Like a Philanthropist: From the Business of Benevolence to the Benevolence of Business*, *in* The Nonprofit Sector: A Research Handbook 100–101 (3d ed. 2021) (Walter W. Powell & Patricia Bromley, eds.); Eleanor Sacks, The Growing Importance of Community Foundations 11–12 (2014), https://scholarworks.iupui.edu/bitstream/handle/1805/6364/the_growing_importance_of_community_foundations-final_reduce_file_size_2.pdf?.
7. *See* Sacks, *supra* note 6, at 16.
8. *See* Christopher Hoyt, Legal Compendium for Community Foundations 10–11 (Council on Foundations, 1996), https://cof.org/sites/default/files/documents/files/Definition-ofa-Community-Foundation.pdf.
9. *See* Candid, Key Facts on U.S. Nonprofits and Foundations (Apr. 2020), https://www.issuelab.org/resources/36381/36381.pdf (counting 1067 community foundations nationwide); *see also* Sacks, *supra* note 6, at 4 (citing "[a] 2014 study found 'at least 763 community foundations in the United States actively making grants'").
10. *See* Horvath & Powell, *supra* note 6, at 104.
11. *See* New York Community Trust, Our History: 1931: The Trust Develops the First Donor-Advised Fund, https://www.nycommunitytrust.org/about/history/.
12. *See* Lila Corwin Berman, Donor Advised Funds in Historical Perspective 13 (2015), https://lawdigitalcommons.bc.edu/cgi/viewcontent.cgi?article=1014&context=philanthropy-forum; National Philanthropic Trust, *History of Giving*, https://www.historyofgiving.org/1930-1980/1931-new-york-community-trust-pioneers-donor-advised-fund/.
13. Earlier legislation, which singled out certain 501(c)(3) entities for superior tax treatment as public charities, foreshadowed the comprehensive 1969 legislation. *See*

Roger Colinvaux, *Defending Place-Based Philanthropy by Defining the Community Foundation*, 2018 B.Y.U. L. Rev. 1, 9–13 (2018).

14. *See* Corwin Berman, *supra* note 12, at 17–23.
15. *See* Hoyt, *supra* note 8, at 10–11.
16. Treas. Reg. §170A-9(f)(10) (as amended in 2013).
17. *See* Treas. Reg. §§ 1.170A-9(f)(11) (as amended in 2013).
18. *See* Colinvaux, *supra* note 13, at 19.
19. Treas. Reg. §§ 1.170A-9(f)(11)(v)(b)(1) (as amended in 2013).
20. *See* Hoyt, *supra* note 8, at 22.
21. *See* National Standards for U.S. Community Foundations, *Getting Accredited* (2014) https://www.cfstandards.org/getting-accredited/national-standards (listing "An Independent Board that Reflects the Community" and "Foundation Control over Component Funds" as two of its "Mission, Structure & Governance" standards for accreditation).
22. Corwin Berman, *supra* note 12, at 20 (quoting Letter from J.A. Tedesco, Chief, Rulings Section, Exempt Organizations Branch, IRS, to Jewish Community Federation of Cleveland, October 28, 1970). The Federation model pioneered by Jewish leaders first in Boston and later in other cities at the end of the nineteenth century shared much in common with the community foundation. Unsurprisingly, these organizations also were some of the first and are still some of the largest sponsors of donor-advised funds. *See id.* at 12.
23. *See* Roger Colinvaux, *Donor Advised Funds: Charitable Spending Vehicles for 21st Century Philanthropy*, 92 Wash. L. Rev. 39, 71–75 & n. 138 (2017) (noting the double benefit of noncash contributions and the considerable criticism it has received).
24. *See* I.R.C. §170(f)(11)(C).
25. *See* Colinvaux, *supra* note 23, at 76–81.
26. Fidelity Charitable, 2021 Fidelity Charitable Giving Report 5, https://www.fidelitycharitable.org/content/dam/fc-public/docs/insights/2021-giving-report.pdf; *see also* Fidelity Charitable, 2022 Fidelity Charitable Giving Report 5, 19, https://www.fidelitycharitable.org/content/dam/fc-public/docs/insights/2022-giving-report.pdf (reporting contributions of "non-publicly traded assets such as restricted stock, private equity, or limited partnership interests totaled $2 billion" and "donor contributions of digital assets soared nearly twelvefold over the previous year" to "more than $330 million in cryptocurrency assets in 2021").
27. *See* Tax Cuts and Jobs Act of 2017, Pub. L. No. 115–97, 31 Stat. 2054 § 11021 (2017) (increasing the standard deduction to $12,000 for individuals and $24,000 for married couples filing jointly and allowing for inflation-based indexing); Darla Mercado, *About 30 Million People Lost These Tax Breaks When They Filed Last Year*, CNBC.com, Apr. 9 2020, https://www.cnbc.com/2020/04/09/about-30-million-people-lost-these-tax-breaks-in-2018.html.
28. *See* Megan O'Neil & Dan Parks, *Tax Law Eliminates Giving Incentive for 21 Million Americans, Study Says*, Chron. Philanthropy (Jan. 12, 2018), https://www.philanthropy.com/article/Tax-Law-Wipes-Out-Giving/242227 ("Nonprofit advocates are deeply worried about the impact of the tax law, especially the doubling of the standard

deduction for individual taxpayers. As a result of that provision, many Americans will stop itemizing their taxes and will no longer get any tax benefit for charitable giving."); Ann Carrns, *Charities Fear Tax Bill Will Cut Giving*, N.Y. TIMES, Dec. 15, 2017, at B5, https://www.nytimes.com/2017/12/15/business/charities-tax-bill.html ("A higher standard deduction means fewer taxpayers will itemize their deductions on their tax returns, reducing the incentive to give to charities").

29. *See* Ruth McCambridge & Patrick Rooney, *Did the Tax Overhaul Create a Spike in Donor-Advised Funds? Well, It's Complicated . . .*, NONPROFIT Q. (Feb. 7, 2018), https://nonprofitquarterly.org/tax-overhaul-donor-advised-funds-spike-daf/ (describing the bunching technique and how the tax changes in 2017 combined with other factors to swell contributions to DAFs); Mark Hrywna, *DAFs Setting Records for 2017*, NONPROFIT TIMES (Feb. 6, 2018), http://www.thenonprofittimes.com/news-articles/dafs-setting-records-2017/ (pointing to the tax legislation along with other factors as "a perfect confluence of events" leading to huge jumps in donor-advised fund contributions in 2017).
30. Daniel Hemel, Joseph Bankman, & Paul Brest, *Are Donor-Advised Funds Good for the Nonprofit Sector?*, 87 EXEMPT ORG. TAX REV. 297, 292 (2021); *see also* Jillian Grennan, *Social Change Through Financial Innovation: Evidence from Donor-Advised Funds*, 11 REV. CORP. FIN. STUD. 694, 696 (2022) (arguing donor-advised funds could "spur[] greater generosity through social influence" by allowing donors to post on social media both at the moment of contribution and again at the time of future distributions).
31. James Andreoni & Ray Madoff, Impact of the Rise of Commercial Donor-Advised Funds on the Charitable Landscape: 1991–2019 (May 4, 2021), https://www.bc.edu/content/dam/bc1/schools/law/centers/philanthropy/2021-forum-philanthropy-report-daf-impact.pdf (comparing individual giving to operating charities to giving to private foundations and DAFs).
32. While DAF use does shield donors' identities from regulators and the public, evidence suggests donors are not using donor-advised funds to retain anonymity from their gifts' recipients. *See* 2022 FIDELITY CHARITABLE GIVING REPORT, *supra* note 26, at 12 (reporting that 82 percent of DAF grants provided donor names and addresses to the receiving charities).
33. *See e.g.*, Brian Galle, *Pay It Forward? Law and the Problem of Restricted-Spending Philanthropy*, 93 WASH. L. REV. 1143, 1150 (2016); Samuel D. Brunson, *"I'd Gladly Pay You Tuesday for a (Tax Deduction) Today": Donor-Advised Funds and the Deferral of Charity*, 55 WAKE FOREST L. REV. 245, 278 (2020).
34. Not all tax experts agree that immediate deduction for contributions to donor-advised funds even provides tax advantages to donors. *See* John R. Brooks, *The Missing Tax Benefit of Donor Advised Funds*, 150 TAX NOTES 1013 (Feb. 29, 2016). Professor Brooks argues making a current donation to a DAF will often leave donors in a worse position than would making their donations later, as the donor avoids paying tax on any resulting capital gain in the interim and could obtain a larger deduction at the later point. *See id.* at 1016. Brooks thus finds "the rapid growth of DAFs

a bit of a puzzle," *id.* at 1014, though in certain circumstances the immediate deduction can confer benefits on donors—such as donating assets at peak value, *see id.* at 1018–22.

35. Nat'l Found., Inc. v. U.S., 13 Cl. Ct. 486 (U.S. Cl. Ct. 1987).
36. *See id.* at 488–90; NFI also paid a commission to Charitable Development Officers for bringing in new donors and projects, a point the IRS also challenged as private inurement incompatible with tax exemption. *See id.* at 489. The court ultimately found the commission structure permissible. *See id.* at 494–95.
37. *Id.* at 489.
38. I.R.C. § 501(c)(3).
39. *See* I.R.C. § 501(c)(3).
40. For a recent argument that commercially affiliated sponsors of DAFs should be subject to greater scrutiny to secure public charity status, see Colinvaux, *supra* note 23, at 61–67. Colinvaux explains that other fundraising organizations must show that the disbursements they make are "commensurate in scope" with the assets they receive and that they do not serve a substantial private purpose, showings commercially affiliated sponsors might struggle to make.
41. *Nat'l Found. Inc.*, 13 Cl. Ct. at 494.
42. *Id.* at 492 (quoting the government's position).
43. *See* The Fund for Anonymous Gifts v. IRS, No. Civ. A. 95–1629, 1997 WL 198108, at *4–5 (unpublished op., vacated by The Fund for Anonymous Gifts v. IRS, No. 97–5142, 1999 WL 334519 (1999)).
44. *See The Fund for Anonymous Gifts*, 1999 WL 334519 at *1 (unpublished op., page citations to Westlaw version).
45. *See, e.g., id.* at *1 ("We are baffled by the government's apparent intransigence.").
46. *See* New Dynamics Found. v. United States, 70 Fed. Cl. 782, 785–86 (2006) (describing New Dynamics' use of "donor-directed sub-accounts").
47. *Id.* at 803.
48. Diners Club International Ltd, *About Us, History,* https://www.dinersclub.com/about-us/history.
49. I.R.S. Form 990, Schedule O: Supplemental Information to Form 990 or 990-EZ: Fidelity Investments Charitable Gift Fund (2019) (emphasis added).
50. *See Vanguard's Successful March to (c)(3) Exemption, Public Charity Status: A Charitable Gift Fund Case Study*, 3 EO Tax J. 34 (1998). Portions of the IRS Administrative file in the Vanguard matter, along with various articles about donor-advised funds, were published in *The EO Tax Journal*, a monthly publication prepared by tax-exempt organizations expert Paul Streckfus.
51. Then as now, Vanguard had a governance structure unique in the investment industry, which enabled it to provide investment services to its funds at cost and to be "the low cost leader" for investors. *See id.* at 35.
52. *See id.* at 86–87 (estimating these administrative fees would amount to under $100,000 in the first three years, although noting costs would vary by the size of the fund and number of donors).

53. *See* Fairbairn v. Fidelity Inv. Charitable Gift Fund, 2021 WL 754534 (N.D. Cal. 2021); Pinkert v. Schwab Charitable Fund, 2021 WL 2476869 (N.D. Cal. 20121).
54. *See* Brian Galle, *The Quick (Spending) and the Dead: The Agency Costs of Forever Philanthropy*, 74 Vand. L. Rev. 757, 793 (2021). ("By a remarkable coincidence, no major commercial [DAF sponsor] seems to have ever contracted with any partner except the for-profit investment firm that founded the [DAF sponsor], suggesting that there is little genuine competition for management fees.")
55. National Philanthropic Trust, 2020 Donor Advised Fund Report, https://www.nptrust.org/reports/daf-report/.
56. Drew Lindsay, *National Donor-Advised Funds Outpace the Field in Giving*, Chron. Philanthropy (Nov. 14, 2017), https://www.philanthropy.com/article/national-donor-advised-funds-outpace-the-field-in-giving/?.
57. Chronicle of Philanthropy, What Donors Want, Donor-Advised Funds: A Practical Guide to America's Fastest Growing Giving Vehicle 4 (2017).
58. *See* Olsen-Phillips & O'Leary, *supra* note 1.
59. *See* Fidelity, 2018 Fidelity Charitable Giving Report, 2, https://www.fidelitycharitable.org/content/dam/fc-public/docs/insights/2018-giving-report.pdf.
60. *The Data Behind the Chronicle's Ranking of America's Favorite Charities*, Chron. Philanthropy (Nov. 5, 2019), https://www.philanthropy.com/article/the-data-behind-the-chronicles-ranking-of-americas-favorite-charities.
61. *See* Heather Joslyn *$8.5 Billion Poured into Fidelity Charitable Accounts in 2017*, Feb. 14, 2018, https://www.philanthropy.com/article/8-5-billion-poured-into-fidelity-charitable-accounts-in-2017/.
62. Katrina Emergency Tax Relief Act, Pub. L. No. 109–73, 119 Stat. 2016, § 301 (2005).
63. *Id.* § 301(d)(2).
64. Roger Colinvaux, *Charity in the 21st Century: Trending Toward Decay*, 11 Fla. Tax Rev. 1, 58–59 (2011).
65. *See* I.R.C. § 170(p); *see also* CARES Act, Pub. L. No. 116-136, 134 Stat. 281 §§ 2204–05 (2020).
66. National Philanthropic Trust, Donor-Advised Fund COVID Grantmaking Survey (2021), https://www.nptrust.org/reports/daf-covid-survey/.
67. *See* Rob Reich & Mohit Mookim, Opinion, *On #GivingTuesdayNow, Start Unleashing Donor-Advised Funds*, Chron. Philanthropy (May 5, 2020), https://www.philanthropy.com/article/on-givingtuesdaynow-start-unleashing-donor-advised-funds/.
68. #HalfMyDAF, *#HalfMYDAF 2021*, https://www.halfmydaf.com/.
69. Pension Protection Act, Pub. L. No. 109–280, 120 Stat. 780 (2006). The legislation primarily focused on fixing underfunded pension plans and the ailing Pension Benefit Guaranty Corporation, but Senator Grassley attached a package of charitable reforms to the bill, including a series of provisions addressing donor-advised funds.
70. A "sponsoring organization" is defined as a tax-exempt charitable organization that is not a foundation and which maintains a donor-advised fund or funds. I.R.C. § 4966(d)(1)(A) (2006).
71. *Id.* § 4966(d)(2)(A).
72. *Id.* § 4966(c)(1)(B)(ii).

73. *See* Marion Fremont-Smith, Governing Nonprofit Organizations 282 (2004).
74. *See, e.g.*, National Philanthropic Trust, *Specialized Grantmaking Services*, https://www.nptrust.org/wp-content/uploads/2020/12/Specialized-Grantmaking-Services-NPT.pdf (offering to conduct expenditure responsibility to allow donor-advised fund grants to be made to entities other than public charities, and providing sample fees); Vanguard Charitable, *Recommend A Grant*, https://www.vanguardcharitable.org/giving-with-vc/how-it-works/granting (similar).
75. *See, e.g.*, Fidelity Charitable, *Charities You Can Support* (limiting grant recipients to public charities, though recommending intermediary charities who may assist donors in getting funds to their ultimate intended recipients).
76. I.R.C. § 4967(a)(2) (2006).
77. *See* I.R.C. § 4958(a), (c)(2) (2018); *see also* John V. Woodhull, *Major Changes for Donor-Advised Funds*, 18 Tax'n Exempts 217, *11 (2007) (noting that slight differences in language might cause the penalties applied to parties may be stiffer in the donor-advised fund context).
78. *See* I.R.C. § 4943(e) (2018).
79. *See* I.R.C. § 6033(k) (2019).
80. *See* I.R.C. § 508(f) (2006).
81. *See* Pension Protection Act, *supra* note 69, § 1226.
82. *See* U.S. Department of the Treasury, *Report to Congress on Supporting Organizations and Donor Advised Funds* (2011), https://www.treasury.gov/resource-center/tax-policy/Documents/Report-Donor-Advised-Funds-2011.pdf [hereinafter Treasury Report].
83. *See id.* at 81.
84. *Id.*
85. *Id.* at 81–82.
86. Several of its ideas were ultimately adopted as part of the 2017 Tax Cuts and Jobs Act, including the increase to the standard deduction.
87. *See* U.S. House Committee on Ways and Means, Tax Reform Act of 2014 Discussion Draft Section-by-Section Summary, Feb. 26, 2014, 872–73, https://www.govinfo.gov/content/pkg/CPRT-113WPRT89455/pdf/CPRT-113WPRT89455.pdf.
88. *See* Letter from Professors Ray Madoff and Roger Colinvaux to Senator Orrin Hatch, July 17, 2017, https://chronicle-assets.s3.amazonaws.com/7/items/biz/pdf/colinvauxmadofftaxreformsubmission.pdf [hereinafter Madoff/Colinvaux Letter].
89. The study can be found at Paul Arnsberger, *Donor-Advised Funds: An Overview Using IRS Data* (2015), http://lawdigitalcommons.bc.edu/cgi/viewcontent.cgi?article=1017&context=philanthropy-forum.
90. *See* Madoff/Colinvaux Letter, *supra* note 88; *see also* Giving USA, The Data on Donor-Advised Funds: New Insights You Need to Know 29 (2018) ("From 2012 to 2015, DAF-to-DAF granting accounted for 4.4 percent of all dollars from donor-advised fund grants.")
91. The request for comments focused on three far more technical issues: (1) whether using DAFs to purchase tickets to charity-sponsored events would violate the

prohibition on distributions with more than incidental benefits to donors; (2) whether use of DAFs to fulfill a donor's pledge to charity would do the same; and (3) how distributions from DAFs are treated by receiving charities for the purposes of deterring their own level of public support. *See* Request for Comments on Application of Excise Taxes with Respect to Donor Advised Funds in Certain Situations, I.R.S. Notice 2017-73, 1 (2017), https://www.irs.gov/pub/irs-drop/n-17-73.pdf.

92. *See* Initiative to Accelerate Charitable Giving, *About Us*, https://acceleratecharitablegiving.org/about/.
93. See Accelerating Charitable Efforts Act, S. 1981, 117th Cong. (2021), https://www.congress.gov/bill/117th-congress/senate-bill/1981/text. Donor-advised funds held by community foundations receive special and more favorable treatment; *see also* Roger Colinvaux, *Speeding Up Benefits to Charity: Donor Advised Fund and Foundation Reform*, 63 Bos. Coll. L. Rev. __ (forthcoming 2022) (making the case for the ACE Act's reforms), available at https://ssrn.com/abstract=3971067.
94. Alex Daniels, *Donor-Advised-Fund Bill Sparks Fierce Lobbying Clash in Calif.*, Chron. Philanthropy (Jan. 23, 2020), https://www.philanthropy.com/article/donor-advised-fund-bill-sparks-fierce-lobbying-clash-in-calif/.
95. Americans for Prosperity Found. v. Bonta, 141 S. Ct. 2373 (2021).
96. Letter to Senate Finance Committee from Community Foundation Public Awareness Initiative, the Council on Foundations, Independent Sector, and Philanthropy Roundtable (Sept. 6, 2017), http://s3.amazonaws.com/acrwordpress/wp-content/uploads/2017/09/07103950/09_06_2017-DAF-Joint-Response.pdf [hereinafter Joint Letter].
97. *See* Dan Parks, *Coalitions of Foundations and Donors Line Up to Oppose New Senate Measure to Speed Up Giving*, Chron. Philanthropy (June 10, 2021), https://www.philanthropy.com/article/coalitions-of-foundations-and-donors-line-up-to-oppose-new-senate-measure-to-speed-up-giving?.
98. *See* Council on Foundations, *National Standards Advisory Committee*, https://www.cof.org/page/national-standards-advisory-committee.
99. *See* National Standards for U.S. Community Foundations, *Getting Accredited: National Standards*, https://www.cfstandards.org/getting-accredited/national-standards (click on Standard 3 for quoted material).
100. *See* Schwab Charitable, *Program Policies*, 23–24 (2020), https://www.schwabcharitable.org/public/file/P-5252372; Alan M. Cantor, Opinion, *Commercial DAFs Keep Touting Their Donors' Crisis Giving. Here's What They Aren't Saying*, Chron. Philanthropy (Jul. 21, 2021), https://www.philanthropy.com/article/Commercial-DAFs-Keep-Touting/249211? (describing conversations with representatives of Schwab, Vanguard, and Fidelity confirming a $50 donation would be sufficient for a DAF to be considered active).
101. *See* Council on Foundations, *Donor Advised Fund Timeline*, 2, https://www.cof.org/sites/default/files/documents/files/DAF-timeline.pdf.
102. *See* Alex Daniels, *New Donor-Advised Fund Pushes to Keep the Cash Moving*, Chron. Philanthropy (Apr. 11, 2018), https://www.philanthropy.com/article/new-donor-advised-fund-pushes-to-keep-the-cash-moving/?.

103. *See* Amalgamated Foundation, *Rewiring Donor Advised Funds to Move More Money to Frontline Nonprofits*, https://www.amalgamatedfoundation.org/advance-change-funds.
104. *See, e.g.*, Terry W. Knoepfle, *The Pension Protection Act of 2006: A Misguided Attack on Donor-Advised Funds and Supporting Organizations*, 9 FLA. TAX. REV. 221, 223 (2009) (arguing "[t]he impact of this legislation has been to dissuade donors from creating donor-advised funds and, as a result, to negatively impact the ability of public charities to provide the types of assistance and support that communities across the United States have relied on for decades").
105. *See* Vanguard Charitable, *supra* note 74.
106. *See* Debra E. Blum, *Charities Capitalize on the Donor-Advised-Fund Boom by Creating Their Own*, CHRON. PHILANTHROPY (Mar. 27, 2018), https://www.philanthropy.com/article/charities-capitalize-on-the-donor-advised-fund-boom-by-creating-their-own/.
107. *See id.* (noting colleges and universities most frequently offer donor-advised funds); Businesswire.com, *Grants to Charities Exceed $15 Billion as Total Assets Increase 9.7% to $85 Billion: 2017 Donor-Advised Fund Report,* https://www.businesswire.com/news/home/20171114005896/en/Grants-to-Charities-Exceed-15-Billion-as-Total-Assets-Increase-9.7-to-85-Billion-2017-Donor-Advised-Fund-Report (reporting findings of the National Philanthropic Trust's 2017 DAF Report that identified religious charities as the predominant subgroup in its statistics on single-issue sponsors).
108. *See* Ohio Wesleyan University, *Donor Advised Funds*, https://www.owu.edu/alumni-and-friends/give-to-owu/donor-advised-funds/.
109. *See, e.g.*, Morgan Stanley Global Impact Funding Trust, *White Label Donor Advised Fund*, https://advisor.morganstanley.com/the-birdie-group/documents/field/b/bi/birdie-group/MS_Private_Label_DAF_Fact_Sheet_Aegis_.pdf.
110. The Philadelphia Foundation, *Donor Advised Fund*, https://www.philafound.org/givers/start-your-own-fund/donor-advised-fund/.
111. The Philadelphia Foundation, *PhilaImpact Fund: Building Social Impact Together*, https://www.philafound.org/wp-content/uploads/2019/01/Phila-Impact-Fund-Sept-2018.pdf.
112. Emmett D. Carson, *21st Century Community Foundations*, 7 (2015), http://www.grantcraft.org/assets/content/resources/Community_Foundations_web.pdf (quoting his earlier letter at length).
113. Press Release, Silicon Valley Community Foundation, *To Serve Philanthropists' Expanding Definition of Community, SVCF Launches East Coast Branch*, (Mar. 20, 2017), https://www.siliconvalleycf.org/blog/svcf-launches-east-coast-branch.
114. *See* Candid, *CF Insights Columbus Survey Results*, https://columbussurvey.cfinsights.org/dashboard/year/2019/tab/respondents/ (providing a downloadable spreadsheet listing the assets of 287 community foundations in the United States and listing SVCF's assets at more than $10.2 billion, with the next largest Tulsa Community Foundation at just over $4.7billion).

115. *See* Kathleen Pender, *Silicon Valley Community Foundation's Assets Surged in 2017; It Won't Say Why*, S.F. CHRON. (Feb. 23, 2018), https://www.sfchronicle.com/business/networth/article/Silicon-Valley-Community-Foundation-s-assets-12704936.php.
116. *See* David Gelles, *How Tech Billionaires Hack Their Taxes With a Philanthropic Loophole*, N.Y. TIMES (Aug. 3, 2018), https://www.nytimes.com/2018/08/03/business/donor-advised-funds-tech-tax.html.
117. *See* David Gelles, *Inside a Powerful Silicon Valley Charity, a Toxic Culture Festered*, N.Y. TIMES (May 11, 2018), https://www.nytimes.com/2018/05/11/business/silicon-valley-community-foundation.html.
118. *See id.*; *see also* Kerry A. Dolan, *Mark Zuckerberg-Connected Charity at Risk of Implosion*, FORBES (May 2, 2018), https://www.forbes.com/sites/kerryadolan/2018/05/02/silicon-valley-community-foundation-emmett-carson/#77c4036c15f0; Alan Cantor, Opinion, *Growth or Mission? The Silicon Valley Community Foundation Made the Wrong Choice*, CHRON. PHILANTHROPY (May 10, 2018), https://www.philanthropy.com/article/growth-or-mission-the-silicon-valley-community-foundation-made-the-wrong-choice/.
119. *See* Penelope Wang, *5 Things to Know About Donor-Advised Funds*, CONSUMER REPS. (Dec. 7, 2019), https://www.consumerreports.org/charitable-donations/donor-advised-funds-things-to-know/ (discussing account minimums and fee structures); *see also* Press Release, Fidelity Charitable, Effective Immediately, Fidelity Charitable Removes Initial $5,000 Minimum Contribution Requirement (Sept. 30, 2020), https://www.fidelitycharitable.org/about-us/news/largest-grantmaker-eliminates-minimum-contribution-amount.html.
120. *See* Grennan, *supra* note 30, at 697 (reporting "[t]he growth in the DAF space in the last five years has been led by DAFs" engaged in innovation, based on a study of more than 4,000 DAF sponsors between 2013 and 2018).
121. *See* Metcalf, *supra* note 4.
122. *See* Chan Zuckerberg Initiative, *Grants*, https://chanzuckerberg.com/grants-ventures/grants/; Maria Di Mento, *Zuckerberg and Chan Pour $2 Billion in Stock into Charity Accounts*, CHRON. PHILANTHROPY (Nov. 8, 2017), https://www.philanthropy.com/article/zuckerberg-and-chan-pour-2-billion-in-stock-into-charity-accounts/.
123. See Andreoni, *supra* note 3, at 7–8.
124. *See* Joint Letter, *supra* note 96 (describing one such use of the practice).
125. *See* CAIR & SOUTHERN POVERTY LAW CENTER, HATE-FREE PHILANTHROPY: IDENTIFYING OPPORTUNITIES AND OBSTACLES TO SAFEGUARD THE SECTOR (2020), https://www.splcenter.org/sites/default/files/dev_hate_free_philanthropy_final1.pdf; CAIR, HIJACKED BY HATE: AMERICAN PHILANTHROPY AND THE ISLAMOPHOBIA NETWORK (2019), https://ca.cair.com/losangeles/wp-content/uploads/sites/6/2019/05/CAIR-Islamophobia-Report.pdf; Alex Kotch, *America's Biggest Charities Are Funneling Millions to Hate Groups From Anonymous Donors*, SLUDGE (Feb. 19, 2019), https://readsludge.com/2019/02/19/americas-biggest-charities-are-funneling-millions-to-hate-groups-from-anonymous-donors/; Mark Hurtubise,

Philanthropy Must Not Support Hate, STAN. SOC. INNOV. REV. (Winter 2021), https://ssir.org/pdf/Winter2021-Viewpoint-Hurtubise-Philanthropy-Hate.pdf.

126. *See* Peter Olsen-Phillips, *Foundations Move $737 Million to Donor-Advised Funds, Chronicle Study Shows*, CHRON. PHILANTHROPY (May 14, 2018), https://www.philanthropy.com/article/foundations-move-737-million-to-donor-advised-funds-chronicle-study-shows/ (reporting a study showing "six foundations [] distributed more than 95 percent of their grants to a national donor advised fund" but also identifying 557 foundations "that made at least one grant to a donor-advised fund during the 2014 to 2016 fiscal years").
127. *A Philanthropic Boom: "Donor-Advised Funds,"* THE ECONOMIST (Mar. 25, 2017).
128. *See* Musk Foundation, Form 990-PF (2016), available at https://pdf.guidestar.org/PDF_Images/2017/770/587/2017-770587507-0f6e7414-F.pdf?.
129. *See* IRS Notice 2017-73, 13–14 (2017), https://www.irs.gov/pub/irs-drop/n-17-73.pdf.
130. *See* Madoff/Colinvaux Letter, *supra* note 88, at 3; *see also* Brunson, *supra* note 33, at 271–72 (decrying the practice).

Chapter 3

1. *See* TOM C.W. LIN, THE CAPITALIST AND THE ACTIVIST (2022) (documenting a growing willingness by corporate America to embrace the priorities of stakeholders through corporate activism).
2. *See* Giving USA, Giving USA 2022 Infographic, https://store.givingusa.org/a/downloads/-/3e65016bdaf93d22/00a07ad39869332d (free download).
3. *See* MARION R. FREMONT-SMITH, PHILANTHROPY AND THE BUSINESS CORPORATION 4 (1972).
4. *See* NORMAN I. SILBER, A CORPORATE FORM OF FREEDOM 18–25 (2001). In contrast, organizations seeking to form with charitable and religious purposes were still subjected to considerable scrutiny for some time. *See id.* When these restrictions were eventually lifted, such entities came to be governed by separate nonprofit corporation statutes in most states. *See id.*
5. *See* Elisabeth Clemens, *The Democratic Dilemma: Aligning Fields of Elite Influence and Political Life*, 43 RESEARCH IN THE SOCIOLOGY OF ORGANIZATIONS, 223, 229–33 (2015).
6. A.P. Smith Mfg. Co. v. Barlow, 98 A.2d 581 (N.J. 1953).
7. *Id.* at 590; *see also* Union Pac. R.R. Co. v. Trustees, Inc., 329 P.2d 398, 399 (Utah 1958) (upholding corporate authority to make charitable gifts on grounds similar to *A.P Smith*).
8. For detailed history of the legal and legislative treatment of corporate charitable gifts, *see* John A. Pearce II, *The Rights of Shareholders in Authorizing Corporate Philanthropy*, 60 VILL. L. REV. 251, 253–65 (2016), and Faith Stevelman Kahn, *Pandora's Box: Managerial Discretion and the Problem of Corporate Philanthropy*, 44 UCLA L. REV. 579, 594–609 (1997).

9. *A.P. Smith Mfg.*, 98 A.2d at 583.
10. *Id.* at 590.
11. *See* Theodora Holding Co. v. Henderson, 257 A.2d 398, 404 (Del. Ch. 1969).
12. *See* Kahn v. Sullivan, 594 A.2d 48 (Del. 1991).
13. Oliver Zunz, Philanthropy in America: A History 175 (2014).
14. Nancy J. Knauer, *The Paradox of Corporate Giving: Tax Expenditures, The Nature of the Corporation, and the Social Construction of Charity*, 44 DePaul L. Rev. 1, 19 (1994) (citing for quote Charles Clotfelter, Federal Tax Policy and Charitable Giving 171 (1985)).
15. *See* Fremont Smith, *supra* note 3, at 13–15.
16. I.R.C. § 170(c) (2020).
17. *See* Fremont-Smith, *supra* note 3, at 15.
18. *See* I.R.C. § 170(b) (2020); *see also* Charles T. Clotfelter, *Charitable Giving and Tax Legislation in the Reagan Era*, 48 Law & Contemp. Probs. 197, 208–29 (1985).
19. *See* CARES Act, Pub. L. No. 116–136, 134 Stat. 281 § 2205 (2020); Consolidated Appropriations Act of 2020, Pub. L. No. 116-260, § 213 (2020).
20. Comm'r of Internal Revenue v. Duberstein, 363 U.S. 278, 285 (1960); *see also* United States v. Am. Bar Endowment, 477 U.S. 105, 116 (1986) ("a payment of money generally cannot constitute a charitable contribution if the contributor expects a substantial benefit in return").
21. *See, e.g.*, William D. Andrews, *Personal Deductions in an Ideal Income Tax*, 86 Harv. L. Rev. 309, 312–16 (1972).
22. The government's description of the charitable deduction as a "tax expenditure"—an amount the government fails to collect in taxes for policy reasons—offers strong support to the subsidy view. U.S. Treasury Department, Office of Tax Analysis, *Tax Expenditures Report* 1, 15–17 (Oct. 19, 2018), https://home.treasury.gov/system/files/131/Tax-Expenditures-FY2020.pdf.
23. *See* Harnwell Wells, *"Corporation Law Is Dead": Heroic Managerialism, Legal Change, and the Puzzle of Corporation Law at the Height of the American Century*, 15 U. Pa. J. Bus. L. 305, 316–35 (2013) (describing 1950s corporate managerialism and its resonance in emerging permissive corporate charitable contribution law).
24. *See* Stevelman Kahn, *supra* note 7, at 609–10; Victor Brudney & Allen Ferrell, *Corporate Charitable Giving*, 69 U. Chi. L. Rev. 1191, 1200–03 (2002).
25. *See* Stevelman Kahn, *supra* note 8, at 611–13.
26. *See id.* at 616–18 (describing work detailed in Joseph Galaskiewicz, Social Organization of an Urban Grants Economy (1985)).
27. *See* Roy Shapira, *Corporate Philanthropy as Signaling and Co-optation*, 80 Fordham L. Rev. 1889, 1905–18 (2012)(evaluating these various signaling possibilities).
28. *See* Robin Pogrebin, *ChevronTexaco to Stop Sponsoring Met's Broadcasts*, N.Y. Times (May 21, 2003), https://www.nytimes.com/2003/05/21/arts/chevrontexaco-to-stop-sponsoring-met-s-broadcasts.html.
29. *See* Edwin McDowell, *Texaco and the Met: A Long Marriage*, N.Y. Times (Mar. 10, 1979), https://www.nytimes.com/1979/03/10/archives/texaco-and-the-met-a-long-marriage-texaco-and-met-a-39year-tie.html.

30. *See OIL: Exit Rieber*, TIME (Aug. 26, 1940), http://content.time.com/time/subscriber/article/0,33009,764502-1,00.html (describing how revelations in a *Herald Tribune* expose led to the ouster of Texaco's long-time chair, Torkild Rieber).
31. *See* Tiffany Hsu, David Yaffe-Bellany, and Marc Tracy, *Jeffrey Epstein Gave $850,000 to M.I.T., and Administrators Knew,* N.Y. TIMES (Jan. 15, 2020), https://www.nytimes.com/2020/01/10/business/mit-jeffrey-epstein-joi-ito.html; Steve Bradt, *MIT Releases Results of Fact-Finding on Engagements with Jeffrey Epstein,* MIT NEWS (Jan. 10, 2020), https://news.mit.edu/2020/mit-releases-results-fact-finding-report-jeffrey-epstein-0110.
32. Michael E. Porter & Mark R. Kramer, *The Competitive Advantage of Corporate Philanthropy*, 80 HARV. BUS. REV. 56 (Dec. 2002).
33. *Id.* at 58.
34. *See, e.g.*, Stevelman Kahn, *supra* note 8, at 674–75; Shapira, *supra* note 27, at 1896–1900.
35. *See* Rosamaria C. Moura-Leite & Robert Padgett, *Historical Background of Corporate Social Responsibility*, 7 SOC. RESP. J. 528, 529–31 (2011).
36. PETER F. DRUCKER, THE PRACTICE OF MANAGEMENT 337 (Rev. ed. 2007).
37. *See* Moura-Leite & Padgett, *supra* note 35, at 531–36.
38. JP MORGAN CHASE & CO., 2018 ENVIRONMENTAL SOCIAL & GOVERNANCE REPORT 2, https://www.jpmorganchase.com/content/dam/jpmc/jpmorgan-chase-and-co/documents/jpmc-cr-esg-report-2018.pdf (introductory letter by Jamie Dimon).
39. FORD MOTOR CO., OUR FUTURE IS IN MOTION: CORPORATE SUSTAINABILITY REPORT 2018–19, 2, https://corporate.ford.com/microsites/integrated-sustainability-and-financial-report-2021/files/ir21-sr18.pdf (joint letter from William Clay Ford, Jr., Executive Chairman, and Jim Hackett, President and CEO).
40. For an extensive review of the history of the CSR debates in corporate law, *see* C.A. Harnwell Wells, *The Cycles of Corporate Social Responsibility: An Historical Retrospective for the Twenty-First Century*, 51 U. KAN. L. REV. 77 (2002).
41. Milton Friedman, *The Social Responsibility of Business Is to Increase Its Profits*, N.Y. TIMES MAG., Sept. 13, 1970, p. 33; *see also* Wells, *supra* note 40, at 109–10, 123–25 (noting Friedman's opposition was shared by many legal scholars).
42. *See* Adolph A. Berle, *Corporate Powers as Powers in Trust*, 44 HARV. L. REV. 1049, 1049 (1931).
43. *See, e.g.*, Honorable Leo E. Strine, Jr., *The Dangers of Denial: The Need for a Clear-Eyed Understanding of the Power and Accountability Structure Established by the Delaware General Corporation Law*, 50 WAKE FOREST L. REV. 761, 767 (2015) ("It is not only hollow but also injurious to social welfare to declare that directors can and should do the right thing by promoting interests other than stockholder interests."); Leo E. Strine, Jr., *Our Continuing Struggle With the Idea That For-Profit Corporations Seek Profit*, 47 WAKE FOREST L. REV. 135, 153 (2012). ("The natural focus of the managers in such a system is therefore supposed to be on advancing the best interests of the stockholders, subject to the legal constraints within which the firm operates.")
44. Dodge v. Ford, 170 N.W. 668 (Mich. 1919).

45. Revlon Inc. v. MacAndrews & Forbes Holdings, Inc., 506 A.2d 173, 182 (Del. 1986) (describing the role of corporate directors at this point as "auctioneers charged with getting the best price for the stockholders").
46. eBay Domestic Holdings, Inc. v. Newmark, 16 A.3d 1, 34 (Del. Ch. 2010).
47. E. Merrick Dodd, Jr., *For Whom Are Corporate Managers Trustees?*, 45 HARV. L. REV. 1145 (1932).
48. *See, e.g.*, Einer Elhauge, *Sacrificing Corporate Profits in the Public Interest*, 80 N.Y.U. L. REV. 733, 738–39 (2005)(describing the view that corporate leaders must act to maximize profits as canonical, but overstated considering statutory and other legal support for corporate actions motivated by social responsibility).
49. Unocal v. Mesa Petroleum, 493 A.2d 946, 955 (Del. 1985).
50. *See, e.g.*, John Tyler, *Negating the Legal Problem of Having "Two Masters": A Framework for L3C Fiduciary Duties and Accountability*, 35 VT. L. REV. 117, 131–38 (2010); Lisa Fairfax, *Doing Well While Doing Good: Reassessing the Scope of Directors' Fiduciary Obligations in For-Profit Corporations With Non-Shareholder Beneficiaries*, 59 WASH. & LEE L. REV. 409, 459–64 (2002).
51. LYNN A. STOUT, THE SHAREHOLDER VALUE MYTH 11 (2012).
52. ADOLPH A. BERLE, JR., THE 20TH CENTURY CAPITALIST REVOLUTION 169 (1954); *see also* Wells, *supra* note 40, at 101–02, (describing Berle's reversal of position).
53. *See* Wells, *supra* note 40, at 98–99.
54. *Dodge*, 170 N.W. at 984; eBay, 16 A.3d at 34.
55. *eBay*, 16 A.3d at 34.
56. *See* Lisa M. Fairfax, *Easier Said Than Done? A Corporate Law Theory for Actualizing Social Responsibility Rhetoric*, 59 FLA. L. REV. 771, 773 (2007) ("Virtually every corporation not only professes a desire to engage in charitable endeavors but also generates a report regarding those endeavors."); DAVID VOGEL, THE MARKET FOR VIRTUE: THE POTENTIAL AND LIMITS OF CORPORATE SOCIAL RESPONSIBILITY 6–12 (2005) (describing the pervasiveness of CSR); *Just Good Business*, ECONOMIST, Jan. 19, 2008, at 4 (describing CSR as "mainstream" even in 2008).
57. Business Roundtable, *Statement on the Purpose of a Corporation* (Aug. 19, 2019), https://opportunity.businessroundtable.org/ourcommitment/ (providing original statement and an updated list of signatories).
58. BlackRock, *Larry Fink's 2019 Letter to CEOs: Purpose & Profit*, https://www.blackrock.com/corporate/investor-relations/2019-larry-fink-ceo-letter.
59. BlackRock, *Larry Fink's 2021 Letter to CEOs*, https://www.blackrock.com/corporate/investor-relations/larry-fink-ceo-letter.
60. SOPHIA A. MUIRHEAD, THE CONFERENCE BOARD, CORPORATE CONTRIBUTIONS: THE VIEW FROM FIFTY YEARS REPORT 7 (1999) [hereinafter CONFERENCE BOARD REPORT]; *see also* N. Craig Smith, *The New Corporate Philanthropy*, 72 HARV. BUS. REV. 105 (May–June 1994) (describing how leading corporate philanthropy programs' shifts to "an approach that ties corporate giving directly to strategy" and noting that funds to support such "initiatives [came] not only from philanthropy budgets but also from business units").
61. CONFERENCE BOARD REPORT, *supra* note 60, at 9.

62. *Id.* at 52.
63. Council on foundations, Increasing Impact, Enhancing Value: A Practitioner's Guide to Leading Corporate Philanthropy 10–11 (2012) (downloadable at https://www.cof.org/content/increasing-impact-enhancing-value-practitioner%E2%80%99s-guide-leading-corporate-philanthropy).
64. *Id.* at 14.
65. Chief Executives for Corporate Purpose, Giving in Numbers: 2018 Edition 14 (2018) [hereinafter 2018 CECP Report]; *see also* Chief Executives for Corporate Purpose, Giving in Numbers: 2017 Edition 15 (2017) ("Companies are using corporate cash more and more.").
66. Corporate Citizenship, The Game Changers: Corporate Foundations in a Changing World 8 (2016), https://corporate-citizenship.com/wp-content/uploads/The-Game-Changers-Corporate-Foundations-in-a-Changing-World.pdf.
67. *See* CECP, *What Does CECP Stand For?*, https://cecp.co/home/what-does-cecp-stand-for/.
68. Chief Executives for Corporate Purpose, Giving in Numbers: 2020 Edition 1 (2020) [hereinafter 2020 CECP Report] (downloadable at https://cecp.co/home/resources/giving-in-numbers/).
69. *See* Conference Board Report, *supra* note 60, at 19 ("The shift toward strategic philanthropy harkens back to the early days of corporate contributions when companies were legally permitted to contribute only to causes related to their business function. In completing this 50-year cycle, corporate contributions have come full circle.").
70. Doug Guthrie, *Corporate Philanthropy in the United States: What Causes Do Corporations Back?*, *in* Politics and Partnerships: The Role of Voluntary Associations in America's Past and Present, 183, 187 (Elisabeth S. Clemens & Doug Guthrie eds., 2011).
71. *See* Chief Executives for Corporate Purpose, Giving in Numbers: 2021 Edition 26 (2021) [hereinafter 2021 CECP Report] (downloadable at https://cecp.co/home/resources/giving-in-numbers/).
72. Studies find disparate degrees of uptake for the corporate foundation model. *See* Guthrie, *supra* note 70, at 187 (pointing to foundations at "[o]ver 39 percent of corporations in the United States"); 2021 CECP Report, *supra* note 71, at 28 (finding 80 percent of the corporations in its study had a foundation).
73. *See* 2021 CECP Report, *supra* note 71, at 28 (reporting only 5 percent of corporate foundations in its study were "predominantly endowed").
74. Council on Foundations, *supra* note 63, at 12.
75. *See* I.R.C. §170(d)(2).
76. *Compare* CARES Act, Pub. L. No. 116-136, 134 Stat. 281 § 2205 (2020) *and* Consolidated Appropriations Act of 2020, Pub. L. No. 116-260, § 213 (2020) (allowing corporate charitable contributions to be deducted up to 25% of a firm's taxable income) *with* I.R.C. § 170(b)(2) (typically applying a 10% percentage limit for all corporate charitable contributions).
77. Conference Board Report, *supra* note 60, at 33.

78. *See* FREMONT-SMITH, *supra* note 3, at 73 (citing RALPH NELSON, THE INVESTMENT POLICIES OF FOUNDATIONS 138–44 (1967)).
79. In addition to the changes to the standard deduction described in chapter 2, this sweeping legislation cut the highest US corporate tax rate from 35 percent to 21 percent. *See* Tax Cut and Jobs Act, Pub. L. No: 115-97, § 13001 (2017). It also increased tax benefits for certain capital investments, introducing a so-called "full expensing" regime for five years. *See id.* § 13201.
80. *See* GIVING USA FOUNDATION, GIVING USA: THE ANNUAL REPORT ON PHILANTHROPY FOR THE YEAR 2017, 158 (2018) (noting two other examples of similar commitments by other financial entities, but not suggesting this was a widespread trend).
81. *See* WELLS FARGO & COMPANY, CORPORATE RESPONSIBILITY REPORT 5 (2018), https://www08.wellsfargomedia.com/assets/pdf/about/corporate-responsibility/2018-corporate-responsibility-report.pdf (reporting donations of $444 million in 2018 and reasserting the 2 percent target).
82. *See* Giving USA, *supra* note 2 (reporting corporate giving in 2019 rose 13.4 percent over 2018 and represented 5 percent of giving overall); Giving USA, 2019 Infographic (reporting corporate giving in 2018 rose 2.9 percent and represented 5 percent of giving overall).
83. CAF AMERICA, VOICE OF CORPORATE PHILANTHROPY IN RESPONSE TO COVID-19 WORLDWIDE (Vol. 4, 2021), https://www.cafamerica.org/wp-content/uploads/4_CV19_Report_CAFAmerica.pdf.
84. CANDID, PHILANTHROPY AND COVID-19 IN THE FIRST HALF OF 2020, at 9 (2020), https://www.issuelab.org/resources/37232/37232.pdf.
85. *See* CANDID, PHILANTHROPY AND COVID-19: MEASURING ONE YEAR OF GIVING 5 (2021), https://www.issuelab.org/resources/38039/38039.pdf.
86. Anna Koob, What Does Candid's Grants Data Say About Funding for Racial Equity in the United States?, Candid Blog, July 24, 2020, https://blog.candid.org/post/what-does-candids-grants-data-say-about-funding-for-racial-equity-in-the-united-states/?. Corporations also undertook and publicized numerous CSR responses to the call for racial equity, changing their operations to be more inclusive. For example, many large retailers signed on to the "15 percent pledge" to "commit 15 percent of their shelf-space to Black-owned businesses." 15 Percent Pledge, *FAQ*, https://www.15percentpledge.org/.
87. *See* CANDID, *supra* note 85, at 17.
88. I.R.C § 501(c)(3) (2019).
89. *See, e.g.*, I.R.C §§ 4941 (imposing penalty taxes on private foundations and their leaders when they engage in "self-dealing" transactions with substantial contributors and foundation managers), 4946 (defining key terms).
90. *See* Melissa Burden, *GM to End Foundation, Redirect Its Charitable Giving*, DET. MORNING NEWS (June 12, 2017), https://www.detroitnews.com/story/business/autos/general-motors/2017/06/12/gm-giving/102764328/.

91. *See* General Motors, *Social Investment*, https://www.gm.com/our-company/social-investment.html (last visited June 20, 2019); General Motors, *Communities*, https://www.gm.com/commitments/communities.
92. *See* Google Foundation, Form 990-PF (2018), https://pdf.guidestar.org/PDF_Images/2018/201/548/2018-201548253-10481c3e-F.pdf. For a comprehensive review of the early days of Google.org, see Dana Brakman Reiser, *For-Profit Philanthropy*, 77 FORDHAM L. REV. 2437 (2009).
93. *See* Waymo.com, https://waymo.com/ (explaining that "Waymo began as the Google self-driving car project in 2009" and is now a subsidiary of Alphabet and sister company to Google).
94. *See* Shabana Hussain, *Google India Aims to Bring 20 Million SMEs Online by 2017*, FORBES INDIA (May 26, 2015), http://www.forbesindia.com/article/special/google-india-aims-to-bring-20-million-smes-online-by-2017/40347/1 (reporting that Google used multiple approaches to target "creating an online presence for 20 million" Indian SMEs on its platforms by 2017).
95. Google.org, *Our Structure*, https://web.archive.org/web/20090219130655/http://www.google.org/about.html.
96. Google.org, *Our Approach*, https://www.google.org/our-approach/#.
97. *See* Brakman Reiser, *supra* note 92, at 2440 n. 12 (citing Google.org, Searching for Solutions, http://www.google.org/index.html, as of Feb. 20, 2009).
98. Google.org, https://www.google.org/.
99. *See* Brakman Reiser, *supra* note 92, at 2458–59.
100. *See* Lyndsey Layton, *Pearson Pays $7.7 Million in Common Core Settlement*, WASHINGTONPOST.COM (Dec. 13, 2013), https://www.washingtonpost.com/local/education/pearson-pays-77-million-in-common-core-settlement/2013/12/13/77515bba-6423-11e3-aa81-e1dab1360323_story.html?.
101. Valerie Strauss, *Pearson Foundation Closing (After Paying Big Fines for Helping Corporate Parent)*, WASHINGTONPOST.COM (Nov. 19, 2014), https://www.washingtonpost.com/news/answer-sheet/wp/2014/11/19/pearson-foundation-closing-after-paying-big-fines-for-helping-corporate-parent/.
102. *See* Liz Alderman & Steven Erlanger, *As Rich Lavish Cash on Notre-Dame, Many Ask: What About the Needy?*, N.Y. TIMES, Apr. 17, 2019, at A1, https://www.nytimes.com/2019/04/17/world/europe/yellow-vest-notre-dame-fire-donations.html.
103. *See* Rachel Adams, *Walmart Accused of Using Charity to Sway Expansion Targets*, N.Y. TIMES, June 16, 2015, at B2, https://www.nytimes.com/2015/06/16/business/walmart-accused-of-using-charity-to-sway-expansion-targets.html.
104. *See* Press Release, Berkshire Hathaway (July 3, 2003), http://www.berkshirehathaway.com/news/jul0303.pdf (announcing the termination of its shareholder-designated contributions program); *see also* Pearce, *supra* note 8, at 275 (describing decision); Linda Sugin, *Encouraging Corporate Charity*, 26 VA. TAX REV. 125, 166 (2006) (similar).
105. *See* Patrick Temple-West, *Oxford Students Uncover Undisclosed Gifts From Fossil Fuel Companies*, FIN. TIMES MONEY MATTERS (July 28, 2021), https://www.ft.com/content/904d4f91-172d-428c-94ee-bcc6f36c83c0.

106. *See, e.g.*, Porter & Kramer, *supra* note 32, at 58–59.
107. *See* 2018 CECP Report, *supra* note 65, at 14.
108. *See* 2021 CECP Report, *supra* note 71, at 15.
109. *See* 2021 CECP Report, *supra* note 71, at 15 (reporting only 4 percent of respondents had closed their foundations and that "the corporate foundation as a community investment model is still an active tool for community engagement").
110. *See* Stevelman Kahn, *supra* note 8, at 666–74 (critiquing many such practices and advocating disclosure to curb managerial discretion over them).
111. *See* Citigroup, Global Citizenship Report (2018), https://www.citigroup.com/citi/about/citizenship/download/2018/Global-Citizenship-Report-2018.pdf.
112. Citigroup, Environmental, Social, and Governance Report (2020), https://www.citigroup.com/citi/about/esg/download/2020/Global-ESG-Report-2020.pdf.
113. *See* ExxonMobil, 2017 Worldwide Contributions and Community Investments, https://corporate.exxonmobil.com/-/media/Global/Files/worldwide-giving/2017-Worldwide-Contributions-and-Community-Overview.pdf.
114. *See* ArcelorMittal, *Collaboration on the Great Lakes,* https://corporate.arcelormittal.com/media/case-studies/collaboration-on-the-great-lakes ("Being part of SOGL has created positive and helpful working relationships with a number of stakeholder groups, and ensures we have regular communications with important [government] organisations. . . . By supporting the environmental interests of the Great Lakes region, we are building trust with our stakeholders and demonstrating leadership in tackling the issues that matter to them.").
115. ArcelorMittal, Presentation from ArcelorMittal SRI Lunch 20, 23 (June 12, 2015), https://corporate-media.arcelormittal.com/media/kt2kjduq/sri-investor-round-table-june-15.pdf.
116. Press Release, Nike, Girl Effect Embarks on New Chapter (Sept. 1, 2015), https://news.nike.com/news/girl-effect-embarks-on-new-chapter.
117. *See* Girl Effect, https://www.girleffect.org/.
118. Gap, Inc. Global Sustainability, P.A.C.E.—Empowering Women, www.gapincsustainability.com/people/pace-changing-one-million-lives.
119. *See, e.g.*, Kathryn Moeller, *Proving "The Girl Effect": Corporate Knowledge Production and Educational Intervention*, 33 Int'l J. Educ. Dev. 612, 620–21 (2013) (arguing that "employing the logic of 'The Girl Effect' maintains, if not potentially exacerbates, unequal relations of power across multiple axes of difference even as it claims to transform them by perpetuating traditionally inequitable roles of social reproduction").
120. *See* Sustainable Apparel Coalition, *The SAC*, https://apparelcoalition.org/the-sac/.
121. *See* The Ellen MacArthur Foundation, *Mission and Vision*, https://www.ellenmacarthurfoundation.org/our-story/mission.
122. *See* Vogel, *supra* note 56, at 21; Susan Rozensher, *The Growth of Cause Marketing: Past, Current, and Future Trends*, 11 J. Bus. & Econ. Res. 181, 181 (2013).
123. *See, e.g.*, Sarah Dadush, *Profiting in (Red): The Need for Enhanced Transparency in Cause-Related Marketing*, 42 N.Y.U. J. Int'l L. & Pol. 1269 (2010) (critiquing lack of transparency and other issues with the (Product) RED campaign); Terri Lynn Helge,

The Taxation of Cause Related Marketing, 85 CHI.-KENT L. REV. 883, 933–39 (2010) (arguing cause related marketing activities can generate impermissible private benefit for corporate partners).

124. *See* Angela M. Eikenberry, *The Hidden Costs of Cause Marketing*, 7 STAN. SOC. INNOV. REV. 51, 51–52 (Summer 2009).
125. *See, e.g.*, Molly Jackson, *Free Shoes From TOMS: Can Such Philanthropy Hurt More Than Help?*, CHRISTIAN SCI. MONITOR (Feb. 25, 2016), https://www.csmonitor.com/World/Making-a-difference/Change-Agent/2016/0225/Free-shoes-from-TOMS-Can-such-philanthropy-hurt-more-than-help.
126. *See* Christopher Marquis & Andrew Park, *Inside the Buy-One Give-One Model*, 12 STAN. SOC. INNOV. REV. 28 (Winter 2014).
127. COUNCIL ON FOUNDATIONS, *supra* note 63, at 30.
128. *See* Porter & Kramer, *supra* note 32, at 64.
129. Cisco, *Impact Report*, https://www.netacad.com/.
130. *See* 2021 CECP REPORT, *supra* note 71, at 24.
131. *See* Double the Donation, *Top Matching Gift Companies*, https://doublethedonation.com/tips/matching-grant-resources/list-matching-gifts-companies/#.
132. *See* 2020 CECP REPORT, *supra* note 68, at 27.
133. *See id.* at 38; Liz Longley, *Make It a Double: Maximizing Corporate Matching Gifts During COVID-19*, INSIDE PHILANTHROPY (May 8, 2020) https://www.insidephilanthropy.com/home/2020/5/8/make-it-a-double-maximizing-corporate-matching-gifts-during-covid-19.
134. *See* 2020 CECP REPORT, *supra* note 68, at 23, 39; 2018 CECP REPORT, *supra* note 65, at 15.
135. *See* 2021 CECP REPORT, *supra* note 71, at 44.
136. *See* Colleen Olphert, *Corporate Citizenship Responses to COVID-19*, CENTER FOR CORPORATE CITIZENSHIP (Mar. 22, 2021, 7:30 AM), https://ccc.bc.edu/content/ccc/blog-home/2020/03/corporate-citizenship-responses-to-COVID-19.html; *see also* 2021 CECP REPORT, *supra* note 71, at 7 ("Non-cash contributions had the largest increase in median monetary value compared to other funding types. This propelled their increase in share of total community investments in the last five years, driven mainly by product donations.").
137. *See* Kristina Monllos, *Budweiser Highlights Disaster Relief Efforts, Real Employees in 60-Second Super Bowl Spot*, ADWEEK.COM (Jan. 26, 2018), https://www.adweek.com/brand-marketing/budweiser-highlights-disaster-relief-efforts-real-employees-in-60-second-super-bowl-spot/.
138. *See* Andrew Adam Newman, *A Direct Approach to Disaster Relief from Procter & Gamble*, N.Y. TIMES, June 3, 2011, at B3, https://www.nytimes.com/2011/06/03/business/media/03adco.html.
139. *See* Keenan Beasley, *Does Doing Good Do Good For Your Brand?*, FORBES.COM (Oct. 4, 2015), https://www.forbes.com/sites/keenanbeasley/2015/10/04/can-you-measure-roi-on-philanthropy/#498bb0e52166 ("During my tenure at Tide, the campaigns we ran in conjunction with Loads of Hope generated the highest return on investment of any of our marketing efforts. It helped that we had a strong tie

in-store, selling yellow cap bottles to support the cause, which gave us incremental placement and deepened consumer's perceptions of the brand.").

140. *See* Md. M. Islam & John Vande Vate, *Surplus Product Donation and Sustainability Strategy: Channels and Challenges for Corporate Product Donations*, *in* 20TH ADVANCES IN PRODUCTION MANAGEMENT SYSTEMS 54–61 (2013).
141. I.R.C. §170(e)(3)(A)(i).
142. I.R.C. §170(e)(4)(B)(v).
143. *See* Sugin, *supra* note 104, at 156–57.
144. *See id.* at 158; JUSTIN M. ROSS & KELLIE L. MCGIVERIN-BOHAN, THE BUSINESS CASE FOR PRODUCT PHILANTHROPY (2012), http://www.nchv.org/images/uploads/The_Business_Case_for_Product_Philanthropy_WEB(1).pdf.
145. *See* 2021 CECP REPORT, *supra* note 71, at 15 (reporting product donations constituted 81 percent of healthcare companies' noncash funding, which in turn constituted 42 percent of those firms' "total community investments"); *see also* 2020 CECP REPORT, *supra* note 68, at 9 (predicting that "the Health Care industry [would] play[] an outsized role in next year's report, given their efforts in vaccine research and facilitation of health services to the public during the Covid-19 public health crisis").
146. *See* Sugin, *supra* note 104, at 157–60 (addressing the problems with in-kind contributions in an article recommending the removal of special tax advantages for them).
147. *See* 2021 CECP REPORT, *supra* note 71, at 15.
148. *See* Salesforce, *News & Insights: How Far Can the 1-1-1 Model Go?*, https://www.salesforce.com/news/stories/how-far-can-the-1-1-1-model-go-this-tech-darling-has-a-unique-approach/; Salesforce.org, *About Us*, https://www.salesforce.org/pledge-1/.
149. *See* Pledge 1%, *Overview*, https://pledge1percent.org/overview.html.
150. *See* Press Release, WHO Statement on Philip Morris funded Foundation for a Smoke-Free World (Sept. 28, 2017), https://www.who.int/news-room/detail/28-09-2017-who-statement-on-philip-morris-funded-foundation-for-a-smoke-free-world (stating "the Organization will therefore not engage with this new Foundation).
151. Tess Legg, Silvy Peeters, Phil Chamberlain, & Anna B. Gilmore, *The Philip Morris-Funded Foundation for a Smoke-Free World: Tax Return Sheds Light on Funding Activities*, 393 THE LANCET 2487 (June 6, 2019) (opining, based on an analysis of foundation informational tax return filings showing well over a quarter of the annual $80 million contribution by Philip Morris remained unspent, that "the Foundation appears to be struggling to fund research using the money it has received from the tobacco industry").
152. *See Generous to a Fault*, THE ECONOMIST, Aug. 15, 2019, at 22, https://www.economist.com/united-states/2019/08/15/why-americas-biggest-charities-are-owned-by-pharmaceutical-companies; Ruth McCambridge, *Philanthropy of Pharmaceutical Companies Under DOJ Scrutiny*, NONPROFIT Q., Aug. 2, 2016, https://nonprofitquarterly.org/philanthropy-pharmaceutical-companies-doj-scrutiny/.

153. Ben Gose, *After a Scandal, Pearson Dissolves Foundation*, CHRON. PHILANTHROPY, Nov. 18, 2014, https://www.philanthropy.com/article/After-a-Scandal-Pearson/152191.
154. *See* Marianne Bertrand, Matilde Bombardini, Raymond Fisman, & Francesco Trebbi, *Tax-Exempt Lobbying: Corporate Philanthropy as a Tool for Political Influence*, 100 AM. ECON. REV. 2065, 2068 (2020).
155. Marianne Bertrand, Matilde Bombardini, Raymond Fisman, Brad Hackinen, & Francesco Trebbi, *Hall of Mirrors: Corporate Philanthropy and Strategic Advocacy*, 136 Q.J. ECON. 2413, 2416–17 (2021).
156. COUNCIL ON FOUNDATIONS, *supra* note 63, at 14.
157. *See, e.g.*, PATRICK RADDEN KEEFE, EMPIRE OF PAIN 371–75, 411–15 (2021) (describing efforts by cultural and educational charities to distance themselves from Sackler philanthropy); Elizabeth A. Harris, *Met Museum Spurns Family Tied to Opioids*, N.Y. TIMES, May 16, 2019, at A1 (reporting the Metropolitan Museum of Art and American Museum of Natural History would not accept future donations from Sackler family members tied to Purdue Pharma's involvement in the opioid crisis), https://www.nytimes.com/2019/05/15/arts/design/met-museum-sackler-opioids.html.

Chapter 4

1. Rob Reich has compared this system to ancient Athens's system of "private funding by wealthy citizens of state services and activities" known as a liturgy. ROB REICH, JUST GIVING: WHY PHILANTHROPY IS FAILING & HOW IT CAN DO BETTER 29 (2018).
2. *See* Hui Qin, *Understanding China's Third Sector*, STAN. SOC. INNOVATION REV. (Feb. 16, 2017), https://ssir.org/articles/entry/understanding_chinas_third_sector (describing the role and function of kinship organizations in providing social services in imperial China).
3. *See* REICH, *supra* note 1, at 35–45 (offering a history of the *waqf* and comparing and contrasting the concept with US foundations).
4. *See generally* PHILANTHROPY IN EUROPE: A RICH PAST, A PROMISING FUTURE 7–13 (Norine Macdonald & Luc Tayart de Borms eds., 2008).
5. *See* 2 ALEXIS DE TOCQUEVILLE, DEMOCRACY IN AMERICA 106 (1993)
6. *See* OLIVIER ZUNZ, PHILANTHROPY IN AMERICA: A HISTORY 8 (2014).
7. *See id.* at 8–9, 22; Barry D. Karl & Stanley N. Katz, *Foundations and Ruling Class Elites*, 116 DAEDALUS 1, 14–17 (1987); Barry D. Karl & Stanley N. Katz, *The American Private Philanthropic Foundation and the Public Sphere 1890-1930*, 19 MINERVA: REV. SCI. & POL'Y 236, 246–48 (June 1981). For a contemporary account of these gifts and foundations, *see* Daniel C. Gilman, *Five Great Gifts*, 88 OUTLOOK 648–57 (1908).

8. *See* David C. Hammack & Helmut K. Anheier, A Versatile American Institution: Changing Ideals and Realities of Philanthropic Foundations 19–20 (2013).
9. *See* Zunz, *supra* note 6, at 20–21; Evelyn Brody, *Charitable Endowments and the Democratization of Dynasty*, 39 Ariz. L. Rev. 873, 920–24 (1997).
10. *See* Reich, *supra* note 1, at 2–4; Aaron Horvath & Walter W. Powell, *Seeing Like a Philanthropist: From the Business of Benevolence to the Benevolence of Business, in* The Nonprofit Sector: A Research Handbook (Walter W. Powell & Patricia Bromley eds.) (3d ed. 2021).
11. *See* Eric John Abrahamson, Sam Hurst, & Barbara Shubinski, Democracy & Philanthropy: The Rockefeller Foundation and the American Experiment 32–34 (2013).
12. Ron Chernow, Titan: The Life of John D. Rockefeller, Sr. 564–65 (1998); *see also* Horvath & Powell, *supra* note 10, at 82–83.
13. *See* Peter Dobkin Hall, *Philanthropy, the Nonprofit Sector & the Democratic Dilemma*, 142 Daedalus: J. Am. Acad. Arts & Sci. 139, 146 (2013).
14. *See* Reich, *supra* note 1, at 4–7, 138.
15. Frank P. Walsh, *Perilous Philanthropy*, 83 Independent 262, 262 (Aug. 23, 1915), https://archive.org/details/independen83v84newy/page/n265/mode/2up. Walsh's commission issued a 1916 report urging foundations with assets of greater than $1 million and more than a single purpose to be chartered federally, with federal supervision and limitations on size and duration. *See* Marion R. Fremont-Smith, Governing Nonprofit Organizations 68 (2004); Eleanor L. Brilliant, Private Charity and Public Inquiry 11–13 (2000); Joseph C. Kiger, Philanthropic Foundations in the Twentieth Century 22–24 (2000).
16. *See* Abrahamson et al., *supra* note 11, at 40–44.
17. *See* Horvath & Powell, *supra* note 10, at 83.
18. *See* Abrahamson et al., *supra* note 11, at 44.
19. Reich, *supra* note 1, at 140.
20. Fremont-Smith, *supra* note 15, at 70 (quoting the Cox Report at 4–5); *see also* Horvath & Powell, *supra* note 10, at 104 (detailing the Cox Committee's investigation and findings); Abrahamson et al., *supra* note 11, at 146–51 (similar).
21. *See* Fremont-Smith, *supra* note 15, at 71–72 (discussing the Reece Commission and noting one congressman's submission of an addendum reaffirming the positive view of the Cox Commission); *see also* Horvath & Powell, *supra* note 10, at 104 (describing the Reece Commission's "more damning assessments"); Kiger, *supra* note 15, at 28–31 (similar); Abrahamson et al., *supra* note 11, at 151–53 (similar).
22. *See* Zunz, *supra* note 6, at 202–04 (2014); Abrahamson et al., *supra* note 11, at 154–56; James J. Fishman, *The Private Foundation Rules at Fifty: How Did We Get Them and Do They Meet Current Needs?*, 17 Pitt. Tax Rev. 247, 252–53 & n. 27; Brody, *supra* note 9, at 924.
23. *See* Fremont-Smith, *supra* note 15, at 73–74; Jan Z. Krasnowiecki & Alexander Brodsky, *Comment on the Patman Report*, 112 U. Pa. L. Rev. 190, 191–92 (1963).

24. *See* Thomas A. Troyer, *The 1969 Private Foundation Law: Historical Perspective on Its Origins and Underpinnings*, 27 Exempt Org. Tax Rev. 52, at 55 & n. 19 (2000) (describing how Treasury officials were warned to tone down references to him in their later report on foundations for fear invoking Patman as a supporter might hinder congressional responsiveness).
25. *See* Zunz, *supra* note 6, at 201.
26. *See* Francis X. Sutton, *The Ford Foundation: The Early Years*, 116 Daedalus, 41, 42–43 (1987).
27. *See* Ford Foundation, Ford Foundation Annual Report 77 (1965), https://www.fordfoundation.org/media/2435/1965-annual-report.pdf.
28. *See* Zunz, *supra* note 6, at 220–24; Larissa MacFarquhar, *What Money Can Buy: Darren Walker and the Ford Foundation Set Out to Conquer Inequality*, The New Yorker, Dec. 28, 2015, at 14, https://www.newyorker.com/magazine/2016/01/04/what-money-can-buy-profiles-larissa-macfarquhar. For a critique of the Ford Foundation's efforts as undermining the burgeoning Black Nationalism movement, see Karen Ferguson, Top Down: The Ford Foundation, Black Power, and the Reinvention of Racial Liberalism (2013).
29. *See* Troyer, *supra* note 24, at 54–55 (providing examples of marketing campaigns).
30. *See* Paul Arnsberger, Melissa Ludlum, Margaret Riley, & Mark Stanton, *A History of the Tax-Exempt Sector: An SOI Perspective*, Stat. Income Bull., Winter 2008, at 106–07, at https://www.irs.gov/pub/irs-soi/tehistory.pdf.
31. *See* Pollock v. Farmers' Loan & Trust Co., 157 U.S. 429 (1895).
32. *See* Ajay K. Mehrotra, *The Public Control of Corporate Power: Revisiting the 1909 U.S. Corporate Tax From a Comparative Perspective*, 11 Theoretical Inquiries L. 491, 501–05 (2010) (relating the history of the 1909 corporate excise tax).
33. *See* Arnsberger et al., *supra* note 30, at 107.
34. *See* Miranda Perry Fleischer, *Charitable Contributions in an Ideal Estate Tax*, 60 Tax L. Rev. 263, 263 (2008).
35. *See* Congressional Research Service, *The Charitable Deduction for Individuals*, Nov. 13, 2018, https://fas.org/sgp/crs/misc/IF11022.pdf.
36. *See* Fishman, *supra* note 22, at 268–69 (describing the congressional sense that the unlimited deduction "seemed outrageous and unfair" after John D. Rockefeller, Jr.'s casual reference to his long-time qualification for it canceling out his income tax obligations); John Holt Myers & James W. Quiggle, *Charitable Contributions and Bequests by Individuals: The Impact of the Tax Reform Act*, 39 Fordham L. Rev. 185, 206–07 (1970) (explaining that the unlimited deduction "had become a sanctuary in which many of the very wealthy were been [sic] sheltered from tax"). For a detailed description of the unlimited charitable deduction's application and its challenges, see Clyde W. Wellen, *The Unlimited Deduction for Charitable Contributions*, 7 Southwestern L.J. 38 (1953).
37. *See* Revenue Act of 1964, Pub. L. 88–272, 78 Stat. 43 § 209.
38. As noted in previous chapters, Congress provided for an unlimited charitable tax deduction for individual donations of cash to public charities (not private foundations or donor-advised funds), in the wake of both Hurricane Katrina, *see* Katrina

Emergency Tax Relief Act, Pub. L. No. 109-73, 119 Stat. 2016, § 301 (2005), and the COVID-19 pandemic, *see* CARES Act, Pub. L. No. 116-136, 134 Stat. 281 §§ 2204–05 (2020).

39. *See* Tax Foundation, *Federal Individual Income Tax Rates History Nominal Dollars Income Years 1913-2013*, https://files.taxfoundation.org/legacy/docs/fed_individual_rate_history_nominal.pdf.
40. U.S. Department of Treasury, Report on Private Foundations 5 (1965) [hereinafter Treasury Report].
41. *See* Troyer, *supra* note 24, at 53–54.
42. *See* Treasury Report, *supra* note 40.
43. *See generally* Troyer, *supra* note 24.
44. Tax Reform Act of 1969, Pub. L. No. 91-172, 83 Stat. 487 (1969).
45. *See* Brody, *supra* note 9, at 921–23 (describing Rosenwald's stinging critique of perpetual philanthropy and the structure of his foundation); *see also* Joel L. Fleishman, Putting Wealth to Work 102–05 (2017) (describing Rosenwald's approach); John R. Thelin & Richard W. Trollinger, Time Is of the Essence: Foundations and the Policies of Limited Life and Endowment Spend-Down 2–6 (Aspen Institute Program on Philanthropy and Social Innovation 2009), at https://assets.aspeninstitute.org/content/uploads/files/content/docs/pubs/Time%20is%20of%20the%20Essence%20FINAL_0.pdf (offering Rosenwald as a case study of a limited life foundation).
46. *See* Fleishman, *supra* note 45, at 100–02 (describing Carnegie's decision to found a general-purpose foundation when "although Carnegie was determined to give away all of his wealth to specific recipients during his lifetime, by the beginning of his last decade he had run out of opportunities that appealed to him as worthy of supporting"); Abrahamson et al., *supra* note 11, at 26–30 (describing Rockefeller's initially time-limited and issue-specific philanthropic projects and his eventual decision to shift to a general-purpose foundation model).
47. Treasury Report, *supra* note 40, at 55.
48. *See* Troyer, *supra* note 24, at 62.
49. The debate surrounding foundation perpetuity has ebbed and flowed. *See, e.g.*, Fleishman, *supra* note 45 (offering a critique of the risks and costs of spending down); Fishman, *supra* note 22, at 1, 293–94 (pointing to Judge Richard Posner's critique that "'a perpetual charitable foundation a completely irresponsible institution'" and adding that small perpetual foundations are also "inefficient"); Francie Ostrower, *Sunsetting: A Framework for Foundation Life as Well as Death* (2011), https://www.aspeninstitute.org/wp-content/uploads/files/content/docs/pubs/Sunsetting2.pdf (arguing that "when approached in a strategic fashion, sunsetting offers a distinct approach to philanthropy with certain benefits and characteristics") Most recently, some critics called for foundations consider spending down in light of the unprecedented needs generated by the COVID-19 global pandemic. *See, e.g.*, Benjamin Soskis, *Amid the Covid-19 Crisis, Foundations Should Stop Treating the 5% Payout as Holy Writ*, Chron. Philanthropy (Mar. 30, 2020), https://www.philanthropy.com/article/Amid-the-Covid-19-Crisis/248374.

50. *See generally* Fleishman, *supra* note 45; Ostrower, *supra* note 49.
51. The tax code does relieve certain entities deemed private foundations of some typical private foundation burdens. For example, privately funded art museums and other exempt organizations that are funded by just a few individuals but do run substantial operating charitable programs can fall within a special category of "private operating foundations." These organizations are subject to their own distribution rules in lieu of the standard 5 percent foundation payout regime. *See* I.R.C. § 4942(j)(3) (identifying the private operating foundation category and the tests an organization must meet to come within it); *see also* Khrista McCarden, *Private Operating Foundation Reform and J. Paul Getty*, 17 Pitt. Tax Review 387, 394–95 (2020) (describing the current private operating foundation rules).
52. *See* I.R.C. §509; Fremont-Smith, *supra* note 15, at 265–67.
53. *See* Fremont-Smith, *supra* note 15, at 264–65 (noting that despite a House proposal for a higher 7.5 percent tax, the 1969 Act adopted a 4 percent "audit fee," and that the rate had been adjusted downward since that time).
54. *See* I.R.C. § 4940(a) (2019).
55. *See id.* § 11(b) (codifying reduction of corporate tax to the 21 percent level under the Tax Cut and Jobs Act, Pub. L. No. 115–97, 131 Stat. 2054 (2017)). For foundations formed as charitable trusts, the more appropriate comparison is with the trust tax rate, which goes up to 39.6 percent. *See id.* § 1(e).
56. *See* SOI Tax Stats—Domestic Private Foundations and Charitable Trust Statistics, https://www.irs.gov/statistics/soi-tax-stats-domestic-private-foundation-and-charitable-trust-statistics (Statistical Tables, Domestic Private Foundations, 2017).
57. *See* I.R.C. § 170(e)(5) (carving out an exception to the usual rule in cases of contributions of appreciated public company stock up to 10 percent of the stock of the corporation).
58. *See id.* § 170(b). These restrictions trace their provenance not to the 1969 Act, but earlier tax reform legislation enacted in 1964, under which the percentage limitations for donations to foundations first diverged from those applicable to all other qualifying charities. *See* Treasury Report, *supra* note 40, at 11.
59. *See* I.R.C. § 2055.
60. *See id.* § 2010(c)(3)(C) (2017) (setting the credit against the estate tax at $10 million, to be adjusted to reflect changes in the cost of living); *What's New—Estate and Gift Tax*, IRS, https://www.irs.gov/businesses/small-businesses-self-employed/whats-new-estate-and-gift-tax (reporting a "basic exclusion amount" for 2022 of "$12,060,000").
61. *See* I.R.C. § 2522.
62. *See* IRS, *Frequently Asked Questions on Gift Tax*, https://www.irs.gov/businesses/small-businesses-self-employed/frequently-asked-questions-on-gift-taxes.
63. IRS, *A General Explanation of Trusts Subject to Section 4947 of the Internal Revenue Code*, in Exempt Organizations 1980 CPE Text, https://www.irs.gov/pub/irs-tege/eotopico80.pdf; *see also* I.R.C. § 4947 (providing for the private foundation rules and penalties to apply to certain kinds of nonexempt trusts).

64. For comprehensive discussion of this issue, see Brian Galle, *Pay It Forward? Law and the Problem of Restricted-Spending Philanthropy*, 93 WASH. U. L. REV. 1143 (2016).
65. *See* James J. Fishman, *How Big Is Too Big: Should Certain Higher Educational Endowments' Net Investment Income Be Subject to Tax?* 28 CORNELL J. L. & PUB. POL'Y 159, 164–65 (2018). For a comprehensive discussion of intergenerational equity in the charitable context, *see* IAN MURRAY, CHARITY LAW AND ACCUMULATION MAINTAINING AN INTERGENERATIONAL BALANCE (2021).
66. *See* I.R.C. § 4968 (2017).
67. *See* Adam Harris, *A Tax on Endowments Became Law. But Congressmen and Colleges Are Still Fighting It.*, CHRON. HIGHER EDUC. (Mar. 8, 2018) https://www.chronicle.com/article/a-tax-on-endowments-became-law-but-congressmen-and-colleges-are-still-fighting-it (describing some such legislative efforts).
68. TREASURY REPORT, *supra* note 40, at 25.
69. *Compare* Tax Reform Act of 1969, Pub. L. No. 91-172, 83 Stat. 503 (1969) (requiring foundations to distribute "the minimum investment return [set at 6%] or the[ir] adjusted net income (whichever is higher)" but allowing for regulatory revision) *with* Pub. L. No. 94-455, 90 Stat. 1520, §1303 (1976) (revising the minimum distribution amount to 5 percent) *and* I.R.C. § 4942 (2014) (current law imposing 5 percent requirement).
70. *See* I.R.C. §§ 4942(d), 4942(e). Specifically, the 5 percent is applied to "the excess of the aggregate fair market value of all assets of the foundation other than those which are used (or held for use) directly in carrying out the foundation's exempt purpose, over (B) the acquisition indebtedness with respect to such assets (determined under section 514(c)(1) without regard to the taxable year in which the indebtedness was incurred)." *Id.* §4942(e)(1).
71. *See id.* § 4942(a).
72. *See id.* § 4942(b).
73. *See* Galle, *supra* note 64, at 1162 (reporting his findings using tax data from foundations from 1985–2011 that "among foundations without recent gifts, payouts hover close to the statutory minimum of five percent annually"); Brody, *supra* note 9, at 927. *But see* Williams, J., Veach, C., & Kienker, B. *An Evaluation of Private Foundation Model Portfolios, Investment Returns, & Payout Rates*, 5 (Council of Michigan Foundations 2020), https://www.michiganfoundations.org/system/files/documents/2021-09/2020%20Evaluation%20of%20Private%20Foundation%20Payout%20Rates.pdf (finding "[h]alf of Michigan's private foundations paid out 6 percent or more of their corpus during 2018, as did a similar proportion of foundations across the United States.").
74. *See* Alex Daniels, *Foundations Turn to Bond Market in Response to Rising Need*, AP NEWS (Feb. 19, 2021), https://apnews.com/article/business-endowments-coronavirus-pandemic-philanthropy-california-58b9c13fada392117d636cae2054fc90.
75. I.R.C. § 4942(g).
76. *See id.* § 4942(g)(1)(A).
77. *See id.*

78. *See, e.g.*, Ray D. Madoff, *The Five Percent Fig Leaf*, 17 Pitt. Tax Rev. 341, 346–47, 354 (2020).
79. *See* I.R.C. § 4942(d). While not technically a type of expenditure that will be a qualifying distribution, the result is the same.
80. *See* Susan Gary, *Private Foundations and Spending Rules: Is Warehousing a Bad Thing?*, NYU National Center on Philanthropy and the Law Conference Paper 14 (Oct. 2019) (unpublished paper on file with author).
81. *See* I.R.C. § 4942(g); Treas. Reg. §53.4942(a)-3.
82. I.R.C. § 4945.
83. *Id.*
84. *See id.* §§ 4945(d)(1)–4945(d)(2); *see also* Treas. Reg. §§ 53.4945-2, 53.4945-3 (elaborating on the political restrictions and identifying exceptions, such as expenditures to provide technical assistance to a government body in response to a written request or to fund nonpartisan voter registration activities conducted in five or more states).
85. *See Hearings Before the Committee on Ways and Means of the House of Representatives on the Subject of Tax Reform*, 91st Cong. 372–79 (1969) (testimony of McGeorge Bundy, President, Ford Foundation).
86. 115(3) Cong. Rec. 4172–73 (1969), https://www.govinfo.gov/content/pkg/GPO-CRECB-1969-pt3/pdf/GPO-CRECB-1969-pt3-8.pdf (reporting floor statements and press accounts of Bundy's statements in the hearing); *see also* Troyer, *supra* note 24, at 52, 60–61 (describing the real and perceived impact of Bundy's testimony).
87. *See* I.R.C. §§ 4945(d)(3), 4945(g); Treas. Reg. § 53.4945-4(a)(3)(ii).
88. I.R.C. §§ 4945(d)(4)(B).
89. *See* Treasury Report, *supra* note 40, at 53.
90. For a careful and often compelling refutation of the jeopardy investment rule's value in preventing imprudent foundation investments, see Richard Schmalbeck, *Reconsidering Private Foundation Investment Limitations*, 58 Tax L. Rev. 59, 93–96 (2004), and Richard Schmalbeck, The Lesser Foundation Excise Taxes: What Are They Good For? (Not Quite) Absolutely Nothing, NYU National Center on Philanthropy and the Law Conference Paper 25–30 (Oct. 4, 2019) (unpublished paper on file with author.
91. *See* Treasury Report, *supra* note 40, at 53 (quoting former I.R.C. § 504(a)(3)).
92. *Id.* at 54.
93. I.R.C. § 4944(a); *see generally id.* §§ 4944(a)–4944(b).
94. *See* Treas. Reg. § 53.4944-1(a)(2)(i).
95. *Id.*
96. I.R.C. § 4944.
97. *See id.* Both individual and aggregate taxes on managers are capped and manager penalties do not apply if participation in the investment "is not willful and is due to reasonable cause," such as reliance on written advice of counsel. *Id.* § 4944(a)(2); *see also* Treas. Reg. § 53.4944–1(b)(2)(v).
98. I.R.C. § 4944(c).
99. *See* Treas. Reg. § 53.4942(a)-3(a)(2)(i).

100. For an argument for challenging program-related investments' equivalency to grants, Madoff, *supra* note 78, at 350–55.
101. *See* Rachel Wimpee, *The Economics of Empowerment: The Civil Rights Origins of Program-Related Investments* 6–7 (2019), https://cppp.usc.edu/wp-content/uploads/2019/03/Wimpee-Rachel-Wimpee_Civil-Rights-Origins-of-PRIs.pdf; Ford Found., Investing for Social Gain: Reflections on Two Decades of Program-Related Investments 14 (1991), https://community-wealth.org/content/investing-social-gain-reflections-two-decades-program-related-investments.
102. *See, e.g.*, Galle, *supra* note 64, at 1148, 1198 (finding that in a data set of thousands of foundations over twenty-five years "barely one tenth of 1% of foundation assets is given over to" PRIs); Marc Gunther, *Doing Good and Doing Well*, Chron. Philanthropy (Jan. 8, 2019), https://www.philanthropy.com/article/Impact-Investing-Struggles-to/245390 (summing up the Chronicle's findings about slow uptake of impact investing with: "[t]he bottom line is that less than three-tenths of 1 percent of the endowments of those 15 big foundations are invested in ways designed to align with mission").
103. *See* Schmalbeck, Lesser Foundation Excise Taxes, *supra* note 90, at 28–30 (detailing a lack of enforcement breeding a lack of concern among most foundations). The IRS Statistics of Income data show zero dollars were collected from zero private foundations based on jeopardy investment violations in 2018, 2019, and 2020. *See* IRS Statistics of Income, Excise Taxes Reported by Charities, Private Foundations, and Split-Interest Trusts on Form 4720, https://www.irs.gov/statistics/soi-tax-stats-domestic-private-foundation-and-charitable-trust-statistics. Other recent years indicate this data was suppressed to avoid identification of taxpayers. This suggests some tax was collected, though it is unclear why the data would need to be suppressed considering the public nature of foundation disclosures generally. *See* Schmalbeck, Lesser Foundation Excise Taxes, *supra* note 90, at 36 & n. 86.
104. *See* Paul Brest, *Investing for Impact with Program-Related Investments*, Stan. Soc. Innovation Rev. 19, 22–23 (Summer 2016) (describing the Gates Foundation's practice of seeking legal opinions for every PRI); Mission Investors Exchange, Strategies to Maximize Your Philanthropic Capital: A Guide To Program Related Investments 17 (2012), https://community-wealth.org/sites/clone.community-wealth.org/files/downloads/report-benabentos-et-al.pdf.
105. Schmalbeck, *Reconsidering Private Foundation Investment Limitations*, *supra* note 90, at 108; *see also* Schmalbeck, Lesser Foundation Excise Taxes, *supra* note 90, at 34 (describing Section 4944 as "irrelevant").
106. *See, e.g.*, Unif. Trust Code § 804 (Nat'l Conference of Comm'rs on Unif. State Laws 2020); Unif. Prudent Mgmt. Of Institutional Funds Act §§ 3 (Nat'l Conference of Comm'rs on Unif. State Laws 2006).
107. *See* Treasury Report, *supra* note 40, at 31.
108. *See id.*
109. *See id.* at 31–34.
110. *See id.* at 32–33. The Report also noted how many foundations had used exceptions to this unrelated business income tax to their advantage. *See id.* at 31–32.

111. *Id.* at 33.
112. *Id.* at 35.
113. *Id.*
114. *Id.* at 34–35. For counterarguments and a call to repeal the excess business holding rules, see Schmalbeck, *Reconsidering Private Foundation Investment Limitations*, *supra* note 90, at 91–93, and Schmalbeck, Lesser Foundation Excise Taxes, *supra* note 90, at 12–25.
115. *See* Treasury Report, *supra* note 40, at 36.
116. *See id.* at 41–45.
117. *See id.* at 39–40; *see also id.* at 33 (giving additional examples of unproductive business holdings, but without addressing donor involvement in the businesses).
118. Troyer, *supra* note 24, at 57–58.
119. Interestingly, as chapter 1 describes, this is precisely the situation that applies to a philanthropy LLC donor. It also shares significant common ground with some of the recommendations for DAF reform described in chapter 2.
120. I.R.C. § 4943(c)(1).
121. *See id.* § 4943(c)(2).
122. *See, e.g., id.* § 4943(c)(3) (applying similar restrictions on the holdings of unincorporated businesses); § 4943(c)(2)(A) (addressing nonvoting stock); § 4943(c)(2)(C) (providing a de minimis exception for foundation holdings of less than 2 percent).
123. *See id.* §§ 4943(a)(1), 4943(b).
124. *See id.* §§ 4943(c)(4)–4943(c)(7). Treasury regulations further elaborate these matters and provide examples. *See, e.g.,* Treas. Reg. §§ 53.4943-2–53.4943-7 and 53.4943-11.
125. *See* Pension Protection Act of 2006, Pub. L. No. 109–280, § 1233, 120 Stat. 780 (2006).
126. *See* Ana Radelat, *Tax Bill Glitch Endangers Future of Newman's Own and Actor's Foundation*, Conn. Mirror (Dec. 21, 2017), https://ctmirror.org/2017/12/21/tax-bill-glitch-endangers-future-of-newmans-own-and-actors-foundation/ (describing Newman's Own Foundation's failure to obtain an exemption from the excess business holdings regime in the negotiations over the 2017 Tax Cut and Jobs Act); Ana Radelat, *Budget Deal Has Plenty for Connecticut*, Conn. Mirror (Feb. 9, 2018), https://ctmirror.org/2018/02/09/senate-stumbles-on-way-to-vote-on-budget-bill-with-plenty-for-ct/ (explaining the foundation's successful advocacy for such an exemption early the following year allowed it to avoid the 200 percent confiscatory tax).
127. *See* I.R.C. § 4943(g).
128. The Treasury Report called out precisely this concern. *See* Treasury Report, *supra* note 40, at 15 ("The lack of a prohibition upon donor-foundation transactions has led some donors to believe that although the foundation has legal title to assets which they have contributed, such assets still 'belong' to them.")
129. *See id.* at 15 (reporting that some managers "apparently feel that the foundation's funds belong to the donor and should be handled in the manner which the donor wishes, rather than in the manner which would benefit the public).

130. Of course, self-dealing can certainly also arise in public charities. Indeed, Congress added a provision to the Code in 1996 that penalizes transactions in which public charity donors and managers obtain excessive benefits in transactions with their organizations. *See* I.R.C. § 4958. This regime is similar, though not identical to the foundation self-dealing rules. *See* Ellen P. Aprill, *The Private Foundation Excise Tax on Self-Dealing: Contours, Comparisons, and Character*, 17 PITT. TAX REV. 297, 309–12 (2020) (comparing the two regimes).
131. I.R.C. § 501(c)(3).
132. *See, e.g.*, REV. MODEL NONPROFIT CORP. ACT § 8.31 (1987); UNIF. TRUST CODE § 802(b).
133. TREASURY REPORT, *supra* note 40, at 15.
134. *Id.* at 16 (emphasis added).
135. I.R.C. § 4941(d).
136. *Id.* § 4941(a); *see also id.* § 4941(c) (imposing statutory maximum obligations for managers). The 2006 Pension Protection Act doubled the initial tax and foundation manager cap amounts from their original 1969 levels. *See* Aprill, *supra* note 130, at 305.
137. I.R.C. § 4962.
138. *See id.* § 4962(b).
139. *Id.* § 4941(d)(2)(E). The rules as enacted also permit interest free loans, free provision of goods and services to foundations, and foundation provision of goods and services to donors, family members, and related parties on terms "no more favorable than that . . . available to the general public." *Id.* § 4941(d)(2)(B)-(D).
140. *See id.* § 4958; *see also* Aprill, *supra* note 130, at 310 (noting this distinction).
141. I.R.C. § 4941(d)(1)(F). A few additional exceptions were also provided, such as for de minimis payments and travel reimbursement. *See id.* § 4941(d)(2)(E).
142. *See* Lloyd Hitoshi Mayer, *"The Better Part of Valor Is Discretion": Should the IRS Change or Surrender Its Oversight of Tax-Exempt Organizations*, 7 COLUM. J. TAX L. 80, 82–96 (2016).
143. *See* Aprill, *supra* note 130, at 307 & n. 51.
144. TREASURY REPORT, *supra* note 40, at 64.
145. *See* Tax Reform Act of 1969, Pub. L. No. 91-172, 83 Stat. 519–22 (1969).
146. *See* Evelyn Brody, *Sunshine and Shadows on Charity Governance: Public Disclosure as A Regulatory Tool*, 12 FLA. TAX REV. 183, 210 (2012) ("Interestingly, Congress required private foundations to make their Forms 990-PF available on request in 1969, but did not obligate publicly supported charities to make their Forms 990 available until 1987.")
147. *See* I.R.C. § 6104(b) ("Nothing in this subsection shall authorize the Secretary to disclose the name or address of any contributor to any organization or trust (other than a private foundation . . .), which is required to furnish such information"). For a discussion of the IRS' decision to stop collecting donor information from non-charitable tax-exempt entities and its impact on "dark money," see Philip Hackney, *Dark Money Darker? IRS Shutters Collection of Donor Data*, 25 FLA. TAX REV. 140 (2021).

148. *See* Americans for Prosperity Found. v. Bonta, 141 S. Ct. 2373 (2021).
149. *See* Pub. L. 91-172, 83 Stat. 522, 524 (1969).
150. *See* I.R.C. §6033(j)(1)(B); *see also id.* §6652(c)(1) (imposing updated monetary penalties for failure to file).
151. *See* Fishman, *supra* note 22, at 281–82.
152. *See id.* at 283.
153. *See id.* at 288–89.
154. Foundation Center, *Foundation Stats*, http://data.foundationcenter.org/#/foundations/all/nationwide/total/trends:assets/2015 (last viewed June 15, 2020).
155. *See* Maria Di Mento, *Foundation Assets Top $1 Trillion, But Signs Point to Slump*, CHRON. PHILANTHROPY (Aug. 19, 2019), https://www.philanthropy.com/article/foundation-assets-top-1-trillion-but-signs-point-to-slump/ (reporting 2017 numbers in a study by "John Seitz, a former Wall Street portfolio manager who analyzes the investment performance of foundations").
156. *See* CANDID, KEY FACTS ON U.S. NONPROFITS AND FOUNDATIONS (June 2021), https://www.issuelab.org/resources/38265/38265.pdf.
157. *See* HAMMACK & ANHEIER, *supra* note 8, at 119–20.
158. GATES FOUNDATION, *Who We Are: Foundation Fact Sheet*, at https://www.gatesfoundation.org/Who-We-Are/General-Information/Foundation-Factsheet; *see also* Candid, *U.S. Social Sector*, https://candid.org/explore-issues/us-social-sector/organizations (listing the top 50 foundations by assets with Gates ranked number one with over $30 billion more assets than the next largest foundation).
159. *See* CANDID, PHILANTHROPY AND COVID-19: MEASURING ONE YEAR OF GIVING 8 (2021), https://www.issuelab.org/resources/38039/38039.pdf (describing how "funding [for COVID response] from independent foundations more than doubled [over the course of 2020], from $1.7 billion in the first half of the year to $4.7 billion" and noting Gates and Rockefeller as the top donors, focusing to a considerable extent, on vaccines).
160. *See* ROCKEFELLER FOUNDATION, *The Rockefeller Foundation: A Digital History, Rockefeller Sanitary Commission*, https://rockfound.rockarch.org/rockefeller-sanitary-commission.
161. *See* ROCKEFELLER FOUNDATION, *The Rockefeller Foundation: A Digital History, International Health Division*, at https://rockfound.rockarch.org/international-health-division.
162. *See* ROCKEFELLER FOUNDATION, *The Rockefeller Foundation: A Digital History, Childhood Immunization*, at https://rockfound.rockarch.org/childhood-immunization.
163. *See* Press Release, Gates Foundation, Bill & Melinda Gates Foundation Pledges $1.6 Billion to Gavi, The Vaccine Alliance, to Protect the Next Generation with Lifesaving Vaccines (June 4, 2020), https://www.gatesfoundation.org/Media-Center/Press-Releases/2020/06/Bill-and-Melinda-Gates-Foundation-pledges-to-Gavi-the-Vaccine-Alliance.

164. Gates Foundation, Gates Foundation COVID-19 Response FAQ, https://www.gatesfoundation.org/ideas/articles/covid19-faq.
165. *See* Michael P. McCauley, NPR: The Trials and Triumphs of National Public Radio 18–21 (2005).
166. *See* Scott Kohler, *Case 42, The Emergency Medical Services Program of the Robert Wood Johnson Foundation*, https://cspcs.sanford.duke.edu/sites/default/files/descriptive/emergency_medical_services_program.pdf.
167. *See* Lyndsey Layton, *How Bill Gates Pulled Off the Swift Common Core Revolution*, Wash. Post (June 7, 2014), https://www.washingtonpost.com/politics/how-bill-gates-pulled-off-the-swift-common-core-revolution/2014/06/07/a830e32e-ec34-11e3-9f5c-9075d5508f0a_story.html. For extensive discussion of Gates and other foundations' involvement in recent public educational reform efforts, see generally Megan E. Thompkins-Stange, Policy Patrons: Philanthropy, Education Reform, and the Politics of Influence; (2016) and Sarah Reckhow, Follow the Money: How Foundation Dollars Change Public School Politics (2013).
168. *See* Layton, *supra* note 167 (describing challenges from various quarters).

Chapter 5

1. Dana Brakman Reiser & Steven A. Dean, Social Enterprise Law 2 (2017).
2. The Grunin Center for Law and Social Entrepreneurship, The State of Social Enterprise and the Law 6 (2019–2020) (reporting thirty-seven states and the District of Columbia have adopted benefit corporation statutes and eight states have L3C statutes).
3. InfluenceMap, Climate Funds and Fossil Fuels (2019), https://influencemap.org/report/Climate-Funds-and-Fossil-Fuels-8f2c813ed814fe5b1eef61b48497b592 (reporting similar levels of thermal coal investment in "a basket of 118 climate-themed funds" as in traditional funds and urging greater regulation); Aneesh Raghunandan & Shivaram Rajgopal, *Do ESG Funds Make Stakeholder-Friendly Investments?*, Rev. Acct. Stud. 3 (2022), https://link.springer.com/article/10.1007/s11142-022-09693-1 (finding "that ESG funds' portfolio firms have significantly *more* violations of labor and environmental laws and pay more in fines for these violations, relative to non-ESG funds issued by the same financial institutions in the same year") (emphasis in original).
4. T. S. Eliot, The Hollow Men (1925).
5. *See* Henry Hansmann, *The Role of Nonprofit Enterprise*, 89 Yale L.J. 835, 838 (1980) ("A nonprofit organization is, in essence, an organization that is barred from distributing its net earnings, if any, to individuals who exercise control over it, such as members, officers, directors, or trustees.")
6. *See* I.R.C. § 501(c)(3) (defining tax-exempt organizations to require "no part of the net earnings of which inures to the benefit of any private shareholder or individual").

7. Thomas C. Schelling, The strategy of conflict 132 (1960).
8. *Id.* at 147.
9. *Id.* at 142–43 (noting "[t]he use of thugs and sadists for the collection of extortion or the guarding of prisoners . . . exemplifies a common means of making credible a response pattern").
10. Andrew Carnegie, *Wealth*, 148 N. Am. Rev. 653, 664 (June 1889) ("[T]he man who dies leaving behind him millions of available wealth, which was his to administer during life, will pass away. . . . unwept, unhonored, and unsung. . . . no matter to what uses he leaves the dross which he cannot take with him. Of such as these the public verdict will then be: 'The man who dies thus rich dies disgraced.' ")
11. *Id.* at 664.
12. *Id.*
13. *Id.*
14. *Id. at* 660 (insisting that allowing him to serve as a trustee for the public represented "much more potent force for the elevation of our race than if it had been distributed in small sums to the people themselves").
15. *Id.* at 663.
16. *See* Jesse Eisinger et al., *The Secret IRS Files: Trove of Never-Before-Seen Records Reveal How the Wealthiest Avoid Income Tax*, ProPublica (June 8, 2021, 5 AM), https://www.propublica.org/article/the-secret-irs-files-trove-of-never-before-seen-records-reveal-how-the-wealthiest-avoid-income-tax. To the extent these wealthy individuals report little or no income, they derive no benefit from charitable deductions. *See* David S. Miller, *Social Welfare Organizations as Grantmakers*, 21 N.Y.U. J. Legis. & Pub. Pol'y 413, 414 (2018) (noting that when he made his billion dollar donation to the Gates foundation "Buffett could not use any appreciable amount of his charitable deduction").
17. Greg Leiserson & Danny Yagan, *What Is the Average Federal Individual Income Tax Rate on the Wealthiest Americans?*, White House Blog (Sept. 23, 2021), https://www.whitehouse.gov/cea/blog/2021/09/23/what-is-the-average-federal-individual-income-tax-rate-on-the-wealthiest-americans/.
18. Gates's longtime rival, Steve Jobs, did die at the age of 56, but the right arrangements could ensure that even an unexpected death would not subject Gates's fortune to the estate tax.
19. 2000 Annual Report, The Bill and Melinda Gates Foundation 10 (2000), https://www.gatesfoundation.org/-/media/1annual-reports/2000gates-foundation-annual-report.pdf ("the size of the foundation's endowment has grown significantly in recent years, to approximately $21.1 billion at the end of 2000").
20. *See* Andrew I. Gavil & Harry First, The Microsoft Antitrust Cases: Competition Policy for the Twenty-First Century (2014) ("Microsoft faced nearly every one of the panoply of tools available in antitrust's remedial tool bag: fines, damages, injunctions against continued conduct, mandatory injunctions requiring changed conduct, continuing oversight of some of its conduct, and even (for a while) the threat of a court-ordered reorganization.")

21. *See, e.g.*, Lina M. Khan, *The Separation of Platforms and Commerce*, 119 COLUM. L. REV. 973, 977–78 (2019) ("Facebook, equipped with technology that lets it detect which rival apps are succeeding, would often give companies a choice: Be acquired by Facebook, or watch it roll out a direct replica. Competing with one of these giants on the giant's own turf is rife with hazards.")
22. Bill Gates endured a major blow to his reputation and the goodwill accumulated through his philanthropic work with the announcement of his divorce and the attention it brought to marital infidelities and links to Jeffrey Epstein. *See, e.g.*, Emily Kirkpatrick, *Bill Gates's Meetings with Jeffrey Epstein Are Apparently a "Sore Spot" for Melinda*, VANITY FAIR (May 13, 2021), https://www.vanityfair.com/style/2021/05/bill-and-melinda-gates-jeffrey-epstein-meetings-sore-spot-divorce.
23. *Frequently Asked Questions*, ONE WORLD PLAY PROJECT, https://www.oneworldplayproject.com/faq/.
24. TOMS SHOES, https://www.toms.com/us/impact.html.
25. GREYSTON, https://www.greyston.org/about/.
26. EMBRACE GLOBAL, https://www.embraceglobal.org/ ("Embrace has already saved over 350,000 lives."); Little Lotus Baby, *Our Story*, https://littlelotusbaby.com/pages/about-us.
27. *See* BRAKMAN REISER & DEAN, *supra* note 1, at 66–67.
28. *See, e.g.*, Delaware Division of Corporations, *2020 Annual Report Statistics*, https://corpfiles.delaware.gov/Annual-Reports/Division-of-Corporations-2020-Annual-Report.pdf (reporting more than three times as many firms formed as LLCs in 2018–20 than as corporations).
29. William B. Brannan, *Lingering Partnership Classification Issues (Just When You Thought It Was Safe to Go Back in the Water)*, 1 FLA. TAX REV. 197 (1993) (offering a comprehensive survey of issues arising under the Kintner regulations).
30. *See* Prop. Treas. Reg. § 301.7701-2, 45 Fed. Reg. 75,709 (Nov. 17, 1980).
31. Michael L. Schler, *Initial Thoughts on the Proposed "Check-the-Box" Regulations*, 71 TAX NOTES 1679, 1682 (1996).
32. Dana Brakman Reiser, *Foundation Regulation in Our Age of Impact*, 17 PITT. TAX REV. 357, 376 (2020) (explaining that a PRI "not only prevents a foundation investment from triggering jeopardizing investment and excess business holding penalties, but also allows the investment to serve as a qualifying distribution toward the annual 5% payout requirement").
33. *See, e.g.*, 11 Vt. Stat. Ann. § 3001(27)(A). As most state L3C enactments are similar to the inaugural Vermont effort and no model legislation exists, the Vermont statute provides a workable reference.
34. *See, e.g.*, *id.* § 3001(27)(D).
35. B Lab also offers its "B Corp" certification, a standard that a firm can use as its required "third-party standard" under benefit corporation statutes. By persuading states to adopt the forms, B Lab helped enlarge the market for its certification business—though B Lab makes its B Impact Assessment tool freely available, and the statutes do not require adopting firms to be certified by B Lab or, indeed, any third-party certifier.

36. *Frequently Asked Questions*, Certified B Corporation, https://bcorporation.net/faqs. B Lab's one-size-fits-all approach allows it to certify banks and bakeries along with tech and fashion businesses. Rather than focusing on a particular type of social mission, it embraces all of them.
37. Model Benefit Corporation Legislation § 102 (B Lab 2017), available in App. A of "White Paper: The Need and Rationale for the Benefit Corporation," https://drive.google.com/file/d/1QyMrBS9_6fC9guMYotZ5DElsTxuD16K9/view.
38. *See* Maxime Verheyden, *Public Reporting by Benefit Corporations: Importance, Compliance, and Recommendations*, 14 Hastings Bus. L.J. 37, 63–78 (2018) (reporting low compliance rates in Delaware (8 percent), Colorado (11 percent), and Oregon (14 percent) but a 100 percent compliance rate in Minnesota, where the statute unusually penalizes failures to report); Ellen Berrey, *Social Enterprise Law in Action: Organizational Characteristics of U.S. Benefit Corporations*, 20 Transactions: Tenn. J. Bus. L. 21, 85 (2018) (finding a compliance rate of just 6 percent in a nationwide survey); J. Haskell Murray, *An Early Report on Benefit Reports*, 118 W. Va. L. Rev. 25, 35 (2015)(reporting an 8 percent compliance rate using data from California, Hawaii, New York, and Virginia).
39. Jeffrey W. Bullock, *A Message from the Secretary of State*, Delaware Division of Corporations, https://corp.delaware.gov/stats/.
40. Del. Gen. Corp. L. § 362(a) (2021).
41. *See id.* § 365(c) ("[i]n the absence of a conflict of interest, no failure to satisfy [their] balancing requirement shall, . . . constitute an act or omission not in good faith, or a breach of the duty of loyalty, unless the certificate of incorporation so provides").
42. Although a handful of others followed their lead, so few public benefit companies had gone public since their creation in 2013 that when two did in 2020, it generated headlines. *See, e.g.*, Benjamin D. Stone, *Public Benefit Corporations Are Going Public*, Nat'l L. Rev. (Mar. 2, 2021), https://www.natlawreview.com/article/public-benefit-corporations-are-going-public; Sarah Murray, *Stakeholders Incorporated: Can Capitalism Change if Company Charters Stay the Same?*, Fin. Times (Aug. 5, 2021), https://www.ft.com/content/ac563017-a88f-4d41-8941-f35418e08309 (reporting uptick in investor interest in PBCs despite data indicating only a handful of IPOs, fewer than 100 VC deals, and an all-time high of just 600 adoptions of the form).
43. Former Delaware Vice Chancellor Strine takes this view. *See* Leo E. Strine Jr., *Making It Easier for Directors to Do the Right Thing*, 4 Harv. Bus. L. Rev. 235, 242 (2014) (situating the Delaware public benefit corporation in the "liberal tradition of incremental, achievable reform rather than radical renovation, the benefit corporation is a modest evolution that builds on the American tradition of corporate law").
44. *Compare* Model Benefit Corporation Legislation, *supra* note 37, § 105 (requiring two thirds of shareholders to approve a termination) *with* Va. Code Ann. § 13.1-786 (2021) (allowing the articles of incorporation to change a default supermajority threshold to a majority).
45. 79 Del. Laws 122 (2013) (setting entry threshold at 90 percent and exit at two-thirds).
46. 79 Del. Laws 122 (2015) (changing entry threshold to two thirds); 82 Del. Laws 256 (2020) (striking supermajority requirement).

47. Rousseau famously imagined a pair of hunters hoping to catch a stag together but doomed to hunt rabbits alone. He explained that because either could defect at any time, it would be foolish for them not to hunt for rabbits even though they would both be better off with a stag. Social enterprise hybrid entities were designed to facilitate the pursuit of two bottom lines (here the stag to a single bottom line's rabbit). But by allowing shareholders or managers to defect in order to chase rabbits, they ensure the stag hunt will not take place. *See* Dana Brakman Reiser & Steven A. Dean, *Hunting Stag with Fly Paper: A Hybrid Financial Instrument for Social Enterprise*, 54 B.C. L. Rev. 1495 (2013).
48. *See* Stone, *supra* note 42; Murray, *supra* note 42.
49. *See* Del. Gen. Corp. L. §§ 365(a) ("The board of directors shall manage or direct the business and affairs of the public benefit corporation in a manner that balances the pecuniary interests of the stockholders, the best interests of those materially affected by the corporation's conduct, and the specific public benefit or public benefits identified in its certificate of incorporation."), 365(c) ("In the absence of a conflict of interest, no failure to satisfy that balancing requirement shall, for the purposes of § 102(b)(7) or § 145 of this title, constitute an act or omission not in good faith, or a breach of the duty of loyalty, unless the certificate of incorporation so provides.")
50. Benefit corporations and Delaware PBCs also might expand or contract the range of potential constituencies as compared to constituency statutes. Some benefit corporation statutes permit directors to consider not merely those constituencies identified in a statute but also others they deem relevant. *See, e.g.*, Md. Code Ann., Corps. & Ass'ns § 5-6C01 (LexisNexis 2021) (defining public benefit to include "accomplishment of any other particular benefit for society or the environment"). Delaware's PBC instructs adopting entities to identify the specific public benefit or benefits it will promote in its organizational charter. *See* Del. Gen. Corp. L. §362(a)(1).
51. *See* Dana Brakman Reiser, *Benefit Corporations: A Sustainable Form of Organization*, 46 Wake Forest L. Rev. 591, 600 (2011) (suggesting that like constituency statutes, benefit corporations may create a risk of "giving directors unbridled discretion, with which they might pursue social good or might pursue foolish or self-serving practices").
52. Model Benefit Corporation Legislation, *supra* note 37, § 301(c).
53. Del. Gen. Corp. L. § 365(c).
54. *See* Verheyden, *supra* note 38, at 63–78; Berrey, *supra* note 38, at 85; Murray, *supra* note 38, at 35.
55. *See* Berrey, *supra* note 38, at 21 (reporting a 2018 study finding just 7,704 benefit corporations (including Delaware PBCs) had ever been formed across US jurisdictions).
56. *See* Morningstar, Sustainable Funds U.S. Landscape Report 1 (2022), https://www.morningstar.com/lp/sustainable-funds-landscape-report.
57. Michael S. Knoll, *Ethical Screening in Modern Financial Markets: The Conflicting Claims Underlying Socially Responsible Investment*, 57 Bus. Law. 681, 686 (2002)("[T]he most common screen is for tobacco, with ninety-six percent of all screened assets steered away from tobacco. The next most common screens are for

gambling, alcohol, and weapons. According to the SIF, more than eight out of every ten dollars in screened assets are in portfolios that avoid companies in each of these industries" (footnote omitted)).

58. *See, e.g.*, Pieter Jan Trinks & Bert Scholtens, *The Opportunity Cost of Negative Screening in Socially Responsible Investing*, 140 J. Bus. Ethics 193 (2017) (testing a wide variety of negative screens and finding they frequently result in underperformance); Samuel A. Mueller, *The Opportunity Cost of Discipleship: Ethical Mutual Funds and Their Returns*, 52 Soc. Analysis 111 (1991) (finding nine out of ten mutual funds negatively screened for compliance with ethical restrictions underperformed the market).
59. *See* Susan N. Gary, *Best Interests in the Long Term: Fiduciary Duties and ESG Integration*, 90 U. Colo. L. Rev. 731, 752 (2019) (pointing to "two metastudies conclud[ing] that funds using negative screens are more likely to show neutral rather than negative or positive performance when compared to non-SRI benchmarks"); Alexander Monk, *Demystifying Negative Screens: The Full Implications of ESG Exclusions*, Schroders (2017), https://www.schroders.com/en/sysglobalassets/digital/insights/2018/thought-leadership/demystifying-negative-screens---the-full-implications-of-esg-exclusions.pdf (explaining that screening methods vary widely and many need not have significant negative impacts on long-term performance, particularly in the actively managed context).
60. *See, e.g., Vanguard FTSE Social Index Fund Admiral Shares*, Vanguard, https://investor.vanguard.com/investment-products/mutual-funds/profile/vftax.
61. *See* Amir Amel-Zadeh & George Serafeim, *Why and How Investors Use ESG Information: Evidence from a Global Survey*, 74 Fin. Analysts J. 87, 94 (2018)(describing "positive screening").
62. *Id.* (defining "Relative/best-in-class screening").
63. *Id.* (identifying "Thematic investment" as an ESG strategy).
64. *Id.* ("*Engagement/active ownership* is the use of shareholder power to influence corporate behavior through direct corporate engagement (i.e., communicating with senior management and/or boards of companies), filing or co-filing shareholder proposals, and proxy voting that is directed by ESG guidelines.")
65. *See* Annie Lowry, *Could Index Funds Be "Worse Than Marxism"?*, The Atlantic (Apr. 5, 2021) ("Index funds now control 20 to 30 percent of the American equities market, if not more.").
66. *See* Andrew Ross Sorkin, *BlackRock Chief Pushes a Big New Climate Goal for the Corporate World*, N.Y. Times: DealBook (Jan. 26, 2021), https://www.nytimes.com/2021/01/26/business/dealbook/larry-fink-letter-blackrock-climate.html (noting that after the head of Blackrock, one of the largest such investors, urged corporate America to embrace solutions to climate change "Microsoft announced a plan to be carbon-negative by 2030, Salesforce pledged to conserve or restore 100 million trees over the next decade and even Delta Air Lines announced a $1 billion effort to be carbon-neutral in 10 years").
67. Press Release, ExxonMobil, ExxonMobil Updates Preliminary Results on Election of Directors (June 2, 2021), https://corporate.exxonmobil.com/News/Newsroom/

News-releases/2021/0602_ExxonMobil-updates-preliminary-results-on-election-of-directors.

68. Lindsay Delevingne et al., The ESG premium: New Perspectives on Value and Performance 2 (2020), https://www.mckinsey.com/business-functions/sustainability/our-insights/the-esg-premium-new-perspectives-on-value-and-performance#.
69. *See* Morningstar, *Sustainable Funds U.S. Landscape Report* 6, 14–16, 19 (2021), https://www.morningstar.com/content/dam/marketing/shared/pdfs/Research/Sustainable_Funds_Landscape_2021.pdf?.
70. *See id.* at 32; *see also* Morningstar, *supra* note 56, at 19 (reflecting in a report on 2021 results that "[although] some equity funds within our sustainable funds landscape may have suffered during the[] rallies [in traditional energy stock prices], most recovered to deliver handsome calendar-year results").
71. Neil Bhutta et al., *Changes in U.S. Family Finances from 2016 to 2019: Evidence from the Survey of Consumer Finances*, 106 Fed. Res. Bull. 1, 19 (2020), https://www.federalreserve.gov/publications/files/scf20.pdf.
72. Request for Comment on Fund Names, Release No. IC–33809 (Mar. 2, 2020), 85 Fed. Reg. 13221 (Mar. 6, 2020), available at https://www.sec.gov/rules/other/2020/ic-33809.pdf [hereinafter SEC Release No. IC-33809].
73. 17 C.F.R. § 270.35d-1(a) (2001).
74. *See* SEC Release No. IC-33809, *supra* note 72, at 6; Adriana Z. Robertson, *Passive in Name Only: Delegated Management and "Index" Investing*, 36 Yale J. Reg. 795, 825–26 (2019).
75. 17 C.F.R. § 270.35d-1(a) (2021).
76. 17 CFR § 240.10b-5 (2021).
77. Quinn Curtis, Jill Fisch, & Adriana Z. Robertson, *Do ESG Funds Deliver on Their Promises?*, 120 Mich. L. Rev. 393, 411–13 (2021); *see also* Investment Company Names, Release No. IC-34593 (May 25, 2022), 87 Fed. Reg. 36594 (June 17, 2022); Enhanced Disclosures by Certain Investment Advisers and Investment Companies About Environmental, Social, and Governance Investment Practices, Release No. IA-6034 (May 25, 2022), 87 Fed. Reg. 36654 (June 17, 2022).
78. SEC Release No. IC-34593, *supra* note 77, at 13–14; *see also* SEC, Division of Examinations, Risk Alert: The Division of Examinations' Review of ESG Investing (2021), https://www.sec.gov/files/esg-risk-alert.pdf (critiquing the "variability and imprecision of industry ESG definitions and terms" and their potential to confuse investors in a guidance document for investment company compliance programs"). *But see* Curtis, et al. *supra* note 77, at 449 (concluding, based on an empirical study of hundreds of ESG funds, that "with ESG entering the mainstream, regulators are faced with a more mature, competitive market and ever-improving disclosure practices in which investors seem to be getting the information they need").
79. *See* Dana Brakman Reiser & Anne Tucker, *Buyer Beware: Variation and Opacity in ESG and ESG Index Funds*, 41 Cardozo L. Rev. 1921 (2020).

80. Drawing on four different third-party metrics, it found ESG funds consistently rate more highly on environmental, social and governance measures than their conventional counterparts. *See* Curtis et al., *supra* note 77.
81. *Id.* at 439.
82. *See* Raghunandan & Rajgopal, *supra* note 3.
83. Interpretive Bulletin Relating to the Employee Retirement Income Security Act of 1974, 59 Fed. Reg. 32606, 32607 (1994) (formerly codified at 29 C.F.R. § 2509.94-01).
84. Interpretive Bulletin Relating to Investing in Economically Targeted Investments, 73 Fed. Reg. 61734, 61734 (2008) (formerly codified at 29 C.F.R. § 2509.08-1).
85. US Dep't of Labor, Field Assistance Bulletin No. 2018-1, Apr. 23, 2018 (clarifying 2015 guidance).
86. Rules and Regulations for Fiduciary Responsibility; Investment of Plan Assets under the "Prudence Rule," 44 Fed. Reg. 37,221, 37,225 (June 26, 1979) (codified at 29 C.F.R. § 2550.404a-l(c)).
87. US Dep't of Labor Statement Regarding Enforcement of Its Final Rules on ESG Investments and Proxy Voting by Employee Benefit Plans (Mar. 10, 2021), https://www.dol.gov/sites/dolgov/files/ebsa/laws-and-regulations/laws/erisa/statement-on-enforcement-of-final-rules-on-esg-investments-and-proxy-voting.pdf.
88. Larry Fink, 2018 Letter to CEOs, A Sense of Purpose, https://www.blackrock.com/corporate/investor-relations/2018-larry-fink-ceo-letter ("Without a sense of purpose, no company, either public or private, can achieve its full potential. It will ultimately lose the license to operate from key stakeholders.").
89. Andrew Ross Sorkin, *BlackRock's Message: Contribute to Society, or Risk Losing Our Support*, N.Y. Times: DealBook (Jan. 15, 2018), https://www.nytimes.com/2018/01/15/business/dealbook/blackrock-laurence-fink-letter.html (noting that Fink's letter "may be a watershed moment on Wall Street").
90. John C. Coffee, *The Future of Disclosure: ESG, Common Ownership, and Systematic Risk* (Mar. 16, 2021). European Corporate Governance Institute—Law Working Paper 541/2020, at 14–15, https://ssrn.com/abstract=3678197 or http://dx.doi.org/10.2139/ssrn.3678197.
91. *See, e.g.*, Will Feuer, *Here's More Evidence That ESG Funds Outperformed During the Pandemic*, Institutional Inv. (Apr. 7, 2021), https://www.institutionalinvestor.com/article/b1r9gb5p9k10b4/Here-s-More-Evidence-That-ESG-Funds-Outperformed-During-the-Pandemic ("In the first year of the pandemic, large funds with environmental, social, and governance criteria outperformed the broader market, according to a report published this week . . . the latest of such analyses to suggest that ESG risks matter for investment performance, at least during a pandemic.")
92. *See* Lynn A. Stout, The Shareholder Value Myth: How Putting Shareholders First Harms Investors, Corporations, and the Public 2 (2012) (noting the financial implications of the Deepwater Horizon disaster reveal that by "trying to save $1 million a day by skimping on safety procedures at the Macondo well, BP cost its shareholders alone a hundred thousand times more, nearly $100 billion").
93. *See* John E. Tyler II., *Giving Priority to Social Good and Public Benefit with Meaningful Accountability Thereto: "Differentiated Social Good" and the Social Primacy Company,*

88 UMKC L. Rev. 955, 969 (2020) (concluding that "commitment may be indicated by the degree of willingness to accept concessionary returns, tolerate greater risk of losing invested capital, or contribute follow on capital").

94. *See* Brakman Reiser, *supra* note 32, at 366.
95. Tom King, *Philanthropy and ESG: Investing or Charity?* The Asset, https://theasset.com/article-esg/40611/theasset.com ("some investors are still unsure or confused as to how to differentiate between" ESG investing and philanthropy).

Chapter 6

1. Max Chafkin & Jing Cao, *The Barbarians Are at Etsy's Hand-Hewn, Responsibly Sourced Gates*, Bloomberg, (May 18, 2017) https://www.bloomberg.com/news/features/2017-05-18/the-barbarians-are-at-etsy-s-hand-hewn-responsibly-sourced-gates.
2. *See* Thomas Piketty, Capital in the Twenty-First Century (Arthur Goldhammer trans., 2014) (documenting the increasing concentration of wealthy among a small group of elites). Piketty devotes very little space to the question of race, mentioning it in passing, for example, as he contrasts a French Revolution that "abolished all legal privileges" and an American Revolution that "allowed slavery to continue for nearly a century and legal racial discrimination for nearly two centuries." *Id.* at 30.
3. Dorothy Brown shows how color-blind tax laws, even those intended to ameliorate wealth inequality, have hurt some of the most vulnerable Americans. Dorothy A. Brown, The Whiteness of Wealth: How the Tax System Impoverishes Black Americans—And How We Can Fix It (2021) (detailing aspects of the tax law that favor wealth-building by white Americans).
4. *See* Alisha Ebrahimji, *Female Fortune 500 CEOs Reach an All-Time High, But It's Still a Small Percentage*, CNN (May 20, 2020, 10:46 AM), https://www.cnn.com/2020/05/20/us/fortune-500-women-ceos-trnd/index.html.
5. *See, e.g.*, Elise Westhoff, *The Left Wants a Philanthropy of the Few*, Wall St. J. (Dec. 14, 2020, 6:41 PM) (defending commercially affiliated donor-advised funds as tools that support "philanthropic freedom enabl[ing] Americans of all backgrounds, beliefs and bank-account sizes to support worthy causes and benefit their communities and the country").
6. *See* Edgar Villanueva, Decolonizing Wealth: Indigenous Wisdom to Heal Divides and Restore Balance 72–77 (2021) (describing the challenges faced by charities led by people of color and noting that fewer than 10 percent of foundation grants benefit people of color).
7. Greg Bensinger, *Corporate America Says Black Lives Matter. It Needs to Hold Up a Mirror*, N.Y. Times (June 15, 2020), https://www.nytimes.com/2020/06/15/opinion/black-lives-matter-corporate-pledges.html. Although unclear how much progress Corporate America made in reinventing itself, it did significantly boost funding for

efforts to combat systemic racism. *See* Alex Daniels, *Companies Lead Philanthropic Response to Calls for Racial Justice, but Will It Last?*, CHRON. PHILANTHROPY (AUG. 24, 2020); https://www.philanthropy.com/article/companies-lead-philanthropic-response-to-calls-for-racial-justice-but-will-it-last ("businesses and the foundations they support have led the philanthropic push to attack systemic racism" with grants for the first half of 2020 surpassing "the total committed to racial justice over the past nine years combined").

8. *See supra* note 4.
9. *See* Press Release, General Motors, the Largest U.S. Automaker, Plans to be Carbon Neutral by 2040 (Jan. 28, 2021), https://media.gm.com/media/us/en/gm/home.detail.html/content/Pages/news/us/en/2021/jan/0128-carbon.html.
10. *See* Melissa Burden, *GM's Head of Global Philanthropy, Foundation Steps Down*, DET. NEWS (July 31, 2017, 6:46 PM) ("overhauling its $30-million-a year global philanthropy efforts . . . [i]t will eliminate the General Motors Foundation this year and focus on mission related giving including on high-tech education, safety and economic sustainability, including in Detroit") https://www.detroitnews.com/story/business/autos/general-motors/2017/06/12/gm-giving/102764328/.
11. *See* Henry B. Hansmann, *The Role of Nonprofit Enterprise*, 89 YALE L.J. 835, 873 (1980) ("enforcement is placed exclusively in the hands of the state's attorney general; private parties, such as donors and consumers, generally lack standing to bring suit against the organization or its officers").
12. This was not always true. Corporations and individuals have in the past been required to make some or all of their tax return information public. *See* Marjorie E. Kornhauser, *Shaping Public Opinion and the Law: How a Common Man Campaign Ended a Rich Man's Law*, 73 LAW & CONTEMP. PROBS. 123 (2010) (describing the surprisingly complex history of tax publicity in the United States).
13. *See* Mark Zuckerberg, *A Letter to Our Daughter*, FACEBOOK (Dec. 1, 2015).
14. *Id.*
15. The wealthiest Americans need not engage in clever tax planning to avoid the income tax, they can avoid income tax merely by declining to sell assets. *See* Jesse Eisinger et al., *The Secret IRS Files: Trove of Never-Before-Seen Records Reveal How the Wealthiest Avoid Income Tax*, PROPUBLICA (June 8, 2021, 5 AM), https://www.propublica.org/article/the-secret-irs-files-trove-of-never-before-seen-records-reveal-how-the-wealthiest-avoid-income-tax.
16. *See* DALBERG, COUNCIL ON FOUNDATIONS & PHILANTHROPY CA, SHIFTING PRACTICES, SHARING POWER?: HOW THE US PHILANTHROPIC SECTOR IS RESPONDING TO THE 2020 CRISES, (reporting that in a 2020 study of more than two hundred foundations "only 13% of respondents reported an increased commitment to hiring BIPOC"); Cheryl Dorsey et al., *Overcoming the Racial Bias in Philanthropic Funding*, STAN. SOC. INNOVATION REV. (May 4, 2020), https://ssir.org/articles/entry/overcoming_the_racial_bias_in_philanthropic_funding# ("Consider that while only 25 percent of family foundations use formal diversity, equity, and inclusion (DEI) goals or strategies to guide their giving, DEI considerations are significantly more common in family foundations formed in the past 10 years.")

17. James Andreoni, *The Benefits and Costs of Donor-Advised Funds,* 32 Tax Policy And The Economy 1, 7–8, (Robert A. Moffitt ed., 2018).
18. For example, commercially affiliated donor-advised funds consider themselves content neutral, but some advocates have urged them to halt contributions to hate groups. *See, e.g.*, Stephen Gandel, *Fidelity Charitable Fund Bankrolls "Hate Groups," Critics Say*, CBS News (Dec. 10, 2019, 10:54 AM), https://www.cbsnews.com/news/fidelity-401k-provider-criticized-for-funding-hate-groups/.
19. Dorothy Brown documents a US racial wealth gap that leaves white families equally likely to have no assets as to be millionaires, while Blacks are twenty times more likely and Latinx families fourteen times more likely to wind up on the losing end of that economic divide. *See* Brown, *supra* note 3, at 18. The impact of the racial wealth gap on Black and Latinx charities has been profound.
20. Atinuke O. Adediran, *Disclosures for Equity,* 122 Colum. L. Rev. 865, 878 (2022).
21. Dorsey et al., *supra* note 16.
22. *See* CAIR & Southern Poverty Law Center, Hate-Free Philanthropy: Identifying Opportunities and Obstacles to Safeguard the Sector (2020), https://www.splcenter.org/sites/default/files/dev_hate_free_philanthropy_final1.pdf; Alex Kotch, *America's Biggest Charities Are Funneling Millions to Hate Groups From Anonymous Donors*, Sludge (Feb. 19, 2019), https://readsludge.com/2019/02/19/americas-biggest-charities-are-funneling-millions-to-hate-groups-from-anonymous-donors/; CAIR, Hijacked by Hate: American Philanthropy and the Islamophobia Network (2019), https://ca.cair.com/losangeles/wp-content/uploads/sites/6/2019/05/CAIR-Islamophobia-Report.pdf.
23. *See, e.g.*, Mark Hurtubise, *Philanthropy Must Not Support Hate*, Stan. Soc. Innovation Rev. (Winter 2021), https://ssir.org/pdf/Winter2021-Viewpoint-Hurtubise-Philanthropy-Hate.pdf.
24. *See* Dorsey et al., *supra* note 16 ("The unrestricted net assets of the black-led organizations are 76 percent smaller than their white-led counterparts.")
25. Simply listing a handful of well-known Black charities seems a halfhearted effort from an organization with the reach and resources of Fidelity. *See Supporting Racial Equity*, Fidelity, https://www.fidelitycharitable.org/guidance/research-charities/supporting-racial-equity.html. The "upstart" DAFs described in chapter 2 suggest how much more ambitious the leading players could be if they chose. *See* Jillian Grennan, *Social Change Through Financial Innovation: Evidence from Donor-Advised Funds*, 11 Rev. Corp. Fin. Stud. 694, 724 (2022) (finding DAFs held by these upstart sponsors "with an innovative style of services also give more to charities located in high inequality areas").
26. *See* Dorothy Guerrero, *Nonprofit Leadership: Is There a Gender Gap?*, MissionBox (June 20, 2020), https://www.missionbox.com/article/127/nonprofit-leadership-is-there-a-gender-gap (detailing significant shortfalls in the number and compensation of women in leadership positions at US and UK nonprofits); Maria Di Mento, *Lack of Women in Top Roles Hinders Nonprofits, Female Nonprofit Workers Say*, Chron. Philanthropy (Apr. 28 2014), https://www.philanthropy.com/article/lack-of-women-in-top-roles-hinders-nonprofits-female-nonprofit-workers-say.

27. *See* Grant M. Hayden & Matthew T. Bodie, *Codetermination in Theory and Practice*, 73 FLA. L. REV. 321, 324 (2021) ("'Codetermination' is the umbrella term for systems in which workers play an official role in corporate governance. Germany has the most well-known codetermination regime, but other European countries, such as Austria, Poland, Denmark, and Sweden, have their own varieties.")
28. *See id.* at 325 ("In the United States, corporate boards have been almost exclusively the domain of shareholders.")
29. Although far from common, some state laws gesture toward such input. Hawaii's sustainable business corporation law, for example, requires annual benefit reports to be posted in draft form on firm web sites for comment for 60 days before being made final. *See* HAW. REV. STAT. ANN. § 420D-11(b) (LexisNexis 2021); *see also* Emily R. Winston, *Benefit Corporations and the Separation of Benefit and Control*, 39 CARDOZO L. REV. 1783, 1833–39 (2018) (advocating benefit corporation statutes mandate adopting firms create a Public Benefit Plan, with input from and enforcement by their beneficiaries).
30. *See* David S. Miller, *Social Welfare Organizations as Grantmakers*, 21 N.Y.U. J. LEGIS. & PUB. POL'Y 413, 416 (2018) (noting that when structuring their philanthropic vehicles donors like Chan and Zuckerberg would need to be mindful of the fact that "expenses of an LLC owned by individuals and not engaged in a business are not generally deductible").
31. I.R.C. § 162(a) (providing a deduction for "all the ordinary and necessary expenses paid or incurred during the taxable year in carrying on any trade or business").
32. B Lab calls its B Impact Assessment the "most credible tool a company can use to measure its impact on its workers, community, environment, and customers." B Impact Assessment, B LAB, https://bimpactassessment.net/.
33. *See* J. Haskell Murray, *An Early Report on Benefit Reports*, 118 W. VA. L. REV. 25, 34–35 (2015) (finding compliance rates with requirements to make benefit reports public below 10%).
34. *See Our Approach*, OMIDYAR NETWORK, https://omidyar.com/our-approach/ ("Omidyar Network has a hybrid structure that combines a limited liability company (LLC) with a private philanthropic foundation . . . [o]ur LLC enables us to invest in innovative for-profit startups that are tackling social challenges with an entrepreneurial spirit. It also allows us to invest in not-for-profits beyond public charities, such as 501(c)(4) social welfare organizations.")
35. I.R.C. § 4958.
36. I.R.C. § 4958(c)(1).
37. *See* Treas. Reg. § 53.4958–6(a).
38. *See* VILLANUEVA *supra* note 6, at 4 (concluding that while philanthropy "indulge[s] those who say that diversity is important" it "does not actually change, not more than superficially").
39. *See id.* at 57 (noting that only 7 percent of foundation board members are Black).
40. GIVING GAP, https://givinggap.org/.

41. *See* Paul Sullivan, *As Donations Shift in the Pandemic, New Databases Aim to Help*, N.Y. Times (Sept. 25, 2020), https://www.nytimes.com/2020/09/25/your-money/donations-social-causes-coronavirus.html.
42. *See* Ibram X. Kendi, *What the Racial Data Show*, Atlantic, Apr. 6, 2020.
43. *Communities in Crisis: How Donors Are Responding to COVID-19*, Fidelity Charitable 3 (2020), https://www.fidelitycharitable.org/insights/communities-in-crisis-covid-19.html.
44. *See* Ruth McCambridge, *High-Powered Coalition Advances Plan to Reform Philanthropy*, Nonprofit Q. (Dec. 2, 2020) (at the initiative of Professor Ray Madoff and with the support of John Arnold, "a high-powered coalition of institutional and individual philanthropists and analysts published a plan that seeks to reform donor-advised funds (DAFs), promote an increased payout from private foundations, and expand the charitable deduction"), https://nonprofitquarterly.org/high-powered-coalition-advances-plan-to-reform-philanthropy/.
45. Treas. Reg. § 1.501(c)(3)-1(d)(2).
46. *See, e.g.*, *How Often Do I Have to Recommend a Grant?*, Fidelity Charitable, https://www.fidelitycharitable.org/faqs/all/how-often-do-i-grant.html ("After two years in which no grants are distributed from a Giving Account, Fidelity Charitable will grant 5% from the Giving Account balance to an IRS-qualified public charity approved by the Trustees of Fidelity Charitable."); *see also* Ruth McCambridge, *Do Donor-Advised Funds Require Regulatory Attention?*, Nonprofit Q. (Aug. 27, 2019), https://nonprofitquarterly.org/do-donor-advised-funds-require-regulatory-attention/ (noting at that time that "Fidelity Charitable, for example, sweeps funds that have been dormant for three years or more"); *But see* Alan M. Cantor, Opinion, *Commercial DAFs Keep Touting Their Donors' Crisis Giving. Here's What They Aren't Saying*, Chron. Philanthropy (Jul. 21, 2021), https://www.philanthropy.com/article/Commercial-DAFs-Keep-Touting/249211? (describing conversations with representatives of Schwab, Vanguard and Fidelity confirming a $50 donation would be sufficient for a DAF of any size to avoid being treated as dormant).
47. Internal Revenue Service, 2021 Form 990-EZ Instructions 29. Unlike the instructions for the smallest, least sophisticated charities, the instructions for private foundation returns make no mention of the importance of the returns on public perception, presumably because that would be self-evident to sophisticated private foundations. https://www.irs.gov/pub/irs-pdf/i990ez.pdf.
48. *See* Elizabeth Arias et al., Provisional Life Expectancy Estimates for January through June, 2020, Centers for Disease Control and Prevention (2021) (showing non-Hispanic whites typically live six years longer than Blacks).
49. Dorsey et al., *supra* note 16.

Chapter 7

1. Andrew Carnegie, *Wealth*, N. Am. Rev. 664 (June 1889).

2. As a "disabling device," it imposes a clear prohibition on a charity's contributors, leaders or employees accessing the entity's funds. *See* Thomas C. Schelling, *Enforcing Rules on Oneself*, 1 J. L Econ. & Org. 357, 370 (1985). It also allows no ambiguity, encompassing virtually all payments or benefits insiders might reach and bolstered by safeguards on particularly risky transactions. *See id.* at 366 ("Rules are best observed if you can easily tell the difference between compliance and violation.") Finally, the state serves as a "judge," empowered not only to criticize violations but to compel compliance. *Id.* at 373.
3. The notion of precommitment, with an individual or group choosing to restrict their own freedom of action in order to achieve an important goal, often draws on the story of Ulysses binding himself to the mast to listen to the sirens without jeopardizing his ship or his crew. Jon Elster, Ulysses Unbound: Studies in Rationality, Precommitment, and Constraints 1 (2000)(describing the "proposition that sometimes less is more or, more specifically, that sometimes there are benefits from having fewer opportunities rather than more").
4. *See* Dana Brakman Reiser & Steven A. Dean, Social Enterprise Law: Trust, Public Benefit, and Capital Markets 151 (2017) (explaining the role private ordering played in defying expectations that Ben & Jerry's purchase by Unilever in 2000 would compromise its values by showing that the "sale contracts included several specific terms to institutionalize Ben & Jerry's social commitments postsale").
5. David Gelles, *How the Social Mission of Ben & Jerry's Survived Being Gobbled Up*, N.Y. Times, Aug. 21, 2015, https://www.nytimes.com/2015/08/23/business/how-ben-jerrys-social-mission-survived-being-gobbled-up.html.
6. In 2015, Unilever published its first human rights report and continues to publish them. *See* Unilever, Human Rights Report: Enhancing Livelihoods, Advancing Human Rights (2015); Unilever, Human Rights Report: Creating a Fairer and More Socially Inclusive World (2020).
7. *See* Brakman Reiser & Dean *supra* note 4, at 151–53 (noting that although Unilever owns all of Ben & Jerry's shares, its "board has 11 seats, and Unilever selects the people who fill only two of them. The remaining seats were initially filled by Cohen, Greenfield, and others with history and commitment to Ben & Jerry's and its social mission. When vacancies arise, the board itself—not Unilever—selects and appoints new members to fill them.")
8. Brad Edmonson, Ice Cream Social: The Struggle for the Soul of Ben & Jerry's 171 (2014).
9. *See* Ross Kerber, *New York Pension Fund Joins Exit from Unilever over Israel Restrictions*, Reuters (Oct. 28, 2021), https://www.reuters.com/business/new-york-pension-fund-divest-104-mln-stake-unilever-2021-10-29/ (reporting the decision announced by the New York State Common Retirement Fund to divest its over $100 million stake in Unilever in response to the issue).
10. *Unilever to Cut 15% of Senior Managers as Peltz Adds Pressure*, Bloomberg.com, Jan. 25, 2022 (pointing to the restructuring as enabling Unilever to sell off some brands, including Ben & Jerry's, "speculated by some analysts as a potential disposal target"); Ariel Zilber, *Unilever Spinning off Ben & Jerry's into Separate Unit in Corporate*

Overhaul, N.Y. Post (Jan. 25, 2022), https://nypost.com/2022/01/25/ben-jerrys-breyers-to-run-as-standalone-unit/ (reporting that "[i]t is unclear if the public backlash to Ben & Jerry's decision played a role in the parent company's restructuring").

11. As chapter 8 details, ancient Athens maintained elaborate protections designed to ensure that wealthy citizens "volunteered" to provide warships in times of need.
12. Danone's North American subsidiary became a noteworthy exception in 2017 and would go on to acquire a B Corp certification from B Lab. *See* Press Release, DanoneWave, DanoneWave Established as the Largest Public Benefit Corporation in the U.S. (Apr. 25, 2017), https://www.prnewswire.com/news-releases/danonewave-established-as-the-largest-public-benefit-corporation-in-the-us-300445182.html.
13. Elizabeth Warren's "Ultra-Millionaire Tax" became a signature of her presidential campaign. *See* Warren Democrats, *Ultra-Millionaire Tax*, Warren Democrats, https://elizabethwarren.com/plans/ultra-millionaire-tax (noting that the "plan was originally released during Senator Elizabeth Warren's presidential campaign").
14. Thomas C. Schelling, The strategy of Conflict 122 (1960) (describing the value of "a player to find a way to commit himself, to 'enforce' the commitment against himself" in gaining an advantage over another person).
15. A private foundation must, for example, disclose the names and addresses of its donors not only to the IRS but to the public.
16. *See, e.g.*, Press Release, Rockefeller Foundation, The Rockefeller Foundation Gives Nearly $3 Million to Support Local New York City Artists (July 10, 2012), https://www.rockefellerfoundation.org/news/rockefeller-foundation-gives-nearly-3-2/ (detailing a number of grants, including to the Museum of Contemporary African Diasporan Arts); Press Release, Ford Foundation, Sixteen Major Donors and Foundations Commit Unprecedented $156 Million to Support Black, Latinx, Asian and Indigenous Arts Organizations (Sept. 24, 2020), https://www.fordfoundation.org/the-latest/news/sixteen-major-donors-and-foundations-commit-unprecedented-156-million-to-support-black-latinx-asian-and-indigenous-arts-organizations/ (detailing $81 million in grants by the Ford Foundation and other donors to cultural institutions such as the Alaska Native Heritage Center, the Alvin Ailey American Dance Theater, the Apollo Theater, the Arab American National Museum, and the Ballet Hispánico); Press Release, JPMorgan Chase, JPMorgan Chase Makes Catalytic $1 Million Donation to Support Museum's Expansion and Growth, https://www.jpmorganchase.com/news-stories/pr-columbus-museum-art.
17. One of the most dramatic instances of a profound disconnect between a corporation's virtuous words and unsavory actions that left customers feeling "betrayed as well as cheated" was the revelation that Volkswagen had widely used software—known as "defeat devices"—to hide pollution from environmental regulators. *See* Rena Steinzor, *How Criminal Law Can Help Save the Environment*, 46 Envtl. L. 209, 227 (2016) ("Had the brand been less self-consciously righteous, EPA's public announcement at the end of September 2015 that VW had installed software that turned off 'air emission control devices' (AECD) in 500,000 cars driven in America might have inspired somewhat less outrage.")

18. Treas. Reg. § 1.501(c)(3)-1(c)(3)(iii). Lobbying is also restricted to "no substantial part" of an exempt organization's activities under I.R.C. § 501(c)(3).
19. 100 Cong. Rec. 9604 (1954).
20. *See* Robert M. Penna, *The Johnson Amendment: Fact-Checking the Narrative*, STAN. SOC. INNOVATION REV., Aug. 24, 2018. Several other origin stories for the Johnson Amendment have been offered. *See* Ellen P. Aprill, *Amending the Johnson Amendment in the Age of Cheap Speech,* 2018 U. ILL. L. REV. ONLINE 1, 2–3 (2018) (relating several alternatives).
21. *Justice Department Settles with Conservative Groups Over IRS Scrutiny*, REUTERS, Oct. 26, 2017, https://www.reuters.com/article/us-usa-tax-conservative-idUSKBN1CV1TY ("In a pair of lawsuits filed in federal court in 2013, the conservative groups accused the IRS of targeting organizations with such words as 'Tea Party' or 'patriots' when they applied to the agency for tax-exempt status starting in 2010.")
22. *See* TREASURY INSPECTOR GENERAL FOR TAX ADMINISTRATION, REVIEW OF SELECTED CRITERIA USED TO IDENTIFY TAX-EXEMPT APPLICATIONS FOR REVIEW 5 (2017) (noting that "progressive" was one of the labels the IRS used to identify groups for extra scrutiny).
23. *See* Evelyn Brody & Marcus Owens, *Exile to Main Street: The I.R.S.'s Diminished Role in Overseeing Tax-Exempt Organizations*, 91 CHI.-KENT L. REV. 859 (2016) (describing the significant repercussions of the scandal).
24. *See* Branch Ministries v. Rossotti, 211 F.3d 137 (D.C. Cir. 2000) (upholding a church's loss of tax-exempt status over its vocal opposition to a pro-choice presidential candidate).
25. *See* Regan v. Taxation with Representation, 461 U.S. 540, 551 (1983) (upholding lobbying restrictions on charities).
26. President Trump's criticism of the Johnson Amendment focused on its impact on the freedom of religious leaders to freely express their political views. *See* Aprill, *supra* note 20, at 4–5.
27. Emily Glazer, *Melinda French Gates No Longer Pledges Bulk of Her Wealth to Gates Foundation*, WALL ST. J. (Feb. 2, 2022, 8:30 AM).
28. *See* Bryan Walsh, *Google's Flu Project Shows the Failings of Big Data*, TIME (Mar. 13, 2014), https://time.com/23782/google-flu-trends-big-data-problems/ (describing how Google Flu Trends seemed "like a perfect use of the 500 million plus Google searches made each day" but proved a major disappointment); *see also* David Lazer, Ryan Kennedy, Gary King, & Alessandro Vespignani, *The Parable of Google Flu: Traps in Big Data Analysis* 343 SCI. 1203 (2014) (describing the Google Flu Trends problems as part of a larger critique of big data). *But see* Alexis C. Madrigal, *In Defense of Google Flu Trends,* THE ATLANTIC (Mar. 27, 2014), https://www.theatlantic.com/technology/archive/2014/03/in-defense-of-google-flu-trends/359688/ (pointing to the value of Google Flu Trends as a complement to traditional disease surveillance programs).
29. ELSTER, *supra* note 3, at 1.
30. As described in chapter 2, like their mirror image alternates, Visa and MasterCard, these commercially affiliated donor-advised funds alter the timing of cash flows.

31. *See* Brian Galle, *Pay It Forward: Law and the Problem of Restricted-Spending Philanthropy*, 93 Wash. U. L. REV. 1143, 1199 (2016) ("Contributors to a qualified DAF can claim a full charitable contribution deduction at the date of transfer, even if the fund itself never distributes any money. Furthermore, because the organizations that sponsor DAFs are usually treated as public charities for tax purposes, donors get an even more generous tax subsidy than is usually available to private foundation contributors.").
32. Early-twentieth-century requirements that tax information be made public were successfully targeted by opponents highlighting threats such as kidnapping. *See* Marjorie E. Kornhauser, *Shaping Public Opinion and the Law: How a Common Man Campaign Ended a Rich Man's Law*, 73 LAW & CONTEMP. PROBS. 123, 131 (2010) (highlighting the success of a "massive campaign . . . aimed at the common man—appealing to his patriotic sense of freedom and a democratic way of life, warning of invasions of privacy and preying on his fears of crime . . . adeptly focused on kidnapping, a crime to which the public was particularly attuned, given the Lindbergh baby kidnapping trial then in progress").
33. In response to Nixon's abuse of tax return information, Congress amended I.R.C. § 6103 to ensure that tax return information would be kept private.
34. *See* BRAKMAN REISER & DEAN, *supra* note 4, at 50 (noting that "[o]nly state governments that invest significant time and resources" in design and enforcement will be able "to bring impact investors and social entrepreneurs together" and none yet have chosen to do so).
35. FIDELITY CHARITABLE, https://www.fidelitycharitable.org/.
36. Penelope Wong, *5 Things to Know About Donor-Advised Funds*, CONSUMER REPORTS (Dec. 7, 2019), https://www.consumerreports.org/charitable-donations/donor-advised-funds-things-to-know/.
37. *See* Michael Theis, *Donor-Advised Funds Saw Rapid Growth in 2020*, CHRON. PHILANTHROPY (Nov. 9, 2021), https://www.philanthropy.com/article/donor-advised-funds-saw-rapid-growth-in-2020 ("Only a few donor-advised funds account for the majority of 2020's contributions. The five largest donor-advised fund sponsors—Fidelity Charitable, National Philanthropic Trust, Schwab Charitable Fund, Vanguard Charitable Endowment, and the Silicon Valley Community Foundation—raised roughly $24.5 billion in 2020, more than half of the total amount contributed to such funds last year.").
38. *See* Fidelity Charitable, FAQs, https://www.fidelitycharitable.org/faqs/all/how-often-do-i-grant.html; *see also* Fidelity Charitable, Program Guidelines, Aug. 2021, at 17, https://www.fidelitycharitable.org/content/dam/fc-public/docs/programs/fidelity-charitable-program-guidelines.pdf (providing for distribution of grants following two years of dormancy, but not indicating the 5 percent amount) [hereinafter Fidelity Program Guidelines]. In practice it remains unclear how such policies play out. *See* Alan M. Cantor, Opinion, *Commercial DAFs Keep Touting Their Donors' Crisis Giving. Here's What They Aren't Saying*, CHRON. PHILANTHROPY (July 21, 2020), https://www.philanthropy.com/article/commercial-dafs-keep-touting-their-donors-crisis-giv

ing-heres-what-they-arent-saying (observing much more relaxed attitudes toward minimum giving by Fidelity employees).

39. *See* Schwab Charitable, Program Policies, Nov. 2020, at 23, https://www.schwabcharitable.org/public/file/P-5252372 (stating that "[i]If no account holders recommend grants during a period of 30 months, the account will be considered inactive" and Schwab Charitable seek a donor recommendation, if none is forthcoming, it will enact the donor's succession plan if that will trigger a grant and if not will issue a grant to its Philanthropy Fund); Vanguard Charitable, Policies and Guidelines, 2018, at 17, https://www.vanguardcharitable.org/sites/default/files/upload/2018%20Policies%20and%20Guidelines_112618_ABW.pdf ("If after four years an account has not granted, Vanguard Charitable will attempt to contact account advisors to initiate at least one $500 grant. If repeated contact attempts are unsuccessful after one year, Vanguard Charitable reserves the right to" make a grant of 5 percent of the fund balance according to the donor's "succession plan" on file or through Vanguard's.) Successive grants in later years up to and including the entire fund balance are possible if it continues to fail to make grants. *See* Schwab Charitable *supra*; Vanguard Charitable *supra*.
40. Goldman Sachs Philanthropy Fund, Program Circular, Dec. 5, 2017, at 9, https://gspf.goldman.com/gspf/Portals/29/docs/2017.11%20GSPF%20Program%20Circular.pdf.
41. *See* Fidelity Program Guidelines, *supra* note 38, at 17; Schwab Charitable, *supra* note 39, at 24; Vanguard Charitable, *supra* note 39, at 23; Goldman Sachs Philanthropy Fund, *supra* note 40, at 9.
42. Critics worry that imposing one-size-fits-all regulations on commercially affiliated donor-advised funds would make them less useful to clients of modest means. *See, e.g.*, Elise Westhoff, *The Left Wants a Philanthropy of the Few*, WALL ST. J. (Dec. 14, 2020, 6:41 PM) (warning that regulation of commercially affiliated donor-advised funds would "stifle Americans who want to support worthy causes but aren't superrich").
43. *See* Tom Metcalf, *Billionaires Funding a Goldman Charity Unmasked by IRS Snafu*, BLOOMBERG (Mar. 14, 2018), https://www.bloomberg.com/news/articles/2018-03-14/peek-into-goldman-s-black-box-charity-reveals-tech-billionaires.
44. Schelling, *supra* note 2, describes the characteristics of precommitment strategies likely to succeed. Such a kill switch could be crafted as the kind of bright-line, disabling rule overseen by a judge with enforcement authority, whereby losing P Lab certification or some other transparency metric would result in a loss of tax nothing status. By Schelling's standards, such a commitment would be quite robust.
45. *See* ELSTER, supra note 3, at 35 ("When Ulysses tied himself to the mast, he also put wax in the ears of his rowers, to prevent them from hearing the songs of the sirens. In the usual reading, his intention was to insulate them from noncognitive aspects of the songs, such as the allure of the melody or of the voices of the sirens.").

Chapter 8

1. *See* Rob Reich, Just Giving: Why Philanthropy Is Failing Democracy and How It Can Do Better (2018) (surveying philanthropic technologies from a wide range of eras and places around the globe).
2. As Carnegie observed long ago, tax law can promote elites' giving by threatening them. *See* Andrew Carnegie, *Wealth*, N. Am. Rev. 659 (June 1889). ("By taxing estates heavily at death the state marks its condemnation of the selfish millionaire's unworthy life.") The Grand Bargain's strategic move aimed to prompt elites into philanthropic action rather than to collect revenues from them, a task recent disclosures have shown to be all but impossible for tax authorities. *See* Thomas C. Schelling, The strategy of conflict 123 (190) ("The distinctive character of a threat is that one asserts that he will do, in a contingency, what he would manifestly prefer not to do if the continency occurred, the contingency being governed by the second party's behavior."). The Grand Bargain's strategic approach warily accepts Carnegie's view that elite philanthropy represents the preferred solution to directing private wealth toward public problems, seemingly reflecting a lack of confidence that the government could succeed in extracting revenues from the very wealthy.
3. Fact Sheet: The American Families Plan, The White House (Apr. 28, 2021) (promising to "[r]evitalize enforcement to make the wealthy pay what they owe").
4. *See* Reich, *supra* note 1, at 35.
5. *See* Roger Lowenstein, When Genius Failed: The Rise and Fall of Long-Term Capital Management (2000). Lowenstein explains that although the Federal Reserve enforces Regulation T to limit borrowing to purchase equities to 50 percent of the value of the securities, Long-Term Capital accumulated leverage in one trade of 20 to 1. "When Long-Term Capital purchased stocks, it of course was subject to Reg. T. But for the most part, Long Term built its equity positions *without purchasing actual securities.*" *Id.* at 102–03 (emphasis in original).
6. *Id. at* 102.
7. Laura Davison, *Wealthy Americans Escape Tax Hikes But Would Face Beefed-Up IRS*, Bloomberg L. News (Aug. 5, 2022), https://www.bloomberg.com/news/articles/2022-08-05/wealthy-americans-escape-tax-hikes-but-will-face-beefed-up-irs. ("Wealthy Americans dodged getting hit by tax increases in the Democrats' economic package, but they likely will face a much better-funded Internal Revenue Service equipped with new auditors and technology to uncover tax avoidance.")
8. *See* Dorothy A. Brown, The Whiteness of Wealth: How the Tax System Impoverishes Black Americans–And How We Can Fix It (2021).
9. *Alexandria Ocasio-Cortez: The Rookie Congresswoman Challenging the Democratic Establishment*, 60 Minutes (Jan. 6, 2019), https://www.cbsnews.com/news/alexandria-ocasio-cortez-the-rookie-congresswoman-challenging-the-democratic-establishment-60-minutes-interview-full-transcript-2019-01-06/ ("you look at our tax rates back in the '60s . . . sometimes you see tax rates as high as 60 or 70 percent").

10. Zelenak sees "Tax Day and Voting Day symboliz[ing] the fulfillment of the two great responsibilities of citizenship." LAWRENCE ZELENAK. LEARNING TO LOVE FORM 1040: TWO CHEERS FOR THE RETURN-BASED MASS INCOME TAX 4 (2013).
11. The idea of a negative income tax is credited to Milton Friedman.
12. *See* BROWN, *supra* note 8, at 27 (describing "the role that tax policy plays in perpetuating the black-white wealth gap").
13. Diamond and Saez do note that over the long term, high rates could affect choices about education and careers in ways that would be decidedly suboptimal. *See* Peter Diamond & Emmanuel Saez, *The Case for a Progressive Tax: From Basic Research to Policy Recommendations* 25 J. ECON. PERSP. 165 (2011).
14. *Id.* at 173.
15. The overall audit rate was 400 percent higher in the 1960s than a decade ago. JOEL SLEMROD & JON BAKIJA, TAXING OURSELVES: A CITIZEN'S GUIDE TO THE DEBATE OVER TAXES 181 (2008).
16. *See* Kim Bloomquist, *Regional Bias in IRS Audit Selection*, TAX NOTES 987, 988–98 (Mar. 4, 2019).
17. Treasury Inspector General for Tax Administration, *High-Income Nonfilers Owing Billions of Dollars Are Not Being Worked by the Internal Revenue Service* (2020), https://www.treasury. gov/tigta/auditreports/2020reports/202030015fr.pdf.
18. *See* Davison, *supra* note 7.
19. *See Charitable Contributions: Optimize Your Charitable Planning for Maximum Tax Savings*, FIDELITY CHARITABLE, https://www.fidelitycharitable.org/guidance/charitable-tax-strategies/charitable-contributions.html.
20. *See* Michael Cohn, *Donor-Advised Funds Grow in Popularity Thanks to Tax Reform*, ACCOUNTING TODAY (Nov. 12, 2019), https://www.accountingtoday.com/news/donor-advised-funds-grow-in-popularity-thanks-to-tax-reform ("Contributions to DAFs totaled $37.12 billion, a 20.1 percent increase compared to $30.90 billion in 2017.").
21. *See* Stanley S. Surrey, *The Congress and the Tax Lobbyist: How Special Tax Provisions Get Enacted*, 70 HARV. L. REV. 1145, 1150 (1957).
22. *See* Steven A. Bank, *When Did Tax Avoidance Become Respectable?*, 71 TAX L. REV. 123 (2017) (documenting the growing respectability of tax avoidance over the 1950s and 60s).
23. *See* Surrey, *supra* note 21, at 1178 n.30.
24. Surrey offers the following stylized example describing the treatment the Canon Foundation might generate in the 1950s:

    > If a person in the 70 percent top bracket informs the Government he is selling fully appreciated stock to pay his tax bill or to obtain cash for other reasons and would like $100 paid to a philanthropy, the Government pays the $100 to that philanthropy and also pays the person $5—or perhaps $6.50 or even $15.50.

    STANLEY S. SURREY, PATHWAYS TO TAX REFORM: THE CONCEPT OF TAX EXPENDITURES 227 (1973).
25. *See* REICH, *supra* note 1, at 30.

26. *See* Jesse Eisinger et al., *The Secret IRS Files: Trove of Never-Before-Seen Records Reveal How the Wealthiest Avoid Income Tax*, ProPublica (June 8, 2021, 5 AM), https://www.propublica.org/article/the-secret-irs-files-trove-of-never-before-seen-records-reveal-how-the-wealthiest-avoid-income-tax (noting that the wealthiest Americans often pay no income tax at all).
27. Emmanuel Saez & Gabriel Zucman, *Progressive Wealth Taxation*, Brookings Papers Econ. Activity (Fall 2019), at 492 (proposing that assets in private foundations controlled by funders should be attributed to funders and subject to a wealth tax).
28. Laura Raicovich, Culture Strike: Art and Museums in an Age of Protest 10 (2021).
29. *See* Saez & Zucman *supra* note 27, at 492.
30. *See* Reich, *supra* note 1, at 140.
31. Neil Bhutta et al., *Disparities in Wealth by Race and Ethnicity in the 2019 Survey of Consumer Finances*, Feds Notes (Sept. 28, 2020), https://www.federalreserve.gov/econres/notes/feds-notes/disparities-in-wealth-by-race-and-ethnicity-in-the-2019-survey-of-consumer-finances-20200928.htm.
32. *Ultra-Millionaire Tax*, Warren Democrats, https://elizabethwarren.com/plans/ultra-millionaire-tax (describing Senator Warren's initial proposal as well as its revised version adding additional nuance and anti-abuse features).
33. Wojciech Kopczuk, *Comment on Progressive Wealth Taxation*, Brookings Papers Econ. Activity (Fall 2019), at 519 (arguing that since "wealth taxation fundamentally relies on taxing a base that cannot be fully covered by information reporting, it is bound to have problems").
34. *See* Saez & Zucman, *supra* note 27, at 440. ("European wealth taxes had low exemption thresholds, creating liquidity problems for some moderately wealthy taxpayers with few liquid assets and limited cash incomes.")
35. *Tax on Extreme Wealth*, https://berniesanders.com/issues/tax-extreme-wealth/.
36. Sen. Ron Wyden, *Treat Wealth Like Wages: A Plan to Fix Our Broken Tax Code, Ensure the Wealthy Pay Their Fair Share, and Protect Social Security* 10, https://www.finance.senate.gov/imo/media/doc/Treat%20Wealth%20Like%20Wages%20RM%20Wyden.pdf ("taxpayers would be required to annually pay income taxes on unrealized gains").
37. *See* Saez & Zucman, *supra* note 27, at 492.
38. *See* Roger Fisher et al., Getting to Yes: Negotiating Agreement Without Giving In (2011). The authors distinguish between the classic vision of bargaining (over positions such as price) and bargaining over interests. Bargaining over interests allows two sides to reach agreement by focusing on aspects of an arrangement that are not zero sum. They offer an example of farmers and oil producers realizing that by waiting three months to evict farmers after oil was discovered, they could allow the farmers to harvest their crops without delaying oil production. *See id.* at 5–6.
39. Reich, *supra* note 1, at 29.
40. *Id.* at 31.
41. *Id.* at 32 ("one option was the antidosis, in which the appointed person could attempt to resist liturgical service by pointing out the fact that other citizens with even greater

resources were not volunteering and had not performed any significant liturgy recently").

42. Thomas C. Schelling, The strategy of conflict 122 (1960).
43. *Id.* at 137–38 (describing a "set of tactics that consists of maneuvering one's self into a position in which one no longer has any effective choice over how he shall behave or respond. . . . to get rid of an embarrassing initiative, making the outcome depend solely on the other party's choice").
44. *Id.* at 124 (explaining that a "threat differs from the ordinary commitment . . . in that it makes one's course of action conditional on what the other player does" here allowing wealthy elites to act first by voluntarily undertaking a liturgy).
45. *Id.* at 134 (explaining that successful enforcement arrangements are ones that "provide no incentive to cheat or that make noncompliance automatically visible or that incur the penalties on which the possibility of enforcement rests").
46. *Id.* at 142–43 (rather than "using thugs and sadists for the collection of extortion or the guarding of prisoners" delegating antidosis authority to fellow wealthy citizens "exemplifies a common means of making credible a response pattern that the original source of decision might have been thought to shrink from").
47. Reich, *supra* note 1, at 34.
48. *Voting Rights Restoration*, Brennan Center for Justice, https://www.brennancenter.org/issues/ensure-every-american-can-vote/voting-rights-restoration.
49. *See, e.g.*, Michael Wines, *In Statehouses, Stolen-Election Myth Fuels a G.O.P. Drive to Rewrite Rules*, N.Y. Times (Feb. 27, 2021), https://www.nytimes.com/2021/02/27/us/republican-voter-suppression.html ("[l]ed by loyalists who embrace former President Donald J. Trump's baseless claims of a stolen election, Republicans in state legislatures nationwide are mounting extraordinary efforts to change the rules of voting . . . raising new barriers to casting votes").
50. *See* Citizens United v. FEC, 558 U.S. 310 (2010) (upholding a corporation's right to spend on political campaigns on free speech grounds).
51. *See* Karl Evers-Hillstrom et al., *More Money, Less Transparency: A Decade under Citizens United*, Open Secrets (Jan. 14, 2020), https://www.opensecrets.org/news/reports/a-decade-under-citizens-united ("The 10 most generous donors and their spouses injected $1.2 billion into federal elections over the last decade. That tiny group of major donors accounted for 7 percent of total election-related giving in 2018, up from less than 1 percent a decade prior.")
52. *See* Kenneth P. Vogel & Laurie Goodstein, In *Tax Debate, Gift to Religious Right Could Be Bargaining Chip*, N.Y. Times (Nov. 26, 2017), https://www.nytimes.com/2017/11/26/us/politics/johnson-amendment-churches-taxes-politics.html (describing the history of attempts at repeal in the context of the House of Representatives passing its version of the tax reform bill).
53. *See, e.g.*, Elizabeth Landers, *Trump: I Will 'Destroy' Johnson Amendment*, CNN Politics (Feb. 2, 2017), https://www.cnn.com/2017/02/02/politics/johnson-amendment-trump/index.html.
54. *See, e.g.*, LaShawn Y. Warren, *3 Reasons the Johnson Amendment Should Not Be Repealed*, Center for Am. Progress (Apr. 6, 2017), https://www.americanprogress.

org/issues/religion/news/2017/04/06/430104/3-reasons-johnson-amendment-not-repealed/.

55. S. 3215, Accountable Capitalism Act, 116th Cong. (2020); S. 3348, Accountable Capitalism Act, 115th Cong. (2018).
56. Shareholder Protection Act. S.530, 117th Cong. (2021).
57. Lucian A. Bebchuk & Robert J. Jackson Jr., *Shining Light on Corporate Political Spending*, 101 GEO. L.J. 923 (2013); Lucian Bebchuk & Robert J. Jackson, Jr., *The Million-Comment-Letter Petition: The Rulemaking Petition on Disclosure of Political Spending Attracts More than 1,000,000 SEC Comment Letters*, HARVARD LAW SCH. FORUM ON CORP. GOVERNANCE AND FIN. REGULATION (Sept. 4, 2014), http://corpgov.law.harvard.edu/2014/09/04/the-million-comment-letter-petition-the-rulemaking-petition-on-disclosure-of-political-spending-attracts-more-than-1000000-sec-comment-letters.
58. Soyoung Ho, *SEC Likely to Take Up Political Spending Disclosure Rulemaki*ng, THOMSONREUTERS ACCOUNTING AND COMPLIANCE ALERT (Mar. 17, 2021), https://tax.thomsonreuters.com/news/sec-likely-to-take-up-political-spending-disclosure-rulemaking/.
59. Americans for Prosperity Found. v. Bonta, 141 S. Ct. 2373 (2021).
60. *See id.* at 2392 (Sotomayor, J., dissenting) ("Today's analysis marks reporting and disclosure requirements with a bull's-eye."); Lloyd Hitoshi Mayer, *Justices Open the Door Wider for Donor Info Law Challenges*, LAW 360 (July 2, 2021), https://www.law360.com/articles/1400104/justices-open-the-door-wider-for-donor-info-law-challenges.
61. Inti Pacheco, *Capitol Riot: See the Full List of Companies Halting PAC Donations*, WALL. ST. J. (Jan. 12, 2021), https://www.wsj.com/articles/capitol-riot-see-the-full-list-of-companies-halting-pac-donations-11610471235.
62. Elizabeth Warren, *Accountable Capitalism Act*, https://www.warren.senate.gov/imo/media/doc/Accountable%20Capitalism%20Act%20One-Pager.pdf.
63. Grant M. Hayden & Matthew T. Bodie, *Codetermination in Theory and Practice*, 73 FLA. L. REV. 321, 324 (2021).
64. Steven Mufson, *A Bad Day for Big Oil*, WASH. POST. (May 26, 2021, 10:24 AM), https://www.washingtonpost.com/climate-environment/2021/05/26/exxonmobil-rebel-shareholders-win-board-seats/.
65. Even the now-infamous philanthropists who make up the Sackler family will manage to sustain little damage to their wealth despite revelations about their misdeeds in "helping to precipitate the opioid crisis." Patrick Radden Keefe, *How Did the Sacklers Pull This Off?*, N.Y. TIMES (July 14, 2021), https://www.nytimes.com/2021/07/14/opinion/sackler-family-opioids-settlement.html. For a comprehensive account of this role, *see* PATRICK RADDEN-KEEFE, EMPIRE OF PAIN (2021).
66. REICH, *supra* note 1, at 29.

Conclusion

1. Shelby County v. Holder, 570 U.S. 529, 554 (2013).
2. Carnegie believed that the estate tax would save wealthy Americans from the threat of "dying disgraced" not because they would patriotically pay taxes, but because they would avoid the threat of taxes by engaging in philanthropy during their lives. *See* Andrew Carnegie, *Wealth*, N. Am. Rev. 664 (June 1889).

Index

For the benefit of digital users, indexed terms that span two pages (e.g., 52–53) may, on occasion, appear on only one of those pages.